CHILDREN AND THE EUROPEAN UNION

This book examines in detail the status of c   ge
of disciplinary perspectives, including th   an
rights discourse, it offers a critical analys   ork
underpinning EU children's rights across a range of areas, including   .aw,
education, immigration and child protection.

Traditionally children's rights at this level have been articulated primarily in the context of the free movement of persons provisions, inevitably restricting entitlement to migrant children of EU nationality. In the past decade, however, innovative interpretations of EU law by the Court of Justice, coupled with important constitutional developments, have prompted the development of a much more robust children's rights agenda. This culminated in the incorporation of a more explicit reference to children's rights in the Lisbon Treaty, following by the Commission's launch, in February 2011, of a dedicated EU 'Agenda' to promote and safeguard the rights of the child.

The analysis presented in this book therefore comes at a pivotal point in the history of EU children's rights, providing a detailed and critical overview of a range of substantive areas, and making an important contribution to international children's rights studies.

Volume 32 in the series Modern Studies in European Law

For the complete list of titles in this series, see 'Modern Studies in European Law' link at www.hartpub.co.uk/books/series.asp

Children and the European Union

Rights, Welfare and Accountability

Helen Stalford

·HART·
PUBLISHING
OXFORD AND PORTLAND, OREGON
2012

Published in the United Kingdom by Hart Publishing Ltd
16C Worcester Place, Oxford, OX1 2JW
Telephone: +44 (0)1865 517530
Fax: +44 (0)1865 510710
E-mail: mail@hartpub.co.uk
Website: http://www.hartpub.co.uk

Published in North America (US and Canada) by
Hart Publishing
c/o International Specialized Book Services
920 NE 58th Avenue, Suite 300
Portland, OR 97213-3786
USA
Tel: +1 503 287 3093 or toll-free: (1) 800 944 6190
Fax: +1 503 280 8832
E-mail: orders@isbs.com
Website: http://www.isbs.com

British Library Cataloguing in Publication Data
Data Available

ISBN: 978-1-84113-765-0

Typeset by Compuscript Ltd, Shannon
Printed and bound in Great Britain by
TJ International Ltd, Padstow, Cornwall

For Iwan, Mairéad, Bethan, Siôn and Mair.
Mae hwn i chi, gyda'r fy holl gariad.

Acknowledgements

I have benefited from much support and assistance in writing this book. The research fellowship I received from the Arts and Humanities Research Council enabled me to complete the formative research on which it is based, for which I am very grateful.

Final completion would simply not have been possible were it not for the wondrous editorial skills of Keleigh Coldron. Her contribution far exceeded the reasonable expectations of an editor, providing thoughtful and invaluable feedback on all aspects of the book, as well as much-needed encouragement and motivation in the final stages. I am thankful also to Richard Hart, Rachel Turner and all at Hart Publishing for their patience, professionalism and efficiency in preparing it for publication.

I am immensely grateful to and appreciative of colleagues at the School of Law and Social Justice, University of Liverpool for their collegiality and friendship over the years. I am particularly indebted to those of you who helped shape my thoughts and approach to this book. Thanks, in particular, go to Louise Ackers who kick-started my interest (and career) in EU children's rights; to Sammie Currie and Fiona Beveridge who provided invaluable feedback on aspects of EU enlargement and mainstreaming; to Ruth Lamont for the many engaging discussions we have had on aspects of EU family law and citizenship and for commenting so diligently on chapters four and five; and to Barry Goldson, Tony Dobson and Mike Jones for teaching me so much about the true impact and value of children's rights on the ground. I will be forever grateful also to Michael Dougan for his generous counsel on various aspects of my research and, indeed, on my career generally, and for patiently advising me on the more technical intricacies of EU law; to Dominic McGoldrick for his great friendship and for stretching my understanding of fundamental rights, and to Eleanor Drywood who, through our various research and writing collaborations and through her own work, has exerted such a positive influence on my analysis of EU children's rights.

Thanks must also go to a number of individuals external to Liverpool too whose input has proved so influential: Clare McGlynn at Durham University willingly shared her thoughts and expertise on many aspects of EU child and family law in the early stages; Jean Grugel and Ingi Iusmen at the University of Sheffield provided a welcome sounding board in the latter stages of writing this book and Nigel Lowe at the University of Cardiff has provided ongoing advice and feedback on the family law aspects of my research. A number of others have introduced me to new perspectives on EU children's rights, including Amandine Garde, Nuno Ferreira and Wouter Vandenhole. I am grateful to Nigel Thomas for providing me with a deeper insight into child participation and for breaking my isolation with those fleeting visits to North Wales. I have also benefited significantly from and enjoyed discussions with Ursula Kilkelly and Laura Lundy on theories and methodologies associated with the Convention on the Rights of the Child. I have been especially privileged to have had the opportunity to work closely with Sandy Ruxton and Mieke Schuurman whose long-established research and campaigning have made such an important contribution to the development of the EU children's rights agenda. I look forward to many more years of collaboration and friendship with you.

During the course of writing this book, I, along with an international team of researchers, completed a project on behalf of the EU Fundamental Rights Agency to develop a set of indicators to measure the impact of EU law and policy on children's rights. The insights gained from that experience have truly enhanced this book and it was a privilege to work with such a dedicated and well-informed group of experts. Helmut Sax of the Ludwig Boltzmann Institute in Vienna was an excellent research partner, Margaret Wachenfeld, formerly of the UNICEF Brussels office, was a true inspiration, and Ioannis Dimitrakopoulos of the Fundamental Rights Agency was refreshingly open to our approach.

A special acknowledgement must go to my family: I will be eternally grateful to my mother, Colette, whose love truly knows no bounds. She has been such an enormous support on so many levels: travelling over at the drop of a hat to help us out at home; offering such wise and uplifting advice and encouragement and even enduring the painstaking process of proof reading. I am grateful, as ever, for the love, support and good humour of my brothers and sisters too. Thank you, in particular, Matt and Siobhán, for reading through those final chapters so attentively when you had more than enough work of your own to do.

The final word of thanks must go to Iwan, whose unstinting love, patience and faith made completion of this book possible and to our children, Mairéad, Bethan, Siôn and Mair, whose very existence makes it meaningful.

Helen Stalford
December 2011

Contents

Table of Cases

European Court of Justice

European Court of Human Rights

UK Cases

Table of Legislation

European Treaties and Conventions

International Treaties and Conventions

Regulations

Decisions

UK Law

Introduction:
Children and the European Union

C HILDREN ACCOUNT FOR over one-fifth (over 107 million) of the EU
population and an estimated 5.4 million children are born every year
across the 27 Member States.[1] The aim of this book is to explore the extent
to which EU law and policy acknowledges, accommodates and regulates their
lives. It represents the first attempt to present a comprehensive and critical analysis of the constitutional, cultural, social, ideological and political issues underpinning children's rights at EU level. In doing so, it is inspired by and builds upon
previous efforts to map out EU activities in relation to children,[2] but does so in
the light of the significant changes to have taken place over the past 20 years, not
only in relation to the institutional and constitutional architecture of the EU, but
also against the readiness of EU legal and policy actors to engage more boldly with
children's rights issues. These developments are symptomatic of the extended
'reach' of the EU more generally: physically, through the expansion of the EU territory, as well as legally and politically through its growing social and fundamental
rights agenda and through the gradual erosion of internal borders. Such factors
have enhanced the legitimacy and value of EU action insofar as it offers not only
a supra-national response to a range of children's rights concerns that transcend
national boundaries, but also insofar as it offers a platform for political dialogue,
best practice exchange and resource-pooling between the Member States in relation to children's rights issues of common concern.

The reference to 'Rights' and 'Welfare' in the title of this book acknowledges
that children's interests and needs are multi-faceted and interlinked, and that they
interact with the rights and interests of others (notably those of their parents and
other children). The reference to 'Accountability' suggests that children's rights
are upheld not simply as a result of being articulated in law or policy, but by
virtue of coherent mechanisms for implementation, enforcement and evaluation.

---

[1] M Marcu, 'Population and Social Conditions' in, *Statistics in Focus,* 38/2011 (Brussels, Eurostat, 2011).

[2] Notably S Ruxton, *Children and the EU* (London, NCH Action for Children, 1996); S Ruxton, *What About Us? Children's Rights in the European Union: Next Steps* (Brussels, The European Children's Network, 2005) and C McGlynn, *Families and the European Union: Law, Politics and Pluralism* (Cambridge, Cambridge University Press, 2006).

Essentially, children's 'rights'—including measures to protect them—mean very little unless individuals, bodies and public institutions can be held to account for upholding them and unless there are mechanisms in place to enable children to enforce them.

This perspective raises a number of questions. Most crucially, what is the added value of children's rights at EU level? What mechanisms are at the EU's disposal to advance children's rights? And how can we ensure that any children's rights measures developed by the EU do not unnecessarily duplicate or, worse still, undermine the activities of international bodies such as the Council of Europe and the United Nations, or indeed, of domestic authorities? Such issues are interrogated from an explicitly children's rights perspective insofar as it makes a concerted effort to locate the analysis within a children's rights ideological and normative framework and, where possible, to draw upon research and campaigns that actively and directly engage with children's life experiences. This approach also provides some insight into the EU's interpretation of children's rights. For instance, to what extent is the EU children's rights agenda dominated by a paternalistic preoccupation with protecting children as opposed to empowering them? Are children's rights at EU level addressed in a manner that is synonymous or coterminous with those of their parents or other adults? In short, is there sufficient and meaningful EU provision that endorses and supports children as independent actors rather than as merely passive objects of control and care?

The substantive focus of the chapters reflects prevalent EU legislative, judicial, policy and campaign activities and covers issues such as child custody and maintenance, immigration and asylum, education and social exclusion, child protection and EU enlargement. This is by no means presented as an exhaustive list. Indeed, at the time of writing, further programmes and provisions are being developed on a range of issues that are excluded from the scope of this book and that have, in the past, appeared somewhat incongruous to EU law and policy, including youth justice, international adoption, missing children and international development.

Adopting a children's rights approach is not simply a question of determining the scope and content of EU provision though; it demands some interrogation of the methods by which those rights are expressed and transposed into law and policy. As such, the following analysis will scrutinise the extent to which procedures, as they are currently framed, can realistically respond to the children's rights deficit at EU level; the decision-making process, the use and value of other methods of governance beyond the law, and the institutional mechanisms in place to enable children and young people to engage with the institutions or seek redress for alleged violations of their rights.

With this in mind, the chapters in this book are organised to allow for a comprehensive and critical analysis of the nature, scope and value of EU measures in relation to children. The first two chapters set the scene by establishing the historical, constitutional and ideological context in which children's rights are pursued at EU level. **Chapter one** charts how EU children's rights has developed from a relatively marginal aspect of EU free movement and consumer law, largely detached from international children's rights discourse, into a distinct and far-reaching discipline in its own right. In the process, it explores the motivations for and added value of EU action in the field of children's rights and ponders whether the EU is possessed of the necessary capacity, expertise and resources to deliver on its children's rights commitments. The discussion then considers how the balance between action at EU and the national level is negotiated before establishing the definitional parameters of the EU's concept of 'child'. **Chapter two** explores the ideological and conceptual contexts in which children's rights have been pursued at EU level. While recent formulations of the EU 'children agenda' are dominated by a normative 'rights'-based model, the analysis explores what this really means in substance and, indeed, in practice. It then moves on to question the robustness of a purely rights-based approach and suggests other normative and conceptual frameworks within which children's interests might be more effectively pursued.

Subsequent chapters illustrate how the normative and methodological tools identified in the first two chapters have been used by the EU to enact measures in relation to substantive children's rights issues. Chapters three, four and five explore various aspects of children's rights in the context of transnational family life, an area which has seen the most explicit and far-reaching EU legal intervention. Specifically, **chapter three** focuses on the extent to which children's right to family life is protected under EU free movement and immigration law. This involves a critical analysis of the EU's persistently narrow legal conceptualisation of 'family', the conditions placed on those seeking family reunification, and of the extent to which EU migration law reinforces or, indeed, challenges the construction of children as inexorably dependent on adults. **Chapters four and five** consider the extent to which the (now well-established) legal and jurisprudential framework regulating cross-national divorce and separation sustain and protect the rights and welfare of children implicated in such processes.

Chapter six moves on to examine how the educational rights and welfare of children are perceived and protected at EU level. In doing so, the analysis considers the role of children as valuable economic and social capital: not only as guarantors for the future stability of the European economy but as active, everyday protagonists in the cultural, political and social life of the EU. **Chapter seven** examines the various measures put in place to protect the welfare of some of the most socio-economically, physically, emotionally and politically vulnerable children in the EU. It considers the effectiveness and limitations of legislative measures in areas that fall within EU competence (such as immigration and asylum), and the range of alternative tools at the EU's disposal to address issues that fall outside its legislative remit. The analysis also points to some of the structural obstacles that impede effective EU protection of children, particularly in relation to inter-departmental incoherence within the Commission, the quality, consistency and subsequent use of research data, and the efforts made to co-ordinate EU activities with the labours of parallel international human rights bodies. **Chapter eight** considers the extent to which children's rights feature in the EU enlargement process. In particular, it highlights how the accession process presents the EU with an exceptional mandate for scrutinising national human rights (including children's rights) systems. In the same token, EU membership can act as a potent incentive for effecting important changes to such systems. The discussion considers the nature and scope of accession states' children's rights obligations during the accession process, as well as the political and legal challenges of enforcing and sustaining these commitments once membership is achieved. The final chapter brings all of the preceding analysis together with an examination of the various mechanisms that can be used by children to actively represent and enforce their rights at EU level. It also makes some suggestions as to the future direction and effects of EU action relating to children.

1

The Value and Scope of EU Action in Relation to Children

INTRODUCTION

T
O SET THE scene for the remainder of this book, this chapter explains why children's rights issues are a concern at EU level and, specifically, examines the value and nature of EU intervention in this regard. As a starting point, it is fair to say that the EU seems an unlikely context within which to pursue children's rights. Historically, children's rights have barely featured on the EU agenda which, since its inception, has been primarily concerned with forging political and economic alliances between the Member States. Changes to the EU's constitutional, legal and institutional landscape over the years, however, have generated new opportunities and, indeed, a necessity to engage with a range of broader social and rights-related issues, including those affecting children.

The following discussion critically assesses the content and scope of this unlikely alliance. It begins by making the case for EU action in relation to children's rights issues. The reasons put forward in this regard go some way towards explaining how children's rights at EU level have progressed over time, from a handful of fairly random measures that were merely instrumental to the operation of other (primarily adult) entitlement, to the bold and potentially far-reaching children's rights strategy that exists today. The analysis will then consider the tensions inherent in an approach that seeks to encourage EU regulation of children's rights whilst safeguarding nation states' competence to determine both the substance of those rights and the process by which they are administered. The discussion will conclude by setting out the conceptual boundaries of EU children's rights, examining in particular how 'child' is defined under EU law.

IS THERE A NEED FOR EU ACTION IN THE FIELD OF CHILDREN'S RIGHTS?

Any suggestion that the EU should develop measures in relation to children can be easily dismissed as indefensible. Objections might point to both a lack of need and capacity for an EU-level response to children's rights issues. The 'lack of need' argument contends that EU activities, because of their predominantly internal market focus, are primarily concerned with maximising adults' capability to contribute to the economy, chiefly through their participation in employment and as providers and recipients of services. Such issues, it is argued, impact upon children only to a very limited extent and largely indirectly, such that their interests will be automatically accommodated 'by proxy' by virtue of any (adult-targeted) EU provision enacted in these areas. Furthermore, it is presumed that international and domestic child law and procedure act as an additional safety net to capture and accommodate children's rights issues that may be incidentally affected by the normal operation of EU law. Most persuasively, Member States' allegiance to the 1989 UN Convention on the Rights of the Child (UNCRC) ensures that all EU legislation, when enforced at domestic level, automatically complies with minimum children's rights principles as set out in the UNCRC. In other words, consistent with Dworkin's celebrated vision of rights as 'trumps',[1] existing children's rights provision as enshrined in the constitutional traditions of the Member States and in international human rights instruments act as a natural brake on the potentially adverse effects of EU law without the need for further duplicate measures at EU level.[2]

Despite these objections, a number of arguments can be put forward in support of more direct EU regulation of children's lives. These arguments relate first and foremost to the legal and moral obligation to act in children's best interests and, specifically, to avert any potential breaches of children's rights arising out of the operation of EU law. Even the blandest and seemingly most innocuous of EU measures can have significant implications for children's rights. Internal market measures aimed at removing barriers to the free circulation of goods and services between the Member States, for instance, have to be balanced against the need to subject such goods and services to sufficient scrutiny with a view to protecting the welfare of children who may be exposed to them.[3] Similarly, the gradual erosion of administrative checks on workers, tourists and other EU citizens crossing EU internal borders undoubtedly facilitates the more nefarious pursuits of international child abduction, child trafficking and human smuggling. EU equality measures aimed at enabling mothers to re-enter the labour market following childbirth and at enabling working parents to continue to organise their employed activities around their family responsibilities thereafter have important knock-on effects for the quality and amount of contact children have with their parents and for the way in which childcare is funded and administered at the domestic level. Even the multiplicity of EU environmental, agricultural or transport initiatives will carry consequences for all consumers and residents of the communities in which they are implemented regardless of their age. Indeed, these examples illustrate that almost every aspect of EU regulation has at

---

[1] R Dworkin, 'Rights as Trumps' in J Waldron (ed), *Theories of Rights* (Oxford, Oxford University Press, 1984) 153.

[2] The relationship between fundamental rights and EU law is explored fully in ch 2.

[3] Case C-244/06 *Dynamic Medien Vertriebs GmbH v Avides Media AG* [2008] ECR I-505.

least indirect consequences for children thereby reinforcing the EU institutions' responsibility to put in place appropriate mechanisms to mitigate any potential threat to children's welfare.

THE ADDED VALUE OF EU ACTION IN RELATION TO CHILDREN'S RIGHTS

Such observations link in with the second argument in favour of EU action in relation to children's rights. This acknowledges the potential of the EU to make a unique contribution to the protection of children's rights in ways that simply cannot be achieved at the national or, indeed, at the international level. This is particularly the case for children's rights issues that cross jurisdictional and geographical boundaries, such as immigration, the free movement of goods, services and people, child trafficking, or parental child abduction. The development of a supra-national, uniform response is essential to achieving an appropriate level of procedural and legal consistency for those implicated in such issues. Crucially, EU measures in this regard represent a level of consensus between the Member States as to how such issues should be addressed and are generally accompanied by the a range of co-operative mechanisms to facilitate their effective administration on the ground.[4] But beyond the more pragmatic value of supra-national regulation of children's rights issues that intersect so markedly with the EU's cross-border/internal market competences, is the wider value of the political and economic resources at the EU's disposal. These resources can be usefully harnessed by domestic and international stakeholders to forge a constructive dialogue on issues of common domestic concern, even if they do not have any explicit cross-national implications—issues such as poverty, child-friendly justice, violence or media literacy providing notable examples. The EU offers a unique forum and source of funding to bring together a range of actors at international, European and domestic level to share experience and best practice on such issues, set mutually-agreed benchmarks, and stimulate wide dissemination, awareness-raising and policy exchange.[5]

---

[4] EU measures regulating cross-border divorce and parental responsibility (discussed in ch 3) are an example of the interplay between the EU and the domestic family law systems. This relationship is significantly aided by the establishment of an EU-wide judicial network and by a designated 'central authority' in each Member State.

[5] See notably, the activities of the European Forum on the Rights of the Child, created in 2007 with the assistance of the German Presidency, to bring together Member States, EU institutional representatives, NGOs and children's ombudspersons, to discuss and identify priorities for action in the field of children's rights (ec.europa.eu/justice/fundamental-rights/rights-child/european-forum/index_en.htm). More specific action programmes have been implemented by the Safer Internet Programme. Additionally, a range of initiatives aimed at tackling child poverty are being implemented through the Commission's Europe 2020 programme—see European Commission, The Social Dimension of the Europe 2020 Strategy: A Report of the Social Protection Committee 2011 (Brussels, European Commission, 2011) 7–8.

THE STRATEGIC IMPORTANCE OF INVESTING
IN CHILDREN'S RIGHTS AT EU LEVEL

The final main argument in support of EU children's rights measures is more strategic in nature and responds to the need to invest in the youth to secure the economic, civic, political and social future of the EU. The notion of childhood as an 'investment' is defined by Piper as a process whereby 'resources are designed and used specifically to bring benefits in the future by reducing the risk of future detriments'.[6] This approach is particularly pervasive at EU level: nurturing productive workers, carers and childbearers of the future is essential for offsetting the economic and social incohesion associated with a perceptible Europe-wide demographic decline and an ageing population.[7] Indeed, this is a significant concern driving the Commission's Growth Strategy, Europe 2020, which underlines the long-term effects as follows:

> Demographic ageing is accelerating. As the baby-boom generation retires, the EU's active population will start to shrink as from 2012/14. The number of people aged over 60 is now increasing twice as fast as it did before 2007—by about two million every year compared to one million previously. The combination of a smaller working population and a higher share of retired people will place additional strains on our welfare systems.[8]

Certainly, the focus on the investment potential of children is regarded by many commentators as legitimising public intervention in children's lives at all levels. In the words of Dingwall and Eekelaar, 'the survival of the liberal social order we enjoy is integrally bound up with the conditions under which children are raised'.[9] The state, therefore, shares responsibility with parents to protect that investment, since it is the state as much as the family and the child that will reap the benefits. In the same token, insofar as the EU benefits from children's future contribution to its economy, labour force, and cultural and political life, it has a responsibility to intervene and support domestic authorities and parents in nurturing this potential in them.

On a more abstract level, the EU has a vested interest in inculcating in children and young people a sense of European identity and membership—including a sense of political consciousness and social responsibility—with a view to securing their allegiance to the European project and sustaining a sufficient level of

---

[6]   C Piper, 'Investing in a Child's Future: Too Risky?' (2010) 22 *Child and Family Law Quarterly* 1, 1.

[7]   See the rather bleak demographic predictions of the EU Social Protection Committee in European Commission, *Child Poverty and Well-being in the EU: Current Status and Way Forward* (Brussels, European Commission, 2008) 10 and S Ruxton, 'What about Us? Children's Rights in the European Union: Next Steps' (Brussels, EURONET, 2005). On children as economic investments more generally, see A Aiyagari, J Greenwood and A Seshandri, 'Efficient Investment in Children' (2002) 102 *Journal of Economic Theory* 290.

[8]   Commission, 'Europe 2020: A Strategy for Smart, Sustainable and Inclusive Growth' (Communication) COM (2010) 2020 final, 7.

[9]   R Dingwall and J Eeklaar, *Rethinking Child Protection* (Oxford, Centre for Socio-Legal Studies, 1984) 108.

political credibility. This is evidenced, in particular, in activities of DG Education and Culture, many of which are focused on mobilising the potential of young Europeans, garnering their views on a range of European issues, and funding a number of formal and informal learning and exchange experiences.[10] As Ferreira notes, 'Having 27 different legal frameworks regulating a range of aspects of children's lives may be an extremely valuable arsenal of inspiration and best practices for lawyers, policy-makers and activists alike'.[11]

VALUING AND FACILITATING CHILDREN'S PRESENT
CONTRIBUTION TO THE EU

While the priorities discussed above point to children's *potential* value as contributors to the future EU project, EU investment in children's rights also serves an important way of acknowledging and supporting children's role as active protagonists in the here and now. Adopting an approach that values children's current contribution to society is consistent with developments in the sociology of childhood research and literature, with the tenor of children's rights campaigns and, indeed, with the direction of law and policy at the domestic level. These movements demonstrate that approaches to children and childhood have shifted away from an overwhelmingly paternalistic preoccupation with safeguarding their welfare towards a more acute awareness of children's status as powerful social actors. Children are no longer viewed exclusively as vulnerable and passive recipients of services and care, but as agents who play an active and valuable role in sustaining family welfare, culture and economic and political stability.[12] There are a number of practical illustrations of this. For instance, there is now a substantial body of research revealing the extent of children's direct contribution to European domestic economies both through their engagement in formal, paid employment,[13] as consumers and clients of a vast range of services, notably education, leisure and sport,[14] and in less quantifiable yet

---

[10] Notable examples include the Youth in Action programme which runs from 2007–13 and targets the 15–28 age-group. It aims to encourage civic participation and nurture the creative and entrepreneurial skills of more hard-to-reach, disadvantaged children, including those with physical or mental disabilities (Dec 1719/2006/EC [2006] OJ L327) and DG Education and Culture, *Looking Behind the Figures of the Main Results of the Eurobarometer 2007 Survey on Youth* (Brussels, European Commission, 2007).

[11] N Ferreira, 'The Harmonisation of Private Law in Europe and Children's Tort Liability: A Case of Fundamental and Children's Rights Mainstreaming' (2011) 19 *International Journal of Children's Rights* 571, 575.

[12] C Smart, B Neale and A Wade, The Changing Experience of Childhood: Families and Divorce (Cambridge, Polity Press, 2001) 12; A Solberg 'Negotiating Childhood: Changing Constructions of Age for Norwegian Children' in A James and A Prout (eds), *Constructing and Reconstructing Childhood* (Basingstoke, Falmer Press, 1997). The extent of children's contribution to the political and economic sphere will be evaluated further in the context of free movement and citizenship (chs 2 and 3) and education (ch 6).

[13] M Lavalette, Child Employment in the Capitalist Labour Market (Aldershot, Avebury, 1994).

[14] H Wintersberger, 'Work, Welfare and Generational Order: Towards a Political Economy of Childhood' in J Qvortrup (ed), *Studies in Modern Childhood* (Basingstoke, Palgrave Macmillan, 2005)

equally valid domestic caring and house-working arrangements[15] and community-based voluntary activities.[16] In a social context, children's personal networking and linguistic knowledge can provide important opportunities for their family to interact with the local community. This is particularly critical for immigrant families, where linguistic and cultural differences can obstruct integration. As Zelizer notes:

> By connecting households with powerful outside institutions, children's mediation sometimes greatly affects the family's social position. Immigrant families, for example, often depend on their…children to establish a wide range of connections between the household's adults and the alien environment. Counter-intuitively, this means that a household lacking children will in certain circumstances accumulate less capital than those with children.[17]

This extensive body of evidence has forced us to question conventional assumptions about children's passive and deficient dependency on adults, and to acknowledge the variety of ways in which children take responsibility for their own and others' welfare; how they act as 'practitioners' of economic and social life,[18] both individually and collectively. In underlining these issues, the aim is not to deny children's inherent dependency on adults but to illustrate the complex dynamics of that dependency. Indeed, children's relationship with their parents and even with their wider community might be more accurately defined in terms of 'interdependency'. This reflects the fact that children's dependency does not simply imply passive receipt of care and services and inherent subjugation, but rather, holds valuable economic and social capital. Consider, for example, the economic value of those industries that profit from children's inherent dependency and need, such as childcare and education and broader charitable campaigns. Parallels can be drawn in this regard to observations made in the context of disability studies, which have commented on the gradual emergence of the 'disability industry' (in the form of disabled people's caring and support services, charities and educational programmes, for instance). The sustainability of this multi-billion pound industry relies on a particular conception of disability, founded on dependence and vulnerability.[19] Similar arguments can be applied to children: children's dependency and need generates work for educationalists, health care workers, domestic carers, and countless others engaged in the consumer and leisure industry with the effect that they are equally dependent on children for their livelihood as children are for their services.

201; R Kränzl-Nagl and U Zartler, 'Children's Participation in School and the Local Community' in B Percy-Smith and N Thomas (eds), *A Handbook of Children and Young People's Participation: Perspectives from Theory and Practice* (London, Routledge, 2010).

[15] W A Corsaro, The Sociology of Childhood, 2nd edn (California, Pine Forge Press, 2005) 36–40; V A Zelizer, 'The Priceless Child Revisited' in Qvortrup (n 14) 184.

[16] D Roker, K Player and J Coleman, 'Young People's Voluntary and Campaigning Activities as Sources of Political Education' (1999) 25 *Oxford Review of Education* 185.

[17] Above n 15, 189

[18] Smart et al, n 12.

[19] J Campbell and M Oliver, Disability Politics: Understanding our Past, Changing our Future (London, Routledge, 1996).

The EU has yet to clearly acknowledge the full extent of children's contribution to the economy and culture of the Member States in any persuasive legal or policy development. It has at least recognised, however, that children should play a more *active* role in policy development and evaluation which, in turn, requires the development of more meaningful and direct opportunities for consultation. The Commission's Agenda for the Rights of the Child asserts in this regard: 'Full recognition of the rights of the child means that children must be given a chance to voice their opinions and participate in the making of decisions that affect them'.[20] The extent to which the EU has the skills, resources and capacity to respond persuasively to this ideal will now be considered.

DOES THE EU HAVE THE CAPACITY TO REGULATE CHILDREN'S RIGHTS?

Notwithstanding the strategic and pragmatic arguments in favour of EU action in children's rights, the potential for that investment to effect valuable improvements in children's lives is significantly undermined by the fact that the EU has limited experience and insight into how children's rights should be formulated, implemented and upheld.

THE EU'S INSTITUTIONAL CAPACITY TO DRIVE CHILDREN'S RIGHTS FORWARD

Up until relatively recently, there has not been a single institution or expert at EU level appointed with the specific task of representing children's rights, nor do any members of the EU's judiciary, the European Court of Justice, claim any insight into the international children's rights standards to which the EU must adhere in interpreting and applying EU law. Rather, children's rights issues have been—and continue to be, to some extent—addressed as a relatively niche aspect of the broader mandates of a select number of Directorate Generals within the Commission. DG Justice,[21] DG Education and Culture, DG Employment, Social Affairs and Inclusion and the former DG for External Relations (DG RELEX[22]) have driven the most significant legal and policy progress in relation to children's rights but in a largely fragmented and mutually exclusive manner.[23] There have been some attempts to

---

[20] Commission to the European Parliament, the Council, the European Economic and Social Committee and the Committee of the Regions, 'An EU Agenda for the Rights of the Child' (Communication) COM (2011) 60 final, 14.

[21] Formerly DG Justice, Freedom and Security until July 2010 when it was divided into two separate DGs, the other DG being DG Home Affairs.

[22] In 2010, in accordance with the Lisbon Treaty, issues formerly addressed under DG RELEX were integrated into the European External Action Service. Certain policy issues have since been integrated into the Foreign Policy Instruments Service.

[23] For a critique of how EU institutional political and communication 'blockages', particularly within the Commission, are hampering progress in relation to children's rights, see J Grugel and I Iusmen, '

stimulate greater co-operation and communication between these departments on children's rights matters, notably through the appointment of a children's rights co-ordinator and through the launch of the European Forum on the Rights of the Child in 2006. While there is little evidence to date of the former performing much more than a high level administrative function, the latter has at least stimulated dialogue between key internal and external stakeholders through a series of annual meetings aimed at responding to clearly defined children's rights priorities.[24]

The Commission, and particularly DG Justice, has been presented as the 'face' of the EU children's rights agenda. However, it is the European Parliament that has been the driving force behind many of the children's rights achievements of which the EU boasts to date. Since the 1980s, it has issued myriad resolutions[25] and research reports,[26] and even appointed a mediator to assist children in the context of international parental child abduction proceedings.[27] The Parliament's commitment to children's rights is evidenced most strongly in the establishment, in March 2011, of the European Parliament Alliance for Children. This is significant not only insofar as its stated aim is 'to create a synergic action that always puts the interests and wellbeing of the child into the heart of all European Parliament'[28] but because it is grounded in a cross-departmental, inter-agency ethic. Thus, the Alliance comprises a genuine partnership between the European Parliament,[29] UNICEF and a network of international NGOs;[30] and will liaise

The European Commission as Guardian Angel: Agenda-Setting for Children's Rights' (forthcoming 2012) *Journal of European Public Policy*; and H Stalford and E Drywood, 'Coming of Age? Children's Rights in the European Union' (2009) 1 *CML Rev* 143.

[24] The Forum includes representatives from the Member States, Ombudspersons for children, the Committee of the Regions, the European Economic and Social Committee, the Council of Europe, UNICEF and other European children's rights NGOs: ec.europa.eu/justice/fundamental-rights/rights-child/european-forum/index_en.htm.

[25] European Parliament resolution of 16 January 2008: Towards an EU Strategy on the rights of the child (2007/2093 (INI)).

[26] Examples include: European Parliament, *Integrating Children in the Development Policy of the European Union*, Directorate General for Research, internal study iv/2003/14/02 of 14 July 2003; European Parliament *Report on a special place for children in EU external action* (2008/2203 (INI)), Committee on Development, 29 January 2009; European Parliament *Report on the exploitation of children in developing countries, with a special focus on child labour* (2005/2004 (INI) Committee on Development, 15 June 2005; European Parliament *Report on promoting social inclusion and combating poverty, including child poverty, in the EU* (2008/2034 (INI), Committee on Employment and Social Affairs, 24 September 2008.

[27] europarl.europa.eu/parliament/public/staticDisplay.do?id=154. This appointment was made in 1987 and preceded the EU's enactment of concrete legislation governing cross-national child abduction by over 15 years. Chapter 4 discusses the children's rights implications of cross-border family law more broadly.

[28] Statement from the Vice-President of the European Parliament, Roberta Angelilli, europarl. europa.eu/news/en/headlines/content/20110328STO16533/html/EP-alliance-to-protect-children-in-Europe-and-beyond.

[29] This will involve a number of nominated child-rights contact people from the various Parliamentary committees, commensurate with the issues being discussed.

[30] The NGOs include Save the Children, Plan International, Eurochild and World Vision and operate collectively under the banner, the Children's Rights Action Group.

with the European Commission to ensure that any recommendations developed by the Alliance are communicated cross-institutionally. While time will tell how effective this Alliance will be in achieving a more coherent and robust EU response to children's rights issues, there is a much more genuine, child-focused tenor to its declarations so far,[31] aided significantly by the fact that its membership has a long-standing interest and expertise in this area.

Another key institutional innovation that bodes well for the future of children's rights at EU level is the establishment in 2007 of the EU Agency for Fundamental Rights (FRA).[32] The function of this independent agency is two-fold: to advise the European Union institutions on how to uphold and promote fundamental rights within the scope of its activities and to collect evidence regarding various aspects of fundamental rights across the Member States to inform any advice it offers. Significantly, the FRA has adopted 'child rights' as one of its key themes and has already funded and published an impressive body of research on issues such as separated asylum-seeking children[33] and child trafficking.[34] Moreover, it has funded the first comprehensive attempt to develop a series of indicators aimed at assessing the extent to which EU law and policy is compatible with children's rights and at measuring the extent to which they are implemented, protected and promoted across the EU.[35]

These institutional developments are clearly to be welcomed: they have provided a range of new forums specifically focused on considering how children's rights might be further advanced at EU level and can exert a powerful influence over key decision-makers when it comes to proposing and adopting law and policy. Ultimately, their activities contribute forcefully to the essential, albeit gradual, cultural and attitudinal shift in the way that children's rights are perceived at EU level. These forums have no decision-making powers, however, nor are they accountable in any sanctionable way for failing to meet the commitments to which they have ascribed. Indeed, the only office that the EU supports that remotely resembles an accountable children's rights representative is the European Ombudsman, charged with investigating allegations of maladministration and, even on the rare occasion when a matter might be brought to his attention that relates to children's rights, the tendency is merely to defer the matter to national children's rights Ombudsmen.[36]

---

[31] The Alliance has explicitly declared that its actions will be firmly rooted in the UNCRC. The precise implications of such an approach are critically examined in ch 2.

[32] Reg 168/2007 of 15 February 2007 establishing a European Union Agency for Fundamental Rights [2007] OJ L53/1.

[33] *Separated Asylum-Seeking Children in European Union Member States* (Summary and Comparative reports) (Vienna, Fundamental Rights Agency, 2010).

[34] *Child Trafficking in the EU: Challenges, Perspectives and Good Practices* (Vienna, Fundamental Rights Agency, 2009).

[35] H Stalford, H Sax and E Drywood, Developing Indicators for the Protection, Respect and Promotion of the Rights of the Child in the European Union—*Updated Post-Lisbon Treaty Conference version* (Vienna, Fundamental Rights Agency, 2010).

[36] National Children's Ombudsmen engage in ongoing exchange and dialogue under the auspices of the European network of Ombudsmen for Children (ENOC), a network that receives substantial

THE IMPORTANCE OF A RELIABLE EVIDENCE BASE

Aside from these institutional developments, an equally important feature of the EU's capacity building in relation to children rights is the development of a sufficiently coherent body of qualitative or quantitative data to provide the empirical basis for a persuasive and coherent supra-national children's rights strategy. Ruxton's observation in 1996 that 'Union statistics on children and childhood are often inadequate compared to data gathering on other issues'[37] still very much reflects the position today. In spite of the significant advancements in the scope of and methodological approaches to data collection and analysis at EU level, coupled with the enhanced availability of national and international data on child-related issues, EU statistics still fail to adequately represent the situation of children. Instead, the position of children is routinely subsumed within more general statistical groupings, and any child-related data is rarely disaggregated further to reveal the distinct experiences of different childhood age-groups.[38]

The importance of establishing a reliable evidence base on which to develop children's rights is not simply a matter of generating more statistical data, however. Equally important are other forms of more qualitative information and research to facilitate an assessment of the domestic legal and institutional frameworks within which EU measures will be applied, and to provide some insight into how EU measures affect children's experiences on the ground.[39] There is an abundance of international, comparative and domestic research on virtually every aspect of children's rights. However, this is not sufficiently exploited to inform related legal and policy strategies at EU level. Moreover, and somewhat ironically, much of this work has been funded by the Commission itself.[40]

There are positive signs of improvement, however, which should address the dearth of persuasive research in relation to certain children's rights issues and, it is hoped, trigger more responsive legal and policy developments. For example, the most recent (November 2011) meeting of the European Forum on the Rights of the Child adopted the theme of 'developing evidence-based child-friendly policies'. Accordingly, it announced the launch, by the Commission with the support

financial support from the European Commission and is involved in the activities of the European Forum on the Rights of the Child (above n 23). For a detailed analysis of the role of this network and other independent children's rights institutions in the EU, see N Thomas, BB Gran, and KC Harnson, 'An Independent Voice for Children's Rights in Europe? The Role of Independent Children's Rights Institutions in the EU' 19 *International Journal of Children's Rights* 429.

[37] S Ruxton, *Children in Europe* (London, NCH Action for Children, 1996).

[38] Stalford, Sax and Drywood, above n 35, 22.

[39] U Kilkelly, 'Operationalising Children's Rights: Lessons from Research' (2006) 1 *Journal of Children's Services* 35.

[40] The Commission's failure to fully exploit the findings of research programmes such as DAPHNE (aimed at preventing and combat violence against children, young people and women), is a case in point and is discussed further in ch 7.

of the European Parliament, of a new pilot to gather reliable data in relation to children involved in legal proceedings across the 27 Member States. In supporting this initiative, the Forum asserted:

> The data should give real insight into the situation of children when they are involved in the justice systems and enable the development of evidence-based EU policies…The EU should bring added value through the collection of data, identification of indicators and promotion of best practices to make a concrete different when children are involved with the justice system, *without duplicating* the work already carried out.[41]

The FRA child-related projects referred to above have also responded to calls to establish a stronger evidence base by engaging in more child sensitive data gathering and analysis. The importance of disaggregating statistics according to age is also reflected, albeit to a modest degree, in EU legislative developments. For example, EU law governing the compilation of migration statistics imposes an obligation on Member States to disaggregate such data in accordance with age to reveal trends in child migration that can be usefully compared and analysed at EU level.[42]

KEY DYNAMICS SHAPING THE DEVELOPMENT
OF CHILDREN'S RIGHTS AT EU LEVEL

In the light of the institutional and methodological limitations referred to above it is perhaps not surprising that children's rights at EU level have historically been pursued in a somewhat haphazard, half-hearted manner—as something of a sideline to, and arguably even a distraction from, the EU's rather broader political and economic pursuits. Such observations have been proffered by the EU institutions as much as by those external to the EU[43] and have, up until relatively recently, conspired to produce a cycle of inertia and ambivalence: as long as children are perceived as contributing relatively little value to the economic and political objectives of the EU, the impetus to invest in research or campaigns aimed at drawing out the impact of EU law on children remains relatively weak. Without such an evidence base, the needs, interests and contribution of children to the EU project remain invisible. This, consequently, perpetuates the perception that there is a lack of need to campaign for more direct EU intervention in relation to

---

[41] Emphasis included in the original. Draft Background Paper for the 6th European Forum on the Rights of the Child: Developing Evidence-Based Policies for Child-friendly Justice, Brussels, 2011, 2 and 4.

[42] Reg 862/2007/EC of the European Parliament and of the Council on Community statistics on migration and international protection and repealing Reg 311/76/EC on the compilation of statistics on foreign workers [20077] OJ L199/23, Art 3(1).

[43] The Commission remarked in the 2011 EU Agenda for the Rights of the Child that the lack of reliable, comparable data poses 'a serious obstacle for the development and implementation of genuine evidence-based policies. Improving the existing monitoring systems, establishing child rights-related policy targets, and monitoring their impact are one of the key challenges' COM (2011) 60 final, 5.

children such that they remain largely peripheral and incidental to mainstream EU law and policy.

Notwithstanding the chaotic and, in some respects, reluctant evolution of children's rights at EU level, there are three key dynamics that have driven and shaped what has now emerged as discrete and legitimate aspect of EU law and policy. They are: the market integration dynamic; the social integration dynamic and the fundamental rights dynamic. The true extent and implications of these influences on the development of children's rights will be explored in subsequent chapters of this book. Suffice to say that one of the first areas in which explicit account was taken of children's needs at EU legal and judicial level was in the context of the free movement of persons provisions. Child-related provision was enacted from the late 1960s onwards, primarily with a view to encouraging the migration of EU workers between the Member States. This body of law has been heavily criticised for its instrumental approach insofar as it endowed children with merely 'parasitic rights' that were highly dependent on and vulnerable to the decisions of their parents.[44] The parameters of this framework have been significantly extended over the years, however, as a result of both judicial ingenuity and legislative enhancement, to endow children, at least in a migration context, with the most direct, independent access to social, civil and economic entitlement thus far available at EU level.[45]

The same internal market imperative underpinned the development of EU measures to regulate jurisdictional and enforcement issues relating to cross-national divorce and parental responsibility arrangements. The logic is that the free movement of people—which is so central to developing and sustaining the EU economy—if it is to be fully effective, has to be accompanied by the free movement of legal decisions regulating individuals' personal relationships.[46] Provision aimed at protecting the interests of children implicated in such proceedings was necessarily introduced to reflect parallel private international and domestic family law in this area, thereby forcing the EU to engage in children's rights in a much more direct way.[47]

In the same token, the EU's internal market activities have triggered the implementation of a range of children protection measures aimed at averting the potentially injurious effects brought about by the gradual erosion of EU internal borders. Thus, the EU has introduced a range of protective measures aimed at addressing the increased threat in cross-border trafficking in children, child abduction and illegal

---

[44] McGlynn, Families and the European Union: Law, Politics and Pluralism (Cambridge, Cambridge University Press, 2006), particularly ch 3; and HL Ackers and H Stalford, *A Community for Children? Children, Citizenship and Migration in the European Union* (Aldershot, Ashgate, 2004).

[45] The evolution of children's rights in the context of free movement and citizenship is discussed in chs 2 and 3.

[46] For a detailed analysis of the interplay between EU family law and EU free movement law, see H Stalford, 'For Better, For Worse: The Relationship between EU Citizenship and the Development of Cross-border Family Law' in N Shuibhne, M Dougan and E Spaventa (eds), *Empowerment and Disempowerment of the EU Citizen* (Oxford, Hart Publishing, forthcoming 2012).

[47] See further chs 4 and 5.

immigration. Such measures have been gradually extended to cover the associated issues of labour and sexual exploitation which, in turn, has prompted a review of the level of protection and support afforded to child victims in these situations.[48]

A similar pattern of children's rights 'overspill' has emerged in the context of the EU's social agenda which finds its origins in the European Social Action Programme of the 1970s. This programme, like the internal market agenda, initially targeted the needs of the EU adult population in acknowledgement of the negative correlation between unemployment and poverty. This agenda, which was primarily aimed at maximising labour market participation, started to interrogate the effects of social exclusion on children, ultimately with a view to developing a range of early intervention strategies that would militate against their social exclusion (and, by implication, economic incapacity) as they progressed into adulthood. Child poverty was thus adopted as a key priority of the EU's Social inclusion agenda at the turn of the millennium and stimulated a series of co-ordinated action plans and research that are still ongoing.[49] Increasingly broad conceptualisations of 'poverty' have, in turn, extended the reach of EU activity into a range of measures aimed at promoting child 'well-being' in ways that were never fully anticipated when the EU embarked on this project.[50]

This brief overview illustrates the sprawling nature of children's rights: what was conceived as a confined set of measures that were incidental and instrumental to the achievement of the EU's broader internal market and social-integration imperatives generated a legal and policy domino effect that the EU has struggled to contain. This stimulated a diverse range of child-related measures in legislative, policy and judicial contexts that were previously ambivalent to children's rights issues. However, there was still no evidence of any strategic approach to this process or a clear statement of the aims and objectives of EU child law or policy; nor was there much evidence that EU children's rights were being constructed within a specific ideological framework endorsed by domestic and international law, policy and discourse. The turn of the millennium marked a turning point in this regard since it was at this point that a more explicit reference to fundamental rights emerged. The introduction of the Charter of Fundamental Rights of the European Union in 2000[51] sparked a more profound engagement by the EU legislature and judiciary with fundamental rights issues.[52] Children's rights were necessarily implicated in this process, not least because the Charter included express provision for children.[53] It was the introduction of the Lisbon Treaty in December 2009,[54] however, that elevated the status of fundamental rights—and,

---

[48] See further ch 7.
[49] Lisbon European Council Presidency Conclusions, Council of the European Union, SN/100/00, 23–24 March 2000.
[50] See further ch 2.
[51] [2000] OJ C/303/17, as amended, [2010] OJC 83/02).
[52] The history and impact of fundamental rights at EU level are considered in more detail in ch 2.
[53] Notably in Art 24.
[54] [2007] OJ C306/1 of 13 December 2007.

by implication, children's rights—within the EU's constitutional order, thereby adding fresh momentum to the EU children's rights campaign. Specifically, as a result of the Lisbon Treaty, the Charter is afforded the same legal status as the Treaties and thereby produces legally binding effects. As a result, the EU institutions and Member States alike can be directly held to account for failing to comply with the children's rights principles and provisions contained within the Charter when implementing EU law.[55] As if to reinforce the point that the changes to the EU's fundamental rights framework also captures children's rights, the Lisbon Treaty also added 'protection of the rights of the child' to the list of general objectives of the European Union,[56] an objective that is echoed in the context of the EU's external relations policy.[57]

These developments have undoubtedly enhanced the legitimacy and coherence of the EU children's rights campaign. Fundamental rights now offers a powerful constitutional 'hook' on which to hang any initiatives aimed at promoting or protecting the rights of the child, even in the more sterile contexts in which children's rights feature. Indeed, there is barely a reference to children's rights at EU level without an accompanying reference to either the Charter or Article 3(3) TEU (Treaty on European Union) or both. Such is the pervasiveness of fundamental rights that it now underpins the operation of internal market and social-integration initiatives too, potentially threading a coherent, rights-based ethic through all the EU children's rights measures in the future.

The gradual, somewhat awkward history of EU children's rights reached something of a peak with the announcement of plans to launch a comprehensive children's rights strategy. The flagship initiative in this regard was the Commission's Communication, 'Towards a Strategy on the Rights of the Child' published in July 2006.[58] This document not only catalogued the various ad hoc legal and policy initiatives and research programmes that had accumulated over the previous decade or so, but also articulated a series of ambitions aimed at achieving a more coherent, transparent and long-term approach to addressing various children's rights issues at EU level. This has been superseded by the EU Agenda for the Rights of the Child[59] which identifies 11 concrete areas for EU action in the coming years[60] which are underpinned by three general principles to guide the institutions in their development, namely: integrating children's rights into the EU's fundamental

---

[55] H Stalford and M Schuurman, 'Are We There Yet? The Impact of the Lisbon Treaty on the EU Children's Rights Agenda' (2011) 19 *International Journal of Children's Rights* 381, 397.

[56] Art 3(3) TEU.

[57] Art 3(5) TEU. These declarations are symbolically important rather than legally forceful; they merely serve to inform the interpretation of other aspects of the Treaty and do not provide a new legal basis for child-focused legislative developments at EU level.

[58] COM (2006) 367 final. See also Commission Staff Working Document Accompanying the Communication from the Commission, 'Preliminary Inventory of EU Actions Affecting Children's Rights' (Brussels, 2006) 889.

[59] Above n 20.

[60] Primarily in relation to child-friendly justice, Roma integration, missing children, vulnerable victims and online safety.

rights policy; building the basis for evidence-based policy and co-operating with external and internal stakeholders.

DEFINING THE BOUNDARIES BETWEEN EU ACTION AND DOMESTIC ACTION IN THE FIELD OF CHILDREN'S RIGHTS

These latter developments have been welcomed by campaigners as indicative of a much more considered approach to children's rights at EU level.[61] It is important, however, not to lose sight of the fact that there are limitations on the extent to which the EU can and should interfere in children's rights issues. The majority of issues remain firmly within the regulatory purview of the Member States to account for the fact that children's needs and interests respond to a range of contextual factors that are specific to the environment in which they live—factors such as culture, religion, politics and economics. Beyond this, the boundary between EU and national regulation of children's rights is determined by reference to a number of core principles.

First and foremost, EU action must be grounded in the treaties: the EU can only enact legal and policy measures within the limits of the competences conferred upon it by the Member States. These competences are articulated in the treaties[62] which specify both the areas in which the EU can act, as well as the process by which that action must be performed.[63] Identifying a legal basis on which to enact child-related measures is not a straightforward process, however, primarily because there are very limited treaty references to children. Article 3(3) TEU, referred to above, offers the most explicit endorsement in declaring that '[The Union] shall... promote...protection of the rights of the child' but it does not confer authority on the EU to effect unlimited measures in relation to children's rights; it is merely a declaration of the EU's basic values and objectives.[64] The fact that few power-conferring provisions within the treaties refer explicitly to 'children' does not mean, however, that the EU has no competence to enact child-related measures; technically it is no more correct to say that the EU has no competence to regulate children's rights than it is to say that the EU has no competence to regulate women's or men's rights. Ultimately the EU has the authority to act in relation to any matter that intersects with an issue prescribed in the treaties, even if the link is relatively tenuous. Moreover, the fact that many treaty provisions are framed

---

[61] Although some still argue that the Commission's Agenda does not go far enough in responding to the diverse needs of children in the EU in a way that fully accommodates the UNCRC. See Eurochild, Policy Position: EuroChild's Proposals for the Development of the EU's Strategy on the Rights of the Child (Belgium, Eurochild, 2010).

[62] Specifically the Treaty on European Union (TEU) and the Treaty on the Functioning of the European Union (TFEU).

[63] Art 3(6) TEU.

[64] A Dashwood, M Dougan, B Rodger, E Spaveta and D Wyatt, *Wyatt and Dashwood's European Union Law*, 6th edn (Oxford, Hart, 2011) 99.

in general, sometimes quite abstract terms makes it relatively easy to establish some correlation with children's rights. For example, EU action to address child poverty finds its legal basis in a much broader treaty reference to 'combating social exclusion',[65] whilst support for programmes aimed at addressing violence against children are grounded, rather inventively, in the Treaty's broad public health provisions.[66]

There are limits, however, on the lengths to which the EU can go in regulating children's rights. Specifically, on determining that the EU has competence to act in a particular aspect of children's rights, the nature and scope of that action are assessed by reference to the principles of subsidiarity and proportionality.[67] The principle of subsidiarity dictates that the EU can only act in relation to a particular children's rights issue if it will be more effective than action at the purely domestic level. This interrogates in the first instance the adequacy of domestic action, which is why so much children's rights provision responds to cross-national phenomena affecting children. Furthermore, the principle of proportionality states that even if EU action in relation to a particular children's rights issue is more appropriate and effective than Member State action alone, the EU must not go beyond what is necessary to achieve its objectives. Implicit in this is the requirement that EU action must add value to what is being achieved at the national level or, indeed, at the international level.

It is easier to satisfy these tests in relation to some issues than others: child-related matters that cross national boundaries such as immigration, trafficking or free movement, clearly demand a level of supra-national co-ordination to achieve an effective, consistent response from the various domestic authorities with which these children interact.[68] Other issues, such as child poverty, juvenile justice, violence or exploitation, demand a little more ingenuity and are generally limited to 'softer' interventions that seek to support and encourage rather than supplant Member States activities.

DEFINING 'CHILD' UNDER EU LAW

Before embarking on a detailed analysis of the content and scope of children's rights in various substantive areas, it is important to define what is meant by 'child' under EU law.[69] In short, there is no established EU definition of 'child' contained in the treaties or secondary legislation, the case law[70] or, indeed, in the

---

[65] Art 153 TFEU, formerly Art 137 EC.
[66] Art 168 TFEU, formerly Art 152 EC.
[67] Art 5 TEU.
[68] N Ferreira, above n 11, 208.
[69] Ch 3 will develop some of the issues relating to the EU definition of child.
[70] AG Tesauro observed with some surprise in Case C-7/94 *Lubor Gaal—Landesamt für Ausbildungsförderung Nordrhein-Westfalen v Lubor Gaal* [1996] ECR I-1031—that the free movement provisions did not contain a single definition of the 'child', para 7.

EU Agenda for the Rights of the Child.[71] In fact, the only explicit attempt to define 'child' at EU level is a sentence on the website of DG Justice: 'As laid down in the UN Convention on the Rights of the Child, a child is any human being below the age of 18'.[72]

This is surprising given the claims by the Commission to develop a 'coherent approach' to the rights of the child across all relevant EU actions[73] and contrasts with many other notions in relation to which the EU has adhered to a universal, 'supra-national' definition to determine the scope of EU entitlement.[74] Consequently, in contrast with the universal definition of 'child' ascribed by the UNCRC and claimed by DG Justice, the legal formula and issues taken into account in determining what constitutes a 'child' under EU law vary according to the context: in some circumstances, 'child' is a biological construct, determined by reference to the minor's blood tie with the adult; in other circumstances, 'child' is an age-based construct, by which the nature and level of the child's rights differ according to their age-group; and, in a limited number of cases, 'child' is a dependency-based construct, determined by reference to the child's economic or social relationship with their parent or legal guardian.

'CHILD' AS AN AGE-BASED CONSTRUCT UNDER EU LAW

Notwithstanding the EU's reluctance to endorse a concrete, universal definition of 'child' it has readily defined the age parameters of 'young person'. The EU's concept of 'young person', however, is not confined to 'minors' or even teenagers under the age of 18 as one might expect. Instead, it includes children from the age of 13 up to adulthood. Examples of this are scattered across EU law and policies that promote the social and civic rights of children and young people. For instance, the Commission's Youth Agenda, the aim of which is to facilitate and encourage more active participation of young people in democratic processes by eliciting their views on a range of Community matters, targets the 13 to

---

[71] Above n 20.

[72] ec.europa.eu/justice/fundamental-rights/rights-child/index_en.htm.

[73] EU Agenda, above n 20, 4.

[74] Eg a formula for determining whether or not an individual qualifies as a 'worker' for the purposes of the free movement provisions has been developed by the ECJ in isolation from any Member State notion of worker (Case 53/81 *Levin v Staatsecretaris van Justitie* [1982] ECR 1035 and Case 75/63 *Hoekstra (née Unger) v BBD* [1964] ECR 177). Thus, it is has long been accepted that a worker is anyone who performs services under the direction of another in return for some form of remuneration (Case 66/85 *Lawrie-Blum v Land Baden-Württemberg* [1986] ECR 2121, paras 16 and 17). A similar, albeit more restrictive supra-national, formula has been established in relation to the concept of 'marriage' under Community law to establish the boundaries of those who can benefit from the various Community rights associated with that status (Art 2 Dir 2004/38, below n 76). (Joined Cases C-122/99 and C-125/99 *D and Sweden v Council* [2001] ECR I-4319; Case C-13/94 *P v S and Cornwall CC* [1996] ECR I-2143). See also L Tomasi, C Ricci and S Bariatti, 'Characterisation in Family Matters for the Purposes of European Private International Law' in J Meeusen (eds), *International Family Law for the European Union* (Antwerp, Intersentia, 2007) 341.

30 age-group.[75] Similarly the free movement provisions apply an age test in determining which family members derive certain rights of entry, residence and other social rights from the migrant worker parent although, again, this is not consistent with the global majority threshold. Thus, under EU law governing the free movement rights of EU citizens and their family members, 'child' is defined as 'direct descendants who are under the age of 21'.[76] A similar model is applied to secondary legislation relating to the free movement of services.[77]

Other EU legislation, particularly in relation to issues in which EU action is complementary to that of Member States, defers to national law to determine what constitutes a child. For example, legislation facilitating cross-border access to social security entitlement for migrants and their families makes provision for 'minor' children implying deference to domestic thresholds of majority.[78] EU immigration law governing the qualification and reception conditions of asylum seekers provides that 'minors shall be younger than the age of legal majority in the Member State in which the application for asylum was lodged or is being examined'.[79] Indeed, most of the EU immigration measures pertaining to unaccompanied minors consistently define this group of children as under-18s.[80] In the same vein, EU law regulating audiovisual media services includes specific provision aimed at protecting the physical, mental and moral development of 'minors', again implying the universal majority threshold espoused by the UNCRC.[81]

There are a number of instances, however, in which the same instrument prescribes different EU entitlement according to the age of the child. For instance,

---

[75] The impetus for this programme came from the 2001 White Paper on Youth, 1444/01 COM (2001) 681. This led to the implementation of Council Resolution of 27 June 2002 regarding a framework of European Co-operation in Youth Matters [2002] OJ C168/2, the signing in March 2005 of the European Youth Pact, and the launch of the Youth in Action Programme 2007–13.

[76] Dir 2004/38 on the Right of Citizens of the Union and their Family Members to Move and Reside Freely within the Territory of the Member States, OJ L158/77 [2004], Art 2(2)(c). The significance of dependency in this context will be discussed below.

[77] Dir 73/148/EEC on the abolition of restrictions on movement and residence within the Community for nationals of Member States with regard to establishment and the provision of services [1973]; Dir 2006/123/EC on services in the internal market [2006] OJ L376/36, para 36 preamble.

[78] Reg 883/2004/EC of the European Parliament and of the Council on the co-ordination of social security systems, [2004] OJ L200/1, Art 1(i)(2).

[79] Dir 2003/9/EC laying down minimum standards for the reception of asylum seekers [2003] OJ L31/18, Art 10(1); and Dir 2004/83 on minimum standards for the qualification and status of third country nationals or stateless persons as refugees or as persons who otherwise need international protection and the content of the protection granted [2004] OJ L304/12, Art 15.

[80] See notably Reg 343/2003 establishing the criteria and mechanisms for determining the Member State responsible for examining an asylum application lodged in one of the Member States by a third-country national [2003] OJ L50/1, Art 2(h); Dir 2003/9 (above n 79) Art 2(h) and Dir 2004/83 (above n 79) Art 2(1).

[81] Dir 2010/13/EU of the European Parliament and of the Council of 10 March 2010 on the co-ordination of certain provisions laid down by law, regulation or administrative action in Member States concerning the provision of audiovisual media services [2010] OJ L95/1, Arts 3(4)(i); 9(1)(e) and (g); 12; 22 and 27. For a full analysis of the children's rights implications of EU consumer protection legislation, see A Garde, 'Advertising Regulation and the Protection of Children-Consumers in the European Union: In the Best Interest of…Commercial Operators?' (2011) 19 *International Journal of Children's Rights* 523.

in the context of employment, children are afforded different rights (primarily linked to health and safety in the workplace) in accordance with their age. The most notable example of this is the Young Workers Directive.[82] The tenor of this instrument is primarily that of protection, ensuring that children are not exposed to harmful working conditions and that an appropriate balance is achieved between work and formal education. Thus, while the directive as a whole applies to all under young people under the age of 18, it distinguishes between 'young people' (a blanket term for all minors under the age of 18), 'adolescents' (any young person of at least 15 years of age but less than 18 years of age who is no longer subject to compulsory full-time schooling) and 'children' (defined as those under the age of 15).[83] Only those who fall within the latter category are prohibited from undertaking formal employment.[84] A similar, albeit less defensible, tiering of children's rights in accordance with their age is evident in EU legislation governing the family reunification rights of third country nationals who are lawfully resident in the EU.[85] While 'child' for the purposes of family reunification refers to those who have not reached the age of majority in accordance with the law of the host Member State,[86] a number of exceptions are applied: a child over the age of 12 who arrives in the host state independently of the rest of the family must satisfy an integration test in accordance with national law before being authorised to enter and reside in the host state.[87] Moreover, the legislation enables Member States to request that applications by parents to be joined by their minor children must be submitted before the child reaches the age of 15.[88]

'CHILD' AS A BIOLOGICAL CONSTRUCT UNDER EU LAW

In certain areas of EU law 'child' is determined according to additional factors other than age. In those areas in which children's rights are derived from those of their parents, notably the free movement provisions or EU immigration law, 'child' is a biological construct that operates alongside the age-based criteria discussed above. The importance of establishing a biological link between the child and his/

---

[82] Dir 94/33 of 22 June 1994 on the protection of young people at work [1994] OJ L216/12.

[83] Art 3.

[84] The Directive allows for certain derogations from the general prohibition on children working. For instance, a greater degree of flexibility is applied during the school holiday periods, and for work related to artistic, sporting, advertising and cultural activities, family business and 'light' work (Art 5).

[85] Dir 2003/86 on the right to family reunification [2003] OJ L 251/12.

[86] Art 4.

[87] Art 4(1).

[88] Art 4(6). Note that while no Member State actually applied such a restrictive policy, these provisions were regarded as so blatantly discriminatory on grounds of age that they were the subject of legal action initiated by the European Parliament against the Council (Case C-540/03 *Parliament v Council* [2006] ECR I-5769). This is discussed further in ch 3. See also E Drywood, 'Giving with One Hand, Taking with the Other: Fundamental Rights, Children and the Family Reunification Decision' (2007) 32 *EL Rev* 396; and E Drywood, 'Challenging Concepts of the "Child" in Asylum and Immigration Law: The Example of the EU' (2010) 32 *Journal of Social Welfare and Family Law* 309.

her parents is evident as much in how the parental relationships are defined as in how children are defined in the legislation. Thus, Directive 2004/38 governing the rights of citizens to enter and reside in other EU Member States provides that 'family member' includes 'the direct descendants who are under the age of 21... of *either* the [EU citizen's] spouse or partner'.[89] This implies that children with no direct biological link to EU migrant adults (the primary beneficiaries of free movement entitlement) can now benefit from the panoply of entitlement previously restricted to their biological children. This more liberal definition, which includes step children, adopted or foster children, or even the children of the migrant's unmarried partner, reflects earlier decisions of the Court of Justice[90] and represents a welcome acknowledgement, not only of the significant variety of family constellations that exist across Europe today, but also of the fact that family life implies rather more complex dynamics than the mere existence of a biological tie. Indeed, it is the existence of a relationship of 'dependency' rather than age or biology that has become the defining feature of 'child' under EU law. A similarly broad approach is also endorsed in EU immigration law governing the rights of third country nationals and particularly refugees, in recognition of the very specific impact that civil war, poverty and disease in primary sending countries has on parental mortality.[91]

'CHILD' AS A DEPENDENCY-BASED CONSTRUCT UNDER EU LAW

Adult-targeted EU provision has been readily extended to children on the basis that they are 'dependent' family members of the primary beneficiaries. This is a particularly important feature of EU free movement and immigration law. The reference to dependency as a basis on which to claim 'child' status is significantly broader than the alternative age-based assessment. Indeed, much of the case law involving claims to derived family rights under the free movement provisions involved young *adults* seeking to stake a claim in their parents' migration legacy rather than 'minors';[92] they have very little to do with 'children's rights' in the conventional sense of the term. There is still no clear guidance, however, on how

---

[89] Above n 76, Art 2(2)(c), emphasis added. Previously, only the joint children of both the EU migrant citizen and his/her legally married heterosexual spouse were entitled to derive mobility entitlement under the free movement provisions. This inevitably excluded some step children from the scope of EU free movement law. See further C McGlynn, *Families and the European Union* (above n 44) 47.

[90] Case C-60/00 Carpenter [2002] ECR I-6279 and Case C-413/99 *Baumbast v Secretary of State for the Home Department* [2002] ECR I-7091. These cases are discussed in more detail in ch 3.

[91] See further the discussion in ch 3.

[92] Joined Cases 389 and 390/87 *Echternach and Moritz v Netherlands Minister for Education and Science* [1989] ECR 723; Case 197/86 *Brown v Secretary of State for Scotland* [1988] ECR 3205; Case 9/74 *Casagrande v Landeshauptstadt München* [1974] ECR 773. While later cases have involved young children, the claims have been brought by their parents on the basis of their caring responsibilities rather than by the children directly. These cases are discussed in ch 3.

'dependency' is defined or, indeed, how heavy that dependency needs to be.[93] In many respects, a loose approach to dependency is to be welcomed insofar as it recognises the many dimensions (including, financial, emotional, practical and physical) of dependency that do not simply expire once a child reaches the age of 18. However, the concept is used rather more selectively by the EU according to the category of children at issue: in free movement cases concerning EU migrant workers and their families, interpretations of dependency are somewhat more generous if there is a perceptible economic gain to be had for the EU. Children may be regarded as a good investment, for example, if the dependency-related entitlement they are claiming will facilitate their or their parents' entry into the labour market. The approach will be less generous, however, if it is likely to give rise to an ongoing relationship of dependency, not on the parents so much as on the public resources of the state in which the child is living.

Some broader concerns emerge from this brief synopsis of the EU's formal conceptualisation of 'child'. First, as McGlynn points out, the shifting and unpredictable definition of child illustrates the difficulties of drafting a coherent set of rights for children that successfully balance and reconcile competing rights, interests and conceptions of childhood.[94] In that sense, one could simply argue that the definition of 'child' necessarily fluctuates to meet the diverse objectives of each aspect of EU law and policy. The fact that this definition has been moulded to fit within the personal and material scope of EU law rather than the converse, however, does not sit comfortably with the EU's current efforts to champion children's rights. It merely serves to highlight the haphazard and disconnected manner in which EU children's rights has historically been developed. Moreover, is raises questions as to whether it is the appropriate for the EU to associate itself so explicitly with the UNCRC[95] when the very concept of child endorsed by aspects of EU law deviates so readily from the definition prescribed by the UNCRC.

CONCLUSION ·

With such a patchwork of provision and a history of incoherence and uncertainty, it is a wonder that we can convincingly talk of 'EU children's rights'. The EU is still grappling with the legacies of this history, and has yet to reconcile some of its more limiting features with the more sensitised and confident tone of the current EU Agenda for the Rights of the Child.

The EU has presented a persuasive rationale for assuming a key role in driving children's rights forward. Commitment to this project demands not only a concrete

---

[93] In Case C-7/94 *Landesamt fur Ausbildungsforderung Nordrhein-Westfalen v Lubor Gaal* [1996] ECR 1-1031, the claimant was the adopted child of a deceased EU migrant who sought to rely on his relationship of dependency on the state (acting in loco parentis) to access entitlement in the host state.

[94] McGlynn, *Families and the European Union* (above n 44) 72.

[95] This relationship will be explored further in ch 2.

legal basis on which to enact legal and policy measures, but also significant investment in capacity building, not only in institutional terms but evidentially too. The 'empirical vacuum' within which EU children's rights have been developed to date can be addressed by simply calling for more relevant, methodologically rigorous research to evaluate how EU law affects children's lives, for better dissemination of work that has already been carried out, and for greater investment in capacity building, training and awareness-raising within the EU institutions. Other obstacles are more pervasive, however, and are the symptom of entrenched perceptions of the mutual exclusivity of the protection and development of children's rights on the one hand and the achievement of EU integration, on the other. These perceptions are reinforced by children's rights campaigners as much as by actors internal to the EU. Indeed, there is a latent concern among the former that by integrating children's rights into the EU's legal and policy mandate as it is currently framed, children's interests are vulnerable to being lost within and perhaps even corrupted by the EU's 'core', resolutely adultist objectives. These concerns reinforce the need to embed the future development of EU children's rights within a firm ideological framework that departs from a purely internal market approach that views children as economic investments, towards one that values children's contribution and rights for what they are. The nature and value of this ideological framework will provide the focus of the analysis in chapter two.

2

The Ideology of EU Children's Rights

INTRODUCTION

H AVING ESTABLISHED THE definition and legal scope of EU children's rights in the previous chapter, this chapter explores the ideological and constitutional foundations of EU activity in relation to children. It has already been explained how the EU's historical inertia in relation to children's rights was partly symptomatic of a political uneasiness with regulating such an intimate, context-specific range of issues that were largely detached from the economic imperative driving the EU. Linked to this was the lack of any explicit legal basis on which to enact direct, justiciable children's rights measures. Not surprisingly, therefore, EU children's rights has traditionally been characterised by a handful of piecemeal initiatives, some formulated on more tenuous legal bases than others, and all of them, for the most part, endowing children with 'indirect' and relatively frail entitlement. The chaotic nature of this journey suggests that EU children's rights have evolved in an ideological vacuum; there has been relatively little attempt, up until now, to think through the values and methods that should underpin the future development of children's rights at this level.

The Commission's publication, in February 2011, of its seminal Communication, 'An Agenda for the Rights of the Child'[1] galvanises the EU's commitment to children's rights. It sets out its overarching purpose as follows:

> [T]o reaffirm the strong commitment of all EU institutions and of all Member States to promoting, protecting and fulfilling the rights of the child in all relevant EU policies and to turn it into concrete results.[2]

In order to achieve this, the Agenda identifies a series of objectives relating both to developments in substantive law and policy affecting children and to the changes that have to be made to the institutional and procedural architecture of the EU to enable these developments to take place. The Commission is very explicit in asserting that 'the "child rights perspective" must be taken into account in all EU

---

[1] Commission, 'An EU Agenda for the Rights of the Child' (Communication) COM (2011) 60 final.
[2] Ibid 3.

measures affecting children'.[3] It offers very little guidance, however, as to what a 'child rights perspective' really entails, leading to questions as to whether the rhetorical capital of 'rights', so easily endorsed by the Agenda, is accompanied by the necessary insight, practical mechanisms and resources to enable the EU to achieve the ambitions associated with such an approach.

Such observations suggest that the time is now ripe to consider, in more depth, the ideological framework underpinning current and planned EU action in the field of children's rights. In doing so, the analysis begins with the somewhat sceptical observation that, in a matter of a few years, the EU has affected a dramatic shift from one extreme to another: it has gone from a position of largely marginalising children's interests in favour of the more mainstream interests of the economically active adult population, to positively embracing the language of children's 'rights', but on a rather superficial and sentimental level. In drawing attention to this shift, the intention is not to malign the EU's newfound commitment to children's rights, but, rather, to illustrate that, in fact, the EU's existing constitutional architecture is really quite amenable to the pursuit of children's rights and has significant capacity to transpose this rhetoric into concrete action. In doing so, the aim, ultimately, is to identify the ideological building blocks for a much more robust, sustainable and persuasive EU children's rights campaign.

With this in mind, the following discussion begins with a consideration of the currency and scope of a 'rights' based approach to protecting children's interests in the EU. It will move on to identify the sources of children's fundamental rights as well as the extent to which these rights are integrated into EU law and policy to produce legally enforceable effects. The analysis will then suggest some additional conceptual and constitutional tools that are at the EU's disposal to pursue the objectives of the EU children's agenda equally, if not more effectively than a literal rights-based approach. The fundamental norms of non-discrimination, citizenship and social inclusion are singled-out in this regard. The analysis will conclude with an examination of how all of these approaches intersect with fundamental rights to produce a coherent and sturdy framework for the advancement and protection of children's interests in a range of contexts.

DEFINING A RIGHTS-BASED APPROACH
TO REGULATING CHILDREN'S LIVES

The 2011 EU Agenda on the Rights of the Child suggests, from its very title, that it is firmly ensconced in a 'rights' framework. Indeed, such is the rhetorical, legal

---

[3] Ibid.

and political value of rights that it seems an obvious discourse within which to locate action in relation to children. As Freeman notes:

> The language of 'rights' can make visible what has for too long been suppressed. It can lead to different and new stories being heard in public ... Rights are important because they are inclusive: they are universal, available to all members of the human race.[4]

But what does a rights-based approach really mean in practice? And what does this involve in the specific context of *children's* rights?

Notwithstanding the extensive literature and guidance on the subject,[5] a 'rights' based approach is notoriously difficult to define but has been variously associated with notions of accountability, universality, international co-operation, participation and non-discrimination.[6] Tun and colleagues have stated:

> A rights-based approach is concerned with the application of human rights standards and principles to both the goal and the process of development—the means becoming as important as the end.[7]

With this in mind, a rights-based approach involves not simply achieving a particular outcome that is compatible with the standards prescribed by human rights law, but also implies an obligation to adhere to human rights standards in the course of achieving that goal. It is a *process* as much as a *product*. It entails a degree of accountability on those who bear the duty—states parties, the EU institutions, authorities at the regional level, as well as other public and private actors—both in terms of respecting and upholding human rights obligations, but also in terms of adapting or instituting processes that facilitate fulfilment of those rights.[8]

This interpretation begs the question as to the degree to which the EU lends itself to the processes and obligations inherent in a rights based approach to regulating children's lives. The following discussion will consider, first of all, the legal

---

[4] M Freeman, 'Why It Remains Important to Take Children's Rights Seriously' (2007) 15 *International Journal of Children's Rights* 5, 6–7.

[5] There is a burgeoning literature that examines the rights based approach, much of which focuses on international development where the concept finds its genesis. This has been adapted to a children's rights context in more recent years, primarily through the programming and campaigning activities of the NGO sector. See, Save the Children, *Child Rights Programming: How to Apply Rights-Based Approaches in Programming* (Stockholm, Save the Children, 2002); G Lansdown, *What's the Difference? Implications of a Child Focus in Rights Based Programming—A Discussion Paper* (London, Save the Children, 2005). See specifically, J Tobin, 'Beyond the Supermarket Shelf: Using A Rights Based Approach to Address Children's Health Needs' (2006) 14 *International Journal of Children's Rights* 275.

[6] J Tobin, 'Understanding A Human Rights Based Approach to Matters Involving Children: Conceptual Foundations and Strategic Considerations' in A Invernezzi and J Williams (eds), *The Human Rights of Children: From Visions to Implementation* (Farnham, Ashgate, 2011) 61, 68.

[7] AA Tun, G Cave, D Trotter and B Bell, 'The Domestic Fulfilment of Children's Rights: Save the Children's Experience in the Use of Rights-Based Approaches' in A Alen, H Bosely and M De Bie (eds), *The UN Children's Rights Convention: Theory Meets Practice* (Netherlands, Intersentia, 2007) 33, 34.

[8] P Alston, 'Ships Passing in the Night: The Current State of the Human Rights and Development Debate Seen Through the Lens of the Millennium Development Goals' (2005) 27 *Human Rights Quarterly* 755.

status of rights within the EU more generally. It will then identify the principles and provisions that form the substance of the children's rights-based approach of which the EU Agenda boasts. In the process, there will be some consideration of how these resources are influencing EU legal and policy *processes* in a way that renders them more sensitive to children's rights, thereby enhancing the EU's accountability in this regard.

THE LEGAL CURRENCY OF FUNDAMENTAL RIGHTS AT EU LEVEL

Implicit in the language of rights is the notion of entitlement: there is little point in asserting one's rights in the abstract if they do not entail enforceable claims.[9] The capacity of the EU to transpose abstract, international children's rights provisions into justiciable entitlement is discerned by reference to the impact of fundamental rights within the EU legal order more broadly. Certainly, the EU institutions have established a reputation as 'staunch defenders of human rights'[10] and now boast a highly developed and coherent constitutional and procedural framework in this regard. In fact, fundamental rights have been part of the EU legal fabric for almost as long as the EU has existed. Initially, they were one aspect of the 'general principles of EU law': written and unwritten principles drawn from the common, constitutional traditions of the Member States that supplement and guide interpretations of the Treaties.[11] Like many other general principles of EU law, the currency and scope of fundamental rights at EU level was established and refined by the Court of Justice through a line of cases dating back to the late 1960s.[12] These cases confirmed that, insofar as the constitutional traditions of the Member States recognise specific key rights, so too should those rights be integrated into the EU legal order. In addition to the rights recognised by the Member States' constitutions, the Court of Justice also established that international human rights treaties and conventions to which the Member States

---

[9] Although international human rights commentators would argue that expectations of enforceability apply mainly to civil and political rights, rather than to economic, social and cultural rights. See further D McGoldrick, 'The Boundaries of Justiciability' (2010) 59 *ICLQ* 981.

[10] P Alston and J Weiler, 'A European Union Human Rights Policy' in P Alston, M Bustelo and J Heenan (eds), *The European Union and Human Rights* (Oxford, Oxford University Press, 1999) 6.

[11] See generally, T Tridimas, *The General Principles of EU Law*, 2nd edn (Oxford, Oxford University Press, 2007).

[12] Case 26/69 *Stauder v City of Ulm* [1969] ECR 419; Case 11/70 *Internationale Handelsgesellschaft* [1970] ECR 1125. For a more detailed analysis see G De Búrca, 'Fundamental Rights and the Reach of EC Law' 13 (1993) *Oxford Journal of Legal Studies* 283; G De Búrca, 'Convergence and Divergence in European Public Law: The Case of Human Rights' in P Beaumont, C Lyons and N Walker (eds), *Convergence and Divergence in European Public Law* (Oxford, Hart, 2002) 131; N Neuwahl and A Rosas, *The European Union and Human Rights* (The Hague, Martinus Nijhoff Publishers,1995); J Weiler and Lockhart, 'Taking Rights Seriously: The European Court and its Fundamental Rights Jurisprudence' (1995) 32 *CML Rev* 51 (Pt 1) and 579 (Pt II); T Ahmed and I de Jesús Butler, 'The European Union and Human Rights: An International Perspective' (2006) 17 *European Journal of International Law* 771.

are signatories are likewise part of the fundamental rights landscape and, by implication, the EU general principles framework.[13] There was a simple logic to this: any obligation arising out of membership of the EU should not conflict with Member States' obligations arising out of their domestic constitutional orders and, indeed, their international commitments.

Such is the importance of fundamental rights that they are now firmly entrenched in all of the EU's institutional processes and continue to exert a powerful regulatory influence not only on the legal and administrative activities of the EU institutions, but on the Member States as well insofar as they are acting within the scope of EU law.[14] Furthermore, their status has been set in constitutional stone, initially by virtue of the 1992 Maastricht Treaty (the Treaty on European Union, or TEU),[15] and later by the Treaties of Amsterdam[16] and Nice,[17] and, most recently, the 2009 Lisbon Treaty.[18]

SOURCES OF CHILDREN'S RIGHTS AT EU LEVEL

Three principal human rights instruments form the bedrock of EU children's rights insofar as they contain direct reference to or have an established jurisprudence and guidance that apply to children and young people. These are the 1989 UN Convention on the Rights of the Child (UNCRC), the 1950 European Convention of Human Rights and Fundamental Freedoms (ECHR) and the Charter of Fundamental Rights of the European Union (the Charter).

---

[13] Case 7/73 *Nold v Commission of the European Communities* [1974] ECR 491, para 13.

[14] *Solange II* (*Re Wuensche Handelsgesellschaft*, BVerfG dec of 22 October 1986) [1987] 3 CMLR 225; Case 5/88 *Wachauf* [1989] ECR 2609. See further: Nic Shuibhne, 'Margins of Appreciation: National Values, Fundamental Rights and EC Free Movement Law' (2009) 34 *EL Rev* 230; G De Búrca, 'The Language of Rights and European Integration' in J Shaw and G More (eds), *New Legal Dynamics of European Union* (Oxford, Clarendon Press, 1995); A Arnull, 'From Charter to Constitution and Beyond: Fundamental Rights in the New European Union' (2003) *PL* 774 and N Krisch, 'The Open Architecture of European Human Rights Law' (2008) 71 *MLR* 183.

[15] [1992] OJ C191. The original Art F(2) TEU stated that 'the Union will respect fundamental rights in accordance with the European Convention on Human Rights and the constitutional traditions common to the Member States'.

[16] [1997] OJ C340. This reinforced the commitment established by the Maastricht Treaty, stating 'that the Union is founded on the principles of liberty, democracy, respect for human rights and fundamental freedoms, and the rule of law, principles which are common to the Member States' (Art 6 TEU). It also afforded jurisdiction to the ECJ to hold the Member States and the EU institutions to account for failure to comply with fundamental rights (ex Art 46 TEU) and introduced a new procedure for dealing with such breaches (ex Art 7 TEU).

[17] [2001] OJ C80. This reinforced the sanctions introduced by the Treaty of Amsterdam (ex Art 7).

[18] [2007] OJ C306/01. The discussion will return to the impact of the Lisbon Treaty on the EU's fundamental rights obligations. For an in-depth analysis of the extent to which the Lisbon Treaty impacts upon the capacity of the EU to pursue children's rights, see H Stalford and M Schuurman, 'Are We There Yet? The Impact of the Lisbon Treaty on the EU Children's Rights Agenda' (2011) 3 *International Journal of Children's Rights* 7.

THE UNCRC AS AN EU CHILDREN'S RIGHTS TOOL

The UNCRC was adopted by the United Nations General Assembly on 2 November 1989 and came into force less than a year later on 2 September 1990. It is, without doubt, the most exhaustive, extensively endorsed human rights instrument having been ratified by 193 state parties.[19] It is now universally acknowledged as the 'fulcrum' upon which all children's rights activities are developed and measured,[20] its 54 provisions presenting an extensive catalogue of children's civil, political, economic, social and cultural rights. These include so-called 'protective' rights—such as the right to be protected from torture (Art 37), and from economic and sexual exploitation (Arts 32 and 34)—as well as 'participatory' rights (the right to education (Art 28), the right to profess and practise their own cultural and religious identity (Art 30) and a right to freedom of association).[21] The interpretation and application of these provisions are underpinned by four 'general principles': that all children should enjoy equal enjoyment of his/her rights (Art 2); that the best interests of the child be a primary consideration in all matters concerning the child (Art 3); that all children have a right to life, survival and development (Art 6); and that all children have a right to express their views and to participate in decisions that affect them in accordance with their age and capacity (Art 12).[22]

The EU Agenda on the Rights of the Child identifies the UNCRC as one of the main building blocks of its rights' framework, and specifically pinpoints 'the best interests of the child' as the overarching, guiding principle:

> In the future, EU policies that directly or indirectly affect children should be designed, implemented, and monitored taking into account the principle of the best interests of the child enshrined in the UNCRC ... All EU Member States ratified the UNCRC ... The standards and principles of the UNCRC must continue to guide EU policies and actions that have an impact on the rights of the child.[23]

Explicit reference to this instrument is highly symbolic, affirming the EU's willingness to draw on it in a much more direct and far-reaching way to supplement the hitherto rather vague references to children in the Treaties. Moreover, it adds a new legitimacy to the EU children's rights agenda by providing a specific

---

[19] The US and Somalia are the only remaining countries that have not ratified the Convention despite signing it in 1995 and 2002 respectively.

[20] Freeman, 'Why It Remains', above n 4, 55.

[21] For a detailed analysis of the content of the Convention, see D McGoldrick, 'The United Nations Convention on the Rights of the Child' (1991) 5 *International Journal of Law and the Family* 132 and D Balton, 'The Convention on the Rights of the Child: Prospects for International Enforcement' (1990) 12 *Human Rights Quarterly* 120.

[22] U Kilkelly, 'Operationalising Children's Rights: Lessons from Research' (2006) 1 *Journal of Children's Services* 36, 40.

[23] Above n 1, 3.

normative context, as well as a language with which international stakeholders[24] are familiar and which can frame their discussions with key EU protagonists. Certainly the UNCRC offers the more purist response to the children's rights-based approach in that the instrument was specifically framed with children in mind and is comprehensive in its coverage, encompassing the entire gamut of civil, political, social and economic rights.

Equally as important to the EU as the UNCRC provisions is the accompanying guidance provided by the UN Committee on the Rights of the Child through its many monitoring reports, recommendations and general comments.[25] These act as an invaluable guide in interpreting and implementing key provisions and principles in areas of EU children's rights activity and are an essential resource in framing new legislative and policy initiatives.

THE LEGAL STATUS OF THE UNCRC AT EU LEVEL

Although the EU is not a party to the UNCRC—currently there is no mechanism for this to occur—it is bound, by virtue of the general principles of EU law described above to adhere to all of the principles and provisions set out in the Convention in relation to all matters that fall within the scope of EU competence. But in order to understand how the relationship between the EU and the UNCRC is negotiated in practice, and to appreciate its impact on children's rights on the ground, it is useful to look at the legal effects of the UNCRC in relation to the Member States that have ratified it.

The UNCRC is a legal document that imposes binding standards on state parties. Thus, by ratifying the instrument, states undertake to 'respect and ensure the rights set forth in [the Convention] to each child within their jurisdiction'[26] and to take 'all appropriate legislative, administrative and other measures for the implementation of the rights recognized in the Convention'.[27] To facilitate domestic fulfillment of the standards set out therein, each state is obliged to establish

---

[24] Such as UNICEF, the Council of Europe, and the many international NGOs such as Eurochild and Save the Children that have been intensively lobbying the EU on a range of children's rights issues since the early 1990s.

[25] Eg General Comment, 'The Right of the Child to Freedom From all Forms of Violence' UNCRC/C/GC/13, 18 April 2011—can inform EU activities in the field of cross-border crime against children (discussed in ch 8); General Comment, 'The Treatment of Unaccompanied and Separated Children Outside their Country of Origin' UNCRC/GC/2005/6, 1 September 2005—can offer useful guidance in relation to the EU immigration and asylum acquis (see ch 3); while General Comment, 'The Aims of Education' UNCRC/GC/2001/1, 17 April 2001—can inform EU activities in the field of education (see ch 6). See more generally, General Comment, 'General Measures of Implementation of the Convention on the Rights of the Child' CRC/GC/2003/5, 27 November 2003.

[26] Art 2 UNCRC.

[27] Art 4 UNCRC.

and maintain appropriate administrative and judicial mechanisms.[28] Critically, however, as an international treaty the UNCRC is not of itself directly enforceable on state parties, at least in the sense that in the absence of implementing domestic legislation, there are no sanctions imposed on states who fail to comply with the obligations to which they have agreed.[29] Rather, the approach of the UNCRC is heuristic, setting out a series of clear benchmarks by which national provision for the promotion and protection of children's rights can be amended and monitored.[30]

This begs the question as to whether the UNCRC can hope to hold any persuasive force at EU level when its enforceability by the very Member States that have ratified it remains so fragile and inconsistent. Cullen, in acknowledging the legal bluntness of the UNCRC at domestic level, has suggested that the best means of giving the instrument 'teeth' is by using it as a 'child-proofing' tool within the EU legal order. She asserts that by integrating relevant aspects of the UNCRC into the fabric of EU law and policy at an early stage entrenches compliance as an obligation rather than leaving it as an optional aspiration.[31] Certainly, there is no doubt that the UNCRC has become an increasingly common reference point within official EU texts in recent years.[32] Child-related legislative instruments, almost without exception, are accompanied by some allusion to the UNCRC either explicitly[33] or more implicitly, for example through their endorsement of broader children's rights canons such as the 'best interests' principle,[34] the child's right to

---

[28] Arts 4, 42 and 44(6) UNCRC. See also UN Committee on the Rights of the Child General Comment no 5 (2003) on the general measures of implementation of the Convention on the Rights of the Child and D Balton, 'The Convention of the Rights of the Child: Prospects for International Enforcement' (1990) 1 *Human Rights Quarterly* 120.

[29] The extent to which the UNCRC gives rise to justiciable rights at the domestic level depends very much on the constitutional order of the state concerned.

[30] State compliance with the Convention is monitored at five year intervals by the UN Committee on the Rights of the Child. For further details of this procedure and an archive of monitoring reports, see ohchr.org/english/bodies/UNCRC/. For an overview of the other mechanisms deployed by the UN to achieve compliance with the UNCRC see Balton, above n 28, 126–27. Note also that in June 2011 the UN Human Rights Council adopted an Optional Protocol on a communications procedure for children's rights. This will take effect in 2012 and will enable individuals to submit complaints to the UN Committee on the Rights of the Child in respect of alleged violations of their UNCRC rights by state bodies. Official Records of the General Assembly, Sixty-sixth Session, Supplement no 53 (A/66/53) ch I.

[31] H Cullen, 'Children's Rights' in S Peers and A Ward (eds), *The EU Charter of Fundamental Rights: Politics, Law and Policy* (Oxford, Hart 2004) 323, 343.

[32] For a fuller analysis of how the UNCRC has shaped EU law, policy and procedure, see H Stalford and E Drywood, 'The Use of the UNCRC in EU Law and Policy-Making' in A Invernizzi and J Williams (eds), *The Human Rights of Children: From Visions to Implementation* (Aldershot: Ashgate, 2011) ch 9.

[33] See for instance Art 28(3) Dir 2004/38 on the right of citizens of the Union and their family members to move and reside freely within the territory of the Member States [2004] OJ L158/77, which prohibits the deportation of migrant children unless it is in their best interests.

[34] As enshrined in Art 3 UNCRC. See, eg Art 17(6) Dir 2005/85 on minimum standards on procedures in Member States for granting and withdrawing refugee status [2005] OJ L326/13; Art 10 Dir 2004/81 on the residence permit issued to third country nationals who are victims of trafficking

participate in decisions that affect him or her,[35] or the right to be protected against discrimination.[36]

Embedding the UNCRC into EU legislative texts is symbolically significant, but the extent to which such references have stimulated tangible changes in the way that EU law is interpreted and implemented is highly debatable. On the one hand, it can enable the EU to act as an important driver of the UNCRC in that by embedding its provisions within legally binding instruments, the EU can endow the UNCRC with a much more potent legal force than is otherwise possible.[37] The eventual impact of this process is constrained, however, by the fact that such references generally fall short of imposing any specific obligations on the Member States because of the EU's limited legal competence to affect substantive changes to domestic children's rights measures and systems.[38]

The impotence and, indeed, reluctance on the part of the EU to fully engage the provisions of the UNCRC, notwithstanding their incorporation into legislative instruments, is reflected in the case law of the Court of Justice. In contrast with the now fairly routine reference to children's rights considerations in EU law and policy, there have only been a handful of specifically child-related cases brought before the Court, and fewer still have prompted any direct engagement with children's rights principles as enshrined in the UNCRC. It was not until 2006, for instance, that the Court acknowledged that the UNCRC should be a primary reference point in assessing the compatibility of EU law with children's fundamental rights[39] and there has only been one case to date—in the field of the free movement of goods—in which the Court has attached decisive weight to the instrument.[40]

in human beings or who have been the subject of an action to facilitate illegal immigration who co-operate with the competent authorities [2004] OJ L261/19. Discussed further in ch 3.

[35] As enshrined in Art 12 UNCRC. See, for instance, arts 11(2), 23(b) and 41(2)(c) Reg 2201/2003 concerning jurisdiction and the recognition and enforcement of judgments in matrimonial matters and the matters of parental responsibility [2003] OJ L338/1 and Art 19(1) Dir 2003/9/EC laying down minimum standards for the reception of asylum seekers [2003] OJ L31/18.

[36] As enshrined in Art 2 UNCRC. See, eg Arts 8(2)(a) and 9(2) Dir 2005/85 [2005] OJ L326/13. This states that, *regardless of age*, reasoned, individual, objective and impartial decisions relating to their residence status must be communicated to the asylum applicant; and Arts 10(1)(a) and (b) which provides that asylum procedures must be sensitive to the linguistic needs and limitations of the applicant. See further Stalford and Drywood, 'The Use of the UNCRC', above n 32.

[37] Stalford and Drywood, 'The Use of the UNCRC', above n 32.

[38] The discussion will return to the issue of EU competence at p 44 below.

[39] Case C-540/03 *European Parliament v Council* [2006] ECR I-5769. The case concerned an (unsuccessful) action by the European Parliament against the European Council on the legitimacy of certain age-related conditions imposed by the Family Reunification Directive and is discussed further in ch 3. See also E Drywood, 'Giving with One Hand, Taking with the Other: Fundamental Rights, Children and the Family Reunification Decision' (2007) 32 *EL Rev* 396.

[40] Case C-244/06 *Dynamic Medien Vertriebs GmbH v Avides Media AG* [2008] ECR I-505. The Court concluded that whether German labeling restrictions on DVDs and videos via mail order constituted a lawful restriction to the free movement of goods given that the restrictions were aimed at protecting the welfare of young people. In drawing this conclusion, the Court referred to Art 17 UNCRC which encourages signatory states to develop appropriate guidelines for the protection of children from media-generated information and material injurious to their well-being.

But it is not only through explicit reference to the UNCRC that children's rights at EU level are upheld and developed. The ECHR is an increasingly valued source in this regard and it is to this instrument that the analysis now turns.

THE ECHR AS A CHILDREN'S RIGHTS TOOL

The ECHR, which was signed in 1950 and came into force in 1953, is the flagship instrument of the Council of Europe. It has been ratified by 47 European states, including all of the Member States of the EU, all of which have incorporated it into their constitutional legal orders. It is a beacon of European democracy and public order,[41] containing a comprehensive checklist of civil and political rights, all of which have been teleologically interpreted through the extensive jurisprudence of the European Court of Human Rights (ECtHR).[42]

The ECHR and its accompanying case law have, since the 1970s, exerted significant influence over the EU in ensuring compliance with its fundamental rights obligations.[43] The instrument has been firmly entrenched in the constitutional fabric of the EU since the Maastricht Treaty formalised its commitment to respecting fundamental rights, as guaranteed by the ECHR 'as general principles of Community Law'.[44] However, notwithstanding the EU's obligations to achieve compatibility between its measures and those of the ECHR, up until now the EU's pursuit of its internal market and political goals have not always sat comfortably with fundamental rights and have, on rare occasions, created discernible 'clashes' between the two regimes.[45] In the process, this has enabled Member States to circumvent or, at least compromise, their fundamental rights obligations under the ECHR on the pretext of meeting obligations under the parallel EU legal order.[46]

---

[41]   *Loizidou v Turkey (Preliminary Objections)* App no15318/89 (1995) 20 EHRR 99, para 75.

[42]   E Dubout, 'Interprétation Téléologique et Politique Jurisprudentielle de la Cour Européenne des Droits de L'homme' (2008) 19 *Revue Trimetrielle des Droits de L'Homme 383*; A Kaczorowska, *Public International Law*, 4th edn (Oxford, Routledge, 2010).

[43]   Case 7/73 *Nold v Commission* [1974] ECR 491; Case C-94/00 *Roquette Frères SA v Directeur Général de la Concurrence, de la Consommation et de la Répression des Frauds* [2002] ECR I-9011.

[44]   Art F(2) Maastricht Treaty.

[45]   For a notable example of such a clash which saw EU economic freedoms effectively trump fundamental rights, see Case C-341/05 *Laval un Partneri Ltd v Svenska Byggnadsarbetareförbundet* [2007] ECR I-11767 and Case C-438/05 *International Transport Workers' Federation and The Finnish Seamen's Union v Viking Line* [2007] ECR I-10779. For an analysis see E Spaventa, 'Federalisation versus Centralisation: Tensions in Fundamental Rights Discourse in the EU' in M Dougan and S Currie (eds), *50 Years of the European Treaties* (Oxford, Hart Publishing, 2009) 343.

[46]   Although several cases have reaffirmed the authority of the ECtHR to curtail any attempts by the EU to undermine the ECHR. See, in particular: *Bosphorous v Ireland* App no 45036/98 ECHR 2005–VI; *Matthews v United Kingdom* App no 24833/94 (1999) 28 EHRR 361 and, more recently, *MSS v Belgium and Greece* App no 30696/09 (unreported) Judgment of 21 January 2011. For a detailed examination of how the EU and ECHR systems have been reconciled, see D Spielmann, 'Human Rights Case Law in the Strasbourg and Luxembourg Courts: Conflicts, Inconsistencies and Complementarities' in P Alston (ed), *The EU and Human Rights* (Oxford, OUP, 1990) 757 and FG Jacobs, 'Human Rights in the European Union: The Role of the Court of Justice' (2001) 26 *EL Rev* 331.

It is significant, then, that the Treaty of Lisbon has paved the way for formal EU accession to the ECHR.[47] This process will go some way towards repairing the loophole in the current system of fundamental rights insofar as it implies that the EU will become a direct signatory to the instrument and will, therefore, be subject not only to the scrutiny of the Court of Justice in Luxembourg, but also to the external restraint of the ECtHR in Strasbourg. It will also enable individuals to bring the EU directly before the ECtHR for failure to observe the ECHR.

Such developments have added significant momentum to the children's rights campaign at EU level but the extent to which they are exercised is clearly determined by the nature and scope of ECHR allegiance to children's rights per se. Commentators have drawn attention to the lack of any direct ECHR provision targeting children,[48] and to the fact that the ECHR is confined to civil and political rights while remaining relatively silent on social or economic rights.[49] Equally problematic is the tendency of the ECtHR to consider children's rights as synonymous with other group or individuals' rights (typically those of the family or their parents),[50] a tendency which is explained by Fortin:

> Clearly the Convention has not often been considered as a means of promoting children's independent claims, as opposed to those of their parents. This is not surprising given the Convention's history and objectives. Its drafters were very obviously considering the needs of post-war Europe rather than children's special requirements. Whilst at least some of its Articles can be utilised on their behalf, children's applications have to be fitted into Articles that could have been far better worded had the Convention been designed with them specifically in mind.[51]

Fortin comments that children are further hampered in bringing a claim for an alleged breach of their rights under the ECHR because they tend to lack the legal

---

[47] Art 6(2) TEU, Protocol 14 ECHR amended to allow for this.

[48] Art 2 Protocol 1 recognises a universal right to education and supports this with the guarantee that children should have a right to be educated in accordance with their parents' (rather than their own) religious and cultural beliefs; Art 5(1)(d) sets out the circumstances in which lawful detention of a minor is justifiable and Art 6(1) restricts public access to trials in the interests of juveniles. Of course, generic provisions such as Art 1 which guarantees the Convention rights and freedoms to 'everyone', and Art 14 which prohibits discrimination on various grounds including age, extend the scope of the instrument to a range of groups not expressly mentioned in the remaining provisions. See U Kilkelly, 'The Impact of the Convention on the Case Law of the European Court of Human Rights' in D Fottrell (ed), *Revisiting Children's Rights: 10 Years of the UN Convention on the Rights of the Child* (Dordrecht, Kluwer, 2000) 87.

[49] See also J Williams, 'Incorporating Children's Rights: The Divergence in Law and Policy' (2007) 27 *Legal Studies* 261, in which she highlights the theoretical and political barriers to implementation of a rights-based approach to developing children's rights at domestic level by reference to the ECHR and the UNCRC.

[50] See, eg the body of case law relating to the application of Art 8 which provides a right to respect for private and family life, discussed at length in A Opromolla, 'Children's Rights under Articles 3 and 8 of the European Convention: Recent Case Law' (2001) 26 *EL Rev, Human Rights Supplement* 46. The potential implications of Art 8 will be explored further in ch 3.

[51] J Fortin, 'Rights Brought Home for Children' (1999) 3 *MLR* 350, 357. See also Fortin, *Children's Rights and the Developing Law,* 2nd edn (Cambridge, Cambridge University Press, 2009) 50 and J Fortin, 'Accommodating Children's Rights in a Post Human Rights Act Era' (2006) 3 *MLR* 299.

and procedural knowledge and support to bring such an action, and because violations of children's rights are commonly confined to the private, family sphere, where direct enforcement of the ECHR by children is more problematic.[52]

In spite of these inherent limitations, the ECtHR has demonstrated a growing willingness to interpret the ECHR dynamically to ensure adequate protection for children in a range of contexts, a willingness that is evidenced in the 250 or so child-related decisions it has issued to date.[53] This ingenuity has been manifested in the ECtHR's—and, until its abolition, the Commission's—deference to relevant provisions of the UNCRC to achieve a more child-focused interpretation of the ECHR provisions.[54] For example, Article 7 of the UNCRC which acknowledges the child's right to know and be cared for by his/her parents, was referred to in support of a father's challenge to his son's adoption which had occurred without his knowledge.[55] In *Sahin v Germany*[56] and *Sommerfield v Germany*[57]—both concerning applications for child contact—the ECtHR referred to Article 12 of the UNCRC in determining both the extent to which the child should be allowed to participate in proceedings and the weight that should be attached to the views expressed. Equally, in the context of juvenile justice, the ECtHR has referred to Article 40(3) UNCRC[58] to inform its interpretation of Article 6 ECHR concerning the right to a fair trial.[59]

---

[52] The ECHR obliges national courts and other public authorities to act in a manner that is compatible with it in matters concerning private individuals. Thus, the state can be held to account for breaches of rights inflicted by one individual against another, simply by failing to put in place the appropriate legal and policy mechanisms to prevent such breaches occurring. Such a breach is rather more difficult to establish in the context of private, family relationships. Indeed, too much state intervention in family life may expose the authorities to allegations that they are in breach of Art 8. See, further, M Hunt, 'The Horizontal Effect of the Human Rights Act' (1998) *PL* 423; A Mowbray, *The Development of Positive Obligations under the European Convention on Human Rights by the European Court of Human Rights* (Oxford, Hart Publishing, 2004) and Fortin, 'Children's Rights and the Developing Law' above n 51, for a review of relevant case law.

[53] All ECtHR cases relevant to children are now accessible through the specialised Council of Europe Database, *Theseus*: coe.int/t/transversalprojects/children/caselaw/caselawchild_EN.asp.

[54] For a comprehensive analysis of the extent to which the UNCRC has informed the ECtHR, see Kilkelly, 'The Impact of the Children's Convention' above n 48; U Kilkelly, 'The Best of Both Worlds for Children's Rights: Interpreting the European Convention on Human Rights in the Light of the UN Convention on the Rights of the Child' (2001) 23 *Human Rights Quarterly* 308 and U Kilkelly, 'Effective Protection of Children's Rights in Family Cases: An International Approach' (2002) 12 *Transnational Law and Contemporary Problems* 336.

[55] *Keegan v Ireland* App no 16969/90 (1994) 18 EHRR 342.

[56] *Sahin v Germany* App no 30943/96 [2003] ECHR 340.

[57] *Sommerfield v Germany* App no 31871/96 ECHR 2003–VIII 341.

[58] This requires states parties to promote the establishment of laws, procedures, authorities and institutions specifically applicable to children who are alleged accused or recognised as having infringed the penal law.

[59] *Nortier v Netherlands* App no 13924/88 (1994) 17 EHRR 273. For further examples see: *Pini and Bertani, Manera and Altripaldi v Romania* App nos 78028/01 and 78030/01 (2005) 40 EHRR 13, para 157; *Havelka v Czech Republic* App no 23499/04 (unreported) Judgment of 21 June 2007; *Saviny v Ukraine* App no 39948/06 (unreported) Judgment of 18 December 2008; *EP v Italy* App no 31127/96 (unreported) Judgment of 16 November 1999; *KA v Finland* App no 27751/95 (unreported) 14 January 2003 and *Haase v Germany* App no 11057/02 (2005) 40 EHRR 19.

Kilkelly emphasises the value of 'cross-fertilising' humanitarian instruments in this way in that it serves, on the one hand, to redress the gap in child-specific provision in the ECHR, and, on the other, to enhance the legal force of the UNCRC:

> The use of the UNCRC to guide the interpretation of the ECHR in children's cases, either implicitly or expressly, holds real promise for maximising the potential of both treaties to protect and promote children's rights.[60]

This has important connotations for the EU given the readiness, and indeed, obligation of the Court of Justice to defer to ECHR case law for enlightenment on the human rights implications of EU law more generally. Indeed, as far as children's rights are concerned, the Court of Justice is rather more amenable to the influence of the ECHR than it is to the UNCRC. This is probably because the EU has historically developed a stronger institutional and legal correspondence with the Council of Europe than it has with the UN. Moreover, it is able to capitalise on the legal authority of the ECHR jurisprudence, a jurisprudence which simply does not exist in relation to the UNCRC. But the Court of Justice's preference for the ECHR over the UNCRC is immaterial insofar as the former has established a prominent and persuasive children's rights jurisprudence which is grounded in the latter. In that sense, the ECHR simply acts as another channel through which the UNCRC can permeate the EU legal order. In the process, the Court of Justice has at its disposal a rich and ideologically robust concentration of children's rights which, in turn, can guide interpretations of EU law in accordance with the same principles.

The potential of this cross-fertilisation process to stimulate a gradual alignment of the EU's approach to children's rights with that of international human rights bodies is epitomised in the Charter of Fundamental Rights of the European Union.

CHILDREN'S RIGHTS AND THE CHARTER OF FUNDAMENTAL RIGHTS OF THE EUROPEAN UNION

Alongside the UNCRC, the Charter has been identified by the Commission as a central plank of its EU children's rights programme. Indeed, it is referred to no less than 22 times in the EU Agenda on the Rights of the Child,[61] and is seen as reinforcing the EU's authority to act in the field of children's rights:

> In view of the strong and reinforced commitment to the rights of the child in the Treaty of Lisbon and in the Charter of Fundamental Rights, the Commission believes it is now

---

[60] Kilkelly, 'The Impact of the Children's Convention' above n 48, 100. See also C Breen, 'The Emerging Tradition of the Best Interests of the Child in the European Convention on Human Rights' in C *Breen, The Standard of the Best Interest of the Child* (Dordrecht, Martinus Nijhoff, 2002).

[61] Above n 1, as compared with eight references to the UNCRC.

the time to move up a gear on the rights of the child and to transform policy objectives into action.[62]

The Charter was adopted by a joint proclamation of the European Council, the Parliament and the Commission at the Nice summit on 7 December 2000.[63] Importantly, its legal status has been significantly elevated as a result of the Lisbon Treaty: while it was initially a merely declaratory, interpretative guide with no legally binding effects on the EU institutions, it is now recognised as having equal legal force to the Treaties.[64] In effect, this means that the EU institutions and the Member States must respect the rights, observe the principles and promote the application of the Charter in accordance with their respective powers.[65]

In substance, the Charter is comprised of 54 Articles, most of which correspond to rights and principles that were already recognised under EU law and arising out of Member States' constitutional traditions and obligations under international law. It also introduces a number of new rights and principles in response to specific social, cultural, scientific and technological advances.[66]

One of the most significant innovations of the Charter is that it contains direct and detailed provision relating to children, many of which are heavily inspired by the UNCRC and the ECHR. Thus the Charter grants children a specific right to: such protection and care as is necessary for their well-being, the opportunity to express their views freely and assurance that such views shall be taken into consideration on matters which concern them in accordance with their age and maturity.[67] Article 24(2) further provides that 'in all actions relating to children, whether taken by public authorities or private institutions, the child's best interests must be a primary consideration'; while Article 24(3) acknowledges children's right 'to maintain on a regular basis a personal relationship and direct contact with both his or her parents, unless that is contrary to his or her interests'.

Additional provisions directly addressing children's rights and interests include: the right to receive free compulsory education (Art 14(2)); the prohibition of discrimination on grounds of, inter alia, age (Art 21) and the prohibition of exploitative child labour (Art 32). Provision targeting the family unit is also of relevance to children such as the right to respect for private and family life, home and communications (Art 7) and the family's right to enjoy legal, economic and social protection (Art 33). Some of the more age-neutral provisions can also

---

[62] Above n 1, 3.

[63] Solemn Proclamation of the European Parliament, the Commission and the Council at Nice on 7 December 2000 [2000] OJ C346/1, amended in 2007 [2010] OJ C83/2, 389.

[64] Art 6(1) TEU [2010] OJ C83/19. See further T Hickman, 'Beano No More: The EU Charter of Rights After Lisbon' (2011) 16 *Judicial Review* 113.

[65] Art 51, see A Dashwood, M Dougan, B Rodger, E Spaveta and D Wyatt, *Wyatt and Dashwood's European Union Law*, 6th edn (Oxford, Hart, 2011) 382.

[66] Including Art 26 relating to the integration of persons with disabilities; Art 3 prohibition of eugenic and practices and the cloning of human beings and Art 8 on the protection of personal data.

[67] Art 24(1).

be construed in favour of children in line with parallel ECHR interpretations. Notable examples include Article 4 which prohibits torture and inhuman or degrading treatment[68] and Article 5(1) prohibiting slavery, forced labour and human trafficking.[69]

The Charter's association with other fundamental rights instruments, and particularly with the ECHR, is critical not only in informing its substance, but in determining its scope and application too.[70] First and foremost, the level of protection conferred by the rights and principles set out in the Charter must at least equate to that offered by the ECHR and can only be restricted in the interests of the general public or in order to protect the rights and freedoms of others.[71] Implicit in this proviso is the notion that the Charter can underpin more far-reaching children's rights provision than the corresponding ECHR measures. Certainly the catalogue of children's rights captured by the Charter has been described by McGlynn as the 'success story' of the instrument insofar as they provide the scaffolding for a much more 'integrated and thoughtful' construction of an EU children's rights agenda.[72] The Charter is also celebrated for acknowledging children's needs and interests as distinct from other (EU adult) citizens or the family more generally, marking a welcomed departure from the highly derivative body of rights historically associated with children's entitlement at EU level.[73]

A further benefit associated with the Charter as compared to other children's rights mechanisms relates to its impact on the EU law and policy-making process, particularly following its legal elevation by the Treaty of Lisbon. Specifically, it has been adopted as a 'proofing tool' to enable the institutions to scrutinise all legislative proposals and internal procedures to ensure their compatibility with

---

[68] Applied successfully by the ECtHR in the context of corporal punishment under Art 3 ECHR, see *A v United Kingdom* App no 25599/94 (1999) 27 EHRR 611.

[69] The parallel provision of Art 4 ECHR having been interpreted by the ECtHR to impose a positive obligation on the state to prevent child trafficking and domestic servitude, see *Siliadin v France* App no 73316/01 (2006) 43 EHRR 16; see further H Cullen, '*Siliadin v France*: Positive Obligations under Art 4 of the European Convention on Human Rights' (2006) 6 *Human Rights Law Review* 585 and, more generally, D Scullion, 'Gender Perspectives on Child Trafficking: A Case Study of Child Domestic Workers' in H Stalford, S Currie and S Velluti (eds), *Gender and Migration in 21st Century Europe* (Surrey, Ashgate, 2009) 45.

[70] For an analysis of the relationship between the Charter and international human rights treaties, see D McGoldrick, 'The Charter and United Nations Human Rights Treaties, in S Peers and A Ward (eds), *The EU Charter of Fundamental Rights: Politics, Law and Policy* (Oxford, Hart, 2004) 83.

[71] Art 52(3).

[72] C McGlynn, *Families and the European Union: Law, Politics and Pluralism* (New York, Cambridge University Press, 2006) 21.

[73] C McGlynn 'Rights for Children: The Potential Impact of the European Union Charter of Fundamental Rights' (2002) 3 *European Public Law* 387; H Stalford, 'Constitutionalising Equality in the EU: A Children's Rights Perspective' (2005) 1/2 *International Journal of Discrimination and the Law* 53.

fundamental rights.[74] In the same token, the EU Agenda on the Rights of the Child reinforces the Commission's commitment to:

[W]orking with the European Parliament and the Council to ensure that ... amendments introduced during the legislative process are fully respecting the Charter. The Commission is also working with Member States that they comply with the Charter when implementing EU legislation into national law, as required by Article 51(1) of the Charter in the EU Agenda on the Rights of the Child.[75]

Indeed, the institutions have already made considerable progress in integrating the Charter into their legislative process, as evidenced in the now routine reference to the Charter in newly proposed and adopted legislative texts, policy proposals,[76] as well as in the deliberations of the Advocates General and Court of Justice.[77] But is this enough? Is a more liberal, explicit allusion to the Charter in the various EU regulatory contexts likely to produce the transformative effects envisaged by the EU Agenda on the Rights of the Child?

The answer to this partly lies in the EU and the Member States' understanding of obligations inherent in the Charter provisions. In reality, there is an alarming paucity of guidance on how the child-related provisions contained within the Charter should be interpreted. Most notably, Article 24 represents the most explicit EU constitutional endorsement of children's rights more generally, and yet the perfunctory manner in which it is referred to by the EU institutions belies the highly complex and contested nature of the rights it enshrines. The provision clearly marks an attempt to amalgamate the normative principles of best interests (Art 3 UNCRC), child participation and freedom of expression (Arts 12 and 13 UNCRC) with the child's substantive right to live with and/or enjoy a relationship with his or her parents (Art 9 UNCRC). This comes across, however, as a rather ill-considered and 'uneasy compromise'[78] between different conceptions of

---

[74] European Commission, 'Strategy for the effective implementation of the Charter of Fundamental Rights by the European Union' (Communication) COM (2010) 573. This mechanism is the product of almost a decade of discussions between the institutions. See Commission, 'Compliance with the Charter of Fundamental Rights in Commission legislative proposals—methodology for systematic and rigorous monitoring' (Communication) COM (2005) 172 final, Brussels 27 April 2005 and European Parliament Resolution on the impact of the Charter of Fundamental Rights of the European Union and its future status (2002/2139 (INI)), [2003] OJ 300E 11/12/03P 432.

[75] Above n 1, 4–5.

[76] Eg Dec 2001/903 on the European Year of People with Disabilities 2003 [2001] OJ L335/15; Dec 2002/187 setting up Eurojust with a view to reinforcing the fight against serious crime [2002] OJ L63/1; Framework Dec 2002/584 on the European Arrest Warrant and the surrender procedures between Member States [2002] OJ L190/1 and Resolutions on languages [2002] C50/1 and life long learning [2002] C163/1.

[77] Examples of judicial references to Art 24 of the Charter include: Case C-149/10 Zoi Chatzi v Ypourgos Oikonomikon 16 September 2010; C-491/10 PPU Joseba Andoni Aguirre Zarraga v Simone Pelz [2011] OJ C63; Case C-200/10 PPU J McB v LE [2011] WLR 699; Case C-403/09 PPU Jasna Detiček v Maurizio Sgueglia [2009] ECR I-12193 and Case C-34/09 Zambrano v Office National de l'Emploi [2011] 2 CMLR 46. In Case C-208/09 Ilonka Sayn-Wittgenstein v Landeshauptmann von Wien ECJ (second chamber) 2010, the Court drew inspiration from Art 7 of the Charter (respect for private and family life).

[78] McGlynn, above n 72, 70.

children's rights as articulated by different instruments. There is little explanation of why these principles are presented together in such a way—why not group the child's right to have contact with his/her family with Article 7, for instance?—or of how they might be differentiated or, indeed, reconciled in practice.

There is an established and detailed children's rights literature, not to mention a burgeoning domestic jurisprudence, dedicated to such questions,[79] all of which reveal a high level of divergence in attitudes and approaches to what are acutely nebulous principles. Insofar as the EU institutions continue to apply the children's rights measures contained in the Charter in isolation from this theoretical and evidential research base, there is a concern that the Charter will not be engaged to its full effect, or that it will be used in the pursuit of one aspect of children's rights to the neglect of others.[80] EU activities to date, for instance, suggest an EU preference for the more predictable (albeit noble) pursuit of child protection issues to the exclusion of the more empowering (albeit challenging) goals of promoting child autonomy and active participation.[81]

The difficulties inherent in defining and interpreting children's rights are further compounded when viewed across different cultural and legal contexts.[82] As Buck notes,

> Childhood is a culturally transmitted idea … [The] universal norm-creation underlying … [international children's rights] may not necessarily be consistent with the core notion of childhood prevalent in any one society at any one time in history.[83]

Such challenges are particularly apparent in an EU context: EU children's rights, if they are to have any relevance, have to take into account the diversity of contexts within which children are situated, not only according to the EU Member State in

---

[79] Distinguished commentaries include: J Locke 'Some Thoughts Concerning Education' in J Adamson (ed), *The Educational Writings of John Locke* (London, Edward Arnold, 1912); P Aries, *Centuries of Childhood. A Social History of Family Life* (New York, Vintage Books, 1962); J Holt, *Escape from Childhood: The Needs and Rights of Children* (Harmondsworth, Penguin, 1975); M Freeman, *The Rights and Wrongs of Children* (London, Frances Pinter, 1983); M Freeman, *The Moral Status of Children: Essays on the Rights of the Child* (The Hague, Kluwer Law International, 1997); B Bandman, *Children's Right to Freedom, Care, and Enlightenment* (London, Routledge, 2007); D Archaud, *Children: Rights and Childhood*, 2nd edn (London, Routledge, 2004); J Eekelaar, *The Emergence of Children's Rights* (Oxford, University Press, 1986) and again J Eekelaar, 'The Interests of The Child and the Child's Wishes: The Role of Dynamic Self-Determinism' (1994) 8 *International Journal of Law and the Family* 42. Notable challenges to common conceptualisations of children's 'rights' have been presented by M Guggenheim, *What's Wrong with Children's Rights* (Cambridge, Harvard University Press, 2005) and LM Purdy, 'Why Children Shouldn't Have Equal Rights' (1994) 2 *International Journal of Children's Rights* 223.

[80] Eurochild, *The European Commission's 2010 Report on the application of the EU Charter of Fundamental Rights and its contribution to protecting children's rights in the EU* (May 2011): eurochild. org/fileadmin/ThematicPriorities/ChildrensRights/Eurochild/Eurochild_assessment_of_2010_Report_on_application_of_EU_FRC_final.pdf.

[81] Cullen, 'Children's Rights' above n 31, 331. Such an assertion will be discussed more fully in chs 6 and 7.

[82] R Franklin (ed), *The Handbook of Children's Rights: Comparative Policy and Practice* (London, Routledge, 1995).

[83] T Buck, *International Child Law*, 2nd edn (Abingdon, Routledge, 2010) 5.

which they reside, but the regions and communities within those Member States too; the socio-economic, political and cultural systems with which they interact; and the other contexts to which they have been exposed as a result of migration. The suggestion is not that the EU should define precisely how these contextual variables are to be accommodated—an impossible and probably undesirable prospect—but that it should at least acknowledge more confidently that such variables necessarily influence the interpretation and application of the Charter.

Having established that the EU and the Member States have to adhere to fundamental rights when acting within the scope of EU law, and having confirmed that this obligation extends to international treaties which the Member States have ratified, the emphasis on 'rights' within the EU's child-related plans is highly persuasive, both legally and politically. Moreover, it chimes with the approach of parallel international polities such as the UN and the Council of Europe, thereby endowing EU efforts in relation to children with an immediate force and ideological legitimacy, effectively providing the ideological framework that EU measures in relation to children have been lacking up to now.

But there are two important points to emphasise regarding the effect of these measures on the actual scope and application of EU law and policy. First, the enhanced visibility of fundamental rights as a result of the constitutional changes summarised above does not serve in any way to extend the competence of the EU beyond those areas identified in the Treaties.[84] Linked to this is the fact that most EU children's rights measures will only produce tangible effects for children if Member States are sufficiently amenable to their implementation.

THE EU'S CAPACITY TO ADVANCE CHILDREN'S RIGHTS: A QUESTION OF COMPETENCE

It has already been established in chapter one that the EU derives its competence to act in any given area from the Member States, not the other way around.[85] Chapter one has also highlighted how, once a legal basis for action is identified in the Treaties, the *nature and extent* of the EU's competence to enact measures in that area are determined by reference to the principles of subsidiarity and proportionality.[86] These principles are absolutely central to the operation of EU law insofar as they determine, first of all, whether a particular objective will be better achieved as a result of EU action as opposed to action at the Member State level and secondly, how far the EU needs to go to achieve that objective. In a children's rights context, the starting point is as follows: children's experiences and needs are largely dictated by the environment in which they live. Thus, their rights should

---

[84]   Case C-249/96 *Grant v South-West Trains Ltd* [1998] ECR I-621; Art 6(1) TEU and Art 51(2) of the Charter of Fundamental Rights of the European Union.
[85]   Art 5(2) TEU.
[86]   Art 5 TFEU.

be determined at the most intimate and sensitive level of governance to the child as possible. It is generally only deemed appropriate for the EU to intervene legally in issues affecting children where they cannot be adequately addressed at the local or national level (notably issues that straddle legal and geographical boundaries, such as free movement, immigration or trafficking).

It is important to understand these core principles in order to fully appreciate the legal significance of the EU's children's rights obligations under the Charter, the UNCRC and the ECHR. All of these instruments, but particularly the Charter as the definitive EU code of fundamental rights, have had some bearing on the institutions' approach to children's rights. The Court of Justice, in particular, has demonstrated an increasing readiness to bring the Charter provisions to bear on decisions relating to children. It remains reluctant to attach any persuasive force to those provisions, however, deferring instead to the Member States' judicial, legislative and administrative processes to effect the necessary changes in the way that children's rights are interpreted at the national level.[87] This confirms that unless a children's rights issue intersects clearly with a substantive area of EU competence, the Charter is confined to making abstract, aspirational declarations as to how children's rights should be upheld within the territory of the EU. It does not confer any new powers or competences on the EU institutions and cannot be used as a legal basis for any new legislative measures. It can only support action founded on the legal bases included within the Treaties.

Furthermore, judicial enforcement of the Charter is limited to interpreting and reviewing the legality of measures adopted by Member States in the process of *implementating* EU law.[88] In that sense, the Charter is narrower in scope than the broader EU general principles framework within which the UNCRC falls, the latter applying to Member States when they act within the *scope* (rather than merely in their implementation) of EU law.[89] It follows, then, that the incorporation of tailored children's rights provisions within the Charter does not extend the institutions' powers to enact children's rights measures in areas in which they would otherwise have no competence, nor does it encroach on Member State sovereignty to determine the substance and scope of domestic child law. The force of the Charter depends, rather, on the nature and scope of child-focused measures that are already in place at EU level as well as on the amenability of domestic systems to them.

These points are illustrated further by reference to the UNCRC. The discussion above has provided a number of examples in which the principles of the UNCRC have become embedded in EU legislative texts. However, the material impact of

---

[87] eg see Case C-403/09 PPU *Deticek v Sgueglia* [2009] ECR I-12193 and Case C-400/10 PPU *J McB v LE* [2011] WLR 699.

[88] R Bray, K Lenaerts and P Van Nuffel (eds), *Constitutional Law of the European Union*, 2nd edn (London, Sweet and Maxwell, 2005) 733.

[89] A Arnull, A Dashwood, M Ross, D Wyatt, E Spaventa and M Dougan, *European Union Law*, 5th edn (London, Sweet & Maxwell, 2006) 285. See also, Dashwood et al, *Wyatt and Dashwood*, above n 65.

this process is constrained by the fact that such references generally fall short of imposing any specific obligations on the Member States. This, in turn, is attributed to the EU's limited legal competence to affect substantive changes to domestic children's rights measures and systems. For example, EU family law upholding children's right to be heard in proceedings relating to which parent should have custody or residence[90] do not enable the EU to scrutinise and impose changes to domestic child consultation procedures; they merely echo Member States' existing obligations under the UNCRC as articulated already in domestic law.[91] EU immigration and asylum law which requires that children are provided with appropriate legal assistance and representation during immigration proceedings[92] presumes that appropriately child-sensitive domestic processes are already in place in this regard. It does not authorise the EU to scrutinise or to make unilateral amendments to such processes. The same is true of family legislation which, it is declared, should be interpreted and applied in the light of the 'best interests of the child'.[93] While such a commitment resonates with Article 3 UNCRC, the EU has absolutely no competence to scrutinise whether or not the 'best interests of the child' have, in fact, been upheld in the process of applying such measures, nor, indeed, does it provide any guidance on how such assessments might be made.[94] This resonates with the point made earlier that EU legislative references to the UNCRC do not create *enforceable* free-standing rights but rather are only as effective as the domestic measures and processes with which they interact.

   A basic understanding of these constitutional issues lends itself to a much more realistic appreciation of what the EU can and cannot achieve in relation to children. But the transformative power of the 'rights' rhetoric should not be underestimated either, even if its legal effect may be limited. When framed within a 'rights' discourse children are pushed to the forefront of the EU's consciousness. 'Rights' offers a discursive language with which key protagonists within the institutions can engage with external children's rights experts and lobbyists. It capitalises on the international and domestic legal and political community's receptiveness to rights-related obligations and it implies a degree of moral accountability, even if the legal sanctions are relatively weak. With that in mind, fundamental rights might be more accurately viewed as acting as a *constraint* on EU activity: they ensure that the EU does not violate or undermine fundamental rights in the

---

[90]   Arts 23(b) and 41(2)(c) Regulation 2201/2003.

[91]   The discussion will return to this issue in chs 4 and 5.

[92]   Art 19(1) Dir 2003/9 laying down minimum standards for the reception of asylum seekers [2003] OJ L31/18 and Art 30(1) Dir 2004/83/EC on minimum standards for the qualification and status of third country nationals or stateless persons as refugees or as persons who otherwise need international protection and the content of the protection granted [2004] OJ L304/12.

[93]   Arts 12(3)(b), 15(1) and (5) and 23(a) of Regulation 2201/2003.

[94]   The fact that UNCRC-sensitive EU measures create no enforceable obligations in the abstract probably explains why many are framed within directives rather than regulations, insofar as they leave a large degree of discretion to the Member State as to how they will be implemented and are subject to certain constraints regarding their enforceability. Article 288 TFEU.

course of its legal and policy activities rather than impose a positive obligation on the EU to actively develop human—including children's—rights measures.[95]

ADDITIONAL CONCEPTUAL FRAMEWORKS FOR PURSUING CHILDREN'S RIGHTS AT EU LEVEL

The tenor of the EU Agenda on the Rights of the Child suggests a distinct preoccupation with this explicit and formal 'rights' framework—manifested, in particular, in the UNCRC and the Charter especially—as the primary context within which to pursue its objectives. In the process, however, it overlooks additional normative frameworks that are at the EU's disposal, notably those of EU citizenship, non-discrimination and social inclusion, all of which can be deployed as part of *a children's rights-based* approach. Indeed, it could be argued that these frameworks encapsulate the nuances of children's rights and interests in a much more direct and legally and politically empowering way insofar as they are familiar to the EU institutions, are firmly grounded in the Treaties, and are supported by a well-developed network of legal, judicial and policy resources. To complete this mapping out of the ideological framework underpinning EU children's rights, the content and scope of these additional concepts will now be briefly considered.

EU CITIZENSHIP AS A CHILDREN'S RIGHTS MECHANISM[96]

EU Citizenship is a status bestowed automatically on those who are nationals of any of the 27 Member States as a supplement to national citizenship. It also implies a discrete set of legal and political entitlement, associated primarily with the exercise of free movement within the territory of the EU.[97] The nature and scope of this entitlement has developed considerably over the years by virtue of expansive judicial interpretations which have enabled individuals to enter and reside within

---

[95] Stalford and Schuurman, 'Are We There Yet?' above n 18, 25. But for a discussion of the ways in which international human rights law might impose positive obligations on the EU see Ahmed and Butler, above n 12.

[96] The status of children in the context of EU citizenship has been explored in greater depth by the author elsewhere, most notably in: H Stalford, 'The Relevance of EU Citizenship to Children' in A Invernizzi and J Williams (eds), *Children and Citizenship* (London, Sage, 2008); and HL Ackers and H Stalford, *A Community for Children? Children, Citizenship and Migration in the European Union* (Aldershot, Ashgate, 2004) and H Stalford, 'The Citizenship Status of Children in the European Union' (2000) 8 *International Journal of Children's Rights* 101. Aspects of this framework will also be considered in ch 3.

[97] Arts 20 and 21 TFEU. Art 21(1)TFEU can be relied on directly by individuals against the national courts without the need for any implementing legislation following Case C-413/99 *Baumbast and R v Secretary of State for the Home Department* [2002] ECR I-7091. The personal and material scope of citizenship as defined by much of this jurisprudence is now codified in Dir 2004/38 [2004] OJ L158/77 on the right of citizens of the Union and their family members to move and reside freely within the territory of the Member States.

other Member States, and to access a wide range of social,[98] economic[99] and civil advantages[100] whilst there.[101] Indeed, such is the importance attached to EU citizenship that it is now regarded as a 'fundamental status'.[102]

Historically, children's status as EU citizens has been regarded as rather vacuous and incidental: given that children do not, for the most part, migrate independently, they only benefit from the rights associated with free movement as a consequence of their parents' decision to live and work in another Member State.[103] More recent case law, however, has seen the Court of Justice heightening the currency of children's status as EU citizens in their own right. Indeed, this has occurred to such a degree that the tables have turned: while children have traditionally derived their citizenship entitlement from their parents, it is becoming increasingly common for parents to derive valuable entry and residence rights within the EU from their children. This is particularly decisive, for instance, for adults of third country nationality who, having lived and perhaps even worked for a period in the host state with their family, no longer qualify for ongoing residence under national immigration law. In such cases, the Court of Justice has willingly extended the residence rights of third country national parents who have children of EU nationality. This is in acknowledgement of the fact that the entitlement accruing to their children by virtue of their EU citizenship status—notably their right to pursue education in the host state[104]—can only

---

[98] In Case C-85/96 *María Martínez Sala v Freistaat Bayern* [1998] ECR I-2691, the Court of Justice granted a Spanish woman resident in Germany access to child-raising allowance, despite the fact that she was not employed and did not have a proper residence permit and Case 76/72 *Michel S v Fonds National de Reclassement Social des Handicapes* [1973] ECR 457 and Case 9/74 *Donato Casagrande v Landeshauptstadt München* [1974] ECR 773 affirmed the migrant child's right to access all educational provision in the host state, as well as any financial support aimed at facilitating education attendance.

[99] Including the right of children to access employment and all associated entitlement in the host state (subject to national age-restrictions), see Art 11 of Reg 1612/68 and Case C-165/05 *Commission of the European Communities v Grand Duchy of Luxembourg* [2005] OJ C132 and Art 23 of Dir 2004/38.

[100] In Case C-148/02 *Carlos Garcia Avello v État Belge* [2003] ECR I-11613, Avello successfully claimed to name the children in accordance with their Spanish heritage, as opposed to the law of Belgium in which the family were residing.

[101] Developments in EU citizenship jurisprudence as well as the academic commentary are usefully summarised in S Currie, 'The Transformation of Union Citizenship' in S Currie and M Dougan (eds), *50 Years of the European Treaties: Looking Back and Thinking Forward* (Oxford, Hart, 2009) 365.

[102] Case C-184/99 *Rudy Grzelczyk v Centre Public d'Aide Sociale d'Ottignies-Louvain-la-Neuve* [2001] ECR I-6193, para 31.

[103] In order to qualify for residence of more than three months in another Member State, EU adult nationals must demonstrate that they are either engaged in employment or have sufficient financial resources and health insurance to avoid becoming a burden on the public resources of the host state. Article 7 Directive 2004/38 on the right of citizens of the Union and their family members to move and reside freely within the territory of the Member States [2004] OJ L158/77.

[104] Formerly Art 12 Reg 1612/68 [1968] OJ L257/2. Rights pertaining to the migrant worker's children are now enshrined in Art 10 of the revised version of this instrument, Reg 492/2011 on the freedom of movement for workers within the Union [2011] OJ L141/1. The entitlement of other accompanying family members is captured by Arts 1 and 2(2) Dir 2004/38 on the right of citizens of the Union and their family members to move and reside freely within the territory of the Member States [2004] OJ L158/77.

be exercised if their primary carers (usually the parents) are allowed to remain with them.[105]

This development in the case law is significant in that it establishes, first and foremost, that EU citizenship yields tangible and direct entitlement for individuals regardless of their age or level of dependency.[106] Furthermore, it explicitly acknowledges the important social, emotional and material interdependence between family members. On the one hand, the application of EU citizenship is a key illustration of how children's rights are operable largely by virtue of the support and assistance of their parents. The very existence of that dependency, on the other hand, can 'anchor' their parents to the host state too.[107] This conceptualisation provides a useful illustration of the distinction between child autonomy and self-sufficiency that pervades children's rights and citizenship literature more broadly:[108] children have an autonomous right to reside in a Member State founded on their status as EU citizens but are not expected to exercise that right without appropriate parental support, even if recognition of this might serve to undermine domestic immigration law, and even, it seems, if it implies an additional burden on the host state's welfare system.[109]

This extension of EU citizenship to children is largely welcome insofar as it yields direct and tangible benefits to children. Furthermore, a key variable shaping the case law in this area is the Court's respect for fundamental children rights principles, notably the right to family life and the right to education. However, EU citizenship is also inherently limited as a framework within which to pursue children's rights by virtue of its exclusivity to certain categories of children under certain defined conditions. First, it is confined largely to children who are the national of a Member State.[110] Second, inasmuch as the rights implied by EU

---

[105] See: *Baumbast and R*, above n 97; Case C-200/02 *Zhu & Chen v Secretary of State for the Home Department* [2004] ECR I-9923; *Zambrano*, above n 77; Case C-127/08 *Blaise Baheten Metock v Minister for Justice, Equality and Law Reform* [2008] ECR I-6241; Case C-310/08 *Harrow LBC v Nimco Hassan Ibrahim* [2010] ECR I-1065 and Case C-480/08 *Maria Teixeira v Lambeth LBC and Secretary of State for the Home Department* [2010] ECR I-1107. In the same token, children can 'anchor' a non-custodial parents' right to reside in the host state in the context of divorce where it is necessary for retaining regular contact with them (Art 13 Dir 2004/38). These issues and case law are discussed in further detail in chs 3 and 6.

[106] See C Forder, 'Family Rights and Immigration Law: A European Perspective' in H Schneider (ed), *Migration, Integration and Citizenship: A Challenge for Europe's Future*, vol II (Maastricht, Forum Maastricht, 2005).

[107] C O'Brien, 'Case C-310/08 *Ibrahim*, Case C-480/08 *Teixiera*' (2011) 48 *CML Rev* 203; C Sawyer, 'Citizenship is Not Enough: The Rights of Children of Foreign Parents' (2005) 35 *Family Law* 224.

[108] B Neale, *Young Children's Citizenship: Ideas into Practice* (York, Joseph Rowntree Foundation, 2004); R Lister, 'Unpacking Children's Citizenship' in A Invernizzi and J Williams (eds), *Children and Citizenship* (London, Sage, 2008) 9.

[109] Following the previous authority of *Baumbast* on this issue, EU child citizens could only enjoy ongoing residence in another Member State for the purposes of pursuing their education if they could demonstrate that they had access to health insurance and sufficient private financial means to cover their living costs. This requirement was significantly undermined by the cases of *Ibrahim* and *Teixera*. For a commentary of these cases, see O'Brien, above n 107.

[110] It only extends to children of third country nationality if at least one of their parents on whom they are dependent or with whom they reside are of EU nationality (Dir 2004/38 Art 2(2)(c)).

citizenship are primarily triggered as a result of EU nationals' exercise of free movement, children only enjoy the benefits of EU citizenship following their move (with a parent) to another EU Member State.[111] Children who do not move between the Member States—the vast majority, in fact—barely engage their EU citizenship entitlement during their childhood.[112] Such limitations imply that EU citizenship falls far short of the universality implied by a rights-based approach to regulating children's lives. But it is a useful vehicle all the same for those who do fall within its scope and remains the most prolific source of direct, tangible, justiciable children's rights at EU level.

NON-DISCRIMINATION AS A NORMATIVE FRAMEWORK FOR PURSUING CHILDREN'S RIGHTS

An arguably more inclusive framework within which children's rights might be developed is that of non-discrimination. This essentially provides that those in comparable situations must not be treated differently, and those in different situations must not be treated in the same way, unless such treatment is objectively justified.

The principle of non-discrimination is a pervasive element of EU law. It is identified as a 'founding value' of the European Union in the TEU[113] and is expressly prohibited by the TFEU in a range of contexts, including on grounds of nationality,[114] sex, racial or ethnic origin, religion or belief, disability, age or sexual orientation.[115] Discrimination is also recognised as a discrete general principle of EU law to the same extent as fundamental rights, although it is a central feature of the EU fundamental rights regime too. Notably, Article 21(1) of the Charter of Fundamental Rights of the European Union extends the grounds on which discrimination is prohibited to include social origin, genetic features, language, political or any other opinion, membership of a national minority, property and birth.[116] In the same token, non-discrimination is an essential element of international human rights law.[117] For example, under the ECHR, it operates both in

---

[111] The case of *Zambrano*, above n 77, is a rare exception and is discussed further in ch 3.

[112] There are other political rights associated with EU citizenship—including the right to vote in municipal and European Parliamentary elections (Arts 22–24 TFEU)—but these are exercisable only by those who have reached the age of 18 in all Member States (with the exception of Austria where the voting age is 16).

[113] Art 2.

[114] Art 18 TFEU.

[115] Art 19 TFEU.

[116] It is important to note that this provision does not serve to alter or extend the powers conferred by Art 19 TFEU to enact anti-discrimination laws in these areas of Member State or private action. Instead, it only addresses discrimination by the EU institutions on these grounds when exercising powers conferred under the Treaties, and by Member States only when they are implementing Union law. See further, Explanations relating to the Charter of Fundamental Rights 2007/C 303/02 [2007] OJ C303/17.

[117] For example, Art 1 of the 1948 Universal Declaration of Human Rights (UDHR) proclaims: 'All human beings are born free and equal in dignity and rights'. This is reinforced by Art 7 UDHR which

tandem with substantive rights to reinforce the level of protection available to individuals[118] and as a standalone right;[119] it is integral to the UN Convention on the Rights of Persons with Disabilities (UNCRPD) to which the EU is a signatory;[120] and forms one of the general principles of the UNCRC,[121] thereby underpinning all other rights protected by the instrument.

Yet despite the ubiquity of non-discrimination at EU level, and despite its importance to the UNCRC, explicit reference to the principle is conspicuously absent from the EU Agenda for the Rights of the Child[122] or, indeed, from any formative discussions around the development of EU children's rights. Certainly adherence to non-discrimination is a central component of a *rights-based approach* but, as far as children are concerned, it is by no means straightforward. Children, like adults, do not enjoy an absolute right to protection against discrimination. In some cases, discrimination can be justified on wider public policy grounds, or with a view to upholding the rights and interests of others, or, indeed, to protect the individual against him or herself. These justifications are more persuasively argued in the context of children: measures that deny children access to rights that are routinely made available to adults—such as employment, sex, marriage, driving a car or consuming alcohol, for instance—are based on a persuasive moral and social consensus that such activities are not in children's best interests, or at least not until they reach a certain level of maturity.

Insofar as such arguments are based primarily on a paternalistic desire to protect children, they have legitimised routine and endemic discrimination against

states: 'All are equal before the law and are entitled without any discrimination to equal protection of the law. All are entitled to equal protection against any discrimination in violation of this Declaration and against any incitement to such discrimination'; and perhaps most importantly, see Art 26 of the 1966 International Covenant of Civil and Political Rights (ICCPR) which states that 'All persons are equal before the law and are entitled without any discrimination to the equal protection of the law. In this respect, the law shall prohibit any discrimination and guarantee to all persons equal and effective protection against discrimination on any ground such as race, colour, sex, language, religion, political or other opinion, national or social origin, property, birth or other status'. For examples of similar declarations in other international instruments, see Breen, above n 60, 13–15.

[118] Art 14 ECHR prohibits discrimination only with regard to the 'enjoyment of the rights and freedoms' set forth in the Convention and is, therefore, more limited than comparable non-discrimination provisions of other international instruments. The ECtHR has found that discrimination on grounds of age falls within the protection of the ECHR (see *Schwizgebel v Switzerland* App no 25762/07 (unreported) Judgment of 10 June 2010).

[119] Protocol 12 ECHR, ETS No 177 was adopted in November 2000, and entered into force on 1 April 2005, following its tenth ratification. This prohibits public authorities from discriminating against individuals 'on any ground such as sex, race, colour, language, religion, political or other opinion, national or social origin, association with a national minority, property, birth or other status' (Art 1). This provision echoes the substance of preceding international human rights measures, notably Art 26 of the 1966 International Covenant on Civil and Political Rights. It is worth noting that, to date, this Protocol has only been ratified by seven of the 27 Member States.

[120] See notably paras c, h and p, Preamble, Arts 3(b), 4(1), 5 and 7 for the purposes of the analysis in this book.

[121] Art 2 UNCRC.

[122] A single, cursory reference to discrimination—as a common experience of Roma children—features in the main text of the Agenda, above n 1, 10.

children on grounds of age.[123] It is now universally accepted that, as children mature and develop an understanding of the world around them, so too does their capacity to exercise autonomous choices. The freedom to make their own mistakes is part and parcel of this formative process. It does not necessarily follow a strict chronology, however, and there is generally a case to be made for extricating an *individual* child's capacity and maturity from more stereotypical, age-based inferences as to what children should or should not be capable of doing.[124]

This fine balance—between the desire to protect children's well-being and the need to encourage an incremental level of autonomy, and the wish to achieve universal standards of rights whilst allowing for the child to be valued and protected in his or her own right—is embedded in the UNCRC and its accompanying guidance.[125] But discrimination in the context of children's rights extends far beyond the well-trodden debate as to where the line between protectionism and self-determinism should be drawn.[126] It is now more widely concerned with identifying and weeding out unjustifiable differences in treatment on a range of grounds, not only of children as compared to adults, but also of some groups of children as compared to other groups of children. Thus, the UNCRC has drawn attention to widespread discriminatory practices against particular communities of children, for example as a result of disability, refugee or asylum-seeking status, HIV/AIDS infection or ethnicity,[127] whilst reinforcing the need for 'affirmative action'—by definition, an exercise in positive discrimination—to offset such disadvantages. These observations beg the question as to how the EU's non-discrimination legal architecture can be exploited to ensure an appropriate parity of treatment between children in comparable situations or, indeed, to afford 'special consideration' to those living in exceptionally difficult circumstances in the EU.

USING EU NON-DISCRIMINATION LAW TO PROTECT CHILDREN'S RIGHTS

The previous discussion has already established that non-discrimination is a canon of EU law, having been constitutionally endorsed within the general principles

[123] For a detailed history of how attitudes towards children's capacity and vulnerability, and the consequent impact on their legal treatment *vis-à-vis* adults has been rationalised, see C Breen, *Age Discrimination and Children's Rights: Ensuring Equality and Acknowledging Difference* (Oxford, Hart, 2005) ch1.

[124] S Fredman, 'The Age of Equality' in S Fredman and S Spencer (eds), *Age as an Equality Issue: Legal and Policy Perspectives* (Oxford, Hart, 2003) 21.

[125] Not least in Arts 3 and 12 as two of the four general principles of the UNCRC. See also General Comment, 'The Right of the Child to be Heard' UNCRC/C/GC/12, 20 July 2009; and Eekelaar, *The Interests of The Child and the Child's Wishes*, above n 79.

[126] See G Lansdown, *The Evolving Capacities of the Child* (Florence, UNICEF Innocenti Research Centre, 2005) for further analysis of this particular line of argument.

[127] R Hodgkin and P Newell, *Implementation Handbook for the Convention on the Rights of the Child*, 3rd edn (Geneva, UNICEF, 2007). The endemic discrimination against the most socio-economically vulnerable is also highlighted in the UNICEF annual reports, *The State of the World's Children* available at unicef.org/sowc/.

framework, in the Treaties and in the Charter of Fundamental Rights of the EU. It is not surprising, then, that the principle suffuses much of EU substantive law, including a range of measures of direct relevance to children. Specifically non-discrimination forms the bedrock of EU citizenship law, in that, subject to the conditions identified above, EU migrant children and their families can access entitlement including all levels of education, in other Member States on the same basis as nationals. The same principle extends to other internal market measures, for example in the context of the free movement of goods, unless persuasive public policy reasons—including the need to protect children's welfare—justify a derogation from it.[128]

The burgeoning corpus of EU equality law also provides an obvious context within which children can be protected against discrimination, first of all by conferring on children a direct enforceable right to equal treatment or protection against unlawful discrimination. For instance, the Employment Equality Directive,[129] which prohibits discrimination on the basis of sexual orientation, religious belief, age and disability in the area of employment, can be relied upon by teenagers in the course of their formal paid activities.[130] Indeed, all of the employment equality legislation in theory could be used by children, notwithstanding the fact that it was primarily conceived to achieve equality between 'men and women' at work.[131]

Equally, the Racial Equality Directive which prohibits discrimination on the basis of race or ethnicity in the context of employment, welfare provision, or goods and services can be used to support children's claims for equal treatment in the context of education.[132] Indeed, the capacity of the EU to offer direct protection for children against discrimination should be even further enhanced if proposals to implement the principle of equal treatment to a range of other public and private sector contexts are adopted.[133]

---

[128] See *Dynamic Medien*, above n 40.

[129] Dir 2000/78 establishing a general framework for equal treatment in employment and occupation (Employment Equality Directive) [2000] OJ L303/16.

[130] Although this has to be balanced against the welfare considerations implied by Dir 94/33 on the protection of young people at work (Young Workers Directive) [1994] OJ L216/12. This imposes a general prohibition on the employment of children who are below the age of 15 or still in full-time compulsory education and introduces a number of measures to protect young people's health and safety in the workplace. This issue will not be explored further in this book, but see R Rodríguez, *Study on Child Labour and Protection of Young Workers in the European Union: Final Report* (Brussels, DG Employment, Social Affairs and Equal Opportunities, 2006).

[131] Thus, none of the equal treatment instruments—including Dir 92/85 Pregnant Workers Directive [1992] OJ L348/1; Dir 96/34 Parental Leave Directive [1996] OJ L145/4; the (re-cast) Dir 2006/54 Equal Treatment Directive [2006] OJ L204/23 and Dir 2004/113 Goods and Services Directive [2004] OJ L373/37—are explicitly limited to *adult* females. They could, it is presumed, be applied in favour of, eg a 17-year-old girl, in full-time employment who, on discovering she is pregnant, wishes to avail herself of this network of legal protection.

[132] Discussed further in ch 6.

[133] Proposal for a Council Directive on implementing the principle of equal treatment between persons irrespective of religion or belief, disability, age or sexual orientation COM (2008) 426 final.

Aside from conferring very direct entitlement on children, it is important to acknowledge also that EU equality law and policy can confer benefits on children in more indirect ways. For example, implicit in the legislation on flexible working for parents, as well as in the panoply of EU initiatives aimed at promoting the 'reconciliation of work and family life', is the assumption that parents will have more time and energy to spend with their children. Whilst a number of commentators have suggested that such developments merely serve to reinforce gendered stereotypes in the private sphere,[134] McGlynn concedes that:

> Policies ... which support equal parenting may, in some small way, be advanced on the basis that they support children's needs and expectations ... [and that], therefore, it is arguable that the pursuit of equal parenting meets the instruction of the European Union's Charter ... to pursue the best interests of the child.[135]

The indirect benefits that accrue to children under EU equality law is also borne out in the case law. Notably, in *Coleman*, the Court of Justice established that adults can suffer discrimination not only in relation to their own characteristics, but also in relation to those with whom they are associated.[136] In this case, Mrs Coleman successfully argued that, as the primary carer of a disabled child, she had suffered disability discrimination 'by association' in that she was treated less favourably than employees with non-disabled children. Thus, we see a similar trend developing in the context of non-discrimination as has occurred in the context of EU citizenship: children are effectively succeeding not only in deriving an indirect benefit from legal measures which historically remained impervious to them, but, more significantly, are acting as a conduit through which their parents can also stake a claim for equal treatment in their own right.[137]

As a final word on non-discrimination, it is worth noting that, in addition to the many examples of non-discrimination producing enforceable entitlement through its integration into secondary legislation, it can also produce potent legal effects as a free standing general principle of EU law. At the abstract level, as discussed earlier, Member States and the EU institutions must adhere to the general principles, including that of non-discrimination, when acting within the

---

[134] In other words, they merely enable mothers to do more with the same amount of time whilst failing to address the imbalance between men and women's caring duties more broadly. See further, C McGlynn, 'Ideologies of Motherhood in European Sex Equality Law' (2000) 6 *European Law Journal* 29; T Hervey (ed), 'Thirty Years of EU Sex Equality Law' (2005) 12 *Maastricht Journal of European and Comparative Law* 307 and E Caracciolo di Torella and A Masselot, *Reconciling Work and Family Life in EU Law and Policy* (Basingstoke, Palgrave Macmillan, 2010).

[135] McGlynn, *Families and the European Union*, above n 72, 91.

[136] Case C-303/06 *Coleman v Attridge Law and Steve Law* [2008] ECR I-5603. For a commentary, see T Connor, 'Case C-303/06 *Coleman v Attridge Law and Steve Law* Judgment of the ECJ' (2010) 32 *Journal of Social Welfare and Family Law* 57.

[137] For a broader analysis of how the principle of non-discrimination operates in EU law, see E Ellis, *EU Anti-Discrimination Law* (Oxford, Oxford University Press, 2005). For a more descriptive summary, see European Court of Human Rights and the European Union Agency for Fundamental Rights, *Handbook on European Non-Discrimination Law* (Luxembourg, Publications Office of the European Union, 2011).

scope of EU law (as defined by the Treaties). But some notable decisions have established that the principle of non-discrimination can also be relied upon to impose direct substantive obligations, not just on the Member States' authorities, but on private individuals too. Thus, in *Mangold,* the Court of Justice determined that the principle of non-discrimination on grounds of age could be invoked by an individual against his private employer to challenge age-discriminatory working regulations.[138] This was notwithstanding the fact that national legislation had yet to be implemented to give effect to this principle. It follows, therefore, that the principle of non-discrimination on grounds of age might conceivably be relied upon to challenge discrimination based on youth rather than on seniority, even in the absence of enforceable, implementing legislation on which to hang such a claim.[139]

SOCIAL INCLUSION AS A FRAMEWORK FOR PROTECTING CHILDREN'S RIGHTS

A final conceptual framework that lends itself to the promotion and protection of children's interests at EU level, but which is often overlooked in EU children's rights programming, is that of social inclusion. Social inclusion is the remedial response to social *exclusion,* the process by which individuals and groups are excluded from taking part in the social, economic, legal and political exchanges of everyday life which are necessary for social integration and personal fulfillment.[140]

As the previous chapter has highlighted, promoting social inclusion is a central objective of the EU's social agenda[141] but insofar as these provisions were originally aimed at maximising employment and social opportunities for *adults* in the EU, they were not particularly child-focused. However, as EU social policy expanded beyond the strictly economic parameters of the internal market, a range of issues were drawn into the EU regulatory frame. Significantly, it was quickly acknowledged that poverty was at the root of most social exclusion: by tackling the causes of poverty, the EU could make significant inroads into addressing unemployment and achieving greater social cohesion. Moreover, the EU recognised that poverty is experienced particularly acutely by children and has detrimental consequences for their immediate and future development. Thus, the correlation between the incidence and extent of child poverty and the future security and prosperity of

---

[138] Case C-144/04 *Werner Mangold v Rüdiger Helm* [2005] ECR I-9981, affirmed in Case C-555/07 *Seda Kücükdeveci v Swedex GmbH & Co KG* [2010] ECJ I-365.

[139] For a detailed analysis of the implications of *Mangold* see M Dougan, 'In Defence of Mangold?' in A Arnull, C Barnard, M Dougan and E Spaventa (eds), *A Constitutional Order of States? Essays in EU Law in Honour of Alan Dashwood* (Oxford, Hart, 2011).

[140] European Commission, 'Towards a Europe of solidarity' (Communication) COM (92) 542 final.

[141] Art 3(3) TEU, as amended by the Lisbon Treaty, pledges the EU's commitment 'to combating social exclusion and discrimination, and to promoting social justice ... and protection of the rights of the child'.

the EU soon became apparent. It was not until the turn of the millennium that child poverty was included more explicitly within the EU's Social Inclusion Process,[142] but during the decade that followed, significant progress was made in establishing a comprehensive EU-wide strategy for tackling and monitoring child poverty.[143] Efforts have been redoubled in this regard since the publication in March 2010 of the European Council's revised strategy for growth, the Europe 2020 Agenda, which identifies social inclusion and poverty reduction among its core targets.[144]

So, how can a seemingly quite narrow focus on children in vulnerable socio-economic circumstances provide the backdrop for a broader EU children's rights agenda? The answer to this lies in our conceptualisation of child poverty. Research and policy has long since departed from the notion that child poverty is merely an issue of material deprivation.[145] Rather, action to tackle child poverty is now regarded as synonymous with action to promote child 'well-being', life-chances and access to legal, social, welfare, cultural and civic processes more broadly.[146] In the same token, social inclusion, with its child well-being and anti-poverty connotations, is the favoured rhetoric of children's rights NGOs that have been at the forefront of the campaign for more meaningful EU intervention in relation to children.[147] Similarly, the EU Agenda for the Rights of the Child draws, to some degree, on the concept of social inclusion, framing its objectives within the broader context of the Europe 2020 Strategy, and identifying a clear correlation between economic deprivation, educational exclusion, cultural marginalisation and physical, mental and emotional vulnerability.[148]

But it is not just the far-reaching concept of social inclusion that offers an attractive framework for promoting children's rights. The method of governance

---

[142] Lisbon European Council, March 2000.

[143] See further Social Protection Committee, *Child Poverty and Well-Being in the EU: Current Status and Way Forward* (Luxembourg, European Communities, 2008).

[144] European Commission, 'Europe 2020: a strategy for smart, sustainable and inclusive growth' (Communication) COM (2010) 2020 final, 3 March 2010.

[145] P Townsend, *The Concept of Poverty: Working Papers on Methods of Investigation and Life-styles of the Poor in Different Countries* (Michigan, Heinemann Educational, 1970); P Townsend, *The International Analysis of Poverty* (New York, Harvester Wheatsheaf, 1993) and J Bradshaw, 'The Understanding of Poverty Transformed' in A Walker, A Sinfield and C Walker (eds), *Fighting Poverty, Inequality and Injustice: A Manifesto Inspired by Peter Townsend* (Bristol, Policy Press, 2011).

[146] This broader conceptualisation of child poverty is evidenced in the myriad studies and indicators that have emerged in recent years devoted to measuring and monitoring such issues, see: UNICEF, *Child Poverty in Perspective: A Overview of Child Well-Being in Rich Countries—Innocenti Report Card 7, 2007* (Florence, UNICEF, 2007) and J Bradshaw, P Hoelscher and D Richardson, 'An Index of Child Well-Being in the European Union' (2007) 80 *Social Indicators Research* 133. Similar studies within the EU include: Social Protection Committee, *Child Poverty*, above n 143; H Stalford, H Sax and E Drywood, *Developing Indicators for the Protection, Respect and Promotion of the Rights of the Child in the European Union: Updated Post-Lisbon Treaty Conference* (Vienna, Fundamental Rights Agency, 2010) and TÁRKI, *Child Poverty and Child Well-Being in the European Union: Report for the European Commission* (Budapest, TÁRKI, 2010).

[147] See notably the network NGO, Eurochild, based in Brussels: eurochild.org/.

[148] Above n 1, 8–9.

associated with it is also highly innovative and effective too: the Open Method of Co-ordination (OMC) was launched at the Lisbon Council in March 2000 as an intergovernmental mechanism to support cross-national co-ordination, evaluation and the implementation of common objectives in various aspects of social policy, including social exclusion and child poverty. It is the participatory, devolved nature of this process that renders it a particularly attractive tool for promoting children's rights in that it relies on the collaborative will of the Member States rather than on top-down, heavy-handed legal prescription to achieve clearly defined goals in areas of mutual interest.[149] Suffice to say, in an area that is characterised by frail legal bases as well as significant opposition to direct EU intervention, the OMC provides a coherent, politically mollifying opportunity for progress in relation to all manner of child-related issues. Moreover, although this process is not generally associated explicitly with 'rights' in the broader sense, it necessarily adheres to the same children's rights principles and provisions that underpin the other conceptual frameworks referred to above.[150]

CONCLUSION

The aim of this chapter has been to map out the ideological framework underpinning EU children's rights, using the EU's flagship programme—the Agenda for the Rights of the Child—as its primary reference point. The tone of the Agenda is quite impressive: it clearly endorses a rights-based approach to the pursuit of its objectives. However, in doing so, the EU assumes some responsibility for both articulating and delivering on it. Scratching beneath the surface, however, the Commission offers little insight into what a rights-based approach actually involves, leading to the (perhaps cynical) conclusion that it is merely exploiting the rhetorical capital of children's rights—and particularly that of the UNCRC—to add some weight or legitimacy to its Agenda.

Linked to this is the contention that a rights-based approach should imply more than just an expressed allegiance to the UNCRC. As Tobin notes, the UNCRC is 'the primary but not the only instrument from which the principles of an international human rights based approach to children are to be derived'.[151] This is certainly true at EU level where there is significant mileage in other human rights instruments, notably the ECHR and the Charter of Fundamental Rights.

---

[149] Stalford and Drywood, above n 32. For a wider, detailed analysis of the OMC, see F Beveridge and S Velluti, (eds), *Gender and the OMC: Perspectives on Law, Governance and Equality in the EU* (Dartmouth, Ashgate, 2008). See also E Szcszyzak, 'Experimental Governance: The Open Method of Coordination' (2006) 12 *European Law Journal* 486.

[150] On the correlation between child well-being, which is implicit in the social inclusion process, and children's rights, see L Lundy, 'The United Nations Convention on the Rights of the Child and Child Well-being' in A Ben-Arieh, F Casas, I Frones and J Korbin (eds), *International Handbook on Child Well-being* (Springer, forthcoming 2012).

[151] Tobin, 'Understanding A Human Rights Based Approach', above n 6, 68.

The former now boasts a well-developed children's rights jurisprudence, while the latter underpins all stages of the legal and policy-making process, from formation through to implementation and judicial interpretation. But the pointed issue of EU competence will always dictate the extent to which abstract children's rights principles can effect tangible, meaningful changes to children's lives on the ground.

This observation has prompted some consideration of whether there are other ideological and conceptual frameworks within which children's rights might be more effectively pursued by the EU. This has revealed not just one explicitly rights-based framework for protecting children's rights, but a conceptual 'quad' of social inclusion, non-discrimination, citizenship and fundamental rights. Indeed, by broadening the EU children's rights debate to encompass these additional frameworks, alternative methods of governance have been identified that circumvent the legal, cultural and political obstacles to direct EU legal intervention in so many children's rights issues. But exploiting these alternatives does not imply an obfuscation of the rights-based approach. Indeed, rights are integral to each and every one of them. It is suggested, rather, that the EU endorses a more blended approach: one that unashamedly picks-and-mixes between the normative frameworks already at the EU's disposal depending on the circumstances, thereby producing a much sturdier, more persuasive system of EU children's rights protection. The extent to which this children's rights framework is articulated in substantive areas of EU law will provide the focus of subsequent chapters.

3

Children, Family Life and EU Migration Law

INTRODUCTION

THIS CHAPTER EXPLORES children's status under EU migration law. This is an area with a long and extensive history of EU legislative and judicial intervention, resulting in a broad and complex web of regulatory instruments. Unlike many other issues covered in this book, EU migration measures are underpinned by an explicit legal framework aimed at stimulating the mobility of primarily EU nationals between countries internal to the EU. This, in turn, has necessitated the progressive fortification of external borders to stem the flow of less economically productive migrants into the EU and, indeed, to distribute such migrants more evenly between the Member States.

All EU migration instruments acknowledge to varying degrees the particular interests of children, for example, in terms of their access to education, healthcare or social welfare benefits. The discussion in this chapter, however, will focus specifically on the extent to which one of the most basic and fundamental of children's rights is articulated and facilitated within this body of law: the right to family life. While the contexts within which different groups of children move remain diverse, the needs and values pertaining to 'family' are a common dynamic shaping the migration experiences of *all* children, impacting in a variety of ways on the application and enforcement of domestic immigration policies and on the level of formal and informal support available to migrant children.

The importance attached to family life in a migration context is evident in the extensive jurisprudence at international, European and national level, with family life providing the principal basis for the entry and residence of many migrants. This, in turn, has prompted some consideration of the specific needs and interests of children as part of the migrant family unit. This chapter explores the extent to which such issues are accommodated within EU law in various migration contexts. To situate the analysis, the discussion first outlines the international children's rights framework relevant to migration. Against this legal backdrop, it then examines how the various EU migration instruments articulate and respond to children's right to family life. In particular, the analysis will argue that children's rights under EU migration law are rooted in conflicting presumptions that neither correspond with international standards nor reflect the reality of migrant children's lives. The final section argues that the EU's failure to respond appropriately to migrant children's needs—and particularly their family-related needs—is partly attributable to the limited body of research relating to children, both within the wider discipline of migration studies, and within the specific body of research on family migration.

ADOPTING A RIGHTS-BASED APPROACH TO MIGRANT CHILDREN'S FAMILY LIFE

Migrant children's right to family life is enshrined in a number of generic international instruments including the 1948 Universal Declaration of Human Rights,[1] the 1966 International Covenant on Civil and Political Rights,[2] the 1996 European Social Charter,[3] and the 1950 European Convention on Human Rights and Fundamental Freedoms (ECHR).[4] Inherent in the right to family life is the right to family unity. Although this is not explicitly identified as a right in international law, the concept of family unity denotes a range of migration entitlements relating to admission and residence which are aimed at ensuring that the family remains together following migration. In contrast, family reunification or 'reunion' refers to the efforts of family members already separated by forced or voluntary migration to regroup in a country—usually in one other than their country of origin—thereby implying a level of state discretion over admission exercised in favour of otherwise excluded individuals.[5]

Underpinning both of these statuses—family unity and family reunification— is the assumption that if members of the family do not have a right to live together or to enjoy direct contact with one another, there would be little family life to respect or protect.[6] Cholewinski states as follows:

> The smallest, closest and yet most important community to many persons is the family unit. The enjoyment of many rights, particularly economic, social and cultural rights,

---

[1] Art 16(3).

[2] Art 23(1). Both this and Art 16(3) of the 1948 Universal Declaration provisions ordain the family as 'the natural and fundamental group unit of society … entitled to protection by society and the State'.

[3] ETS 163 revising the 1961 European Social Charter, Art 16. This provides that 'with a view to ensuring the necessary conditions for the full development of the family, which is a fundamental unit of society, the Parties undertake to promote the economic, legal and social protection of family life by such means as social and family benefits, fiscal arrangements, provision of family housing, benefits for the newly married and other appropriate means'.

[4] Art 8(1) provides that 'everyone has the right to respect for his private and family life, his home and his correspondence'.

[5] The additional umbrella term 'family union' is used throughout the rest of this chapter to denote all measures that enable the family to live together in the host state, by moving together as a unit, being reunited after a period of separation, or by staving off deportation of one or more family members on the basis of their personal ties in the host state.

[6] E Feller, V Türk and F Nicholson, *Refugee Protection in International Law: UNHCR's Global Consultations on International Consultation* (Cambridge, Cambridge University Press, 2003) 23.

would be meaningless without affording protection to this wider context in which individual human beings locate and express themselves.[7]

With this in mind it is now universally acknowledged that meaningful protection of the right to family life requires a commitment on the part of states to ensure immigration policies do not unduly interfere with the exercise of that right.[8] In Europe, Article 8(2)[9] of the ECHR has played a particularly key role in defining the boundaries of state immigration control vis-à-vis the family, and has been extensively interpreted as imposing both positive and negative obligations on state signatories. Thus, there is now a considerable body of case law demonstrating the extent to which concerns around family life, and particularly around the welfare of children, can be used to restrain the application of domestic immigration control, either by admitting family members into the host state for the purposes of family reunification (the so-called 'positive obligation') or by precluding deportation of an individual from the host state if doing so would have an adverse effect on the exercise and enjoyment of family life (the 'negative obligation').[10]

In cases concerning children, the European Court of Human Rights (ECtHR) has demonstrated an increasing willingness to uphold an (adult, usually parent) applicant's residence status, acknowledging that the trauma of deportation could unduly jeopardise the family, and particularly the child's educational, social and emotional stability.[11] This represents a departure from the previous, more hard line approach by which deportation was sanctioned as the standard course of action unless there were insurmountable legal, political, cultural or social obstacles preventing the family from re-locating with the applicant to another state. More recently, the ECtHR has developed a relatively straightforward test which focuses on the quality of the relationship between the family members over and

---

[7] R Cholewinski, 'Family Reunification and Conditions Placed on Family Members: Dismantling a Fundamental Human Right' (2002) 4 *European Journal of Migration and Law* 271, 274.

[8] This obligation is endorsed, inter alia, by Art 8(2) of the ECHR; Art 10(1) of the 1966 International Covenant on Economic, Social and Cultural Rights; Arts 17(1)(c) and 19(6) of the Revised 1996 European Social Charter, ETS 163; Art 12 of the Universal Declaration of Human Rights; Art 16 of the 1989 UNCRC; Art 44(2) of the UN Convention on the Protection of All Migrant Workers and Members of their Families, UN GA Res 45/158 of 18 December 1990 and Art 12 of the European Convention on the Legal Status of Migrant Workers, 24 November 1977, ETS 93.

[9] This states that 'there shall be no interference by a public authority with the exercise of [the right to family life] except such as is in accordance with the law and is necessary in a democratic society in the interests of national security, public safety or the economic well-being of the country, for the prevention of disorder or crime, for the protection of health or morals, or for the protection of the rights and freedoms of others'.

[10] This may even be the case where deportation is motivated by the serious criminal misconduct on the part of the applicant. See: *Gül v Switzerland* App no 23218/94 (1996) 22 EHRR 93; and *Ahmut v Netherlands* App no 21702/93 (1997) 24 EHRR 62, paras 70–73. For an extensive analysis of the ECHR case law in this area, see C Forder, 'Family Rights and Immigration Law: A European Perspective' in H Schneider (ed), *Migration, Integration and Citizenship: A Challenge for Europe's Future*, vol II (Maastricht, Forum Maastricht, 2005).

[11] D Thym, 'Respect for Private and Family Life under Article 8 ECHR in Immigration Cases: A Human Right to Regularize Illegal Stay?' (2008) 57 *ICLQ* 87.

above peripheral matters relating to length of residence, or even the personal conduct of the applicant. As Forder notes:

> The recent trends in the deportation cases and the family reunification cases can be summarized as follows: in both situations the duration of residence of the person is relatively unimportant. What matters is the strength of family bonds and the degree of disruption to those bonds likely to be occasioned or already occasioned by the state's actions.[12]

Central to this test, is judicial evaluation as to the actual and potential impact national immigration responses to family dislocation and fragmentation might have on children's well-being.[13] Before even reaching this point, however, individuals have to fall within the definitional boundaries of 'family' imposed by the law in order to benefit from protection. The ECHR case law has endorsed a broad conceptualisation of the 'family' and of 'family life' for the purposes of family union rights to include extra-marital cohabiting and non-cohabiting relationships,[14] post-divorce parent–child relationships,[15] sibling relationships[16] and even children's relationships with their grandparents.[17] EU migration law, on the other hand, has been less comprehensive in accommodating different family relationships, carrying important consequences for children, as the following discussion will demonstrate.

THE NATURE AND SCOPE OF CHILDREN'S FAMILY RIGHTS UNDER EU MIGRATION LAW

The true currency of children's rights under EU migration law is visible in the provision relating to the family union entitlement of both EU and third country nationals, including asylum seekers. That said, family union means different things in different EU migration contexts. In relation to labour market mobility, and particularly that of EU nationals, a fixed, permanently resident non-national population in the host state has been established as a natural consequence of

---

[12] Above n 10, 87.

[13] See *Slivenko v Latvia* App no 48321/99 (2004) 39 EHRR 24. The Court upheld the applicants' appeal against deportation on the basis of Art 8, even though the family was being deported collectively. The Court found that such expulsion would constitute an interference with their private life and their 'home' since they had established strong social, economic and personal relations in the host state. The Court noted, however, that such broad interpretation of Art 8 in immigration cases applies mainly to the 'core' or nuclear family and will only include wider kin or personal bonds in the most exceptional of cases. See further Thym, 'Respect for Private and Family Life' above n 11.

[14] *Abdulaziz, Cabales and Balkandali v United Kingdom* App nos 9214/80, 9473/81 and 9474/81 (1985) 7 EHRR 471.

[15] *Berrehab v Netherlands* App no 10730/84 (1989) 11 EHRR 322.

[16] *Boughanemi v France* App no 22070/93 (1996) 22 EHRR 228. A relationship between the applicant and a minor sibling is more likely to benefit from the protection of Art 8(2) unless a special relationship of dependency between adult siblings is established, see *Ezzouhdi v France* App no 47160/99 13 February 2001. See also Forder, 'Family Rights', above n 10, 77.

[17] *Marckx v Belgium* App no 6833/74 (1979-80) 2 EHRR 330, para 45.

a fluid free movement agenda.[18] EU enlargement and the globalised market economy have further extended the need for expeditious family reunification, generating a new wave of primary labour migrants, many of whom anticipate being joined by family members once they are settled in the host state. In the context of irregular and forced migration, on the other hand, heightened controls on immigration have rendered family reunification for many migrants the most likely lawful pathway into the host country.

Each of these migration contexts are governed by a distinct political and economic agenda. The former is very much concerned with the now well-embedded concept of facilitating and sustaining labour market mobility within the EU. The latter is linked to more basic concerns around ensuring compliance with international human rights obligations whilst also responding to the perceived threat migration poses to welfare and labour market systems, not to mention national security. It follows then that the family union measures included in the free movement of persons legislation is broader and significantly more accessible than the more defensive measures governing immigration and asylum of third country nationals. The critical question for this chapter is the impact of these divergent agendas on children's rights and welfare.

CONCEPTUALISATIONS OF 'CHILD' AND 'FAMILY' UNDER EU MIGRATION LAW

Generally, the definition ascribed to the 'family' and 'child' by EU migration legislation is a critical starting point in determining the extent of children's right to enter, reside and to access social entitlement in the host state, or indeed, in determining which family members can join them after they themselves have moved to the host state.

The free movement provisions governing the migration status and entitlement of EU nationals and their families are relatively straightforward. Directive 2004/38 on the right of citizens of the Union and their family members to move and reside freely within the territory of the Member States reaffirms family members' permanent right to enter the host state either with or following the primary EU migrant's move there.[19] 'Family', for the purposes of this instrument, is defined as: the primary EU migrant's legal spouse; their partner with whom they have contracted a registered partnership (provided such a partnership is recognised by the

---

[18] Cholewinski, 'Family Reunification' above n 7.

[19] Art 5(1) Dir 2004/38 on the right of citizens of the Union and their family members to move and reside freely within the territory of the Member States amending Reg 1612/68 and repealing Dirs 64/221, 68/360, 72/194, 73/148, 75/34, 75/35, 90/364, 90/365 and 93/96 [2004] OJ L158/77; Corrigendum published as Directive 2004/58 on the right of citizens of the Union and their family members to move and reside freely within the territory of the Member States amending Reg 1612/68 and repealing Dirs 64/221, 68/360, 72/194, 73/148, 75/34, 75/35, 90/364, 90/365 and 93/96 [2004] OJ L229/35 (hereafter the Citizenship Directive).

legislation of the host Member State);[20] any biological children of either the EU migrant or his or her spouse or partner, provided they are under the age of 21 or are 'dependent' and the dependent direct relatives in the ascending line and those of the spouse or partner.[21] The instrument applies equally to family members of both EU and non-EU nationality (provided the primary qualifying migrant is an EU national) and is unconditional for the first three months of residence.[22] EU citizens who wish their family members to remain in the host state for more than three months must satisfy the resources requirement set out in Article 7,[23] and family members of third country nationality must apply for a residence card.[24]

These rights are far-reaching, not only in terms of their accessibility—they simply need to accompany or join an EU migrant in the host state—but also in terms of their durability.[25] Once family members enter the host state, they can remain

[20] Art 2(2)(b) Dir 2004/38. This provision reflects the Court of Justice's decision in Case 59/85 *Netherlands v Ann Florence Reed* [1986] ECR 1283 and does not grant a general right for all unmarried dependent or third country national partners to enter and reside with the EU migrant worker in the host state.

[21] Art 2(2). For more detailed analysis of the case law relating to the interpretation of 'family' under EU free movement law, see C McGlynn, *Families and the European Union: Law, Politics and Pluralism* (New York, Cambridge University Press, 2006); G Barret, 'Family Matters: European Community Law and Third Country Family Members' (2003) 40 *CML Rev* 369; N Foster, 'Family and Welfare Rights in Europe: The Impact of Recent European Court of Justice Decisions in the Area of Free Movement of Persons' (2003) 25 *Journal of Social Welfare and Family Law* 291.

[22] Art 3(2)(a). The case law relating to the entry and residence rights of third country national spouses is conflicting and rather contentious. The Court of Justice in Case C-109/01 *Secretary of State for the Home Department v Akrich* [2003] ECR I-9607 initially established the rule that a third country spouse could only join an EU national in the host state if their initial entry into the EU had been lawful. Thus, the fact that Mr Akrich had been deported from the UK on two previous occasions for illegally entering precluded the couple from settling together in Ireland. This contrasts with other decisions however. In Case C-459/99 *Mouvement contre le racisme, l'antisémitisme et la xénophobie ASBL (MRAX) v Belgium* [2002] ECR I-6591 for instance, it was held that the ECJ could not refuse entry to a third country national spouse simply on the basis that they were not in possession of a valid identity card or passport, provided they could prove their marriage and identity by other means. The decisions in Case C-60/00 *Carpenter v Secretary of State for the Home Department* [2002] ECR I-6279 and Case C-127/08 *Blaise Baheten Metock v Minister for Justice, Equality and Law Reform* [2008] ECR I-6241further challenge restrictions on spousal rights since both allowed the spouse to remain with the EU migrant in the host state notwithstanding the illegality of their initial entry and residence, and the fact that the 'family life' they purported to preserve had been formed during their illegal stay. For further commentary, see A Tryfonidou, 'Jia or "*Carpenter II*": The Edge of Reason' (2007) 33 *EL Rev* 908; B Olivier and J Herman Reestman, 'European Citizens' Third Country Family Members and Community Law' (2007) 3 *European Constitutional Law Review* 463; S Currie, 'Accelerated Justice or a Step Too Far? Residence Rights of Non-EU Family Members and the Court's Ruling in *Metock*' (2009) 34 *EL Rev* 310; C Costello, '*Metock*: Free Movement and "Normal Family Life" in the Union' (2009) 46 *CML Rev* 587; E Fahey, 'Going Back to Basics: Re-embracing the Fundamentals of the Free Movement of Persons in *Metock*' (2009) 36 *Legal Issues of Economic Integration* 83 and, more generally, R White, 'Conflicting Competences: Free Movement Rules and Immigration Laws' (2004) 29 *EL Rev* 385.

[23] In other words, they must have sufficient resources so that neither they nor their family members become a burden on the social assistance system of the host Member State during their period of residence. They must also be in possession of comprehensive sickness insurance cover in the host Member State.

[24] Arts 6(2), 9 and 10.

[25] It should be noted, however, that EU migrants from the most recent accession states (2004 and 2007) have been subject to certain restrictions on their freedom of movement to allow for a period

there even if the subsequent purpose of their stay is not family union, provided they continue to satisfy the resources requirement. Third country national family members also retain a right of residence in the host state following the death or departure of the Union citizen (Art 12(2)), or following divorce from the Union citizen (Art 13(2)), provided, again, they can satisfy the resources requirement.[26]

Conditions of ongoing residence have been further relaxed in more recent years to accommodate the specific interests of children. Most notably, children and custodial parents are entitled to remain in the host state following the death or departure of the primary EU migrant citizen 'if the children reside in the host Member State and are enrolled at an educational establishment, for the purpose of studying there'.[27] Furthermore, family members, and particularly third country national parents, also enjoy a right to remain in the host state following divorce from the EU citizen if they have primary custody of the couple's children or have been awarded rights of access to the children that must be exercised in the host state.[28] Significantly, the Directive explicitly provides that any exceptional expulsion of minors should accord with the provisions of the UNCRC 'in order to protect their links with their family'.[29]

These developments represent a subtle shift away from an exclusive preoccupation with facilitating the mobility of the migrant worker *adult* towards facilitating and protecting the personal and educational development of the migrant *child*. Such provision therefore supports the assertion that it is parenthood rather than marriage that has now become the central axis of family entitlement under free movement law.[30]

THE FAMILY RIGHTS OF THIRD COUNTRY NATIONALS UNDER EU LAW

By contrast to the increasingly liberal approach endorsed by the free movement of persons' provisions, EU legislation governing the child and family rights of third country national migrants is more mottled, with entitlement shifting in

---

of economic, political and social adjustment for both the new and existing Member States. For a detailed, critical and empirical analysis of these 'transitional measures' see S Currie, *Migration, Work and Citizenship in the Enlarged European Union* (Surrey, Ashgate, 2008).

[26] Although to qualify for permanent residence, the family must have lived in the host state for at least 12 months prior to the migrant worker's death. Family members automatically acquire permanent residence after a period of five consecutive years of residence with the EU citizen (Arts 16(2) and 18). The requisite period of residence to qualify for permanent residence is reduced in cases where the primary migrant reaches the age of retirement (Art 17(1)(a)) or where the primary migrant has been forced to cease working because of permanent incapacity (Art 17(2)(b)).

[27] Art 12(3).

[28] Art 13(2)(b) and 13(2)(d) respectively. These provisions essentially codify the ruling in Case C-413/99 *Baumbast and R v Secretary of State for the Home Department* [2002] ECR I-7091, discussed below.

[29] Art 28(3)(b) further endorses minors' immunity from expulsion unless this is deemed to be in their best interests in accordance with the UNCRC.

[30] I Dey and F Wasoff, 'Mixed Messages: Parental Responsibilities, Public Opinion and the Reforms of Family' (2006) 20 *International Journal of Law, Policy and the Family* 225, 243.

accordance with the nature of the migration. This is hardly surprising given that this body of law governs a range of migration scenarios including long-term work-related migration from highly developed regions for the relatively well resourced,[31] those who are applying for or have been granted refugee status,[32] temporary protective measures for asylum seekers or victims of trafficking[33] and more restrictive procedures aimed at excluding illegal migrants.[34]

Generally, all immigration instruments allow entry and residence to the spouse of the primary migrant. Registered or long-term unmarried partners may also enter and reside in the host state if domestic law recognises such relationships or if national discretion is exercised in their favour.[35] However, this body of law is less forgiving than the free movement provisions to cases of divorce following migration. Under the Family Reunification Directive, for instance, families can subsequently acquire independent right of residence, although the conditions attached to this are more limited. Only after a minimum period of *five* years residence is the spouse or unmarried partner and a child who has reached majority entitled to an autonomous residence permit independently of the sponsor.[36] This implies that partners who divorce or separate from the sponsor during the initial five years of residence will not qualify for any further right to remain in the host state. Member States also have discretion to limit permanent residence 'to the spouse or unmarried partner in cases of breakdown of the family relationship'. No reference is made to the children of such relationships and whether they would retain a right to remain, notwithstanding the fact that they may no longer live with the sponsor.

---

[31] Notably Dir 2003/109 concerning the status of third country nationals who are long-term residents [2004] OJ L16/44 (known as the Long Term Resident Directive); Dir 2003/86 on the right to family reunification [2003] OJ L251/12 (known as the Family Reunification Directive), note it is not binding on UK, Ireland and Denmark.

[32] Dir 2004/83 on minimum standards for the qualification and status of third country nationals or stateless persons as refugees or as persons who otherwise need international protection and the content of the protection granted [2004] OJ L304/12 (known as the Refugee Qualification Directive); Dir 2005/85 on minimum standards on procedures in Member States for granting and withdrawing refugee status [2005] OJ L326/13 (known as the Refugee Status Directive).

[33] Dir 2001/55 on minimum standards for giving temporary protection in the event of a mass influx of displaced persons and on measures promoting a balance of efforts between Member States in receiving such persons and bearing the consequences thereof [2001] OJ L212/12 (known as the Temporary Protection Directive); Dir 2003/9 laying down minimum standards for the reception of asylum [2003] OJ L31/18 (known as the Reception Directive); Reg 343/2003 establishing the criteria and mechanisms for determining the Member State responsible for examining an asylum application lodged in one of the Member States by a third country national [2003] OJ L50/1; Dir 2004/81 on the residence permit issued to third country nationals who are victims of trafficking in human beings or who have been the subject of an action to facilitate illegal immigration, who co-operate with the competent authorities [2004] OJ L261/19 (known as the Trafficking Directive), note in particular Art 10. Trafficking is considered in more detail in the context of EU child protection measures in ch 7.

[34] Dir 2008/115 on common standards and procedures in Member States for returning illegally staying third country nationals [2008] OJ L348/98 (known as the Returns Directive).

[35] Recital 10, Preamble, Family Reunification Directive, above n 31. See further McGlynn, *Families*, above n 21.

[36] Art 15(1). This contrasts with the more flexible thresholds applied by the Citizenship Directive, see above n 19.

Unlike under Directive 2004/38 (Article 12(2)), no reference is made to the need to ensure the child remains in close proximity to the non-custodial (sponsor) parent for the purposes of contact. Indeed, the discretionary withdrawal of residence rights from the ex-spouse/partner implies that any children of whom they have custody would also be forced to return to their country of origin. This is in clear conflict with Recital 11 of the Directive's Preamble which states that 'the right to family reunification should be exercised in proper compliance with the values and principles recognized by the Member States, in particular with respect to the rights of women and of children'.[37]

That said, aspects of EU immigration law do acknowledge the specific family situation of certain groups of migrants. Moreover, they appear amenable to a broader, more context-sensitive approach to family lives and family relationships, particularly for those who have migrated from more culturally, politically and economically diverse regions. In such cases, family relationships often correspond to quite a different model, with wider kin and community routinely assuming caring responsibilities for children and other vulnerable adults, particularly in areas ravaged by war and disease resulting in high levels of adult mortality.[38] Thus the Temporary Protection Directive[39] offers family-related protection to 'other close relatives who lived as part of the family unit, who were wholly or fully dependent on the sponsor'. The Refugee Qualification Directive[40] attaches a similarly broad interpretation to 'family', allowing host Member States to extend entitlement

> [T]o other close relatives who lived together as part of the family at the time of leaving the country of origin, and who were wholly or mainly dependent on the beneficiary of refugee or subsidiary protection status at that time.[41]

These provisions essentially entitle children who are no longer being cared for by their parents in their country of origin to join and be cared for by other 'close' relatives (for example, siblings, aunties and uncles or grandparents) in the host Member State. That said, the specification of 'close relatives' within the concept of family implies an exclusion of other dependents who are not biologically linked, such as children who are being cared for by family friends or 'distant' relatives (such as those linked to the child through marriage only) but who nonetheless occupy an important and, perhaps, the only stable caring figure in the child's life. Such an

---

[37] Of course, Art 8 ECHR could be invoked here, although there is little precedent to indicate how the courts might apply the provision to found a minor child and custodial parent's right to remain since most of the case law involves an application on the part of the non-custodial parent. For an analysis, see Thym, above n 11.

[38] For discussion of the extent to which human rights protection accommodates divergent cultural practices, see HJ Steiner and P Alston, *International Human Rights in Context*, 2nd edn (Oxford, Oxford University Press, 2000) 403.

[39] Dir 2001/55, Art 15.

[40] Dir 2004/83. Two different levels of international protection—refugee status and subsidiary protection—are covered: subsidiary protection is granted to those who need humanitarian protection but fall outside the scope of the Geneva Convention. See the definition in Art 2(e).

[41] Art 23(5). Note that these provisions are largely discretionary.

approach is at odds with the ECHR's attitude to immigration cases, which focuses more on the de facto nature of relationships rather than a more clinical and, in some cases, artificial preference for close blood ties.[42] It is also worth noting that the marginally broader conceptualisation of 'family' in the Temporary Protection Directive and the Refugee Qualification Directive is not shared by other EU immigration instruments which revert to the narrow nuclear model. The obvious explanation for the more restrictive approach is that it militates against any abuse by migrants seeking to gain access to the host state on the basis of bogus personal relationships. This does not explain, however, why other instruments governing the same group of immigrants are more permissive in this regard.

The definition and rights of the 'child' under EU migration law is equally erratic. The free movement provisions have always ascribed to a relatively generous definition of 'child' to include an EU migrant's and their partner's 'descendants under the age of 21 years old', as well as any 'dependent' biological children regardless of their age. Essentially then, free movement law detaches the notion of child from any age limitation, applying a more flexible biological and dependency test instead.[43] EU immigration and asylum law, on the other hand, endorses a rather narrower definition of 'child' that corresponds with the age of minority (generally up to the age of 18).[44] For example, the Directive on Long Term Residents—which, by definition, regulates the most economically active and self-sufficient of migrants—affords associated rights to any *minor* children of both the primary migrant (the 'sponsor') and his or her spouse; *minor* children of whom the primary migrant has custody (presumably following separation or divorce from the other biological parent), provided they are economically dependent and *minor* children of whom the primary migrant's spouse has custody, provided they are economically dependent.[45] The same definition is afforded to the children of those who have obtained refugee status in an EU Member State in that they too are classed as long-term residents.[46]

RESTRICTIONS ON CHILDREN'S RIGHTS UNDER IMMIGRATION LAW

There are some controversial exceptions to allowing minor children access to the host state under EU immigration law. The first exception arises when the child

---

[42] H Stalford, 'Concepts of Family under EU Law: Lessons from the ECHR' (2002) 1 *International Journal of Law, Policy and the Family* 410. See, however, Thym, above n 11 on the limitations of this approach in immigration cases.

[43] The precise meaning of 'dependency' will be discussed in the next section. For further discussion of the free movement concept of 'child', see ch 1.

[44] Note that the Directive allows Member States to exercise their discretion to authorise the entry and residence of adult dependent children and adult unmarried children of the sponsor *or* his or her spouse (Arts 2 and 3).

[45] Art 2(e) Dir 2003/9 note that the Long Term Residents Directive defers to the definition of 'child' provided in Arts 4(1)(a)–(c) of the Family Reunification Directive (2003/86).

[46] Art 4(1) Dir 2003/86.

is married. For instance, the Reception Directive limits entry to the *unmarried* and dependent minor children of the sponsor *and* his or her spouse, and to the *unmarried* and dependent minor children of the sponsor only.[47] Similarly, both the Temporary Protection Directive and the Refugee Qualification Directive apply to minor children on condition that they are *unmarried* and dependent.[48] And the Family Reunification Directive explicitly states that 'the minor children referred to in this Article must be below the age of majority set out by the law of the Member State concerned, and must not be married'.[49] The blanket exclusion on married children is particularly arbitrary and is informed, it seems, by a decidedly western image of marriage as a voluntary and equal undertaking between two economically self-sufficient adults. It also presumes that the child's marriage transfers any dependency from their parents to their spouse. The reality, of course, is that children often do not enter into mutually agreed, fulfilled and enduring marriages. Moreover, their dependency on their parents may well become more acute and complex upon marriage, for example in terms of financial assistance or help with childcare, particularly if they are living in an economically or politically unstable region. The routine exclusion of married children from family union entitlement is likely, therefore, to exacerbate their sense of economic, social and emotional isolation at a time when their need for familial support is most acute.[50]

Further exceptions to the general rule that minor children are allowed to access the host state under EU immigration law are based on age rather than marriage. These are prescribed specifically by Article 4 of the Family Reunification Directive. This states, first, that in cases where a child over the age of 12 applies to join his or her family in the host state, Member States have a discretion to 'verify whether he or she meets a condition for integration' before authorising their entry and residence. The provision offers no guidance on the nature and scope of this integration condition but, rather vaguely, posits that it will be determined by the legislation of the Member State 'existing…on the date of implementation of this Directive'.[51] Moreover, Member States may 'request that applications concerning family reunification of minor children be submitted before they reach the age of 15, as provided for by its existing legislation on the date of the implementation

---

[47] Art 2(d) Dir 2003/9. The definition does not include children of spouse/partner only (such as the sponsor's step-children). Furthermore, in all cases, the family must have already existed prior to the migration of the sponsor, implying exclusion of any relationships that were formed, or of children born, post-migration.

[48] Art 15(1)(a) Dir 2001/55/EC and Art 2(h) Dir 2004/83 respectively.

[49] Art 4(1).

[50] UNICEF reports that globally 36% of women aged 20–24 were married or in a union before they reached 18 years of age. It also notes that marriage of young girls is particularly common in sub-Saharan Africa and South Asia, countries from which many asylum seekers in the EU originate. In Niger, 77% of 20–24 year old women were married before the age of 18 and in Bangladesh, this rate was 65%. See further United Nations Children's Fund, *The State of the World's Children 2006* (New York, UNICEF, 2005) 131 and United Nations Children's Fund, *Early Marriage: A Harmful Traditional Practice—A Statistical Exploration* (New York, UNICEF, 2005) 12–13.

[51] Art 4(1).

of this Directive'.[52] The second part of the provision states that 'if the application is submitted after the age of 15, the Member States which decide to apply this derogation shall authorise the entry and residence of such children on grounds other than family reunification'. Whilst this appears to offer a concession to the otherwise harsh approach to the family reunification rights of teenagers, it provides no elaboration on what those 'other' grounds might be. Indeed, it is difficult to envisage how a 16 year old might qualify for entry into the host state other than on grounds of family reunification. If they wanted to qualify as an asylum seeker, a worker, a student or a volunteer, for instance, they would presumably be subject to the relevant immigration rules which can be even more restrictive than the provisions of the Family Reunification Directive.

Article 8 of the Family Reunification Directive presents a further challenge to children's rights. It enables Member States to require the sponsor 'to have stayed lawfully in their territory for a period not exceeding two years before having his/her family members join him/her'. This can be increased to a maximum waiting period of three years 'where the legislation of a Member State relating to family reunification in force on the date of adoption of this Directive takes into account its reception capacity'. Notwithstanding the damage that such protracted periods of separation from a parent might cause to children's well-being, it is difficult to see how such provisions can be reconciled with the UNCRC. Notably, Article 9(1) provides that:

> States Parties shall ensure that a child shall not be separated from his or her parents against their will, except when competent authorities subject to judicial review determine, in accordance with applicable law and procedures, that such separation is necessary for the best interests of the child.

And Article 10(1) states that:

> In accordance with the obligation of States Parties under Article 9, Paragraph 1, applications by a child or his or her parents to enter or leave a State Party for the purpose of family reunification shall be dealt with by States Parties in a positive, humane and expeditious manner.

Significantly, the Family Reunification Directive provisions were subject to a high-profile action for annulment, initiated by the European Parliament against the Council in 2005.[53] The Parliament argued that they breached fundamental rights, particularly the rights (and best interests) of the child as protected by the UNCRC, as well as the right to protection against discrimination on grounds of age and to respect for family life, enshrined in Articles 14 and 8 of the ECHR and Articles 21 and 7 of the Charter.[54] The reference to the UNCRC, as the ultimate,

---

[52] Art 4(6).

[53] Case C-540/03 *European Parliament v Council* [2006] ECR I-5769.

[54] In fact, this case constitutes the first instance in which the Court explicitly considered the impact of the Charter, in spite of its (then) unbinding nature. For further discussion of the implications of this decision vis-à-vis the status and application of the Charter, see E Drywood, 'Giving with One Hand,

global template for measuring state compliance with fundamental children's rights obligations, provided a particularly important feature of the Parliament's claim. This constitutes the first instance in which an EU institution acknowledged the status of the UNCRC as an influential source of human rights protection at this level.[55] Despite the novel references to both the Charter and the UNCRC, the Court of Justice rejected the Parliament's argument that the Directive provisions breached fundamental rights, essentially concluding that the rights articulated by these instruments could not be used to limit the application of Member States' margin of discretion in defining the legitimate parameters of their immigration policy. Responding in particular to the contention that the age thresholds applicable to children seeking family reunification—Articles 4(1) and 4(6)—constituted age discrimination, the Court of Justice reasoned that they reflected legitimate expectations as to the degree of integration that children of that age could attain in the host state before reaching the age of majority. In other words, the Court was implying that older children would be less inclined to integrate into the host state after the age of 12, rendering family reunification less pressing and beneficial to all concerned.[56] Such assertions are highly disingenuous, not to mention empirically ill-founded. Furthermore, they ignore the much more significant damage that might be caused to young people as a result of being separated from close family for extended periods at what is commonly regarded as a critical point in the life-course. In reality, teenage years are the very time when many young people are most in need of parental support and guidance: through the emotionally turbulent process of maturing, a decisive stage in their education, and a period where many young people are susceptible to negative external influences. As Drywood notes:

> Whilst the view that children reach a crucial point in their development around the age of twelve is widely supported, equally important is that it is not until a much later age that children have fully developed personalities and cognitive abilities. Crucially, it is believed that these developments are nurtured within the support and love of a family. Moreover, child development experts are unanimous in their belief that there is no place for a 'one-size fits all' approach to child development: every child matures and grows differently. In such a complex area, in which the Court has no expertise, it fails to present any supporting evidence or argument for its assumptions.[57]

A further equally tenuous argument put forward by the Court of Justice was that the Directive's selective approach to upholding children's rights was mitigated

---

Taking with the Other: Fundamental Rights, Children and the Family Reunification Decision' (2007) 32 *EL Rev* 396 and T Arnull, 'Family Reunification and Fundamental Rights' (2006) 31 *EL Rev* 611.

[55] Previously, the Advocate General made fleeting reference to the UNCRC in Case C-148/02 *Carlos Garcia Avello v État Belge* [2003] ECR I-11613 in support of a child's right to assume the surname that most represented his cultural heritage but the instrument did not feature at all in the Court of Justice's final reasoning.

[56] Para 48. This rationale is made explicit in the Preamble to the Directive (Recital 12).

[57] Drywood, *Giving with One Hand* above n 54, 405–6.

by the fact that the provisions in question could be applied by Member States on a discretionary basis, enabling Member States to apply more favourable, inclusive provisions. Thus, in what amounts to a legislative passing-of-the-buck, the Directive defers to Member State discretion in determining whether or not the age and residency thresholds will be applied to limit children's right to family reunification—a discretion that will inevitably be exercised in the light of national political and economic exigencies. This supports Cholewinski's claim that the real motivation behind the family reunification provisions, and particularly those targeting children, 'is essentially born of an economic necessity rather than humanitarian principle'[58] and significantly undermines the children's rights impact of the legislation.

THE IMPORTANCE OF 'DEPENDENCY' IN DETERMINING MIGRANT CHILDREN'S FAMILY RIGHTS

A second contention relating to the scope of children and family entitlement under EU migration law is that they are based on arbitrary and unrefined presumptions regarding children's dependency upon adults. Children's entitlement under Directive 2004/38 is largely conflated with that of the family, for instance. In other words, individuals can qualify as 'children' (and therefore, as family members) under the Directive if they are 'under the age of 21 or *dependant*'.[59] Thus the broad conceptualisation of 'child' under Community free movement law implies that essentially anyone of any age whose EU national parent migrates to another EU country can accompany them if they can demonstrate that they are dependent on them.[60] EU immigration law imposes a similar requirement of dependency, although this is generally coterminous with the conditions of minority and non-marriage referred to earlier.[61]

The EU's emphasis on dependency in determining children's rights under EU migration law raises several issues worthy of comment. First, the concept remains—deliberately, it would seem—broad, offering limited guidance on what constitutes 'dependency'. Earlier Court of Justice interpretations of the free movement provisions suggested that dependency denotes a primarily financial relationship with the parent worker which, the Court acknowledges, may well persist even after they reach the age of majority.[62] Interpretations have been refined in more recent years, however, to reflect a more functional model of dependency, focused more on providing for the child's care and welfare. Notably,

---

[58] Cholewinski, 'Family Reunification' above n 7, 290.
[59] Art 2(2)(c), emphasis added.
[60] See ch 1 for further discussion of the implications of this broad definition of 'child'.
[61] See, eg Art 2(d)(ii) Reception Directive; Art 15(1)(b) Temporary Protection Directive; Art 2(h) Refugee Qualification Directive and Art 4(1)(c) Family Reunification Directive.
[62] Cases 389 and 390/87 *Echternach and Moritz v Netherlands Minister for Education* [1989] ECR 723.

in the densely critiqued joined cases of *Baumbast and R*,[63] the Court of Justice upheld two third country national mothers' right to remain with their children in the host Member State even following the departure of the primary EU migrant workers from whom they had derived their initial rights of entry and residence. The Court of Justice rationalised this decision on the basis that the women were the primary carers of their children who were EU nationals in their own right and, therefore, entitled to remain in the host state, not least to pursue their education.[64] Such rights would be impracticable by the children, the Court concluded, unless their mother was also allowed to remain with them in the host state. This more nuanced interpretation of dependency was reinforced in the subsequent case of *Chen*.[65] This case concerned a Chinese migrant who moved initially to Cardiff while she was pregnant with her second child before moving to Northern Ireland with the specific aim of giving birth to the baby there. In doing so, she sought to benefit from unique nationality laws in place at the time which enabled anyone born on the island of Ireland (including Northern Ireland) to acquire Irish nationality. Crucially, by acquiring Irish nationality, baby Chen automatically acquired EU citizenship. Her parents then succeeded in their claim for long term residence in the UK arguing that it would allow them to care for baby Chen, thereby enabling her to exercise her nationality—and EU citizenship—rights.[66] The Court concluded as follows:

> A refusal to allow the parent, whether a national of a member state or a national of a non-member country, who is the carer of a child to whom [ex] Article 18 EC and Directive 90/364 grant a right of residence, to reside with that child in the host member state, would deprive the child's right of residence of any useful effect. It is clear that enjoyment by a young child of a right of residence necessarily implies that the child is entitled to be accompanied by the person who is his or her primary carer.[67]

These decisions not only reinforce the distinct status of children as EU migrant citizens in their own right, but also turn the notion of dependency under free movement law on its head. Essentially, the children in *Baumbast* and *Chen* derived their free movement rights from their migrant parents to enter the host state in the first instance and remained dependent on them for their day-to-day care and well-being. It was that very dependency, however, that subsequently became the

---

[63] *Baumbast* above n 28.
[64] The rights to education pertaining to the child of an EU migrant worker were then enshrined in Art 12 Reg 1612/68 [1968] OJ L257/2. Such rights are now captured in Art 10 of the revised version of this instrument, Reg 492/2011 on freedom of movement for workers within the Union [2011] OJ L141/1.
[65] Case C-200/02 *Zhu and Chen v Secretary of State for the Home Department* [2004] ECR I-9923.
[66] For a more detailed analysis of these cases, and the notion of dependency in the context of free movement and citizenship, see H Stalford, 'The Relevance of European Union Citizenship to Children' in J Williams and A Invernizzi (eds), *Children and Citizenship* (London, Sage, 2008) 159. See also Forder, 'Family Rights' above n 10 and A Tryfonidou, 'Family Reunification Rights of (Migrant) Union Citizens: Towards a More Liberal Approach' (2009) 15 *European Law Journal* 634.
[67] *Chen*, above n 65, para 45.

source of their non-qualifying parents' ongoing right of residence. In other words, the parents relied on their children's dependency to bolster their own legal right to remain,[68] such that the children became the legal 'anchors' preventing their parents from being cut adrift by national immigration law.

This broader approach to dependency is also emerging in relation to legislation regulating third country national migrants, bringing it in line with the abundance of 'anchor' case law and commentary on ECHR-based immigration claims.[69] At EU level, the Family Reunification Directive, in a rare concession to the age or marriage-based conditions pervading the legislation, grants Member States discretion to admit any *adult unmarried* children of the sponsor who are 'objectively unable to provide for their own needs on account of their state of health'.[70] Such provision acknowledges the diverse nature of dependency and the complexity of intra-familial relationships and needs, which extend far beyond economic necessity to accommodate the more subtle and complex dynamics of caring.

EXTRICATING CHILDREN'S FAMILY RIGHTS FROM THE ECONOMIC/SELF-SUFFICIENCY NEXUS?

It was thought, initially, that the *Baumbast* and *Chen* concessions would operate extremely narrowly, and always with a view to protecting the host state's social (welfare) system. Certainly, all of the case law up until 2010 suggested that children would only really benefit from any dispensation from the standard, more restrictive definition of 'family' and 'dependant' if the family was otherwise financially self-sufficient and unlikely to lay claim to the valuable economic and social resources of the host Member State.[71] In both *Baumbast* and *Chen,* for example, the families demonstrated that they had the financial means to guarantee economic self-sufficiency for the duration of their residence in the host Member State. In *Chen,* in particular, the parents had already invested considerably in the EU economy through their business activities. By contrast, the Court of Justice was rather less sympathetic to a claim for residence in the factually similar case of *W (China) and X (China) v Secretary of State for the Home Department.*[72] The facts in this case are distinguished from *Chen* insofar as the parents in question had seemingly entered the UK illegally. They then travelled to the Republic of Ireland where the mother, X, gave birth to their child, Q, who, as a result of

---

[68]   H Stalford, 'The Relevance' above n 66, 164.

[69]   For a review of some of the ECHR-based case law, see C Sawyer, 'Citizenship is Not Enough: The Rights of Children of Foreign Parents' (2005) 35 *Family Law* 224; D Stevens, 'Asylum-Seeking Families in Current Legal Discourse: A UK Perspective' (2010) 32 *Journal Of Social Welfare and Family Law* 5 and Forder, '*Family Rights*' above n 10.

[70]   Art 4(3) Directive 2003/86.

[71]   M Dougan and E Spaventa, '"Wish You Weren't Here" … New Models of Social Solidarity in the European Union' in E Spaventa and M Dougan (eds), *Social Welfare and EU Law* (Oxford, Hart, 2005).

[72]   *W (China) and X (China) v Secretary of State for the Home Department* [2006] EWCA Civ 1494, [2007] 1 WLR 1514.

Irish nationality law at the time, automatically qualified as an Irish national. The parents then returned to the UK and applied for asylum unsuccessfully. On appeal, they argued, on the basis of the *Chen* decision, that their right to remain was instrumental to enabling the child to exercise her rights as an EU citizen. Their claim failed. The court distinguished the two cases on the grounds that in *Chen* the child had access to both health insurance and sufficient resources, albeit provided by her mother, such that she would not be reliant in any way on the host state for her economic welfare. The baby's fate in *W and X* was determined less by the fact that she was an EU citizen and more by her (and her parents') economic capacity. In doing to, it seemed to establish the rule that, although a relationship of dependency can frustrate the normal application of national immigration law (particularly in cases involving children of EU nationality) this will not be permitted if there is any risk that the host state might have to assume any responsibility for the economic welfare of the family.[73] It also reinforced the view that EU national children's migration status, while couched in the cosy terms of care, integration and welfare, was ultimately to be determined by the same economic nexus that has always governed EU migration entitlement: the extent to which children have any rights in this area remained highly contingent on the legal and financial status and decisions of their parents.

A wave of more recent cases, however, has put paid to the notion that economic self-sufficiency is the ultimate determining factor underpinning family reunification entitlement, particularly where children's education and welfare is at stake. The case of *Ibrahim*,[74] for instance, concerned a Danish citizen, Mr Yusuf, who had been working in the UK for a year when his wife, a Somali national, and their three children (all Danish nationals) joined him there. The father subsequently ceased work and claimed incapacity benefit from June 2003 until May 2004. He then left the UK until 2006, leaving his wife and children in the UK surviving on state benefits. The couple had a fourth child in the UK before separating. Mrs Ibrahim applied for housing benefits from the local authority but was turned down on the basis that she no longer qualified under EU free movement law to reside in the UK. The authorities also concluded that she could not rely on the *Baumbast* decision reasoning—that, as her children were enrolled in full-time education, they had a right to remain—because the family were not financially self sufficient. The case was eventually referred to the Court of Justice which supported the mother's claim on the basis that it would enable the children to exercise the rights endowed on them by EU free movement law (specifically their right to

---

[73] Note also that Irish immigration law was subsequently amended such that non-national parents whose children are born there must now be able to claim a substantial connection with Ireland (usually by virtue of having been resident there for a number of years) to acquire long term residence status. See the Nationality and Citizenship Act 2004. See, further, A Tryfonidou, 'Kunqian Catherine Zhu and Man Lavette Chen v Secretary of State for the Home Department: Further Cracks in the "Great Wall" of the European Union?' (2005) 11 *European Public Law* 527. See, more generally, C Barnard, *The Substantive Law of the EU: The Four Freedoms* (Oxford, Oxford University Press, 2007).

[74] Case C-310/08 *Harrow LBC v Ibrahim* [2010] ECR I-1065.

education). Furthermore, the Court confirmed that these residence rights were not to be subjected to a self-sufficiency test, since imposing them might impact adversely on the family's capacity to integrate and, indeed, to remain in the host state.

This controversial extension to free movement law was confirmed by the Court of Justice in the concurrent decision of *Teixeira*,[75] involving a Portuguese couple. who moved to the UK in 1989. After giving birth to their daughter, Mrs Teixeira worked only intermittently and the couple separated soon after the child started school. Mrs Texeira's residence entitlement—and specifically the anchoring potential of her daughter as an EU citizen enrolled in full time education—was considered when she applied for housing assistance from the local authority. The Court of Justice reaffirmed the decision in *Ibrahim* that residence entitlement for family members under the free movement provisions crystallises around the child's educational rights and welfare rather than around any evidence of economic self sufficiency. O'Brien puts it this way: 'By affirming a financially unconditional residence right for children of (former) migrant workers and their primary carers, the Court has strengthened, and sharpened the definition of the hitherto blurry-edged *Baumbast* "Article 12" principle'.[76]

O'Brien reminds us, however, of the essential 'triggers' of this seemingly magnanimous extension of long term residence rights to primary carers: a period of work in the host state at least at some point in the past by at least one of the child's parents and the child's enrolment in education. Less likely to succeed, therefore, are those who claim similar benefits while the child is still a baby, the very period when the need for public assistance is potentially most acute.[77] Thus, by correlating parents' residence rights with compulsory schooling, it could be argued that the case law draws an implicit distinction between family reunion entitlement on the basis of the children's age, raising questions as to its compatibility with Article 2 UNCRC and Article 21 of the Charter.

The subsequent decision in *Zambrano*,[78] however, has questioned the need to establish that the child is in education to support primary carers' rights to reside with them under EU law. This has been achieved not on the basis of children's educational rights under free movement law—indeed, the applicants in *Zambrano* never actually exercised free movement between the territory of the Member States—but on the more abstract basis of EU citizenship, as enshrined in Article 20(1) TFEU.[79] The case concerned two Columbian nationals who had entered Belgium in 1999 with their first child on a visitor's visa. On arriving in Belgium, the father unsuccessfully applied for asylum and, in spite of being issued

---

[75] Case C-480/08 *Teixeira v Lambeth LBC and Secretary of State for the Home Department* [2010] 2 CMLR 50.

[76] C O'Brien, 'Case C-310/08 *Ibrahim*, Case C-480/08 *Teixeira*' (2011) 48 *CML Rev* 203.

[77] Ibid 215–16.

[78] Case C-34/09 *Ruiz Zambrano v Office National de l'Emploi* [2011] All ER (EC) 491.

[79] The specific status of EU citizenship as a conceptual framework within which to pursue children's rights more broadly under EU law is explored briefly in ch 2.

with an order to leave, he continued to reside (illegally) there with his family, making several unsuccessful attempts thereafter to regularise his residence status. Despite having no work permit, Mr Zambrano eventually secured employment in Belgium, while Mrs Zambrano gave birth to two more children in 2003 and 2005. Both of these children automatically acquired Belgian nationality at birth by virtue of Belgian law.

Mr Zambrano sought to rely on his children's status as Belgian nationals (and hence, EU citizens), as the basis for his right of residency in Belgium, despite the fact that (unlike in the previous cases) the family had never moved between the Member States to trigger their free movement entitlement. In a decidedly pragmatic and humane interpretation of EU citizenship, the Court recognised that refusing a residence permit to the parents inevitably implied that 'those children, citizens of the Union, would have to leave the territory of the Union in order to accompany their parents'. In the same vein, it further concluded that refusal of a work permit to Mr Zambrano would risk him not having 'sufficient resources to provide for himself and his family', which would also result in the children, citizens of the Union, having to leave the territory of the Union'.[80]

The Court's judgment in *Zambrano* therefore represents another celebrated boost to the currency of children's status as EU citizens, detaching their rights not only from the economic/self-sufficiency imperative that has long characterised EU citizenship but seemingly from the pre-condition of free movement too.[81] Furthermore, it reinforces the range of rights that cascade down to the parents as primary carers, all *in anticipation of* facilitating the child's '*genuine enjoyment of the substance of the rights*' pertaining to that status.[82] In that sense, as Hailbronner observes, the existence of children within these proceedings has a dramatic liberalising impact on the Court's reasoning, and, indeed, on the parameters of EU citizenship more broadly, even so far as to regularise an otherwise irregular residence to an extent that even a claim under Article 8 ECHR would probably not have achieved.[83]

But while the decision is a minor triumph for children's rights under EU law, it should be viewed in the context of the very specific circumstances of the case.[84] Subsequent case law has highlighted that to enable the child's rights to effectively trump the normal application of national immigration law, there must be evidence of more than a mere 'desirability' on the part of the non-qualifying parent

---

[80] Above n 78, para 44.

[81] On the implications of this more generally, see N Shuibhne, 'Free Movement of Persons and the Wholly Internal Rule: Time to Move On?' (2002) 39 *CML Rev* 731.

[82] Of course, the Court is forced to make an imaginative leap: it is enough that the child *may* exercise free movement in the future given the security and support to reside within the EU now.

[83] K Hailbronner and D Thym, 'Case C-34/09, *Gerardo Ruiz Zambrano v Office National de l'emploi (ONEm)*, Judgment of the Court of Justice (Grand Chamber) of 8 March 2011' (2011) 48 *CML Rev* 1253, 1261.

[84] Inasmuch as the father had previously been issued with a *non-refoulement* clause stipulating that he was not to be repatriated to Columbia, the children would have potentially been rendered stateless. It is unclear, in fact, where the family would have been able to move to had they been deported from Belgium.

to reside in the host state with the child; rather, it must be shown that national law (seeking to deport the family member) will frustrate the 'genuine enjoyment of the substance of citizenship rights' by the child.[85] In other words, the *Zambrano* reasoning is confined to those cases where the child would be prevented, for all practical purposes, from remaining in the Member State if it were not for the support of the parent who is subject to the deportation order.[86]

THE NATURE AND SCOPE OF 'SEPARATED' CHILDREN'S RIGHTS UNDER EU IMMIGRATION LAW

The central importance of the 'family' and dependency in determining children's status under EU immigration law immediately raises questions as to how one defines children's rights if there is no identifiable 'family' unit on which to pin their entitlement—that is, if children are living and/or moving independently of their family, and particularly of their parents. The most obvious example of this is 'unaccompanied minors' or, to use the broader international children's rights terminology, 'separated children',[87] although the point applies equally to children who are left behind in their country of origin following their parents' move for work or asylum-related purposes. In the latter case, the brief analysis of the Family Reunification Directive above shows how presumptions regarding children's dependency on their parents for their personal and economic welfare are conveniently discarded to limit older children's right to join their family members in the host state. Conversely, other provisions of the same instrument adopt a much more generous approach to family reunification in relation to children who have *moved* to another state independently of their parents (rather than just 'stayed' in their country of origin) and who have acquired refugee status. Thus Article 10(3)(a) of the Family Reunification Directive requires Member States to authorise the entry

---

[85] Case C-256/11 *Murat Dereci v Bundesministerium für Inneres* [2011] OJ C219/11. The Court of Justice confirmed in *Dereci* that it is for national courts to determine whether national immigration law, if applied, would interfere with the child's 'genuine enjoyment of the substance of citizenship rights'.

[86] See A Lansbergen and N Miller, 'European Citizenship Rights in Internal Situations: An Ambiguous Revolution? Decision of 8 March 2011, Case C-34/09 *Gerardo Ruis Zambrano v ONEM*' (2011) 7 *European Constitutional Law Review* 287.

[87] Separated children are defined as: 'children under 18 years of age who are outside their country of origin and separated from both parents or previous/legal customary primary care giver. Some children are totally alone, while others may be living with extended family members or other adults. As such, some may appear to be 'accompanied' but the accompanying adults are not necessarily able or suitable to assume responsibility for their care. This concept recognises that children suffer physically, socially and psychologically as a result of being without the care and protection of their parents or previous primary care giver(s). Separated children may be seeking asylum because of fear of persecution or lack of protection due to human rights violations, armed conflict or disturbances in their own country'. Taken from J Kanics and D Sutton, *Save the Children and The Separated Children in Europe Programme Position Paper on Returns and Separated Children* (Norway, Save the Children, 2004). See, also, Separated Children in Europe Programme, *Statement of Good Practice*, 4th edn (Brussels, Save the Children, 2010).

and residence of the unaccompanied minor's first-degree relatives in the direct ascending line (ie their parents). In the absence of any family member meeting this description, Article 10(3)(c) grants Member States discretion to authorise the entry and residence of the child's legal guardian or any other member of the family. The definition and rights attached to 'family' are, therefore, more generous in the context of unaccompanied minors than for most other categories of child migrant. This is no doubt attributable to what is perceived as unaccompanied minors' enhanced vulnerability and a desire to reunite them, as soon as possible, with their family, regardless of what model that might take. This is reflected in other EU immigration instruments. For example, the Refugee Qualification Directive emphasises the need to ensure, where possible, that an unaccompanied minor is placed with adult relatives in the host state, that he or she remains with any siblings, and that absent family members are located in a sensitive and safe manner as soon as is practicable.[88] The Reception Directive makes similar provision for unaccompanied minors who have not yet acquired refugee status.[89] Additionally, the Dublin II Regulation, which sets out the criteria for determining the Member State in which an asylum application lodged within the EU will be heard, provides that if an unaccompanied minor has a relative or relatives living in another Member State who can take care of him or her, Member States are obliged, where possible, to unite the minor with them, unless this is contrary to the child's best interests.[90] The Temporary Protection Directive seeks also to expedite the reunification of family members (including minors) who have been separated from one another following a sudden evacuation from their country of origin.[91] Even the more recent and controversial Returns Directive affords special consideration to the family-related needs of unaccompanied minors, specifying that:

> Before removing an unaccompanied minor from the territory of a Member State, the authorities of that Member State shall be satisfied that he or she will be returned to a member of his or her family, a nominated guardian or adequate reception facilities in the State of return.[92]

The family-related provisions for unaccompanied minors are also supplemented with a range of more substantive social rights, including a right to access education, a right to medical (including appropriate mental health) care and a right to legal assistance and representation in the context of immigration proceedings.

Such measures are to be welcomed for fulfilling the requirements of the UNCRC, notably Article 22, which provides that:

1. States Parties shall take appropriate measures to ensure that a child who is seeking refugee status or who is considered a refugee in accordance with

---

[88] Art 30 Dir 2004/83.
[89] Art 19 Dir 2003/9.
[90] Art 15(3) Reg 343/2003.
[91] Dir 2001/55 Art 15.
[92] Art 10(2).

applicable international or domestic law and procedures shall, whether unaccompanied or accompanied by his or her parents or by any other person, receive appropriate protection and humanitarian assistance in the enjoyment of applicable rights.

2. For this purpose, States Parties shall provide … in any efforts … to protect and assist such a child and to trace the parents or other members of the family of any refugee child in order to obtain information necessary for reunification with his or her family. In cases where no parents or other members of the family can be found, the child shall be accorded the same protection as any other child permanently or temporarily deprived of his or her family environment for any reason, as set forth in the present Convention.

However, as with much EU law relating to children, these provisions remain subject to certain caveats. In some cases, the additional protection and entitlement afforded to unaccompanied minors are explicitly limited to those who are below the age of 16. For example, as an exception to the general rule that all unaccompanied minors be placed with family members in the host state, the Reception Directive offers states the alternative liberty to place unaccompanied minors over the age 16 in detention centres for adult asylum seekers.[93]

A similar age threshold applies to unaccompanied minors' right to legal representation in the course of immigration procedures. Notably, the Refugee Status Directive allows Member States to 'refrain from appointing a legal representative … where the unaccompanied minor is 16 years or older, unless he/she is unable to pursue his/her application without a representative'.[94] Thus, while much of the provision included within EU immigration instruments might reflect the aspirations of Article 22 UNCRC, their rigid, conditional nature potentially brings them into conflict with a number of other UNCRC provisions, notably Article 2 (regarding non-discrimination), Article 3 (relating to best interests) and Article 12 (on the right to participation). This contradiction is magnified by the fact that the EU instruments themselves routinely refer to these principles[95] and yet fail to provide any concrete guidance as to how they might be implemented. This issue was identified by Save the Children in its response to the European Parliament's approval of the Returns Directive, the most recent addition to the EU immigration and asylum acquis. Criticism was levelled, in particular, at the

---

[93] Dir 2003/9. Note, however, that Art 19(2) of this instrument obliges the Member State to place unaccompanied minors with adult relatives, foster family, or accommodation centres suitable for minors whilst their asylum application is being assessed.

[94] Art 17(3) Dir 2005/85. Of course, the decision to provide legal representation for a young person who is 'unable to pursue his or her application' is entirely a matter for national discretion and, therefore, may not offer much in the way of a concession to this otherwise rigid rule.

[95] For references to the best interests of the child, eg see: Art 5(a) Returns Directive; Art 15(3) Dublin II Regulation (Reg 343/2003); Art 5(5) Family Reunification Directive; Art 15(4) Temporary Protection Directive and Art 18(1) Reception Directive. Measures that endorse the child's right to be heard include: Art 30(3) Refugee Qualification Directive; Art 16(1) Temporary Protection Directive and Art 17 Refugee Status Directive.

EU's failure to include within the Directive a proper procedure for assessing the best interests of the child, despite the fact that this very principle, along with the right to family life, was promoted as a 'primary consideration' when implementing the instrument.[96]

Such issues demonstrate the rhetorical nature of EU immigration measures relating to children and how easily provision aimed at safeguarding children's welfare can be trumped by broader concerns to constrain the mobility of less desirable, economically challenged migrants. Equally, however, they underline the role and responsibility of national authorities to add substance to such provisions in a manner that honours the principles of the UNCRC. This is particularly important given the fact that EU immigration measures essentially represent a floor of entitlement which Member States have a discretion to build upon with more favourable entitlement for individuals and families.

THE IMPORTANCE OF DETACHING CHILDREN'S MIGRATION STATUS FROM THAT OF THEIR FAMILY

A final issue that merits some consideration is the contention that migrant children's rights should be assessed in isolation from those of the family. Such a suggestion appears to contradict the accepted wisdom—endorsed by the discussion up to now in this chapter—that the family is the ultimate environment for nurturing children's well-being which must be sustained regardless of the mobility trajectories of individual family members. Nonetheless, automatically subsuming children's rights within more general 'family' provision can serve to obscure the distinct impact of migration, including migration law and policy, on children. In reality, migrant children's interests and needs are not always congruent with those of their parents or siblings, even in cases where migration decisions are seemingly guided by the best interests of children. In most cases, of course, parents make migration choices with regard to the interests of the family as a unit in the short and longer term, determined primarily by reference to the economic gains from accessing new employment, the cultural and social benefits of moving to or from a particular country or a region within that country, and the educational capital to be gained from accessing another country's education system.[97] Such deliberations are fairly typical for migrant families, and reinforce the law's perception of the migrant family as an indivisible unit with interdependent needs and interests. This perception is challenged, however, by the reality of many migrant children's

---

[96] Recital 22 Preamble Returns Directive.

[97] E Kofman, 'Family-Related Migration: A Critical Review of European Studies' (2004) 30 *Journal of Ethnic and Migration Studies* 243; P Raghuram, 'The Difference that Skills Make: Gender, Family Migration Strategies and Regulated Labour Markets' (2004) 30 *Journal of Ethnic and Migration Studies* 303; A Bailey and P Boyle, 'Untying and Retying Family Migration in the New Europe' (2004) 30 *Journal of Ethnic and Migration Studies* 229; AJ Bailey and TJ Cooke, 'Family Migration, Migration History and Employment' (1998) 21 *International Regional Science Review* 99.

lives which are becoming increasingly destabilised rather than enriched by migration. This trend is not exclusive to those caught in the asylum process or at the harder end of economic migration of third country nationals either: it is occurring on a routine basis among financially secure EU and third country national citizens working or studying in other EU Member States, usually at the instigation of well meaning parents. For example, research has revealed a growing propensity among such migrants to leave children behind in the host state, often in the care of their grandparents or other family members, to minimise any disruption to their education or to avoid any anticipated problems in securing appropriate, affordable childcare in the host state.[98] In many cases, this results in quite complex and unsettling migration arrangements; siblings may be separated from one another to enable one of them to accompany the migrant parent to the host country, often for educational purposes, or children may be shuttled back and forth between countries periodically in response to the family's care, work, financial or educational commitments. Such decisions, while they may be motivated by the parents' *best intentions* to improve the quality of life and opportunities of the family as a whole, do not always operate in the *best interests* of children. In the same vein, it does not necessarily follow that children's well-being is secure as a result of parents' enhanced professional and economic status following migration, particularly if children's contact with parents, siblings and friends is fractured as a result, or if the move has required them to adapt to a new linguistic, cultural, social and educational system at a particularly vulnerable stage in their personal development.

On a more extreme level, there are instances in which parents are instrumental in arranging the independent, even illicit, migration of the child for economic or political purposes (including trafficking and unaccompanied asylum seeking), either with a view to obtaining a better future for the child (even if it requires their separation from the family unit), or with a view to exploiting the 'anchoring' potential of the child to secure valuable family reunification rights in the host state (as in the case of *Chen* referred to above).[99]

These situations raise questions as to the role and capacity of immigration law to regulate such complex and private decisions. We know that migration law is premised on particular presumptions as to the sanctity of family life and autonomy, but should it be more prescriptive as to what type of family migration arrangements are conducive to children's best interests specifically, or should this be left exclusively to the discretion of parents? Furthermore, should the right

---

[98] HL Ackers and H Stalford 'Managing Multiple Life-Courses: The Influence of Children on Migration Processes in the European Union' in K Clarke, T Maltby and P Kennett (eds), *Social Policy Review 19* (Bristol, Policy Press, 2007); K Wall and J São José, 'Managing Work and Care: A Difficult Challenge for Immigrant Families' (2004) 38 *Social Policy and Administration* 591.

[99] For a discussion of the complex dynamics of family relationships, care and responsibility in the context of trafficking, see D Scullion, 'Gender Perspectives on Child Trafficking: A Case Study of Child Domestic Workers' in H Stalford, S Currie and S Velluti (eds), *Gender and Migration in 21st Century Europe* (Surrey, Ashgate, 2009) 45.

to family life—the very basis for the right to family reunification—essentially be relinquished by parents once their actions (in engineering the independent migration of their child) compromise the very exercise of that right? The current EU and ECtHR jurisprudence suggests that there are limits to the extent to which states can interfere with family life.[100] It is also accepted, however, that the wider political and economic exigencies of immigration control can, in certain circumstances, take precedence over the family status of migrants. Such exceptions operate in the light of public policy and security concerns which require restrictions on the entry and residence rights of certain individuals, or if there is evidence of bogus or 'opportunistic' family relationships having been formed to circumvent the normal application of immigration law. The application of these exceptions necessarily implies states' authorities making value judgements as to the motivations underpinning individual and family migration, and as to the substance and quality of the family life that ensues. Moreover, the potentially injurious effects of immigration law on family relationships is generally rationalised on the basis that family life can be sustained simply by returning en masse to the applicant's country of origin.[101]

Serious concerns arise, however, when these judgements are made in a way that neglects to consider the distinct needs of any children within that family unit. Currently, the law operates on the basis that children's rights will be automatically catered for if the right to family life is accommodated. In reality, children have quite distinct needs to those of adult migrants, particularly as far as their personal welfare, educational and social integration is concerned, although such issues have yet to be reflected comprehensively in migration law and policy. While it could be argued that this is attributable to the absence of any coherent ideological commitment to children's rights at EU level more generally (an argument that runs throughout this book), the final section of this chapter maintains that it is attributable also to a general failure to locate children specifically within the very research that informs the development of migration law and policy. It is to this issue that the discussion now turns.

SITUATING CHILDREN WITHIN MIGRATION RESEARCH

While the legal and policy framework indicates that children's migration trajectories are characterised by a rich and diverse tapestry of experience and status, there is a surprising dearth of research exploring their distinct experiences of migration. Similarly, there is very little research revealing the impact of migration on children's

---

[100] As illustrated by *Metock*, above n 22.
[101] But see the broader interpretation of 'family life' espoused by the ECHR in the case of *Slivenko v Latvia*, above n 13, and the discussion of this by Thym, 'Respect for Private and Family Life' above n 11.

family relationships.[102] This is in spite of an evident growth in child-focused—particularly empirically-grounded—research relating to children's status within and experiences of family. This body of work has acknowledged both individual childhood experiences of family life, as well as children's role as co-constructors of 'familyhood', on a par with parents and other kin. This body of participatory research has succeeded also in highlighting children's resilience to family change and, in some cases, trauma, and to their ability, given the opportunity, to independently and collectively negotiate family relationships across time and space. Yet in spite of the undisputed social, legal and political influence of such work, it is largely isolated to certain areas of family studies, concentrating to a large degree on family fragmentation and re-structuring as a result of divorce and parental separation.[103]

The diminutive body of research into child migration is characterised by a preoccupation with the most economically, socially and politically marginalised, notably child refugees and asylum seekers and child victims of human trafficking. While not undermining the critical contribution of this work towards raising awareness and prompting political action, or doubting the distinctly impoverished status of such children, it has, on the one hand, perpetuated particular (and in some cases, damaging) 'typologies' of child migrants and, on the other, overshadowed, discouraged and even trivialised equally significant research into the status and experiences of more 'typical' child migrants. In reality, child migrants represent a highly heterogeneous community: migration occurs in response to a range of diverse socio-economic, political and personal factors, all of which interact and impact acutely on an individual's needs, experiences and relationships with kin. This diversity of experience characterises child migration both within and into Europe—for EU and third county national children alike—and challenges the entrenched stereotypes that view child migration through monocular nationality or economic lenses. For instance, the common tendency to view *EU* national child migrants as relatively privileged in comparison to child migrants of third country nationality, is now increasingly challenged by the liberalisation of migration processes and the expanding social and economic gulf between migrants from different Member States, particularly following the most recent phases of enlargement.[104] Economic and social marginalisation can affect EU migrant children in much the same way as it does asylum seeking or refugee children. Equally diverse are the experiences and status of third country national migrant children into the EU. Some migrate with their parents for the purposes of employment, often supported by generous relocation packages (including exclusive housing, and private schooling and healthcare) from global conglomerates. At the other end of the spectrum are those who are forced to seek asylum in the

---

[102] Recent research published by Save the Children represents one of the few attempts to explore the broader migration experiences of children and young people. See J O'Connell Davidson and C Farrow, *Child Migration and the Construction of Vulnerability* (Stockholm, Save the Children Sweden, 2007).

[103] Some of this work is discussed below.

[104] Ackers and Stalford, 'Managing Multiple Life Courses' above n 98.

EU, often placed in sub-standard and isolated accommodation, facing short-term exclusion from education and other social and welfare services, and enduring long periods of separation from family members.

The lack of research exploring child migration is attributable to a number of methodological and ideological factors. First, migration, by its very nature, involves a complex web of contextual variables of a cultural, linguistic, economic and political nature. Any attempt to engage with migrant children on an empirical level demands an acute appreciation and accommodation of their linguistic and cultural background within the design and implementation of the methodology. To be successful, therefore, such research often demands additional time and financial resources, more sophisticated data analysis techniques, and closer attention to the cross-national comparability of data to account for linguistic and methodological differences.[105] Obtaining access to migrant children who face widespread social, legal and economic marginalisation presents a further challenge to participatory research in this context and generally requires close and effective collaboration with key gatekeepers in the NGO and social welfare sectors, often with significant time and funding implications.

Aside from these logistical challenges, the scarcity of participatory research involving migrant children is arguably attributable also to longstanding presumptions around migration decision-making. The traditional tendency to associate both voluntary and forced migration with purely economic (employment; standard of living) or political imperatives (civil unrest; social and economic deprivation), has largely dictated the direction of research in this area towards a focus on the adult, and particularly the adult breadwinner. While research has, since the 1980s at least, acknowledged the extent to which concerns around family welfare determine migration choices,[106] there remains a distinct deficiency of work exploring the specific impact of family migration on children, or indeed, the extent to which children's interests influence migration trajectories.[107] The surge in gender-related migration studies over the past 30 years has addressed this to some extent,[108] but even this work has tended to consider children as merely

---

[105] For more detailed discussion on the methodological challenges of conducting empirical research with children at cross-national level, see HL Ackers and H Stalford, *A Community for Children? Children, Citizenship and Migration in the European Union* (Aldershot, Ashgate, 2004) 13–41.

[106] J Mincer, 'Family Migration Decisions' (1978) 86 *Journal of Political Economy* 749; DT Litcher, 'Household Migration and the Labour Market Position of Married Women' (1980) 9 *Social Science Research* 83; M Boyd, 'Family and Personal Networks in International Migration: Recent Developments and New Agendas' (1989) 23 *International Migration Review* 638; Bailey and Cooke, 'Family Migration'; P Boyle, TJ Cooke, K Halfacree and D Smith, 'A Cross-National Comparison of the Impact of Family Migration on Women's Employment Status' (2001) 38 *Demography* 201; Bailey and Boyle, 'Untying and Retying'; Kofman, 'Family-Related Migration'; E Herman 'Migration as Family Business: The Role of Personal Networks in the Mobility Phase of Migration' (2006) 44 *International Migration* 191.

[107] Ackers and Stalford, 'Managing Multiple Life-Courses' above n 98, 318.

[108] For example, E Kofman, A Phizacklea, P Raghuram and R Sales, *Gender and International Migration in Europe: Employment, Welfare, and Politics* (London, Routledge, 2000); D Bryceson and U Vuorela (eds), *The Transnational Family: New European Frontiers and Global Networks* (New York,

passive appendages or intractable obstacles to women's migration,[109] or to conflate the interests and experiences of children with those of their mothers.

These constraints on child migration research carry with them some important consequences. First, they fuel a tendency to categorise migrant children into artificial, binary groups—internal/international, voluntary/forced, temporary/permanent, accompanied/unaccompanied, legal/illegal, regular/irregular[110]—which, in turn, serves to polarise children's experiences of migration. This tendency fails to acknowledge the dynamic nature of migration, and the fact that legal status, perceptions and experiences of migration can shift significantly during childhood migration. Indeed, it is the ease with which children can acquire a new migration status that is often exploited by more sinister forces within migrant networks. By way of illustration, Anderson and O'Connell Davidson[111] cite cases in which human traffickers advise children to apply for asylum in the host state, only to abduct them later from those caring for them for the purposes of sexual or labour exploitation. The authors comment further on the extent to which such over-simplistic perceptions of migration shape and limit legal and political responses, particularly in the context of child trafficking:

> Though the [law] frames 'trafficking' as a problem of organised criminal involvement in a form of illegal migration, the actions and outcomes covered by its definition (violence, confinement, coercion, deception and exploitation) can and do occur within both legally regulated and irregular systems of migration and employment (also within legal and illegal systems of migration into private households). For instance, researchers report a 'rise in the incidents of unpaid wages, confiscated passports, confinement, lack of job training and even violence' against migrant workers who are legally present in a number of countries under various work permit schemes, [while] the 'anti-trafficking' measures that have recently been adopted by many governments, such as tighter border controls, would clearly offer legal migrants no protection whatsoever against such abuse and exploitation.[112]

A further illustration of the gulf between common typologies of child migration and reality is seen in relation to forced migrants from more recent EU accession states such as Romania and Bulgaria. While there is data to suggest that a significant proportion of child asylum seekers and trafficked children originated from

---

Berg, 2002); S Currie, *Migration, Work and Citizenship in the Enlarged European Union* (Aldershot, Ashgate, 2008) and H Stalford, S Currie and S Velluti (eds), *Gender and Migration in 21st Century Europe* (Aldershot, Ashgate, 2009).

[109] Ackers and Stalford, above n 98.

[110] R King, 'Towards a New Map of European Migration' (2002) 8 *International Journal of Population Geography* 89; B Anderson and J O'Connell Davidson, 'Border Troubles and Invisibility: Child Rights and Migration in Europe' paper presented to Save the Children Sweden Seminar on Rightless Migration, 1 June 2005, 2.

[111] Anderson and O'Connell Davidson, above n 110, 4.

[112] Anderson and O'Connell Davidson, 'Border Troubles' above n 110, 2.

these states, particularly Romania,[113] their status post-accession shifted to one of EU migrant. It did not automatically follow, however, that they enjoyed a more privileged or protected status in the host state. Indeed, in many cases, it implied that the protective benefits provided to asylum seekers, unaccompanied minors and trafficked children were actually withdrawn from them and replaced with the economic self-sufficiency test underpinning the free movement provisions to test their eligibility for residence and other associated rights within the host state. Acknowledging these concerns, Huijsmans has called for a more exhaustive and meaningful study of child migration that goes beyond such polarised extremes of experience and addresses regular migration opportunities and encounters which are less easily classified as either 'good' or 'bad', 'advantageous' or 'exploitative'.[114]

A second consequence of the conceptual myopia that characterises migration studies is that it limits the methodologies applied to child migration research, perpetuating an approach that defers to adult proxy or retrospective accounts of migrant children's experiences. Children's direct accounts of migration are rarely heard: their needs and encounters inevitably remain absorbed within and conflated with those of their parents or family. As such, legal and policy measures remain impervious to their distinct requirements.[115]

CONCLUSION

Migration is a multi-dimensional and complex phenomenon, and the law's response at domestic and EU level is informed by a range of different priorities in the face of an expanding and increasingly heterogeneous population. These include meeting the educational and professional needs of a progressively more mobile workforce, plugging vital skills gaps, encouraging international knowledge and skills exchange, protecting domestic welfare and social regimes and responding to humanitarian and political crises. In responding to the complex dynamics of migration, the need to protect and sustain family life remains a constant preoccupation. In the process, however, the specific rights and interests of children as autonomous and distinct individuals within the family have been largely

---

[113] UNHCR, *Trends in Unaccompanied and Separated Children Seeking Asylum in Europe 2000* (Geneva, UNHCR, 2001) particularly 7–8.

[114] R Hujisman, 'Free Movement of Workers and an Expanding EU: Time to Think about Child Migration' in S Swärd and L Bruun (eds), *Conference Report—Focus on Children in Migration: From a European Research and Method Perspective* (Stockholm, Save the Children Sweden, 2007).

[115] On a more positive note, Art 1(c) Reg 862/2007 on the compilation of statistics on foreign workers [2007] OJ L199/23 specifies that common rules are to be established for the collection and compilation of Community statistics on 'administrative and judicial procedures and processes in the Member States relating to immigration, granting of permission to reside asylum and other forms of international protection and the prevention of illegal immigration'. Such data should shed light on the relative status of children within asylum processes, particularly as the instrument requires Member States to disaggregate migration statistics in accordance with age (Art 3(1)). Chapter 7 touches upon some other developments in relation to data collection and analysis in the context of child protection.

obscured, a situation that is perpetuated by EU migration instruments. Despite the numerous references to children within the various provisions described above, they remain largely insensitive and unresponsive to the specific needs and interests of children. Even the more explicit children's rights measures are characteristically vague, offering considerable scope for national derogation.

Of course, the provisions securing children's right to family union are an important step in safeguarding the welfare of migrant children. Even these measures, however, are awash with contradictions or based on unverified presumptions regarding children's family relationships, best interests, dependency and capacity. Even at the most fundamental level, the narrow and fluctuating definitions of child and family under EU migration law illustrate the extent of the EU's disengagement with migrant children's family life, and particularly their lack of insight into the reality of children's domestic arrangements. Significantly, the discussion has sought to tease out some of the artificial and, in some respects, arbitrary distinctions that are drawn between different categories of EU migrant children and family constellations. Limitations on children's migration rights based on age and marriage are a particularly disturbing illustration of this disengagement and demonstrate how easily notions of 'dependency' and direct contact with close kin can be destabilised by wider political concerns to stem undesirable forms of migration and secure external borders. That said, very recent case law shows signs of the Court of Justice shifting towards a rather more child-focused, rights based approach to assessing children's status in a migration context. Consequently, it is childhood and parenthood rather than marriage or 'family' more broadly that is becoming the defining feature of many EU migration decisions.

This recent trend in the case law reinforces the point that migration law is one of the few areas in which the EU has explicit competence to enact binding measures for the betterment of all citizens, including children, and the efforts made to accommodate children's rights in this process should be acknowledged. This body of law is pledging more confident allegiance to children's fundamental rights as expressed in the UNCRC, the Charter and the ECHR, an allegiance that appears to be permeating the case law with increasing prominence. The landmark ruling in *Parliament v Council*, however, highlights the fragility and vagueness of this commitment, and how very easily children's rights can be undermined. This reinforces not only the need for a review of the impact of EU migration law on children, but perhaps more importantly, enhanced efforts at the national level to ensure that domestic immigration measures compensate for what are still significant shortfalls in EU children's rights provision.

4

Children's Rights under EU Family Law: Custody, Access and Parental Child Abduction

INTRODUCTION

HAVING EXPLORED CHILDREN'S family rights in the context of EU immigration, asylum and free movement law in the previous chapter, this chapter considers how children's rights are addressed in another area in which the EU has developed family-related entitlement: that regulating the cross-national recognition and enforcement of decisions relating to divorce, child custody, access and abduction.[1] Measures in this area, like those in the field of immigration and asylum, have evolved primarily over the course of the last decade, and have generated a substantial body of case law as well as ongoing debate—particularly among academics and legal practitioners—as to their value, legality and technical interpretation. This chapter will explore these developments with a view to evaluating the extent to which the EU, in regulating cross-national family law, actively engages and promotes children's rights as part of the family unit. The first section sets the context for the discussion with a summary of the scope of, and reasons for, EU regulation in the field of family law and a brief statistical overview of the incidence of divorce across the Member States. To pinpoint the significance of children's rights within the family law context, section two considers the wider body of socio-legal research examining approaches to children's rights in the negotiation of custody and access arrangements, and the extent to which family dispersal and reconstitution as a result of parental separation and divorce undermine or challenge children's status as independent contributors to the family decision-making process. The chapter then examines the content and scope of the child-relevant provisions within this legislation and assesses, by reference to the case law, their impact on children's experiences of such processes. A specific point of discussion will be the extent to which EU measures articulate the normative principles of child participation (as enshrined in Art 12 UNCRC)

---

[1] The EU terminology 'custody and access' will be adopted in this chapter instead of the terms 'contact and residence' which are particularly familiar to British family lawyers. The term 'abduction' will be used interchangeably with the alternative term 'wrongful removal or retention'.

and best interests (as enshrined in Article 3 UNCRC—particularly in terms of improving child consultation practices—and expediting the return of a child following wrongful removal or retention.

THE SCOPE OF AND REASONS FOR EU FAMILY LAW

The EU has, for over a decade, been legislating on cross-national family justice issues to accommodate the increasing incidence of international relationship breakdown and to determine procedures for ensuring that divorces and parental responsibility decisions and/or agreements reached in one Member State can be enforced easily in any other Member State to which any of the parties move. In that sense, the EU's recent attention to family law is inextricably linked to its concern to sustain fluid free movement. Because mobility is central to the achievement of the EU's internal market objectives, its aim is to avoid a situation whereby individuals are prevented from moving between the Member States for fear that parental responsibility decisions will not be recognised or enforced in their new country of residence. Equally, its aim is to ensure that the EU's fluid policy on free movement is not exploited by individuals as a means of frustrating the legitimate enforcement of family decisions across jurisdictions. For example, this might occur where a mother who has been granted shared custody of a child moves to her home Member State, the UK for example, in order to limit the father's access to the child due to the geographical, financial and administrative obstacles created by the move, or by virtue of the fact that in England and Wales, mothers are routinely granted more favourable custody rights in comparison to fathers.

A brief survey of the incidence of divorce across the EU highlights the need for regulation in this area. The most recently available statistics reveal that approximately 2.2 million marriages and 875,000 divorces are concluded every year across the EU and that, in general, divorce is on the increase across nearly all EU Member States (England and Wales providing a notable exception). EUROSTAT data also estimates that on average four out of 10 marriages in the EU results in divorce, with more than six divorces for each 10 marriages in Belgium, the Czech Republic and Estonia.[2] Cross-national comparative data on relationship breakdown is deficient in a number of respects, restricting our ability to draw firm conclusions from it.[3] First, it does not account for the breakdown rate of civil or registered

---

[2] Europe In Figures, *Eurostat Yearbook 2006-07*, EUROSTAT Statistical Books (Luxembourg, European Communities, 2007) 68, 70 and 71.

[3] Although there is some European comparative sociological research exploring the impact of social context on divorce. See M Wagner and B Weiß, 'On the Variation of Divorce Risks in Europe: Findings from a Meta-Analysis of European Longitudinal Studies' (2006) 22 *European Sociological Review* 483; J Dronkers, M Kalmijn and M Wagner, 'Causes and Consequences of Divorce: Cross-national and Cohort Differences' (2006) 22 *European Sociological Review* 479 and HJ Andreß, B Borgloh, M Brockel, M Giesselmann and D Hummelsheim, 'The Economic Consequences of Partnership Dissolution: A Comparative Analysis of Panel Studies from Belgium, Germany, Great Britain, Italy, and Sweden' (2006) 22 *European Sociological Review* 533.

partnerships or, indeed, of cohabiting relationships which, in some Member States at least, are much more prevalent than marital relationships.[4] A second limitation, and more relevant to this analysis, is the fact that EU data revealing the incidence of divorce generally across the Member States is not coherently disaggregated to reveal the presence of children in divorcing or separating families. Nor does it tell us much about divorce rates among 'international couples'—that is, couples of different nationalities or who originate from different Member States to one another. Comparability is further hampered by the fact that domestic statistical collation remains inconsistent and patchy, with many gaps in data from the more recent EU accession states in particular. There has, however, been some attempt to assess the incidence of international divorce in the EU. For instance, according to the most recent data there are approximately 2.4 million new marriages in the EU every year, approximately 13 per cent of which (310,000) are international. Annually, the number of divorces across the EU continues to rise. In 2007 (the most recent year for which data is available), there were 1047, 427 divorces of which 137,000 (again, 13 per cent) had an international element. In addition, 28,000 of the estimated 3.5 million married couples living in other EU Member States divorce every year, an experience that typically prompts a further migration (of a return to their country of origin) for at least one of the parties.[5]

Further evidence of the incidence of international breakdown can be gleaned from the research on family migration given the association between 'international' relationship formation, breakdown and mobility (in the sense that migration has occurred for at least one of the parties either prior to or after the relationship was formed). Research conducted by Boyle and colleagues, for instance, identifies a clear correlation between international migration and relationship dissolution:

> The stresses associated with longer distance moves may be greater than more local moves and an extensive literature documents the potential implications of international

---

[4] There is a considerable body of national research to support the proposition that separation rates among cohabiting couples are significantly greater. See, eg A Barlow, S Duncan, G James and A Parks, *Cohabitation, Marriage and the Law: Social Change and Legal Reform in the 21st Century* (Oxford, Hart, 2005); A Mastekaasa, 'Marital Status, Distress and Well-being: An International Comparison' (1994) 25 *Journal of Comparative Family Studies* 183; K Kiernan, 'Cohabitation in Western Europe: Trends, Issues and Implications' in A Booth and A Crouter (eds), *Just Living Together: Implications of Cohabitation on Families, Children and Social Policy* (New Jersey, Lawrence Erlbaum Associates, 2002); A De Maris and W MacDonald 'Premarital Cohabitation and Marital Instability: A Test of the Unconventionality Hypothesis' (1993) 55 *Journal of Marriage and Family* 399.

[5] European Commission, *Impact Assessment Accompanying Document to the Communication from the Commission to the European Parliament, the Council, the European Economic and Social Committee and the Committee of the Regions Bringing Legal Clarity to Property Rights for International Couples*, Commission Staff Working Paper (Brussels, European Commission, 2011) 12 and 59. See also K Granath, *Study to Inform a Subsequent Impact Assessment on the Commission Proposal on Jurisdiction and Applicable Law in Divorce Matters—Draft Final Report to the European Commission DG Justice, Freedom and Security* (Brussels, European Policy Evaluation Consortium, 2006) 6. This report also provides a detailed analysis of the most common nationality combinations of international marriages across different Member States. Note, however, that the report is based on statistics collated during the 2000–03 period and accounts for only 14 of the 27 Member States.

migration on mental health. Even longer distance moves … will likely disrupt local family and friend networks … and there is evidence that children's behaviour may be affected negatively by such disruption, with migrant children apparently suffering higher school dropout rates, poorer educational attainment, more delinquent behaviour, and higher rates of substance abuse. Such outcomes will inevitably impact upon the parents and may contribute to problems in any relationship, and frequent long- or short-distance moving is only likely to exacerbate such potentially negative effects.[6]

Earlier socio-legal research examining the impact of intra-EU migration on children's rights and experiences by the author also explored issues relating to international family breakdown. This research involved 180 interviews with EU migrant children and their parents in Portugal, Sweden, Greece and the UK, and revealed 38 cases of parental separation and divorce—21 per cent of the sample. Custody and access issues were decided informally in the majority of those cases, although there were some instances of ongoing court proceedings resulting in the complete dispersal of the family unit, including separation of siblings, and a growing cultural and linguistic void between children and their non-resident parent.[7]

Apart from these studies, there is very little qualitative or quantitative evidence of the impact of international relationship breakdown on children. In fact, the case law generated so far by EU family legislation provides perhaps the most illuminating insight into the extent to which EU law has and can be used to give effect to children's rights. Before moving on to a detailed analysis of this case law, the next section considers in more sociological terms why it is so critical to uphold children's rights in a family law context, particularly in proceedings surrounding parental separation, custody and access.

THE POSITION OF CHILDREN IN THE DIVORCING FAMILY: SOCIOLOGICAL PERSPECTIVES

The family is a fundamental dimension of children's lives and the cultural, economic and structural context of family life has profound effects on children's sense of identity, well-being and opportunities. There is no doubt that our understanding of family, as an 'institution', has shifted significantly over the past 40 years as a result of variable socio-legal and economic factors, including the liberalisation of divorce processes, an increase in non-marriage-based child-bearing, a growth in intercultural unions, and changes in parental employment and caring patterns.

---

[6] PJ Boyle, TJ Cooke, V Gayle and CH Mulder, 'The Effect of Family Migration on Union Dissolution in Britain' in H Stalford, S Currie, and S Velluti (eds), *Gender and Migration in 21st Century Europe* (Aldershot, Ashgate, 2009) 11.

[7] See further HL Ackers and H Stalford, *A Community for Children? Children, Citizenship and Migration in the European Union* (Aldershot, Ashgate, 2004) 182–85.

Consequently, it is arguably *parenting* rather than marriage that is now commonly regarded as the normative procurement of family life.[8]

Despite universal acknowledgement of the central importance of family to children and of the effects of family-related changes on them, it is only in the past 20 years or so that research has specifically explored children's individual perceptions and experiences of family life, at least in a European context. Certainly the progressive creep towards the privatisation of family life constrained previous attempts to conduct empirical, and particularly observational or ethnographic, research in this sphere.[9] Consequently, child and family laws and policies at all levels have traditionally been constructed on the basis of adult presumptions regarding children's interests, and on the basis of highly generalised and, to some extent, clinically-amassed statistical data.

More recent advancements in the sociology of childhood literature have achieved significant success in addressing this deficit, such that there is now an expectation that child-focused research, if it is to be regarded as legitimate, will involve some form of direct engagement with children and young people. Notably there has been a marked proliferation, particularly since the mid-1990s, of qualitative research exploring the impact of parental separation, divorce and family restructuring on children. This work has challenged embedded notions as to the primarily negative economic, social and psychological impact of such events on children, and exposed an impressive array of coping and negotiation strategies employed by children, as well as the supportive role they assume vis-à-vis their parents and siblings.[10]

A further achievement of this work is the fact that it has shifted attention away from an exclusive preoccupation with the *individual* experiences and needs of children and young people and acknowledged children's role as active co-constructors of family life.[11] Corsaro, for instance, has applauded the 'utility of conceptualising families as local cultures in which children actively participate, contribute to their own social development, and affect the participation of all other family members'.[12]

Some key normative tools have been developed to assist practitioners in accommodating and regulating these complex dynamics of children's family life. First and foremost, the specific protection of children and the promotion of their

---

[8] I Dey and F Wasoff, 'Mixed Messages: Parental Responsibilities, Public Opinion and the Reforms of Family' (2006) 20 *International Journal of Law, Policy and the Family* 225 and C Smart, B Neale and A Wade, *The Changing Experience of Childhood: Families and Divorce* (Cambridge, Polity Press, 2001).

[9] W Corsaro, *The Sociology of Childhood*, 2nd edn (London, Sage, 2005) 86.

[10] I Butler, L Scanlan, M Robinson, GF Douglas and MA Murch, *Divorcing Children: Children's Experience of Their Parents' Divorce* (London, Jessica Kingsley, 2003) 103; GF Douglas and MA Murch, 'Taking Account of Children's Needs in Divorce: A Study of Family Solicitors' Responses to New Policy and Practice Initiatives' (2002) 14 *Child and Family Law Quarterly* 57; B Neale, 'Dialogues with Children: Children, Divorce and Citizenship' (2002) 9 *Childhood* 455.

[11] Corsaro, *The Sociology of Childhood*, above n 9, 87.

[12] Corsaro, *The Sociology of Childhood*, above n 9, 105.

best interests has become a cornerstone of legislation and practice in family law systems across Europe.[13] Equally important, however, are measures aimed at reaffirming children's active *agency* within and contribution to *interdependent* relationships within the family environment. If applied in a balanced and sensitive way, such tools should serve to militate against any tendency to manufacture an artificial notion of, on the one hand, children's exclusive dependence and vulnerability, or, on the other, their complete autonomy.

The image of the family as a collective endeavour in which children are very much protagonists is perhaps difficult to reconcile with a family that has undergone some fragmentation or dispersal as a result of divorce or parental separation, particularly given the common propensity, at least in the course of legal proceedings, to focus on individual and often competing needs and outcomes. However, some of the studies referred to above have demonstrated how such events can nurture a more acute sense of negotiation and mutual support between family members in a way that might never have otherwise occurred.[14] While this research is careful to avoid over-generalising the experiences of children affected by divorce or family reconfiguration as either wholly positive or negative, it does confront assumptions about the submissive, 'docile' and helpless image commonly associated with children in this situation.

The findings of this work have dovetailed with, but also responded to, broader developments in the international children's rights movement, most notably following the introduction of the UNCRC. This instrument endorses the status of the family as 'the fundamental group of society and the natural environment for the growth and well-being of all its members and particularly children' and recognises 'that the child, for the full and harmonious development of his or her personality, should grow up in a family environment, in an atmosphere of happiness, love and understanding'.[15] Such aspirations are not confined to 'intact' nuclear families in the legal sense either. Articles 5, 7, 8, 9, 16 and 20 all uphold children's rights to care, contact and development in various family contexts. Equally, judicial interpretations of certain ECHR provisions have further advanced our understanding of how children's rights to both protection and autonomy can be negotiated within the family.[16]

---

[13]   Dey and Wasoff, 'Mixed Messages' above n 8, 226.

[14]   Smart, Neale and Wade, *The Changing Experience,* above n 8, illustrated particularly well in ch 4 of their book.

[15]   Preamble.

[16]   See, further, Case Comment, 'Children's Rights, Parental Autonomy and Article 5' (1989) 14 *EL Rev* 254 and A Opromolla, 'Children's Rights under Articles 3 and 8 of the European Convention: Recent Case Law' (2001) 26 *EL Rev, Human Rights Supplement* 46 and S Harris-Short, 'Family Law and the Human Rights Act 1998: Judicial Restraint or Revolution' (2005) 17 *Child and Family Law Quarterly* 329. See, more broadly, U Kilkelly, *The Child and the European Convention on Human Rights* (Aldershot, Ashgate, 1998) and, more recently, the Council of Europe programme, *Building A Europe For And With Children,* including a database of child-specific case law, accessible at: coe.int/children.

These developments in research and in the international legal spheres have precipitated important changes in domestic legal systems. Indeed, there has long since been an expectation that all legislative measures and procedures in the field of family justice, particularly those relating to the negotiation of parental responsibility arrangements, will incorporate detailed and focused consideration, not only of the interests and needs of any children involved, but of their expressed views. It is in this context, therefore, that we consider the nature and scope of European family law. To what extent do developments at EU level in regulating cross-national divorce and parental responsibility attend to children's rights and interests in a manner that reflects international children's rights norms, accounts for the substantial mass of empirical research in this area, and consolidates children's position under domestic family law? In exploring this question, the following sections summarise first how EU family law has evolved before critically examining the nature, scope and impact of its child-focused provision.

THE EVOLUTION OF EU FAMILY LAW REGULATING
DIVORCE AND PARENTAL RESPONSIBILITY

It is only since the late 1990s that the EU has showed any particular interest in family justice per se. Prior to that, EU measures relating to the family were largely limited to rights of entry and residence in other Member States under the free movement provisions, and even those rights were coterminous with those of the migrant worker with whom they moved.[17] In fact, until 2004, EU law did not even recognise the legal status of divorcees under free movement law; in order to benefit from any family rights under the free movement provisions you had to move with a migrant worker as either their legally married (heterosexual) spouse or dependent child, and the spouse would be divested of any residence rights in that host country should he or she divorce the migrant worker.[18] So, it came as something of a surprise when the EU started to formulate measures to assist the mutual recognition and enforcement of divorce and associated parental responsibility arrangements between the Member States.

This development came about following the 1997 Treaty of Amsterdam which transferred matters relating to immigration, asylum, visas and judicial and administrative co-operation in civil and commercial matters from the intergovernmental Pillar Three—known then as Justice and Home Affairs—into the Pillar One realm of the EC. This process effectively conferred law-making competence on the EU institutions in relation to cross-national family issues. Prior to that, cross-national

---

[17] As discussed in ch 3.

[18] Divorcees can now retain their right of residence in accordance with the conditions set out in Art 13 Dir 2004/38 on the right of citizens of the Union and their family members to move and reside freely within the territory of the Member States amending Reg 1612/68 and repealing Dirs 64/221, 68/360, 72/194, 73/148, 75/34/EEC, 75/35, 90/364, 90/365 and 93/96 [2004] OJ L158/77. See also Case C-413/99 *Baumbast and R v Secretary of State for the Home Department* [2002] ECR I-7091.

family disputes within the EU were regulated through a network of bi-lateral agreements, intergovernmental conventions and private international laws.[19]

Changes to the family law framework in response to these constitutional developments were introduced at a remarkable pace. As far as divorce, custody and access are concerned, what was a relatively inauspicious mutually-negotiated intergovernmental agreement to facilitate cross-border recognition of matrimonial and associated parental responsibility decisions—with virtually no reference to children[20]—was swiftly transposed into a legislative instrument, automatically and uniformly applicable across all of the Member States (with the exception of Denmark).[21] The Regulation received a mixed response: from practitioners, many of whom bemoaned having to acquaint themselves with a new and seemingly complex supplement to the existing private international law regime; from academics who questioned the appropriateness and legitimacy of EU intervention in an area in which it had seemingly little prior knowledge or expertise and which sought to harmonise such divergent domestic family law regimes and from national

---

[19] Previously applicable instruments include the 1970 Hague Convention on Divorces and Legal Separations, the 1980 European Custody Convention and the 1996 Hague Protection Convention on Jurisdiction, Applicable Law, Recognition, Enforcement and Co-operation in respect of Parental Responsibility and Measures for the Protection of Children. This latter instrument entered into force on 1 January 2002. Member States are no longer free to approve the 1996 Convention on their own because the Brussels II*bis* provisions effectively override domestic law in relation to intra-EU cases (Case 22/70 *Commission v Council* [1971] ECR 263). Nor does the Convention allow for accession by the EU as a whole. By way of exception, therefore, the Council has authorised EU Member States to sign the 1996 Convention in the interests of the EU by virtue of Dec 2003/93/EC authorising the Member States, in the interest of the Community, to sign the 1996 Hague Convention on jurisdiction, applicable law, recognition, enforcement and co-operation in respect of parental responsibility and measures for the protection of children [2002] OJ L48/1. The Member States therefore signed the Convention on 1 April 2003, with the exception of the Netherlands which signed on 1 September 1997. States then had until June 2010 to fully ratify or accede to the Convention (Dec 2009/431 [2009] OJ L151/6) (Council Decision of 5 June 2008 (2009/431/EC) OJ L 151/6). At the same time they made a declaration aimed at ensuring that the Brussels II*bis* Regulation would take precedence over the Convention for intra-EU purposes. See, further, N Lowe, 'New International Conventions Affecting the Law Relating to Children: A Cause for Concern?' (2001) *International Family Law* 171; N Lowe, 'The 1996 Hague Convention on the Protection of Children: A Fresh Appraisal' (2002) 14 *Child and Family Law Quarterly* 191 and N Lowe, 'The Growing Influence of the EU in International Family Law: a View from the Boundary' [2003] 56 *Current Legal Problems* 439.

[20] The Convention on Jurisdiction and the Recognition and Enforcement of Judgments in Matrimonial Matters of May 28 1998 [1998] OJ C221 (commonly referred to as the Brussels II Convention) adopted under the former Pillar Three, Art K3 of the Treaty on European Union 1992.

[21] Reg 1347/2000 on jurisdiction and the recognition and enforcement of judgments in matrimonial matters and in matters of parental responsibility for the children of both spouses [2000] OJ L160/19 (known as the Brussels II Regulation). Note that Denmark, the UK and Ireland negotiated an opt-out clause through the Treaty of Amsterdam enabling them to exempt themselves from any legislative instruments enacted under Title IV, including family measures (see the Protocols on the position of the United Kingdom and Ireland, and on the position of Denmark annexed to the Treaty on European Union and the Treaty Establishing the European Community). So far, Denmark has declined to opt into all Title IV measures while the UK and Ireland have chosen to opt in to most, but not all, family justice legislation (this is discussed further in ch 5).

policy-makers concerned about the additional threats such measures posed to national sovereignty.[22]

As far as children's rights are concerned, a number of deficiencies with the original Brussels II Regulation were immediately identified. For instance, it was confined to regulating jurisdiction, recognition and enforcement of parental responsibility arrangements in relation to the children of *both* parents involved in the associated divorce or separation proceedings. Excluded from its scope were children born to cohabitants, children born to legally resident third country nationals as well as any step children or adopted children of either parent. These and many other criticisms prompted the amendment of the Regulation in the form of Regulation 2201/2003 (hereafter referred to as Brussels II*bis*).[23] One of the most important, but interestingly the least celebrated, innovations of the revised Brussels II Regulation was the range of new provisions it included to address the interests and needs of children affected by cross-national family breakdown and separation.[24] The Brussels II*bis* Regulation thus represented a long overdue, more explicit endorsement of children's rights under EU family law.

THE NATURE AND SCOPE OF CHILDREN'S RIGHTS PROVISION UNDER THE BRUSSELS II*BIS* REGULATION

Before examining in more detail the children's rights provisions contained in Brussels II*bis*, it is important to define the material and personal scope of the instrument. Like its predecessor, Brussels II*bis* governs cross-national jurisdiction, recognition and enforcement of judgments both in matrimonial matters—divorce, separation, annulment—and in matters of parental responsibility. In that sense, because of the nature of EU competence on family law issues, it remains limited to harmonising *procedural* as opposed to *substantive* aspects of family law measures.

---

[22] Some of these arguments are presented by Peter McEleavey, see: P McEleavey, 'The Brussels II Regulation: How the European Community has Moved into Family Law' (2002) *ICLQ* 883; P McEleavey, 'The Communitarisation of Family Law: Too Much Haste Too Little Reflection?' in K Boele-Woelki (ed), *Perspectives for the Unification and Harmonisation of Family Law in Europe* (Antwerp, Intersentia, 2003) 509; and P McEleavey, 'The Communitarisation of Divorce Rules: What Impact for English and Scottish Law' (2004) *ICLQ* 605.

[23] Reg 2201/2003 concerning jurisdiction and the recognition and enforcement of judgments in matrimonial matters and in matters of parental responsibility [2003] OJ L338/1 (known as the Brussels II*bis* Regulation) 1.

[24] The first Brussels II Regulation made only fleeting reference to the best interests of the child in the context of determining which jurisdiction should be competent to deal with the case (Art 3(2)(b)). Reference was also made to children's rights in Art 15(2) which set out the grounds for non-recognition of parental responsibility orders between Member States. This included cases where: '(a) such recognition is manifestly contrary to the public policy of the Member State in which recognition is sought taking into account the best interests of the child' and '(b) except in cases of emergency within the child having been given an opportunity to be heard, in violation of fundamental principles of procedure of the Member State in which recognition is sought'. See, further, H Stalford, 'Brussels II and Beyond: A Better Deal for Children in the European Union?' in K Boele-Woelki (ed), *Perspectives for the Unification and Harmonisation of Family Law in Europe* (Antwerp, Intersentia, 2003) 471.

Once the jurisdiction competent to rule on a particular cross-national dispute has been determined, it is for the courts of that jurisdiction to apply national family law accordingly. Yet the Regulation can also be regarded as accommodating children's rights/interests in a number of procedural and substantive ways. First, and most obviously, its personal scope has been extended to determine jurisdiction, recognition and enforcement of parental responsibility decisions in relation to *all* children regardless of their parents' marital status, thereby detaching parental responsibility decisions from matrimonial proceedings.[25] The material scope of the Regulation has also been significantly extended. It now regulates: private (custody and access) proceedings; protective measures concerning the administration; conservation or disposal of the child's property[26] and cross-national public (care) proceedings[27] as well as decisions relating to jurisdiction and return following parental child abduction.[28]

Aside from the extended scope of the Brussels II*bis* Regulation, it has also introduced some important procedural changes that impact upon children's experiences of international family processes. Notably, disputes regarding jurisdiction in matters of parental responsibility are now generally settled by affording jurisdiction to the Member State in which the child is habitually resident.[29] Notwithstanding the possible difficulties associated with determining habitual residence of children in international families—many of whom make a series of successive moves between different Member States in response to the demands of the labour market[30]—giving preference to the courts of the child's habitual residence avoids the potential injustice associated with the notorious 'first seized'

[25] Para 5 Preamble and Arts 1(b) and (2).

[26] Art 1(2).

[27] Case C-453/06 *Telecom GmbH v Bundesrepublik Deutschland* [2006] OJ C326/41; Case C-523/07 *Re A (Freedom, Security, Justice)* [2009] 2 FLR 1; Case C-403/09 PPU *Jasna Detiček v Maurizio Sgueglia* [2009] ECR I-12193.

[28] Arts 10, 11, 40 and 42.

[29] Para 12 Preamble and Art 8(1). This principle is subject to certain exceptions set out in Arts 9, 10 and 12, notably where the child has transferred habitual residence as a result of a lawful move, or where there is evidence that the child has a 'substantial connection' with another Member State (eg as a result of a parent's habitual residence there or if the child is a national of that state).

[30] Lowe and colleagues describe the various tests that have been applied to determine habitual residence including: the 'dependency' test, whereby the habitual residence of the child depends on where their parents are habitually resident; the 'parental rights' test, whereby habitual residence depends on the wishes of the custodial parent; the 'child-centred' test, which scrutinises the nature and quality of the child's rather than the parents' residence in a particular state and the 'fact-based' test, regarded by Lowe et al as the most eminent of the tests, this reduces determination of habitual residence to a simple question of fact in the light of all of the circumstances of the case. See, further, N Lowe, M Everall and M Nicholls, *International Movement of Children: Law, Practice and Procedure* (Bristol, Jordan Publishing, 2004) 59–66. For an illustration of how habitual residence is determined in the context of Brussels II*bis*, see *T v O (Attorney General, notice party)* [2007] IESC 55. See also R Schuz, 'Habitual Residence of Children under the Hague Abduction Convention: Theory and Practice' (2001) 13 *Child and Family Law Quarterly* 1 and, more generally, R Lamont, 'Habitual Residence and Brussels II*bis*: Developing Concepts for European Private International Family Law' (2007) *Journal of Private International Law* 261.

rule.[31] This rule enables parties to establish jurisdiction in any Member State with which they have a connection, as determined by reference to the criteria set out in Article 3. Where competing claims are brought by each party in different jurisdictions, it is the country in which proceedings have been issued first that will generally have jurisdiction.

By making habitual residence the definitive test in determining jurisdiction for child custody and access, it removes any incentive for the parties to race to establish jurisdiction (at least as matters relating to parental responsibility are concerned), ideally achieving a much less adversarial, more considered approach that places the interests of the child at the heart of proceedings from the outset. Moreover, ensuring that proceedings are conducted in the state of the child's habitual residence is more conducive to child participation, not least because the child is more likely to be physically present in the Member State in which the proceedings are conducted and to be familiar with the language in which proceedings are being conducted.[32]

Additional procedural innovations aimed at safeguarding the welfare of the child include, in the context of child abduction cases, the introduction of a compulsory six-week deadline (from the date of the application) by which a decision on the return of a child should be delivered.[33] In the same spirit of expedience, an accelerated preliminary rulings procedure was introduced on 1 March 2008 to enable the Court of Justice to deliver judgments on urgent matters relating to justice, freedom and security within a much shorter period than would otherwise occur.[34] This procedure has been welcomed by many family judges who were previously reluctant to approach the Court of Justice for guidance on certain aspects of the Brussels II*bis* for fear that it would unduly delay the process, thereby jeopardising the welfare of any children involved.[35]

---

[31] Art 19(2) of Brussels II*bis* states: 'Where proceedings relating to parental responsibility relating to the same child and involving the same cause of action are brought before courts of different Member States, the court second seised shall of its own motion stay its proceedings until such time as the jurisdiction of the court first seised is established'.

[32] Discussed further in H Stalford, 'European Union Family Law: A Human Rights Perspective' in J Meeusen, G Straetmans and M Pertegas-Sender (eds), *International Family Law for the European Union* (Antwerp, Intersentia, 2006) 119. The discussion will return to some of these issues later in the chapter.

[33] Art 11(3). The discussion will return to the implications of the six-week deadline in relation to child participation later.

[34] Introduced by Dec 2008/79 [2008] OJ L24/42, and the amendments to the Rules of Procedure of the Court of Justice adopted by the Court on 15 January 2008 [2008] OJ L24/39. The decision in Case C-195/08 PPU *Inga Rinau* [2008] ECR I-5271 was the first case to be dealt with under this procedure and was heard within eight weeks, as opposed to the average 19 month turn-around period common for applications under the standard preliminary reference procedure. See further C Kumar, 'A Fast-Track to Europe: The Urgent Procedure for Preliminary Rulings' (2008) 3 *International Family Law* 180. Subsequent Brussels II*bis* cases heard under this procedure include: *Detiček*, above n 27, para 30; Case C-211/10 PPU *Povse v Alpago* [2010] ECRI-06673 and Case C-200/10 PPU *J McB v LE* [2010] OJ C328/10.

[35] A Schulz, 'Guidance from Luxembourg: First ECJ Judgment Clarifying the Relationship between the 1980 Hague Convention and Brussels II*bis*' (2008) 4 *International Family Law Journal* 221.

While these amendments are a welcome innovation of the Brussels II*bis* Regulation, the question remains as to how effective such measures are *in practice* in safeguarding and advancing the rights and welfare of the child. The next section seeks to address this question by reference, in particular, to the growing body of case law in this area. The discussion will focus on two linked normative principles that have shaped children's rights under domestic family law: the best interests (welfare) principle and the participation (agency) principle.

EU FAMILY LAW AND THE BEST INTERESTS PRINCIPLE

The best interests principle is a canon of international and domestic child and family law and universally acknowledged as a determining factor underpinning decisions around child custody and access. While Article 3(1) UNCRC is the most commonly cited reference for this principle, it finds expression in a number of earlier international texts, notably the 1959 Declaration on the Rights of the Child,[36] the 1979 Convention on the Elimination of All Forms of Discrimination Against Women,[37] as well as in various other provisions of the 1989 UNCRC itself.[38]

Notwithstanding the global influence of best interests, it remains a highly contested concept on a number of levels. First, long-standing criticisms as to its vagueness and 'indeterminacy' and its vulnerability to highly subjective and variable interpretations remain persuasive today.[39] Specifically it has been contended that such interpretations inevitably reflect the value preferences and, indeed prejudices, of the individual making the decision.[40] Moreover, it has been claimed that the UNCRC's expressions of the principle—with its universalist aspirations—is steeped in a narrow predominantly western vision of child welfare which can be at odds with the experiences of and attitudes towards children from non-western countries and cultures.[41]

A further challenge relating to the practical application of the best interests principle in proceedings involving children is that it requires a high degree of speculation as to how a particular decision will affect the well-being of the child in the immediate future and longer term. As Parker notes, 'child custody cases

---

[36] Principles 2 and 7.

[37] Art 5(b).

[38] Arts 9, 18, 20, 21, 37 and 40. For further examples of where the best interests principle has been referred to, see P Alston, 'The Best Interests Principle: Towards a Reconciliation of Culture and Human Rights' (1994) 8 *International Journal of Law Policy and the Family* 1, 3.

[39] RH Mnookin, 'Child Custody Adjudication: Judicial Functions in the Face of Indeterminacy' (1975) 39 *Law and Contemporary Problems* 226; M Freeman, 'The Best Interests of the Child? Is The Best Interests of the Child in the Best Interests of Children?' (1997) 3 *International Journal of Law Policy Family* 360; C Piper, 'Assumptions About Children's Best Interests' (2000) 22 *Journal of Social Welfare and Family Law* 261; M Freeman, *A Commentary on the United Nations Convention on the Rights of the Child—Article 3: The Best Interests of the Child* (Netherlands, Martinus Nijhoff Publishers, 2007).

[40] Alston, 'The Best Interests Principle' above n 38, 5.

[41] S Parker, 'The Best Interests of the Child: Principles and Problems' (1994) 8 *International Journal of Law, Policy and the Family* 26.

involve the imprecise exercise of appraising peoples' characters and dispositions and then trying to work out how each possible decision might affect them'.[42] Linked to this is the assertion that the principle emphasises and has entrenched a predominantly paternalistic approach to decisions around care, custody and access to the detriment of an approach that values agency, self-determinism and direct participation in decision-making processes. While this imbalance may be attributable partly to the fact that the best interests principle was expressed in international treaties and domestic law long before children's right to participate was ever even acknowledged as possible, let alone desirable,[43] key developments in children-related research over the past 20 years or so have significantly altered the discourse surrounding children's rights. This has served to challenge long-standing presumptions as to children's inherent vulnerability and incapacity and demanded a review of exclusively welfare-based processes.

So how are these issues brought to bear in this analysis of EU family law? Has Brussels II*bis* shed any more light on the content and scope of the best interests' principle? How has the principle been applied in the light of other rights enshrined in the Regulation, notably the child's right to be heard? And how has the supposedly universal notion of best interests been interpreted and applied in cases that straddle national and cultural contexts? With regard to the latter point, certainly a range of practical and cultural issues have to be taken into account in determining international cases, such as ensuring the child can sustain contact with the non-custodial parent if the parties are separated across countries, or the potential impact of international relocation on the child's cultural and religious identity and linguistic capacity. This assessment therefore demands some sensitivity to the broader context of children's lives, beyond their immediate relationships with parents and kin, to include their wider social environment. It is with this in mind that the discussion now turns to explore how the best interests' principle is expressed and applied in the context of Brussels II*bis*. [44]

THE CONTENT AND SCOPE OF THE BEST INTERESTS PRINCIPLE UNDER BRUSSELS II*BIS*

A number of Brussels II*bis* provisions are qualified by the best interests principle—or some derivation of it[45]—in the sense that it underpins decisions

---

[42] Ibid 30.

[43] Alston, 'The Best Interests Principle' above n 38, 18.

[44] For a useful comparative summary of how the best interests principle is determined and applied in European countries see K Boele-Woelki, B Braat and I Curry-Sumner (eds), *European Family Law in Action*, vol III (Antwerp, Intersentia, 2005). For an historical account of how best interests has been determined in French law, see J Rubellin-Devichi, 'The Best Interests Principle in French Law and Practice' (1994) 8 *International Journal of Law, Policy and the Family* 259.

[45] Art 12(1)(b), for no apparent reason other than what is widely accepted as an error of translation, refers instead to the 'superior interests' of the child.

relating to jurisdiction[46] and to some extent recognition too.[47] Best interests is also the primary basis on which an *exception* to the standard rules on jurisdiction, recognition and enforcement can be applied. For example, while jurisdiction is generally determined by reference to the habitual residence of the child, this can be transferred to another Member State provided it is in their best interests.[48] Additionally, a judgment relating to parental responsibility will not be automatically recognised in another Member State if such recognition is deemed to be manifestly contrary to public policy, 'taking into account the best interests of the child'.[49]

These provisions represent a positive endorsement of the best interests principle and are in keeping with other private international instruments in this area. The operation of the principle in practice, however, is limited in two fundamental respects. First, insofar as the Regulation is confined to the procedural aspects of cross-national family justice, determining jurisdiction and ensuring recognition and enforcement of judgments cross-nationally, the courts are explicitly prohibited from reviewing the substance of any decision legitimately reached in another Member State.[50] One might question, therefore, how the best interests principle can be used to guide, or indeed challenge, the application of the rules on jurisdiction, recognition and enforcement if, in practice, courts are precluded from examining the substantive facts relating to the child's welfare.

Indeed, the Brussels II*bis* Regulation appears to operate on the implicit presumption that the rules on recognition, jurisdiction and enforcement as they stand are already consistent with the best interests of the child. For example, questions of jurisdiction that arise in the context of child abduction are governed by an overarching 'policy of return', a policy which is itself based on the presumption that it is in the best interests of children generally for the court of the child's country of habitual residence to determine questions of custody and access.[51] If such rules are based on the implicit presumption that they serve the best interests of the child, it seems somewhat counterintuitive to use the same principle as grounds for allowing any deviation from them. Indeed, the case law suggests that only in the most exceptional of cases will the principle be allowed to frustrate the normal application of the rules.[52]

---

[46] Para 12 Preamble, Arts 12(1)(b),12(3)(b) and 12(4) and Arts 15(1) and 15(5).

[47] Art 23(a).

[48] Arts 12(3)(b) and 15.

[49] Art 23(a).

[50] Arts 26 and 48.

[51] This policy has been captured in the motto 'first return, then concern' quoted by K Siehr, 'The 1980 Hague Convention on the Civil Aspects of International Child Abduction: Failures and Successes in German Practice' (2000) 33 *New York University Journal of International Law and Politics* 207.

[52] Eg in *Re M (Children) (Abduction: Rights of Custody)* [2007] UKHL 55, [2008] 1 AC 1288, Baroness Hale stated of the Convention—and, by implication, the Brussels II*bis* Regulation—that 'the underlying purpose is to protect the interests of the children by securing the swift return of those who have been wrongfully removed or retained' (para 44).

These points are illustrated by *W v W*[53] which concerned a Welsh father and Irish mother who married in Dublin in 1992 and went on to have three children in quick succession. Following a series of moves between Ireland, England, Germany and Japan, the parents decided to separate. The mother returned to Ireland with the children in 1998 with the agreement of the father and he went to live in England. The mother then experienced a number of financial, housing and mental health problems and was ultimately diagnosed with bipolar disorder which resulted in her being hospitalised for five weeks in December 2001 and for two months in March 2002. Her condition was subsequently stabilised with medication. The father assumed care of the three children in London during the mother's first period of hospitalisation and they remained with him until the proceedings in 2004. All were enrolled in schools in England and achieved considerable success, with one of the children winning a scholarship for a prestigious private boarding school.

In May 2002, the mother and father issued competing judicial separation and divorce proceedings in Ireland and England respectively and the mother applied for custody of the children. The Irish judge made a joint custody order awarding primary care of the children to the father but with provision for access in favour of the mother. Access was subsequently obstructed by the father. Thus, on appeal, the mother was granted custody of the two children having agreed that it was in the best interests of the third child to remain in the boarding school to which she had won a scholarship. The father appealed against the decision, arguing that it was so contrary to the welfare of the children that its recognition in England would be manifestly contrary to public policy (on the basis of Art 23(a) of the Brussels II*bis* Regulation).[54] Dismissing the appeal, the English courts stated that the child's best interests was merely one of a number of factors that had to be taken into account in assessing a claim for non-recognition on grounds of public policy. Emphasising the very exceptional use of the public policy argument and of the 'overwhelming duty to enforce a foreign order', the judge concluded:

> There is no basis upon which recognition of this order, made after consideration of detailed evidence, on express welfare principles, and after a lengthy hearing, could possibly be considered to be contrary to public policy. On the contrary, its non-recognition would be contrary to public policy.[55]

Moreover, the court restated the Regulation's embargo on re-visiting the *substance* of other jurisdictions' judgments, asserting that to reassess the welfare of the

---

[53] *W v W (Foreign Custody Order: Enforcement)* [2005] EWHC 1811 (Fam). A number of complicated issues arose in this case as to which international/EU instrument should apply given that the case fell between the two Brussels Regulations. This discussion will not dwell on the specific details of this aspect of the judgment, the intention being merely to illustrate how the court determined what currency should be attached to the children's best interests.

[54] The father also argued that the decision should not be recognised on the grounds that the Irish courts did not have jurisdiction to rule on the issue as the mother had not been resident in the country for the requisite period of time (one full year) when she commenced proceedings there. In his view, therefore, the English courts should have had jurisdiction to rule on the matter.

[55] *W v W*, above n 53, para 38.

children would be to violate that very provision. Indeed, Singer J acknowledged that while the award of custody in favour of the mother may not have been in the children's best interests, he felt unable to conclude that it was so contrary to their best interests that it would be actually contrary, let alone manifestly contrary, to public policy to enforce it.[56]

This case demonstrates the bluntness of the best interests principle as a tool for challenging the application of the standard rules on recognition and enforcement, not to mention its susceptibility to varying interpretations: the Irish courts determined that it was in the best interests of the children to be returned to their mother, whereas the English judge, although duty bound to enforce the order, expressed that he would not have made the same decision himself.[57]

THE GROWING PROMINENCE OF BEST INTERESTS IN CHILD ABDUCTION CASES? RECONCILING *NEULINGER*[58] AND *ZARRAGA*[59]

Subsequent case law suggests, however, a growing willingness on the part of at least some courts to indulge in qualitative child welfare assessments in individual cases on the basis that, to do otherwise, risks breaching human rights standards. This is evidenced most dramatically in the case of *Neulinger,* decided by the Grand Chamber of the European Court of Human Rights in July 2010. While the decision fell within the 1980 Hague Child Abduction Convention rather than the Brussels II*bis* Regulation, the intimate legal association between the two regimes implies that it will inform intra-EU cases too. The case concerned a mother who had wrongfully removed her two-year-old son from Israel to Switzerland following the breakdown of her relationship with the father. In seeking to enforce the father's application for the child's immediate return to Israel, the Swiss Federal Court rejected the mother's claim that there was a grave risk that returning the child to Israel would expose him to physical or psychological harm or otherwise place him in an intolerable situation.[60] On eventual appeal to the Grand Chamber of the ECtHR, however, it was decided that to enforce the return order would amount to an unjustifiable interference with the mother

---

[56] The decision of Holman J in *Re S (Brussels II: Recognition and Best Interests of Child) (No 2)* [2003] EWHC 2974 (Fam), [2004] 1 FLR 582 heavily influenced Singer J's reasoning in this regard.

[57] Similarly, in *Vigreux v Michel* [2006] EWCA Civ 630, [2006] 2 FLR 1180 an order for non-return, on the basis of certain welfare considerations, was reversed on appeal in favour of upholding 'the policy of the Hague Convention, buttressed by the provisions of the Brussels II*bis* (Wall LJ, para 49) and *C v W* [2007] EWHC 1349 (Fam), [2007] 2 FLR 900, the English High Court issued an order for the return of a teenage girl to her mother in Ireland despite 'substantial welfare reservations'.

[58] *Neulinger and Shuruk v Switzerland* App no 41615/07 (unreported) Judgment of 6 July 2010.

[59] Case C-491/10 PPU *Aguirre Zarraga v Pelz* [2011] I L Pr 32.

[60] This exception to automatic return is found in Art 13b of the Hague Convention. The same exception is available in abduction cases under Brussels II*bis* (Art 11). In *Neulinger,* the mother alleged that the father's involvement in an extremist sect posed a palpable threat to the child's well-being. She also argued that she risked being prosecuted for child abduction if she returned to Israel.

and child's right to respect for private and family life as protected by Article 8 ECHR. Even more significantly, the Grand Chamber looked to the requirements of Article 3 UNCRC (the best interests principle) in interpreting and applying Article 8 ECHR: five years had elapsed since the mother's wrongful removal during which period the child had settled well in Switzerland and had not seen his father. Indeed, it was accepted by a majority of 16–1 that there was no benefit to be gained from returning the child (potentially without his mother) to an uncertain family situation in Israel. Thus, while the automatic return endorsed by the Hague Convention is generally regarded as 'marching hand-in-hand' with Article 8 ECHR, this is always subject to an appreciation of whether such a course of action is consonant with the best interests principle as enshrined in Article 3 UNCRC.[61]

This cross-referencing between human rights instruments achieved by *Neulinger* is surely to be welcomed if the ultimate outcome is to provide better protection for the welfare of the individual child. The decision has generated considerable debate, however, with many commentators arguing that it significantly undermines the primary purpose for which the Hague Convention was designed: to uphold decisions of the national courts and to preclude abducting parents from gaining a legal advantage from their wrongdoing.[62] Specifically, *Neulinger* has been criticised not only for undermining the principle of subsidiarity by allowing supra-national courts to engage in substantive determinations of child welfare issues, but also for creating a worrying level of dissonance in approach depending on whether the case is heard before the domestic courts, the ECtHR or the Court of Justice of the EU. This is highlighted by Walker and Beaumont's comparative analysis of child abduction cases brought before the Strasbourg and Luxembourg courts: in contrast with the ECtHR's preoccupation with upholding the rights of the individual child, they have observed a stubborn reluctance on the part of the Court of Justice to deviate from the strict ethic of return traditionally associated with child abduction law and indulge in any consideration of individual welfare assessments. This dissonance, they argue, will be even less defensible given the increasing legal and judicial alignment between the EU and the ECHR, particularly following the EU's inevitable accession to the latter:

> The ECtHR is placing too much emphasis on the best interests of the child, by encouraging 'an in depth-examination of the entire family situation' in abduction proceedings. In stark contrast the [Court of Justice] is placing too much confidence in the principle of mutual trust and not ensuring sufficient protection for the best interests of the child … Further, these two major European courts should not be operating in complete isolation. They should be aware of each other's judgments to try to bring the law back in line. This

---

[61] This approach was confirmed in *Raban v Romania* App no 25437/08 (unreported) Judgment of 26 October 2010.

[62] L Walker, 'The Impact of the Hague Abduction Convention on the Rights of the Family in the Case Law of the European Court of Human Rights and the UN Human Rights Committee: The Danger of *Neulinger*' (2010) 6 *Journal of Private International Law* 629.

is especially true now that there is potential for the European Union to accede to the European Convention on Human Rights which would mean decisions of the ECJ being subject to review by the ECtHR.[63]

The Court of Justice's tendency to support the more politically conventional route of automatic return, even when there are serious child welfare issues that might support a refusal, is illustrated in the case of *Zarraga*. The facts are as follows: Mr Zarraga, A Spanish national, married Ms Pelz, a German national in 1998 in Spain. They had a daughter in 2000 whilst the family still lived in Spain. The couple's relationship deteriorated in the years that followed and in 2007 they issued divorce proceedings before the Spanish courts, with both parties seeking sole custody of the daughter. At first instance, the father was awarded custody and the mother access rights in the light of evidence that the father was best placed to ensure that the family, school and social environment of the child was maintained. As the mother had repeatedly expressed her wish to settle in Germany with her new partner and her daughter, the court considered that the award of custody to the mother would have been contrary to the conclusions of that report and would also have been detrimental to the child's welfare.[64]

The mother moved to Germany permanently with her new partner in June 2008. The daughter visited her later that summer but failed to return home to her father. In the light of the mother's breach of the custody and access arrangements, the Spanish court issued a new judgment at the request of the father, which included a suspension of the mother's access rights, as well as a provisional order prohibiting the child from leaving Spanish territory in the company of her mother or with any member of the mother's family. By January 2009 the child had still failed to return to her father, at which point the Spanish court issued an order for her immediate return under the Brussels II*bis* regime. The mother successfully appealed against this on the grounds that the order for return was contrary to the expressed wishes of the child.[65] Proceedings relating to her custody were reconvened before the Spanish court who requested fresh expert evidence to ascertain what would be in the child's best interests, including evidence from the child herself (who was nine years old by this time). Neither the mother nor the child attended on the requested dates, presumably because the Spanish court had rejected the mother's application that she and

---

[63] L Walker and P Beaumont, 'Shifting The Balance Achieved by the Abduction Convention: The Contrasting Approaches of the European Court of Human Rights and the European Court of Justice' (2011) 7 *Journal of Private International Law* 231, 231. The authors suggest that a more faithful reading of the child abduction provisions is not at odds with the best interests principle, indeed it is quite the opposite: a refusal to return the child based on one of the exceptions already provided for in the Hague Convention and the Brussels II*bis* Regulation automatically implies that the best interests of the child have been accommodated. In the same token, the return of the child will only be ordered if it is in the child's best interests.

[64] *Zarraga*, above n 59, para 19.

[65] Note that even in intra-EU child abduction cases that fall within the scope of Brussels II*bis*, the Regulation (Art 11) defers to the Hague Abduction Convention (Art 13) in determining whether the parties can invoke one of the exceptions to the automatic return of the child.

her daughter be permitted to leave Spanish territory freely after the hearing. Nor did the court agree to the mother's express request that Andrea (her daughter) be heard via video conference. In December 2009, the Spanish court awarded sole rights of custody to the father, a decision that was immediately appealed by the mother. She argued that the custody proceedings were inherently flawed since it was unlikely that an accurate assessment of Andrea's best interests had been made due to lack of relevant information (including her and her daughter's testimony) available to them.[66] The German court upheld this appeal and refused to enforce the order for the child's return on the grounds that the Spanish court had not taken the child's views into account which, it concluded, constituted a breach of the child's fundamental rights as enshrined in Article 24(1) of the Charter of Fundamental Rights.[67]

The German court sought the opinion of the Court of Justice as to whether they were obliged to enforce the order to return or whether they had an exceptional power to review the substance of the case[68] if the judgment issued by the Spanish court contained a serious infringement of the child's fundamental rights as recognised by the Charter. Whilst recognising that the Brussels II*bis* Regulation, in conjunction with Article 24 of the Charter, created an obligation to hear the views of the competent child, the Court of Justice concluded that the assessment of whether there has been such an infringement falls exclusively within the jurisdiction of the courts of the Member State of origin (Spain); the German courts did not, by sole virtue of the alleged infringement, acquire jurisdiction to determine such matters.[69] The main thrust of the Court of Justice's reasoning was that the entire operation of the Brussels II*bis* Regulation was underpinned by the principle of mutual trust between the Member States which extends to a presumption that each jurisdiction will have in place an equally robust legal system 'capable of providing an equivalent and effective protection of fundamental rights'.[70] In its blind loyalty to the principle of mutual recognition, however, the decision totally undermines the capacity of children's rights to serve as a legitimate exception to automatic return,[71] extends already protracted litigation, and places itself at the polar opposite to the ECtHR in its interpretations of exactly the same law.

Notwithstanding the Court of Justice's reluctance to engage fully in this important aspect of children's rights, it remains a critical feature of the Brussels II*bis* regime all the same and is worth considering in more depth.

---

[66] Walker and Beaumont, *Shifting the Balance*, above n 63, 239.
[67] The scope and substance of the children's rights provisions within the Charter is discussed in more detail in ch 2.
[68] Pursuant to Art 42 Brussels II*bis*.
[69] *Zarraga*, above n 59, para 75.
[70] *Zarraga*, above n 59, para 70.
[71] Under Art 13 Hague Abduction Convention 1980.

BRUSSELS II*BIS* AND THE VOICE OF THE CHILD

Alongside the best interests, the other normative principle that has influenced the development of family law is the right of the child to participate in decisions that affect them, as articulated in Article 12 UNCRC.[72] This right is manifested in legal measures that reinforce the child's right to be heard in the course of judicial proceedings, not only in the context of custody, access and abduction, but also in criminal justice and care proceedings. Children's participatory rights have also been interpreted in the context of the right to a fair trial under Article 6 of the ECHR.[73] Together, these measures provide an international 'space' for children's voices but, as Griffiths notes, 'building sensible law and policy in that space requires empirical knowledge of what children do and do not say, and how children are understood or misunderstood in different types of settings'.[74] This 'empirical knowledge' is now well-developed: an extensive body of research has emerged over the last 20 years serving to illustrate how a routine failure to confer with children when it comes to decisions about where and with whom they live can exacerbate the trauma, confusion and isolation commonly associated with relationship breakdown. This research unanimously advocates honest and open dialogue with children from the outset with a view to allaying any misconceptions they may have about their role in events, enabling them to express their views on how post-divorce living and contact arrangements should work, and providing both parents and children with the opportunity to draw on each others' emotional support in a more reciprocal way.[75]

Despite the existence of all of this empirical guidance, the reality is that parents' perspectives on children's participation is often tainted by their own conflicted emotions towards each other or by an overwhelming sense of responsibility to shield them from any further trauma associated with the divorce (particularly in relation to very young children or in cases of domestic abuse). Since formal legal

---

[72] Further guidance on the obligations inherent in Art 12 UNCRC are provided by the UN Committee on the Rights of the Child's General Comment no 12, 'The Right of the Child to be Heard' CRC/C/GC/12, 2009.

[73] See *Airey v Ireland* App no 6289/73 (1979-80) 2 EHRR 305, and *T and V v United Kingdom* App no 24888/94 16 December 1999. See, further, U Kilkelly, 'The Best of Both Worlds for Children's Rights: Interpreting the European Convention on Human Rights in the Light of the UN Convention on the Rights of the Child' (2001) 23 *Human Rights Quarterly* 308; JP Costa, *International Justice for Children* (Strasbourg, Council of Europe, 2009) and K Norrie, 'Human Rights and the Children's Hearing System: An Assessment of Which Aspects of the Children's Hearing System Might be Subject to Challenge under the European Convention' (2000) *The Journal Online* 19.

[74] A Griffiths, 'Hearing Children in Children's Hearings' (2000) 3 *Children and Family Law Quarterly* 283.

[75] Eg see M Maclean (ed), *Parenting after Partnering: Containing Conflict after Separation* (Oxford, Hart Publishing, 2007); L Trinder, 'Maternal Gatekeeping and Gate-Opening in Post Divorce Families: Strategies, Contexts and Consequences' (2008) 29 *Journal of Family Issues* 1298; C Smart, B Neale and A Wade, *The Changing Experience of Childhood: Families and Divorce* (Cambridge, Polity Press, 2001). On the value of and approaches to child participation in a range of other contexts, see B Percy-Smith and N Thomas (eds), *A Handbook of Children and Young People's Participation: Perspectives from Theory and Practice* (London, Routledge, 2009).

proceedings are often the resort for such conflict-ridden cases, account needs to be taken of the extent to which the judicial process provides an opportunity for children to voice their wishes and feelings, particularly if this has not been achieved within the private sphere of the family. This is all the more important in cross-national family disputes since decisions as to custody and access may necessitate the child's relocation to a new, unfamiliar cultural and linguistic environment. It may also create significant geographical distance between them and the non-custodial parent and relatives requiring lengthy but irregular periods of contact (typically confined to the holiday period).[76]

The Brussels II*bis* Regulation acknowledges these concerns by imposing an explicit obligation on national courts to hear children's views on matters relating to custody, access and return. Recital 19 of the Preamble set the tone: 'the hearing of the child plays an important role in the application of this Regulation, although this instrument is not intended to modify national procedures applicable'.[77]

Although this commitment to child participation is worded cautiously—no doubt mindful of the EU's legal incapacity to supplant existing national consultation procedures with harmonised measures—it is reinforced by other substantive provisions. For instance, Articles 23(b) and 41(2)(c) warn that failure to consult with a competent child can be used as a basis for non-recognition and enforcement of parental responsibility decisions. The principle is further echoed in the provisions relating to parental child abduction[78] which make the enforcement of any order to return the child to the country from which they have been abducted conditional upon giving the child an opportunity to be heard.[79] This is a significant provision insofar as it actively obliges Member States to consult with children as a sine qua non of issuing a return order, subject to the child's age or degree of maturity.[80]

The decision in *Zarraga* suggests that, in the eyes of the Court of Justice, the obligation to hear the child presents a relatively flimsy challenge to the overarching policy of mutual recognition and automatic return in child abduction cases, the domestic courts appear rather more amenable to using this provision to uphold children's fundamental rights in such proceedings.[81] Equally, however,

---

[76] Ackers and Stalford, *A Community for Children*, above n 7, 197.

[77] Recital 19 Preamble.

[78] Arts 10–11, 40 and 42. Note that Arts 12 and 13 of the Hague Convention on the Civil Aspects of International Child Abduction of 25 October 1980 are applied to actions brought within the scope of Art 11 of the Brussels II*bis* Regulation, subject to the amendments set out in paras 2–8 of Art 11 of the Regulation.

[79] Arts 11(2) and 42(2)(a).

[80] This represents a subtle amendment to Art 13(2) of the Hague Convention which does not impose an explicit obligation on national courts to consult with a child but rather allows the judicial or administrative authorities to refuse to order the return of the child if it finds that the child objects to being returned and has attained an age and degree of maturity at which it is appropriate to take account of its views. The effect of this provision is to place the onus firmly on the child to submit their objections to return, rather than on the national courts to actively seek the child's views.

[81] Walker and Beaumont note that courts in many parts of Europe have at least heard the views of children younger than 10 and cite some examples in which their views have been upheld, see *Re W*

they reveal a significant difference of opinion among legal practitioners as to the value and ethics of involving children directly. Common objections point to the risks of imposing an inappropriate level of responsibility on children to make life-changing decisions as to custody and access, to the additional trauma to which such practices exposes children, and to the potential for children to be manipulated or 'coached' by one or other parent.[82] Such arguments highlight the delicate balancing act facing judges between two seemingly conflicting principles: children's right to participate and to safeguarding their welfare, particularly in child abduction cases.[83]

In reality, of course, the two are intimately linked: open and direct discussion with children is an essential means of establishing what is in their best interests. This is captured succinctly by Lady Hale and Lord Wilson in their leading judgment in the UK Supreme Court case of *E (Children)*:[84]

> [There are] situations in which the general underlying assumptions about what will best serve the interests of the child may not be valid. We now understand that, although children do not always know what is best for them, they may have an acute perception of what is going on around them and their own authentic views about the right and proper way to resolve matters.

There is an abundance of case law to support this point. *Re F (Abduction)*,[85] for example, concerned two children, aged 12 and 13, who were born in Poland to an English mother and Polish father. The parents divorced in 2002 but the mother, who had primary custody of the children, continued to live and work in Poland. The father had regular access to the children and was granted 'restricted authority' to co-determine vital issues such as the children's education and healthcare. In December 2006, following ongoing disputes between the couple over maintenance arrears and access arrangements, the mother brought the children to England without informing the father. She claimed that this was to enable her to secure a better job so that she could continue to support her children independently. The mother had discussed the move with the children and had their full agreement. She also claimed that the children had informed their father of their plans to move to England which he appeared to accept. On arriving in England, the mother did not notify the father of their new address and the father's first

(Children) [2010] EWCA Civ 520, [2010] 2 FLR 1165, in which the views of siblings aged eight and five were upheld (Walker and Beaumont, *Shifting the Balance*, above n 63, 240).

[82] Thus, the court made the decision to award custody of the children to the mother in *W v W*, above n 53, in spite of the expressed wishes of the children to remain with the father. The court concluded that they had been unduly influence by the father who had deliberately obstructed any previous contact with the mother. Similarly, in *C v W*, above n 57, the court issued an order for the return of a teenage girl to her mother in Ireland in spite of her cogent objections.

[83] See further N Lowe, 'A Review of the Application of Article 11 of the Revised Brussels II Regulation' (2009) *International Family Law* 27 and N Lowe and K Horosova, 'The Operation of the 1980 Hague Abduction Convention—A Global View' (2007) 41 *Family Law Quarterly* 59.

[84] *Re E (Children) (Abduction: Custody Appeal)* [2011] UKSC 27, [2011] 2 WLR 1326, para 16.

[85] *Re F (Abduction: Rights of Custody)* [2008] EWHC 272 (Fam), [2008] 3 WLR 527.

contact with the children was not until the following September, some nine months after the move. The father then made an application under the Hague Child Abduction Convention and Brussels II*bis* for the return of the children in response to which the mother raised the objections of the children as a defence. To support this she relied primarily on the written and oral evidence of the English CAFCASS[86] officer in 2008 which was based on an interview with the boys and on an evaluation of their school reports. The CAFCASS officer relayed their 'clear and emphatic' objections to return and their contentment with their life in England. The evidence also referred to the father's failure to respond to telephone messages and letters the boys had sent since arriving in England. While confirming that the overarching objective of the Hague Convention—and, by implication, of Brussels II*bis*—is to expedite the return of abducted children to enable matters of custody and access to be determined by the courts of the requesting state, the children's objections were deemed to be sufficiently cogent to justify judicial discretion in favour of refusing return. The judge clarified what factors should be taken into account in exercising this discretion, stating:

> If a child's objections to return result solely from a desire to remain with the abducting parent who in turn does not wish to return, then little or no weight should be attached to the child's objection … However, I do not think that is the case here. The objections very considerably rest upon the happiness and feeling of security of the children in their new school where they are doing so well and their general environment and feelings of security in England.[87]

Accordingly, the father's application for return was dismissed and the children were allowed to remain with their mother in England. In reaching this decision the judge relied heavily on the (then) House of Lords decision in *Re M*[88] in which Baroness Hale clarified—and to some extent corrected—previous interpretations of the exception to return based on the child's objections.[89] She stated:

> In child's objections cases   the exception [to return] is brought into play when only two conditions are met: First that the child herself objects to being returned and second, that she has obtained an age and degree of maturity at which it is appropriate to take account of her views. These days, and especially in the light of Article 12 of the United Nations Convention on the Rights of the Child, courts increasingly consider it appropriate to take account of a child's views.[90]

---

[86] CAFCASS is the Children and Family Court Advisory and Support Service, an independent statutory body representing the interests and wishes of children in private and public family proceedings.

[87] *Re F*, above n 85, para 45 (Sir Mark Potter P).

[88] Above n 52.

[89] While *Re M* was a non-European case—in that the children had been abducted from Zimbabwe—the courts have since concluded that the interpretation of the Hague Convention applies equally to the relevant provisions of the Revised Brussels II Regulation. See Thorpe LJ in *Vigreux v Michel*, above n 57.

[90] Above n 52, para 45.

Baroness Hale further elaborated on the factors that should be taken into account by the judge in determining how much weight to attach to children's views in reaching a final decision:

> Taking account does not mean that those views are always determinative or presumptively so. Once the discretion comes into play, the court may have to consider the nature and strength of the child's objections, the extent to which they are 'authentically her own' or the product of the influence of the abducting parent, the extent to which they coincide with or at odds with other considerations which are relevant to her welfare, as well as the general Convention considerations … The older the child, the greater the weight that her objections are likely to carry.[91]

This more child-centric approach[92] is reflected in other Brussels II*bis* judgments. In *Re F (A Child)*,[93] the English Court of Appeal upheld a mother's appeal against a return order issued in respect of her seven-year-old child who had been wrongfully retained in the UK following a Christmas visit to stay with her maternal grandmother. The appeal was allowed on the grounds that the judge at first instance had failed to hear the child's views on the matter. Failure to consult with the child was described by Thorpe LJ as a 'fundamental deficiency' incapable of being ignored.[94] He also emphasised the point that the participation obligation applies to *all* child abduction cases under Article 11 of Brussels II*bis*, regardless of whether the parties are raising a defence on the basis of the child's objections or not.[95] The only exception to the obligation to hear the child in such proceedings is where the child's age or capacity would render it inappropriate.[96]

Such examples represent a refreshing departure from the typically paternalistic approach that has characterised much of the case law in this area, and reflects advancements in the wider children's rights arena, at least in the UK. It is now universally acknowledged that advocating child consultation and participation in family proceedings is not synonymous with conferring decision-making powers on the child Their opinion merely informs the process and is only one part of the evidential jigsaw.[97] As Griffiths notes, 'it is not the wants a child asserts, but the needs a child reveals that are most influential … This places the child who speaks at a hearing in the situation of a (sometimes unwitting) witness about him[/her]self'.[98] Equally persuasive is the argument that participatory rights are instrumental

---

[91]   Above n 71, para 45.
[92]   R Lamont, 'Re M and Beyond: Managing Return When a Child has Settled Following Abduction' (2009) 31 *Journal of Social Welfare and Family Law* 73, 80.
[93]   *Re F (A Child) (Abduction: Child's Wishes)* [2007] EWCA Civ 468, [2007] 2 FLR 697.
[94]   Para 19.
[95]   Paras 16–17 of judgment.
[96]   Eg the House of Lords decision in *Re D (Abduction: Rights of Custody)* [2006] UKHL 51, [2007] 1 FLR 961 and the Court of Appeal decision in *Klentzeris v Klentzeris* [2007] EWCA Civ 533, [2007] 2 FLR 996. For a detailed review of the 'child objections' cases, see P McEleavey, 'Evaluating the Views of Abducted Children: Trends in Appellate Case Law' (2008) *Child and Family Law Quarterly* 230.
[97]   J Eekelaar, 'The Interests of the Child and the Child's Wishes: The Role of Dynamic Self-determinism' (1994) 8 *International Journal of Law, Policy and the Family* 42, 53–54.
[98]   Griffiths, 'Hearing Children' above n 74, 294.

rather than hostile to safeguarding the best interests of the child inasmuch as active consultation with children provides a valuable opportunity for filling in the gaps between the facts as articulated by the parents, identifying any additional factors that have impacted upon the child, and explaining to the child in sensitive and honest terms why a particular decision regarding custody, access or return is likely or has been made.[99]

Notwithstanding evidence of an increasing willingness, at least by the domestic courts, to involve children in Brussels II*bis* proceedings, child participation is still hostage to a number of factors including the arbitrary application of age and capacity tests, restrictive and diverging national provision for child consultation and the time limitations imposed by the Regulation itself.

AGE AND CAPACITY AS A BARRIER TO CHILD PARTICIPATION

All of the decisions referred to above, while appearing to champion direct consultation with children in proceedings,[100] append the standard proviso 'subject to age and capacity of the child'. Of course there are instances in which common sense dictates that it would be clearly inappropriate and even damaging to involve a child directly in proceedings, for example where they have expressed a clear desire not to be involved in proceedings, where they are particularly emotionally or physically fragile, or where the child is still in its infancy and unable to articulate his or her views. However, the age and capacity test entrenched in legislation is rarely interpreted as a presumption in favour of participation that can only be rebutted in the light of the child's clear incapacity or immaturity. In most cases the default position is non-participation. This approach is patently inconsistent with the spirit of Article 12 of the UNCRC which affords children a *right* as opposed to an option to participate in decisions that affect them. As Lundy notes, 'the practice of actively involving [children and young people] in decision-making should not be portrayed as an option which is the gift of adults but a legal imperative which is the right of the child'.[101]

The presumed wisdom underpinning age and capacity thresholds has also been heavily challenged by approaches to child participation in other judicial contexts, notably juvenile justice proceedings where children are expected to publicly

---

[99] See further M Potter, 'The Voice of the Child: Children's "Rights" in Family Proceedings' (2008) 3 *International Family Law Journal* 140, 147 and N Thomas and C O'Kane, 'When Children's Wishes and Feelings Clash with their Best Interests' (1998) 6 *International Journal of Children's Rights* 137. For a comparative perspective on how the courts reconcile these principles, see D Archaud and M Skivenes, 'Balancing a Child's Best Interests and a Child's Views' (2009) 17 *International Journal of Children's Rights* 1.

[100] Note, however, that in the English courts, any attempts to joinder children to proceedings as separate parties are reserved for only the most exceptional of cases.

[101] L Lundy, '"Voice is Not Enough": Conceptualising Article 12 of the United Nations Convention on the Rights of the Child' (2007) 33 *British Education Research Journal* 927, 934.

account for their actions.[102] This contention is supported by extensive research conducted since the early 1980s on child competence, all of which confirms that children's capacity to express their views increases in accordance with the opportunities for participation afforded to them. Freeman summarises the findings of this work:

> Where children have experiences with, and overt permission for, participation in decision-making, their competence in reasoning increases: the more autonomy children are given, the better they are able to exercise it.[103]

Indeed, it is now universally accepted that questions of capacity cannot be determined in an arbitrary and linear fashion in accordance with specific age categories. Rather, it demands a much more nuanced, sensitive and dynamic approach that not only assesses the individual characteristics and circumstances of the child, but also scrutinises whether the family justice process itself can be better adapted to facilitate meaningful child consultation. Indeed, it has been argued that questions of capacity should focus less on the ability of the child to communicate their wishes and needs, and more on the capacity of adults (including practitioners) to elicit those views sensitively and effectively.[104]

DIVERGENCE BETWEEN NATIONAL CHILD CONSULTATION PROCEDURES

Linked to this issue is the fact that Brussels II*bis*, while it endorses child participation, resolutely defers to national law to determine the scope and content of this commitment. It follows then that the strength of children's right to be heard under the Regulation depends entirely on whether measures at the national level give effect to such a right and on how amenable national judges are to interpreting and applying those measures expansively. In reality, significant divergence exists between the Member States in the procedures for consulting with children. Many states (the Netherlands, Denmark, Hungary and Spain) still adhere to a

---

[102] B Goldson and J Muncie (eds), *Youth Crime and Juvenile Justice*, vol 1 (London, Sage, 2009); B Goldson and J Muncie, 'Rethinking Youth Justice: Comparative Analysis, International Human Rights and Research Evidence' (2006) 6 *Youth Justice* 91.

[103] Freeman, 'The Best Interests of the Child?' above n 37, 367. See, further, A Solberg, 'Negotiating Childhood: Changing Constructions of Age for Norwegian Children' in A James and A Prout (eds), *Constructing and Reconstructing Childhood* (Basingstoke, Falmer Press, 1990) and P Alderson and M Goodwin, 'Contradictions within Concepts of Children's Competence' (1993) 1 *International Journal of Children's Rights* 303.

[104] R Hunter, 'Close Encounters of a Judicial Kind: 'Hearing' Children's 'Voices' in Family Law Proceedings' (2007) 3 *Child and Family Law Quarterly* 283; FE Raitt, 'Hearing Children in Family Law Proceedings: Can Judges Make a Difference?' (2007) 2 *Child and Family Law Quarterly* 204; B Percy-Smith and N Thomas, *A Handbook of Children and Young People's Participation: Perspectives from Theory and Practice* (London, Routledge, 2009); C Forder, 'Seven Steps to Achieving Full Participation of Children in the Divorce Process' in JCM Willems (ed), *Developmental and Autonomy Rights of Children: Empowering Children, Care-Givers and Communities* (Antwerp, Intersentia, 2002).

predominantly age-based test in determining whether children should have a right to be heard. Most other countries (Austria, Belgium, Bulgaria, England and Wales, Belgium, Ireland, France, Greece, Sweden, Italy and Lithuania) operate a slightly more 'flexible'[105] policy, based on the child's understanding/maturity/ capacity and age; while only a minority of countries (Portugal, Germany and Finland) dispense with any explicit age/capacity criteria and work on the presumption that all children should be heard unless it is contrary to their best interests. A similar level of diversity exists in relation to how consultation is carried out: some states, such as the UK, typically require written adult proxy accounts of the child's views by independent representatives, while others, such as Germany, advocate much more direct judicial engagement with the child.[106] These differences highlight the lottery presented to children involved in Brussels II*bis* proceedings, in the sense that the form and currency of their participation will depend entirely on the system in place in their country of habitual residence.

Notwithstanding the significant divergence between national procedures, there is evidence to suggest that the Regulation is acting as a type of auditing mechanism for national consultation processes. This has occurred first as a direct result of provisions such as Article 23(b) which enables Member States to refuse to recognise parental responsibility decisions on the basis that the appropriate child consultation procedures were not followed in the issuing state. Similarly, return orders are commonly issued by judges—in spite of the competent child's strong objections—on the basis of their confidence in the child participation opportunities available in the requesting Member State.[107] These obligations, and the additional cross-national co-operation demanded by the Regulation, may well prompt Member States to adopt a more rigorous and consistent approach to their child consultation procedures to facilitate the smooth application of the instrument and to ensure that the policy reasons favouring return are incontrovertible.[108]

---

[105] Bearing in mind that this additional flexibility offers greater discretion to avoid a consultation altogether.

[106] I am grateful to Eberhard Carl, Judge at the Court of Appeal in Berlin and Frankfurt, for his insight into how children's views are heard in Germany. For further detail on the nature of child consultation proceedings in the various EU Member States and surrounding countries, see K Boele-Woeli, B Braat and I Curry-Sumner (eds), *European Family Law in Action* 773.

[107] For an excellent illustration, see *Vigreux v Michel*, above n 57.

[108] It is also worth noting that the establishment in 2001 of the European Judicial Network in Civil and Commercial Matters has undoubtedly encouraged a greater level of cross-national judicial and administrative communication and exchange in relation to children's rights under Brussels II*bis* proceedings. See Dec 2001/470 establishing a European Judicial Network in civil and commercial matters [2001] OJ L174/25, and The European Evaluation Consortium, *Evaluation of the Functioning of the European Judicial Network in Civil and Commercial Matters: Final Report* (Brussels, European Commission, 2005).

CHILD PARTICIPATION AND THE SIX WEEK DEADLINE
IN CHILD ABDUCTION CASES

A further threat to child participation posed by the Brussels II*bis* Regulation is presented in Article 11(3) which obliges courts to expedite decisions relating to return applications following child abduction. The provision states 'the court shall, except where exceptional circumstances make this impossible, issue its judgment no later than six weeks after the application is lodged'.[109] Again, this requirement reflects the overarching policy of the Hague Convention to restore the status quo for the child and to ensure that the courts of the child's habitual residence retain jurisdiction to determine questions of custody and access. On a more practical level, it also reduces the costs of litigation for the parties. the deadline can be criticised, however, for hampering effective consultation with children, a process that often demands more time for establishing trust and adapting processes. This issue has been acknowledged in the case law. In *Re D (Abduction: Rights of Custody)*,[110] for example, Baroness Hale called for a re-appraisal of the way in which the views of abducted children are to be ascertained in order to meet the six week deadline imposed by Article 11(3). In particular she argued for views to be sought at the outset of proceedings to avoid delays rather than the customary practice of eliciting views towards the end of proceedings. Further recommendations in this regard are proffered by Thorpe LJ in *Re F*:[111]

> One thing that is clear to me is that the obligation to hear the child must not override the obligation in the same Article 11 to conclude the proceedings within 6 weeks of issue. It must be implicit in the juxtaposition of the two obligations that the obligation to hear the child will be fulfilled within the 6-week duration of the litigation, particularly since in the majority of Member States the judge hears a child directly at the final hearing ... It seems to me to be necessary that in the future the question of how and when the court will hear the child ... must be considered at the first directions appointment and any subsequent directions appointment to ensure that that central ingredient of the case is never out of the spotlight.

CONCLUSION

In embarking on the regulation of family law the EU, wittingly or otherwise, has assumed an ineluctable responsibility towards children. Despite its initial reluctance to embrace children's rights, the Brussels II*bis* legislation has, in fact, evolved to offer one of the most prolific sources of children's rights at EU level. This is

---

[109] Art 11 of the Hague Abduction Convention 1980 entitles judicial and administrative authorities of the requesting state to enquire as to the reasons for the delay if a decision has not been reached within six weeks from the date of the commencement of proceedings. However, the Brussels II provision is much more direct: it does not merely allow for the authorities to request reasons for a delay but positively obliges judges to meet the deadline.

[110] *Re D (A Child) (Abduction: Rights of Custody)* [2006] UKHL 51, [2007] 1 AC 619.

[111] [2007] EWCA Civ 468, para 24.

attributable less to the real substance of the children's rights provisions contained within the Regulation—which largely echo what was already available under private international law—but more to the way it has interacted with domestic family law processes. As a dynamic and malleable instrument, it is capable of accommodating not only the national legal context in which it is being applied, but also the individual interests and needs of any children implicated in such proceedings. But the extent to which this is achieved depends on the readiness and capacity of those who interpret and apply the law to breathe life and meaning into what are, for all intents and purposes, rather vague and bland provisions. This is no mean feat, particularly where judges are faced with the unenviable task of balancing seemingly competing rights-based claims. Best interests and participation are a prime example of this dilemma and one that is illustrated particularly well by the now abundant case law based on the Brussels II*bis* Regulation. The fact that this is dominated by abduction cases makes it difficult to determine how best interests is applied in the more 'straightforward' custody and access cases. In an abduction context, however, a brief analysis of the English case law reveals ongoing concerns as to the precise scope and currency of the best interests test. This is illustrated by the fact that welfare concerns will rarely successfully challenge a return order on its own merits, primarily because the policy of return underpinning the law on child abduction is presumed to be already firmly embedded in best interests. While such a presumption may well operate in favour of children in the majority of cases, the restrictions imposed by the Regulation are such that judges in the state to which the child has been abducted are precluded from conducting a rigorous assessment of the child's needs, a point illustrated only too well by *Zarraga*. This raises ever more acute concerns that the policy of return espoused by the Brussels II*bis* Regulation is driven more by a desire to achieve comity between the Member States than it is by a genuine desire to act in children's best interests.

The child participation provisions, on the other hand, have been applied more successfully in Brussels II proceedings, although again this has primarily been in the context of child abduction, with limited evidence of children's views being taken into account or even invited in non-abduction cases. Arguably, the positive obligation imposed on the courts to consult with children in return cases has militated against the inconsistent and narrow application of many national child consultation procedures. The currency of this participation, however,—the extent to which children's views are taken into account, the extent to which children are kept informed of what decisions are being made about their future and why, and the application of arbitrary age thresholds which may bear little relation to the actual competence of the child to participate—remains vulnerable to highly subjective, variable and, in some cases, uninformed interpretations of children's needs and capacities.

Of course, child participation in the legal process can never replace effective child consultation between family members on a private level. This reinforces the point that participation is a *process* rather than a *product*: a right that is nurtured and sustained throughout the child's life rather than a privilege to be endowed upon a select few in the course of judicial proceedings. Indeed, many of the challenges associated with determining best interests may well dissipate if adults across the EU, in both public and private contexts, were more amenable to giving children the space and resources they need to contribute to discussions about their own lives.

5

Maintenance, Mediation and the Future of EU Family Law

INTRODUCTION

T HE PREVIOUS CHAPTER has highlighted how EU measures in the field
of divorce and parental responsibility have prompted a reappraisal of the
currency and scope of children's rights, particularly in the course of child
abduction proceedings. In the same vein, this chapter will explore the children's
rights implications of other EU family law developments, notably in relation to
the cross-national recognition and enforcement of child maintenance decisions
and in the field of international family mediation. While these areas of law are less
obvious sites for the articulation of children's rights, even within a domestic law
context, they nonetheless raise questions of direct relevance to children's welfare
and autonomy. The chapter will conclude with some thoughts on how ongoing
developments in the field of EU family law are likely to impact upon children, particularly in the wake of the Lisbon Treaty[1] which came into force on 1 December
2009 bringing with it a radical shake up of the EU's constitutional, institutional
and procedural architecture.

ENFORCING CHILD MAINTENANCE CROSS-NATIONALLY

Child maintenance can be defined as an ongoing obligation for the financial care
and support of children of a relationship or marriage that has been terminated, or
in some cases never existed. The maintenance obligation is based on the premise
that parents have a duty to provide for their children's material needs regardless
of the status of their relationship with one another. This is confirmed by Article
27(2) of the UNCRC which states that 'the parent(s) or others responsible for the
child have the primary responsibility to secure, within their abilities and financial
capacities, the conditions of living necessary for the child's development'. Child
maintenance is, therefore, by definition a children's rights issue: it is concerned
with upholding and protecting children's welfare insofar as its aim is to address

---

[1] [2007] OJ C306, 17 December 2007.

the child's ongoing material needs in the event of parental divorce or separation with a view to avoiding and alleviating child poverty. This is supported by Skinner and others' research comparing child support policy in 14 countries which revealed a positive correlation between child maintenance contributions and poverty reduction.[2] Their study demonstrated that maintenance makes a potential contribution to material poverty reduction[3] in all countries, particularly if there is no other income from parental employment.[4] Equally, one can assume that securing a guaranteed level of parental support for children shields them from the adverse effects of poverty in the broader 'social exclusion' sense of the word, notably by ensuring they have sufficient resources to access educational materials, local recreational services, transport and adequate housing.[5]

Determining child maintenance is a complex and extensively litigated aspect of family law involving a detailed projection of the child's current and future material needs, offset against the parents' employment status, income, access to state support and other financial commitments. While it is now accepted that maintenance arrangements can include lump sum as well as periodical payments,[6] the term normally implies an ongoing economic relationship between the parents and the child which is subject to renegotiation as circumstances change and new needs arise.[7] In the majority of cases, child maintenance arrangements are negotiated and reviewed privately between the parties. However, widespread problems associated with the ongoing enforcement of such agreements—particularly as new relationships and the parties' financial resources are diverted—compel a significant proportion of parents to resort to formal processes.

The challenges associated with determining and enforcing child maintenance are exacerbated in an international situation by the sheer geographical distance between parties and by the problems inherent in navigating foreign legal, administrative and social systems. For example, it may be more difficult to obtain access

---

[2] C Skinner, J Bradshaw and J Davidson, *Child Support Policy: An International Perspective—Research Report No 405* (Leeds, Department for Work and Pensions, 2007). Reported also in C Skinner and J Davidson, 'Recent Trends in Child Maintenance Schemes in 14 Countries' (2009) 23 *International Journal of Law, Policy and the Family* 23.

[3] 'Poverty' here being defined in accordance with OECD guidelines which sets the child poverty threshold at 50% of median net disposable income. See H Frazer and E Marlier, *Tackling Child Poverty and Promoting the Social Inclusion of Children in the EU—Key Lessons* (Brussels, European Commission, 2007).

[4] Of course, it is difficult to make generalisations in this regard given that maintenance contributions are typically offset against welfare benefit entitlement, depending on the calculation methods in place at the national level. See further T Ridge, 'Supporting Children? The Impact of Child Support Policies on Children's Well-being in the UK and Australia (2005) 34 *Journal of Social Policy* 121.

[5] For a detailed analysis of child poverty in this broader sense of the word, see J Bradshaw, P Hoelscher and D Richardson, 'An Index of Child Well-Being in the European Union' (2007) 80 *Social Indicators Research* 133; G Redmond, 'Child Poverty and Child Rights: Edging Towards a Definition' (2008) 14 *Journal of Children and Poverty* 63 and The Social Protection Committee, *Child Poverty and Well-Being in the EU: Current Status and Way Forward* (Luxembourg, European Communities, 2008).

[6] Case C-220/95 *Antonius Van den Boogaard v Paula Laumen* [1997] ECR I-01147.

[7] Memoranda submitted by Mavis Maclean Ev 84 to Work and Pensions Committee (Oral Evidence, Wednesday 17 January 2007).

to information relating to the absent parent's financial assets or employment status, while evaluations of 'wealth' or income may need to account for economic trends and the cost of living in different Member States and, indeed, between regions within those Member States.[8]

There is significant divergence between Member States as to how maintenance is defined, assessed and enforced.[9] In their comparative study, Skinner and others classify maintenance systems into three main categories: first, court-determined agreements, as in Belgium, Austria, Germany, Sweden and France; second,those based on assessments made by an agency or other administrative body which also retains primary responsibility for the collection and enforcement of the agreement, as in Denmark and the UK and third the 'hybrid' systems where responsibility for determining and enforcing maintenance is shared between administrative and judicial authorities, as in Finland and the Netherlands.[10] Practices also differ as to whether pre-tax or net income is taken into account in assessing the non-resident (typically the father's) income,[11] and in how maintenance payments are reviewed.[12]

The diversity of national approaches to child maintenance reinforces the need for clarity and uniformity in cases that straddle jurisdictional boundaries. This has been achieved with varying degrees of success through a number of international instruments including the United Nations Convention on the Recovery Abroad of Maintenance 1956,[13] the Hague Convention on the Recognition and Enforcement of Decisions Relating to Maintenance Obligations 1973,[14] the 2007 Hague Convention on the International Recovery of Child Support and other forms of Maintenance,[15] and the rather more modest Council of Europe Recommendation on payment

---

[8] HL Ackers and H Stalford, *A Community for Children? Children, Citizenship and Migration in the European Union*, (Aldershot, Ashgate, 2004), 187.

[9] N Wikeley, *Child Support: Law and Policy* (Oxford, Hart, 2006) 3.

[10] Above n 1. See also K Boele-Woelki, B Braat and I Curry-Sumner (eds), *European Family Law in Action*, vol II (Antwerp, Intersentia, 2003) for an overview of different Member States' approaches to (primarily spousal) maintenance arrangements. These arrangements are also subject to variation if the case involves cross-national enforcement of child maintenance. For instance, responsibility for recovery of maintenance within England and Wales currently lies with the Child Maintenance and Enforcement Commission (CMEC) whereas cross-national cases are generally dealt with by the court. See C Bradley, 'Resolution: Resolution's International Committee' (2009) 3 *International Family Law Journal* 201.

[11] Skinner et al, *Recent Trends*, above n 2, 38.

[12] Some countries automatically review child maintenance amounts annually in line with inflation or price indexes (such as Belgium, France and Denmark). In the Netherlands and Finland, amounts are increased in line with the cost of raising a child or the cost of living index, while in Austria and the UK, adjustments in maintenance do not occur automatically but rather rely on individual parties requesting a review in the light of a change in their circumstances. Skinner et al, *Recent Trends*, above n 2, 48.

[13] The United Nations Convention on the Recovery Abroad of Maintenance 1956.

[14] The Hague Convention on the Recognition and Enforcement of Decisions Relating to Maintenance Obligations 1973, concluded 2 October 1973.

[15] The 2007 Hague Convention on the International Recovery of Child Support and other forms of Maintenance, concluded 23 November 2007. This is discussed in more detail later in the chapter.

by the state of advances on child maintenance.[16] Measures at the EU level have developed in tandem with these instruments, formerly on the legal basis of Article 65 EC and, since the Treaty of Lisbon, on the basis of Art 81 of the Treaty on the Functioning of the European Union (TFEU), primarily with a view to achieving the EU's internal market objectives of facilitating the free movement of persons.[17]

EU LEGAL FRAMEWORK GOVERNING CROSS-NATIONAL
CHILD MAINTENANCE

EU child maintenance provision boasts a surprisingly long history, pre-dating EU divorce and parental responsibility legislation by some 30 years, although it started life as a rather more general, intergovernmental instrument aimed at ensuring cross-national enforcement of commercial and civil obligations.[18] As with other family measures, it was the Treaty of Amsterdam which marked the turning point in the way that cross-national maintenance issues were regulated since it transferred issues relating to judicial co-operation in civil matters from the third intergovernmental pillar into the law-making scope of the (then) EC Treaty (formerly Title IV, Arts 61–69). This prompted the transposition of the intergovernmental Brussels I Convention into uniformly applicable and binding legislation.[19] Like the preceding Convention, this Regulation—commonly referred to as the 'Brussels I Regulation'—was of general application, limited to harmonising *procedures* for determining jurisdiction as well as cross-national recognition and enforcement in all civil and commercial matters. To the extent that spousal and child maintenance were expressly included within its material scope,[20] the instrument served to ensure that maintenance orders could be enforced by family members regardless of where they lived in the EU. The instrument was not without its critics, however. Objections were levelled primarily at the administrative requirements the Regulation imposed on applicants,[21] and at the

[16] Recommendation 869 (1979) on payment by the state of advances on child maintenance, adopted by the Standing Committee, acting on behalf of the Assembly, on 28 June 1979.

[17] For a more detailed examination of the interplay between EU family law and EU citizenship and free movement, see H Stalford, 'For Better, For Worse: The Relationship between EU Citizenship and EU Family Law' in N Shuibhne, M Dougan and E Spaventa (eds), *Empowerment and Disempowerment of the EU Citizen* (forthcoming Oxford, Hart, 2012).

[18] The Brussels Convention (EC) on Jurisdiction and the Enforcement of Judgments in Civil and Commercial Matters 1968 (commonly referred to as the 1968 Brussels Convention) [1972] OJ L299/32. This Convention was supplemented by the Lugano Convention 1988 to govern the mutual recognition of civil and commercial agreements between EU Member States and those of the European Free Trade Area including Switzerland, Iceland and Norway.

[19] Reg 44/2001 on jurisdiction and the recognition and enforcement of judgments in civil and commercial matters [2001] OJ L12/1.

[20] Art 4. Excluded from the scope of the Regulation were property rights arising out of marriage, wills, succession, bankruptcy, insolvency, social security and arbitration (Art 1).

[21] Art 38 required applicants to obtain a declaration of enforceability in order to enforce them in another Member State. This issue was subsequently addressed by the adoption of further EU legislation rendering the cross-national enforcement of maintenance decisions automatic. However, this

ongoing operation of the 'first seized' rule[22] which, it was claimed, encouraged a race between parties to establish jurisdiction over and above more conciliatory forms of dispute resolution.[23] The failure of the Regulation to resolve differences in applicable law between the Member States was another issue of concern in that couples (and practitioners) remained uncertain as to whether the family law of the forum seized (*lex fori*) or that of another country would be applied by the courts of the state that had been afforded jurisdiction to determine maintenance arrangements. The exclusion of non-maintenance related financial issues, such as matrimonial property, from the scope of the Regulation, as well as the legal disconnection of maintenance from divorce and parental responsibility issued by the Brussels II*bis* Regulation,[24] were equally derided for leading to unnecessary costs and delays and necessitating complex cross-referencing between different court decisions (sometimes issued in different jurisdictions).[25]

Responding to these concerns, the Commission adopted a Green Paper launching a debate on how to improve EU legal provision relating to cross-national maintenance disputes.[26] This eventually led to the adoption of a new Regulation devoted specifically to issues surrounding jurisdiction, enforcement, recognition and, for the first time, applicable law, relating to maintenance obligations.[27] The aim of this instrument is to extricate maintenance issues from the more general scope of the previous instrument with a view to streamlining, simplifying and clarifying procedures for enforcing maintenance decisions cross-nationally. It also introduced some notable amendments. First, it abolished altogether the requirement of a declaration of enforceability (*exequatur*) to render orders enforceable in any other Member State party to the Regulation.[28] It also introduced a range of measures to promote

---

was only applicable to uncontested orders (Reg 805/2004 creating a European Enforcement Order for uncontested claims [2004] OJ L143/15).

[22] Art 27.

[23] D Hodson, 'Fairness in Family Law across Europe: A Pan European Ideal or a Pandemonium of Cultural Clashes?' presented to the European Regional Conference of the International Society of Family Law, University of Chester, 17–21 July 2007.

[24] Formerly Reg 1347/2000 on jurisdiction and the recognition and enforcement of judgments in matrimonial matters and in matters of parental responsibility for children of both spouses [2000] OJ *L160/19*, and subsequently repealed and replaced by Reg 2201/2003 concerning jurisdiction and the recognition and enforcement of judgments in matrimonial matters and the matters of parental responsibility [2003] OJ *L338/1* (discussed fully in ch 4).

[25] M Harper, 'An English (Law) View of Brussels I and Brussels II' (2006) *International Family Law Journal* 9. See, also, I Karsten, 'The State of International Family Law Issues: A View from London' (2009) 1 *International Family Law Journal* 35.

[26] Commission Green Paper of 15 April 2004 on maintenance obligations COM (2004) 254 final.

[27] Reg 4/2009 on jurisdiction, applicable law, recognition and decisions and co-operation in matters relating to maintenance obligations [2008] OJ L7/1.

[28] Art 17 but see further below regarding the particular position of the UK. The Regulation does not prescribe any specific methods of enforcement which are subject to the national laws in question. Mechanisms are likely to include freezing orders and attachment of earnings orders against bank accounts, penalties such as loss of driving license, deductions from social security payments or orders for sale. See, further, D Eames, 'Maintenance Enforcement: The 2007 Hague Convention and the EC Regulation' (2008) 1 *International Family Law Journal* 47.

co-operation between national central authorities aimed, for example, at assisting creditors in obtaining information about the debtors' financial circumstances.[29]

As far as determining *child* maintenance is concerned, the Regulation provides that jurisdiction will be afforded to the same court that has jurisdiction to entertain proceedings concerning parental responsibility (which generally lies with the state in which the child is habitually resident).[30] Of course maintenance raises different issues to custody and access, with many commentators fervently opposing any conflation of the two issues or any suggestion that access be made conditional upon compliance with certain financial obligations.[31] Nevertheless, the determination of all of these issues within the same jurisdiction allows for a more contextualised, pragmatic and holistic assessment of the child's material needs by reference to the cultural, social and welfare environment in which the child is habitually resident, and by more direct reference to the nature of the custody and access arrangements put in place. This provision is limited, however, in that jurisdiction is afforded to the state of the child's habitual residence only in relation to maintenance cases that are *ancillary* to parental responsibility proceedings. Jurisdictional decisions relating to stand-alone child maintenance assessments, on the other hand, are decided in accordance with the general rules set out in the Regulation,[32] implying that they may well be decided in a completely different state in accordance with completely different laws than those applied to the parental responsibility decision.

TOWARDS HARMONISATION OF FAMILY LAW? THE NEW RULES ON APPLICABLE LAW

Perhaps the most contentious innovation of the Maintenance Regulation is the inclusion of harmonised rules on applicable law—that is, the specific national

---

[29] Arts 49–63.

[30] Art 3(d). See also Art 8 Reg 2201/2003 concerning jurisdiction and the recognition and enforcement of judgments in matrimonial matters and in matters of parental responsibility [2003] OJ L338 (hereafter, the Brussels II*bis* Regulation).

[31] LJ Weitzman and M Maclean, *Economic Consequences of Divorce: The International Perspective* (London, Clarendon Press, 1992); K Boele-Woelki (ed), *Common Core and Better Law in European Family Law* (Netherlands, Intersentia, 2005). Note, however, there is a significant body of research that reveals a distinct correlation between non-resident parents' propensity to comply with maintenance arrangements and the level of contact they have with their children. See, A Burgess, *The Costs and Benefits of Active Fatherhood. Evidence and Insights to Inform the Development of Policy and Practice* (Wiltshire, Fatherhood Institute, 2006); H Koball and D Principe, 'Do Non-Resident Fathers Who Pay Child Support Visit Their Children More?' Series B, no B-44 (Washington DC, The Urban Institute, 2002) 1; and N Wikely, E Ireland, C Bryson and R Smith, *Relationship Separation and Child Support Study*: DWP Research Report No 503 (Norwich, HMSO, 2008) and S Andrews, D Armstrong, L McLernon, S Megow and C Skinner, *Maintenance: Research on Instigating Behaviour Change*. Vol 1(London, Child Maintenance and Enforcement Commission, 2011).

[32] For stand-alone maintenance cases, Arts 3(a) and (b) state that jurisdiction will lie with the court or administrative agency where either the defendant or the creditor is habitually resident. Where parents bring maintenance proceedings simultaneously before the courts of different Member States, the court of the Member State first seized shall have jurisdiction and the court of the Member State second seized shall decline jurisdiction (Art 12). This, it is claimed, will encourage further instances of strategic forum shopping, with little or no regard to the specific interests or vulnerabilities of the parties concerned, including the child. See M Thorpe, 'London: The Divorce Capital of the World' (2009) 39 *Family Law* 21.

rules that govern a cross-national dispute once jurisdiction has been determined. Previously such rules were determined on the basis of the applicable law rules in place in the Member State afforded jurisdiction. These rules differ from country to country: most apply applicable law by reference to various 'connecting factors'—such as the common nationality of both parties (*lex patriae*) or the state where the marriage was celebrated (*lex loci celebrationis*)—to ensure that any divorce or related financial proceedings are governed by the legal order with which the marriage has the closest connection. However other Member States, such as the territories of the UK, routinely apply their own law by virtue of the fact that they have jurisdiction (*lex fori*) regardless of the parties' connection with other Member States.

Proposals to harmonise applicable law rules were prompted by concerns as to the legal uncertainty they created, making it difficult for parties to predict which law would apply to their proceedings even after jurisdiction had been determined. For example, a British couple may seize the Portuguese courts to determine child maintenance allocation on the basis that they and their children have lived there for a decade, presuming that the issue will be governed by Portuguese law, only to find that the Portuguese authorities will apply the UK rules on the basis of the couple's nationality. While providing much needed clarity and predictability, these harmonised rules were also aimed at undermining any unfair advantage parties sought to gain from racing to seize jurisdiction: essentially all Member States would be subjected to the same principles in determining which laws would apply to a given case. Such proposals made perfect sense to the majority, but a minority of (primarily *lex fori*) states struggled to see how setting aside their national family laws and applying those of another country would add clarity and predictability to proceedings. The UK, a staunch defender of the *lex fori* approach, objected particularly vociferously, so much so that it resolved to join Denmark in opting out of the Regulation entirely[33] and stalled the process of adoption for the remaining states.

All was not lost, as consultation surrounding the Regulation coincided with negotiations for a new Hague Convention on the International Recovery of Child Support and Other Forms of Family Maintenance.[34] Achieving international consensus on applicable law was an equally prominent ambition of this instrument but to accommodate the UK's dissent it confined the rules on applicable law to an optional Protocol attached to the main Convention which it allowed all states

---

[33] By virtue of Art 1 of the Protocol on the position of the United Kingdom and Ireland, annexed to the (then) Treaty on European Union and to the Treaty Establishing the European Community.

[34] Hague Convention on International Recovery of Child Support and Family Maintenance (done at The Hague November 23, 2007). This was adopted by 57 states, including all of the EU Member States. For a detailed analysis of the relationship between the Hague Maintenance Convention and the Brussels Maintenance Regulation see P Beaumont, 'International Family Law in Europe: The Maintenance Project, the Hague Conference and the EC—A Triumph of Reverse Subsidiarity' (2009) 73 *RabelsZ Bd* 509. Further clarification on the rationale for some of the EU maintenance provisions can be gleaned from A Borrás and J Degeling, 'Convention of 23 November 2007 on the International Recovery of Child Support and Other Forms of Family Maintenance Explanatory Report' (The Hague, Hague Conference on Private International Law, November 2009).

to opt into separately.[35] These rules provide that determination of maintenance obligations shall be governed by the law of the country in whose territory the creditor (usually the custodial mother) is habitually resident. Thus, even if the courts of the debtor's habitual residence have *jurisdiction* to decide on the issue, they will be obliged to apply the *law* of the creditor's—and, by implication, the child's—habitual residence. The Convention provides some exceptions to this principle based variously on the parties' joint choice as to an alternative applicable law, or on the law of a country that has a 'closer connection' to the maintenance claim, although such exceptions are generally only applicable to maintenance claims between adults rather than child maintenance specifically.[36] The EU Regulation was subsequently amended to reflect these measures insofar as the instrument now merely defers to the provisions of the Hague Convention with respect to the rules governing applicable law.[37] Only those states that opt into the Protocol, however, can benefit from the new, more flexible rules relating to automatic recognition of foreign judgments (the abolition of *exequatur*). It follows then that, until such time as it signs the Protocol, the old rules relating to *exequatur* will continue to apply to UK judgments before they will be recognised in other Member States, thus making enforcement more difficult. Conversely, foreign judgments will be automatically recognised in the UK territories.

IS THE EU MAINTENANCE REGULATION COMPATIBLE
WITH CHILDREN'S RIGHTS?

Having summarised the main features of the EU Maintenance Regulation, questions remain as to whether it is truly congruent with children's rights simply by virtue of the fact that it includes child maintenance within its scope. Certainly, the Regulation should be applauded for adding a modicum of clarity and expedience to cross-national maintenance proceedings and for facilitating more vulnerable parties' access to justice. However, having already acknowledged that maintenance is unequivocally about protecting children's rights to an adequate standard of living in the material sense—and to life, survival and development in the broader sense—it is perhaps surprising that the Regulation fails to make a single reference to the welfare needs of the child.[38] The emphasis instead is firmly on enforcing

---

[35]   Eames, 'Maintenance Enforcement' above n 28.

[36]   In general then, maintenance claims involving children will continue to be determined by the law of the state of the creditor's habitual residence.

[37]   Art 15 states that decisions as to the law applicable to maintenance obligations 'are to be determined in accordance with the Hague Protocol of 23 November 2007 on the law applicable to maintenance obligations in the Member States bound by that instrument'.

[38]   The Regulation does make some concessions that suggest an implicit acknowledgement that access to appropriate financial support from parents is a fundamental children's *right*. Notably, in actions involving children under the age of 18, all Member States are obliged to provide legal aid in respect of claims made through the central authority, provided they are not 'manifestly unfounded' (Art 46). Moreover, the freedom of the parties to choose the jurisdiction in which to settle the

parental obligations, protecting the rights of the 'maintenance creditor' (generally the parent with care or the state), and on promoting the proper administration of justice within the European Union.[39] This is perhaps not surprising given the need to delineate EU competence in determining the precise conditions for child maintenance—that is, to ensure that the substance and scope of child maintenance entitlement remains firmly within the preserve of domestic legislatures.

Interestingly, some national family maintenance systems have been similarly criticised for their implicit preoccupation with reducing levels of public expenditure on supporting lone-parent families rather than on upholding the rights of the child per se.[40] An illustration of how easily individual rights are obscured within maintenance cases is provided by the English case of *R (Kehoe) v Secretary of State for Work and Pensions*[41] in which the (then) House of Lords confirmed that child maintenance under English law can only be enforced through the intermediary of the Child Support Agency; the parent with care has no standing in this respect, and children are certainly not allowed to enforce such a right in their own interests.[42] Such an approach has bewildered some commentators, including McKay who has remarked:

> It is a strange world in which the state, which often has no interest in collecting money privately, is the one who has to collect it and the individual who does have the interest in actually receiving it does not have that power.[43]

Wikeley further contends that such a decision is also incompatible with Article 27(4) UNCRC which provides that state parties shall take 'all appropriate measures' to secure the recovery of maintenance for children from their parents. In fact, the position adopted in England and Wales is at odds with other European jurisdictions. In France, for example, parents with care of the child can recoup maintenance arrears directly from the non-resident parent's employer, bank, unemployment benefit agency or pension insurance funds.[44] Direct enforcement

---

maintenance dispute is restricted in cases involving children (Art 4(3)). A likely explanation for this is that the Regulation encourages parties to resolve ancillary child maintenance disputes in the same Member State that is dealing with the question of parental responsibility, and the Regulation already provides that jurisdiction will generally lie with the Member State in which the child is habitually resident (Art 3(d)—referred to above). To allow parties, therefore, to change the jurisdiction by mutual agreement (save where it is patently in the best interests of the child) would be to undermine this principle.

[39] Paras 8, 14 and 15.

[40] J Eekelaar and M Maclean, *The Parental Obligation* (Oxford, Hart, 1997).

[41] *R (Kehoe) v Secretary of State for Work and Pensions* [2005] UKHL 48, [2005] 1 AC 42.

[42] See, however, the powerful dissenting opinion of Baroness Hale, above n 41, para 49, as well as the detailed commentary of N Wikeley, 'A Duty But Not a Right: Child Support after *R (Kehoe) v Secretary of State for Work and Pensions*' (2006) 2 *Child and Family Law Quarterly* 287 and N Wikeley, 'Case Commentary: *R (Kehoe) v Secretary of State for Work and Pensions*: No Redress When the Child Support Agency Fails to Deliver' (2005) 17 *Child and Family Law* Quarterly 113.

[43] Extract taken from House of Commons, Work and Pensions Committee, and Child Support Reform, *Report of Session 2006-07 Together with Formal Minutes* (London, The Stationery Office, 2007) 63.

[44] For a summary of different countries' maintenance procedures, see *A Comparative Study of Child Maintenance Regimes*, available at: york.ac.uk/inst/spru/research/childsupport.

is also available to parents with care in Germany, Austria and Belgium, while in Scotland a child who has reached the age of 12 can issue maintenance proceedings in their own right.[45]

Such divergence in national approaches illustrates the point that children's rights will differ much more markedly in the context of maintenance proceedings depending on the state in which the application is being heard.[46] There is no universal right of either application or enforcement that equates with the competent child's universal right to participate in proceedings concerning custody and access. Children's material welfare following divorce or parental separation is, therefore, entirely subject to the relevant national law, making the likelihood of any financial relief not only dependent on their custodial parent pursuing a maintenance claim, but also on the relevant authorities ensuring such obligations are enforced. The effect of this is to further disenfranchise even the most competent of children, effectively placing any decision to enforce parents' financial obligations in the hands of adult proxies or at the mercy of resource intensive, excessively bureaucratic and, in some cases, dysfunctional national enforcement procedures.[47]

RECOVERY OF CHILD MAINTENANCE UNDER EU FREE MOVEMENT LAW

The state-centric approach of national family law to the regulation of child maintenance may explain the EU's ambivalence to children's rights within the maintenance Regulation, but it also reveals some inconsistency with other areas of EU law addressing child support. In the context of the free movement of persons, for example, the Court of Justice has specifically upheld children's right to claim state-provided maintenance even following a move to another Member State in the event that their parents 'back home' default on payments.[48] This approach is entirely, although perhaps not consciously, in keeping with Article 27(4) of the UNCRC which provides that:

> States Parties shall take all appropriate measures to secure the recovery of maintenance for the child from the parents or other persons having financial responsibility for the child, both within the State Party and from abroad. In particular, where the person having financial responsibility for the child lives in a State different from that of the child, States Parties shall promote the accession to international agreements or the conclusion of such agreements, as well as the making of other appropriate arrangements.

---

[45] Art 7(1). Child Support Act 1991.
[46] H Stalford, 'Old Problems, New Solutions? EU Regulation Of Cross-National Child Maintenance' (2003) 15 *Child and Family Law Quarterly* 269, 269; I Curry-Sumner, 'Transnational Recovery of Child Maintenance in Europe: The Future is Bright, The Future is Central Authorities' in Masaryk University, *Days of Public Law: Collection of Arts* (Brno, Masaryk University, 2007).
[47] H Xanthaki, 'The Judiciary-Based System of Child Support in Germany, France and Greece: An Effective Suggestion?' (2000) 22 *Journal of Social Welfare and Family Law* 295.
[48] Case C-85/99 *Offermans* [2001] ECR-2261; Case C-255/99 *Humer* [2002] ECR-1205.

While the Court of Justice's approach in these cases was concerned much more with ensuring the smooth portability of welfare entitlement under free movement and social security legislation,[49] its recognition of the children's direct claims to cross-border financial support represents a significant endorsement of children as individual rights holders under EU law. This approach also reinforces the congruence between the EU's internal market pursuits and the protection and promotion of children's rights: a congruence that has yet to be fully articulated in the context of the EU Maintenance Regulation.

To conclude this discussion of EU child maintenance provision, it seems fair to say that the development of a harmonised procedure for determining jurisdiction, recognition and enforcement offers much needed clarity and consistency to cross-national child maintenance disputes. This will undoubtedly benefit children who are vulnerable to financial hardship in the wake of parental relationship breakdown. There is little point, however, in developing supra-national regulation in the field of maintenance if, on the ground, national enforcement procedures are selective, overly-bureaucratic and insensitive to children's rights. As such, any remaining limitations of the current EU Maintenance Regulation are largely symptomatic of persistent administrative and ideological shortcomings in national child maintenance processes.[50] While some of these problems should, in time, be ironed out as communication between the central authorities of each Member State becomes more routine and lucid,[51] it is disappointing that, yet again, the EU has declined to exploit the opportunity to articulate more persuasively the children's rights imperative driving maintenance provision.

EU DEVELOPMENTS IN THE FIELD OF FAMILY MEDIATION

Another aspect of family law to have come under the EU legal spotlight since the mid 1990s is that of mediation. Mediation is now widely advocated by family law practitioners as an effective means of resolving matrimonial and parental

---

[49] Specifically, Reg 1612/68 [1968] OJ L257/2 (subsequently revised as Reg 492/2011 on freedom of movement for workers within the Union [2011] OJ L 141/1) and Reg 1408/71 [1997] OJ L28/1, now Reg 883/2004 on the co-ordination of social security systems [2004] OJ L200/1. For a more detailed discussion of the way in which entitlement to welfare provision can be claimed cross-nationally, see M Dougan, 'Expanding the Frontiers of Union Citizenship by Dismantling Territorial Boundaries of National Welfare States' in C Barnard and O Odudu (eds), *The Outer Limits of EU Law* (Oxford, Hart, 2009) 119–65 and for an analysis of how the benefits associated with free movement and EU citizenship can be applied analogously to EU family law, see Stalford , 'For Better, For Worse' above n 17.

[50] It is these very shortcomings that the Hague Conference has been aiming to avoid through its latest intervention. See W Duncan, 'The Development of the New Hague Convention on the International Recovery of Child Support and Other Forms of Family Maintenance' (2004) 38 *Family Law Quarterly* 663; W Duncan, 'The Hague Convention of 23 November 2007 on the International Recovery of Child Support and Other Forms of Family Maintenance: Comments on its Objectives and Some of its Special Features' in G Buono and P Volken (eds), *Yearbook of Private International Law*, vol X 2008 (Germany, Sellier, 2009).

[51] Ch VII (Arts 49–64) Reg 4/2009.

responsibility disputes and of minimising much of the trauma, acrimony and, indeed, financial cost associated with judicial proceedings.[52] The Council of Europe promotes mediation as a means of protecting children, the European Convention on the Exercise of Children's Rights recommends it for all disputes affecting children,[53] and the Committee of Ministers' Recommendation on Family Mediation encourages all Member States' governments to introduce and promote family mediation provision and sets out a series of procedural principles to guide the formulation of such measures.[54] A persuasive message, indeed, although none of these instruments boast many signatories.

The EU's endorsement of mediation began in earnest in 2002 when the European Commission presented a Green Paper reviewing existing mediation methods in Europe and initiating widespread consultations with Member States and interested parties on possible measures to promote its use.[55] This publication drew attention to the specific benefits that mediation could bring to disputes of a cross-national nature:

> Cross-border disputes tend to result in even more lengthy proceedings and higher court costs than domestic disputes. With the completion of the internal market, the intensification of trade and the mobility of citizens, irrespective of the importance of the issue or the monetary value involved, disputes between citizens from different Member States and between persons residing in different Member States, amplified by the expansion of cross-border e-commerce, are steadily increasing, and the number of cross-border disputes being brought before the courts is increasing correspondingly. In addition to the practical problem of overworked courts, these disputes often raise complex issues which involve conflicts of laws and jurisdiction and practical difficulties of finance and language.[56]

Subsequently, in July 2004, the Commission developed a voluntary Code of Conduct for Mediators setting out a number of principles relating to, for example, competence, advertising, impartiality, fees and confidentiality.[57] The proposal for

---

[52] Of course there are instances in which mediation is deemed to be entirely inappropriate, notably where there is a history of domestic violence, or in certain cases of parental child abduction. Also, a number of commentators have criticised the tendency to present the debate about the relative merits of in-court and alternative dispute resolution (including mediation) as entirely polarised. They endorse, instead, a rather more nuanced, holistic approach that responds to the complex needs that families face in the aftermath of family breakdown, which appeals to a range of legal and non-legal interventions, depending on the context. See further M Maclean, 'Family Mediation: Alternative or Additional Dispute Resolution? An Editorial' (2010) 32 *Journal of Social Welfare and Family Law* 1 and R Dingwall, 'Divorce Mediation: Should We Change our Mind?' (2010) 32 *Journal of Social Welfare and Family Law* 107.

[53] ETS 160, 25 January 1996, Art 13.

[54] Recommendation no R (98) 1. Such principles emphasise the need to ensure the impartiality of the mediator, the voluntary nature of participation, the accessibility and flexibility of the process, and the need to provide specific training for mediators, particularly in the context of international family disputes. See also the Council of Europe's Parliamentary Assembly Recommendation 1639 (2003) (1) on family mediation and equality of sexes, 25 November 2003.

[55] COM (2002) 196 final.

[56] Above n, para 6, 7.

[57] European Commission, 'European Code of Conduct for Mediators' (2004) available at: ec.europa.eu/civiljustice/adr/adr_ec_code_conduct_en.pdf.

a Directive on Certain Aspects of Mediation in Civil and Commercial Matters[58] followed rather more swiftly than the final instrument which was not adopted until some four years later, in 2008.[59] The instrument applies to almost all cross-national matters falling within the scope of EU civil and commercial law[60] and, while deliberately thin on detail,[61] it provides a useful framework for negotiating complex and often sensitive matters in a non-adversarial way. Thus, despite its broad scope, it is a potentially valuable mechanism for encouraging a swifter, more conciliatory response to family disputes involving children.

Notwithstanding the likely benefits of an EU mediation instrument, there are a number of procedural and logistical issues that might hamper its effective operation when applied to family proceedings involving children. The first issue relates to what was identified as a lack of professional capacity to deliver an effective international mediation service to the standard envisaged by the Directive. The second concern relates to whether the European Mediation Directive is sufficiently amendable to children's rights. And the third concern questions the *need* for a distinct instrument covering family mediation, particularly in the light of existing EU provision in the family arena.

ACHIEVING EFFECTIVE CROSS-NATIONAL MEDIATION

There is no doubt that mediation is an increasingly favoured alternative to family litigation within most nation states, as highlighted by the Commission's Green Paper referred to above. Despite unquestionable international consensus on the benefits of mediation, national approaches to its regulation, funding, staffing and enforcement vary significantly, as does the status of children in such processes. In some countries, such as France, it is a compulsory pre-requisite of judicial proceedings;[62] in others, like Austria, it is a voluntary undertaking by the parties and in countries such as Ireland and Germany the judge will often adjourn proceedings to enable mediation to proceed.[63] Only a minority of countries, such as

---

[58] COM (2004) 718 final, 22 October 2004.

[59] Dir 2008/52 on certain aspects of mediation in civil and commercial matters [2008] OJ L136/3.

[60] Revenue, customs or administrative matters are explicitly excluded from the scope of the instrument (Art 1).

[61] The lack of detail reflects the Commission and Parliament's desire to adopt a 'light touch' and flexible approach to a process which, for all intents and purposes, remains largely voluntary.

[62] Arts 252–252-3 C.Civ. The reference here is to conciliation (for which legal representation is compulsory) rather than mediation although the provisions refer to the option to appoint an independent mediator should the parties fail to meet an agreement.

[63] For a more detailed cross-national comparative overview of family mediation procedures see the Hague Conference Permanent Bureau, 'Feasibility Study on Cross-Border Mediation in Family Matters' (The Hague Conference on Private International Law, Preliminary Document no 20, 2007) 5–14; S Kiesewetter, 'Emerging Good Practices in the Polish-German Mediation Project' (Strasbourg, Paper to the 7th European Conference on Family Law themed International Family Mediation, Council of Europe, 16 March 2009). On the cross-cultural dynamics of mediation, see S Shah-Kazemi, 'Cross-Cultural

Sweden, have introduced laws enabling children to be involved in mediation as a matter of routine unless it is inappropriate and contrary to their best interests.[64]

Achieving effective mediation in the context of an international dispute raises additional challenges: parties will have to agree on which particular national mediation procedure to adopt, and they may have to appoint a bilingual mediator who is familiar with the legal systems of the countries implicated in the proceedings and has an appreciation of the distinct cultural norms shaping each party's perspective. International mediation also presents logistical challenges, requiring one party to travel across countries to participate, with work and financial constraints potentially restricting the amount of time available to negotiate a satisfactory agreement.[65] To accommodate such constraints, cross-national mediation will often take place over a weekend, placing intense pressure on the mediator and on the parties. Children add a further complication in the sense that any calls to engage in effective and meaningful child consultation may well give way to the more pragmatic desire to negotiate an agreement within the limited time available.[66]

Responding to the popularised assertion that mediation is an effective means of resolving family disputes, coupled with the progressive 'internationalisation' of relationship formation and dysfunction, a number of international regulatory mechanisms have been put in place. Bi-national mediation arrangements have been established between specific Member States[67] and efforts have been made, primarily at the instigation of mediators in France,[68] to develop practical training guidelines and set down minimum procedural standards for mediation practice. The Hague Conference, for its part, has initiated detailed expert consultation on international mediation with a view to developing more comprehensive, uniformly applicable guidelines.[69]

Mediation: A Critical View of the Dynamics of Culture in Family Disputes' (2000) 14 *International Journal of Law, Policy and the Family* 302.

[64] See C Bradley, 'Briefings' (2006) 3 *International Family Law Journal* 162, 164.

[65] Although the increasing availability of new communication technologies, such as online conferencing, addresses many of these problems.

[66] For more detailed discussion of the cultural, ethical and logistical challenges posed to cross-national mediation, see H Stalford, 'Crossing Boundaries: Reconciling Law, Culture and Values in International Family Mediation (2010) 2 *Journal of Social Welfare and Family Law (Special Issue on Mediation)* 155.

[67] The German Federal Ministry of Justice provides specific training for cross-national parental disputes and has established mediation schemes with both France and the United States with varying degrees of success. For further information on the Franco-German bi-national mediation project see S Alles, 'Franco-German Family Mediation: From the Experiences of a Parliamentary Pilot Project to New Prospects' (paper presented to the 7th European Conference on Family Law, Strasbourg, Council of Europe, 16 March 2009). The model developed by the German Federal Association for Family Mediation (Bundesarbeitsgemeinschaft für Familien-Mediation, or BAFM) provides perhaps the best example of cross-border mediation in Europe. Further details at: bafm-mediation.de.

[68] Notably the Association Pour la Médiation Familiale and the Association Internationale Francophone des Intervenants auprès des familles séparées (AIFI) have encouraged and developed cross-national networks of communication and exchange between mediators.

[69] Permanent Bureau of the Hague Conference on Private International Law, 'Feasibility Study on Cross-border Mediation in Family Matters—Responses to the Questionnaire' for the attention of the

EU MEDIATION DIRECTIVE

The EU Mediation Directive follows suit in responding to the persistent logistical and regulatory obstacles to cross-border mediation. First, acknowledging the divergence in national approaches, it begins by establishing a uniform working definition of 'mediation' as:

> Any process, however named or referred to, where two or more parties to a dispute are assisted by a third party to reach an agreement on the settlement of the dispute, and regardless of whether the process is initiated by the parties, suggested or ordered by a court or prescribed by the national law of the Member State.[70]

Similarly 'mediator' is defined as 'any third party conducting mediation, regardless of the denomination or profession of that third party in the Member States concerned and of the way the third party has been appointed or requested to conduct the mediation'.[71]

The Directive addresses the widespread lack of skills and capacity among mediators to respond to the specific demands of international couples by encouraging Member States to enhance training and to introduce quality assurance mechanisms and professional codes of conduct.[72] A further, dominant aim of the Directive is to encourage national courts to refer parties to mediation and to clarify the relationship between mediation and domestic judicial proceedings.[73] However, in contrast with other EU family law legislation, this instrument does not determine issues of cross-national jurisdiction, recognition or enforcement. This is probably because mediation operates on the basis of a voluntary undertaking and consensus between the parties, such that it would be counterintuitive to seek to regulate such matters. Furthermore, agreements made as a result of mediation can be generally transposed into more formal, binding terms by the court in accordance with national law, at which point reference can be made to alternative EU instruments to determine how such agreements can be enforced in other Member States. In that sense, the aims and scope of the Mediation Directive are deliberately confined to providing a non-adversarial framework for *negotiating* family decisions while the conditions of the subsequent *application* and *enforcement* of any formal decisions arising out of mediation will be governed by the Brussels II*bis* Regulation[74] or the Maintenance Regulation.[75]

Council of April 2008 on General Affairs and Policy of the Conference (The Hague, Preliminary Document no 10 of March 2008). See also Permanent Bureau of the Hague Conference on Private International Law, 'Draft Guide to Good Practice under the Hague Convention on the Civil Aspects of International Child Abduction, Part V—Mediation' (The Hague, Preliminary Document no 5 of 5 May 2011).

[70] Art 2(a). This provision explicitly excludes from the scope of the definition any attempts made by the judge to settle a dispute within the course of judicial proceedings.

[71] Art 2(b).

[72] Art 4.

[73] Art 1.

[74] Discussed fully in ch 4.

[75] The Directive states as much in para 20 of its Preamble.

MEDIATION: EMPOWERING ADULTS BUT DISEMPOWERING CHILDREN?

The general absence, at least at national level, of any regulatory scaffolding to support the mediation process is simultaneously its greatest strength and its greatest weakness. On the one hand, it is rather less intimidating, costly or time-consuming for the parties, tipping the balance of power in their collective favour, while providing the context for a more consensual and sustainable outcome. With that flexibility, however, comes a greater margin for deviation from minimum international standards that govern parties' status within decision-making processes. This is particularly true as far as children are concerned: in contrast with judicial proceedings, there is generally no explicit domestic legal obligation to uphold children's rights in the course of mediation. Instead, these obligations are derived from international law, which itself has limited effect unless explicitly incorporated into national law. The principles of best interests and participation are two obvious standards already identified within the family justice context. Article 3 UNCRC reaffirms the best interests' principle as the pre-eminent yardstick against which all family decisions should be made: 'In all actions concerning children, *whether undertaken by public or private social welfare institutions, courts of law, administrative authorities or legislative bodies*, the best interests of the child shall be a primary consideration'.[76] In the same vein, Article 12 imposes an obligation on states parties to assure that the child who is capable of forming his or her own views has the right to express those views freely in all matters affecting him or her. While this imposes a general obligation to consult with the competent child and to afford 'due weight' to that child's views, Article 12(1) further conditions the right, confining it to 'any judicial and administrative proceedings affecting the child'. The extent to which mediation, as an extra-judicial and non-administrative process, falls within the procedural scope of these provisions is unclear, and may explain the widespread failure of states to acknowledge children's status in this context. As a consequence, we are presented with a paradox whereby the flexible, unregulated nature of mediation—which lends itself to a more mutually consensual approach to family decision-making with likely long-term benefits for children—effectively divests children of the valuable rights they otherwise enjoy in the course of more adversarial judicial proceedings.[77]

The EU Mediation Directive reinforces this point by declining to make any reference to children at all.[78] This is perhaps unsurprising given the broad scope of the instrument—it applies to mediation in a range of commercial and civil law

---

[76] Emphasis added.

[77] See further G Dennison, 'Is Mediation Compatible with Children's Rights?' (2010) 2 *Journal of Social Welfare and Family Law (Special Issue on Mediation)* 169.

[78] The only hint of any acknowledgement of 'rights' within the proposal is the routine reference to the Charter of Fundamental Rights in the Preamble (para 27). This, of itself, is unlikely to augment children's individual rights under the instrument but see below for some discussion of the potential impact of the Charter following the Treaty of Lisbon.

settings—but the inclusion of family mediation within its compass should surely have prompted some consideration of children's interests.

The growing support for family mediation at national level is largely driven by the (somewhat contested) wisdom that non-litigious processes are likely to produce better outcomes for children.[79] The majority of its most ardent proponents would also argue that embracing alternative dispute resolution of this nature should not be to the detriment of children's involvement in the decision-making process. These observations are supported by an established body of research indicating that, if competently managed, more direct involvement of children in mediation reduces their anxiety, promotes a better understanding of the factors contributing to the parents' breakdown and assists children in adjusting to future custody and access arrangements.[80] Equally, placing children's best interests more consciously at the centre of mediation proceedings shifts the focus of negotiations away from the parents' experiences and desires, and focuses attention more firmly on the needs and interests of the child.[81] These conclusions are endorsed by the Council of Europe which, over a decade ago, asserted that:

> The mediator should have a special concern for the welfare and best interests of the children, should encourage parents to focus on the needs of children and should remind parents of their prime responsibility relating to the welfare of their children and the need for them to inform and consult their children.[82]

PROBLEMS OF ENFORCING MEDIATED AGREEMENTS RELATING TO CHILDREN

Aside from these empirical and ideological arguments, there is also a more technical reason why EU mediation provision should reflect national approaches to children's rights more consistently. Mediation and judicial family proceedings are not always mutually exclusive processes: mediation will often be promoted as the ideal starting point, and any decisions reached by the parties as a result of this are often submitted to the courts for ultimate approval and transposition into a binding agreement. Ultimate approval, however, may be subject to the observance of certain procedural formalities, including evidence of active consultation with all of the

---

[79] J Cashmore, 'Children's Participation in Family Law Matters' in C Hallett and A Prout (eds), *Hearing the Voices of Children: Social Policy for a New Century* (Bodmin, Routledge Falmer Press, 2003) 157. For a rather more cautious perspective on mediation, see Dingwall, *Divorce Mediation* above n 52.

[80] L Parkinson, *Family Mediation: Appropriate Dispute Resolution in a New Family Justice System*, 2nd edn (London, Family Law, Jordan Publishing, 2011); M Roberts, *Mediation in Family Disputes: Principles of Practice* (Farnham, Ashgate, 2008) ch 10 especially.

[81] See DT Lansky, LH Swift, E Manley, A Elmore and C Gerety, 'The Role of Children in Mediation' (1996) 14 *Conflict Resolution Quarterly* 147; D Saposnek, 'The Value of Children in Mediation: A Cross-Cultural Perspective' (1991) 8 *Conflict Resolution Quarterly* 325 and L Trinder, 'Conciliation, the Private Law Programme and Children's Wellbeing: Two Steps Forward, One Step Back?' (2008) 38 *Family Law* 338.

[82] Recommendation no R (98) 1, Principle III (viii).

parties concerned. EU measures governing cross-national child abduction illustrate this interplay between mediation and judicial proceedings: these provisions place an obligation on the parties to hear the competent child's views before a decision regarding return will be made and rendered enforceable.[83] The Regulation does not confine the obligation to hear children's views solely to judicial proceedings.[84] This is significant, particularly as mediation is now an increasingly favoured platform for resolving even the most complex of international parental responsibility disputes.[85] Indeed, Brussels II*bis* compels national central authorities to 'facilitate agreement between holders of parental responsibility *through mediation or other means,* and facilitate cross-border co-operation to this end'.[86] The instrument does not provide any further guidance on how mediation should be conducted, however. Rather, it seems we are to defer to national measures to fill in the gaps. If national mediation processes are not accompanied by the guidance or, indeed, the resources needed to give effect to the obligation to hear children's views, however, we are presented with an acute legal dilemma: the obligations imposed by EU child abduction law to ensure that the views of the competent child have been heard before an order to return will be enforceable simply becomes inoperable: many national mediation processes simply do not have a mechanism by which children can be consulted to activate this provision.

A second rather more dramatic consequence of the disparity between EU child consultation obligations and domestic mediation processes is that it effectively concedes authority to the EU to create new children's rights that are not endorsed by national family justice regimes. The issue of legal competence—or lack thereof—has routinely been used by the EU to rationalise its inertia in the field of children's rights such that EU measures have tended to merely reiterate rights that are already firmly entrenched in national systems. In this instance, however, the EU is reaching well beyond the boundaries of its competence to impose new children's rights obligations (the right to be heard), albeit in relation to the relatively obscure context of cross-border mediation. This situation is undoubtedly the result of clumsy legal drafting and ill-founded presumptions as to the scope of national mediation measures rather than a strategic endeavour to drive children's rights forward. The solution to this inconsistency, however, should lie not in deleting or ignoring those EU obligations, but rather, in encouraging nation states to reflect on and amend their mediation processes to accommodate

---

[83]   Arts 11(2) and 42(2) BII*bis* Reg—the scope and force of these measures are discussed in the light of the relevant case law in ch 4.

[84]   Nor, indeed, do Arts 12 and 13 of the Hague Convention 1980 to which it refers.

[85]   Reunite, *Mediation in International Parental Child Abduction: The Reunite Mediation Pilot Scheme* (Leicester, Reunite, 2006). See also M Freeman, *International Child Abduction: The Effects* (Leicester, Reunite, 2006).

[86]   Art 55(e), emphasis added. This obligation is presumed to apply equally to the operation of the 1980 Hague Child Abduction Convention in intra-EU disputes dealt with under Art 11 of the Revised Brussels II Regulation. See the Hague Conference Permanent Bureau, Feasibility Study no 20 (2007) (above n 63).

children's rights in a way that responds to the persuasive research in this area and adds some substance to the EU measures.

IS A SEPARATE LEGAL INSTRUMENT GOVERNING
CROSS-BORDER MEDIATION NECESSARY?

A final question on the topic of EU mediation measures relates specifically to the utility of the EU Mediation Directive itself. On a very basic level, it seems paradoxical to seek to impose supra-national regulation on a process of which the very essence is informality, flexibility and party autonomy. The Commission has justified the instrument on the grounds that it merely *encourages* the use of mediation without making it compulsory, that it facilitates access to justice for those less inclined or well-resourced to pursue more litigious routes, and that it promotes greater transparency and coherence as regards the process and effects of national mediation.[87] Notwithstanding these objectives, the likely impact of the instrument remains in doubt, particularly given that the Community operates solely within the confines of existing national procedures and is prohibited from imposing any direct, harmonised legal obligations.[88] In that sense, it could be seen as amounting to little more than a gentle persuasive nudge as to the virtues of mediation. Moreover, given that the instrument makes no reference to children at all, it will have little bearing on attempts to achieve a more child-focused approach to family mediation. This, it seems, remains subject entirely to national prescription, the will of parents and the skill and foresight of mediators.

A final issue that questions the necessity of including family issues within a separate Mediation Directive picks up on a point raised in the previous section relating to its interplay with other EU family instruments. The Brussels II*bis* Regulation requires central authorities to facilitate agreement between holders of parental responsibility through mediation. A parallel obligation, 'to encourage amicable solutions with a view to obtaining voluntary payment of maintenance, where suitable by use of mediation, conciliation or similar processes', features within the Maintenance Regulation too.[89] These provisions suggest that including family

---

[87] See Explanatory Memorandum accompanying the initial proposal for the Mediation Directive, 5–6 (above n 58).

[88] Explanatory Memorandum accompanying the initial proposal for the Mediation Directive, 3 (above n 58). Although this Directive covers mediation in family law matters, it extends only to the rights available to the parties under the law of the Member State in which mediation takes place. Moreover, if the content of an agreement resulting from family mediation is not enforceable in the Member State where it was concluded, this Directive does not enable the parties to circumvent the law of that Member State by having the agreement rendered enforceable in another Member State. This is supported by Reg (EC) 2201/2003 which specifically provides that such agreement must be enforceable in the Member State in which it was concluded. See European Parliament Legislative Resolution of 29 March 2007 on the proposal for a directive on certain aspects of mediation in civil and commercial matters COM (2004) 718—C6-0154/2004—2004/0251(COD), para 14.

[89] Art 51(2)(d).

issues within a more generic, stand-alone Mediation Directive which is decidedly ambivalent to children's rights is somewhat superfluous and perhaps even counter-productive. For the purposes of clarity, context and consistency, provisions relating to mediation should arguably be contained within the instruments that regulate the specific legal context to which they refer, which themselves should be amended to reflect more closely children's status in such processes. States need then look no further than the Commission's existing Code of Conduct on Mediation for supplementary guidance on appointment, procedure and content.[90]

CHILDREN, THE LISBON TREATY AND THE FUTURE OF EU FAMILY LAW

The discussion up to now has revealed a notable proliferation of EU activity in the field of family law since the late 1990s, and it appears that the EU institutions are showing no signs of relenting in their efforts to amend existing and develop new instruments. Most recent efforts for reform have focused on the procedural harmonisation of applicable rules concerning divorce and legal separation concluded under Brussels II*bis*.[91] Developments in this regard sought to address the legal confusion arising from the divergent conflicts of law rules in operation across the Member States. This divergence, it was argued, precluded most people involved in cross-national family disputes (and particularly those without the legal know-how and resources) from making an informed and confident choice about which country's system might best respond to their interests. This inevitably aggravated the delays and the legal costs typically associated with such proceedings. The EU's solution—harmonised rules on applicable law that would operate alongside the Brussels II*bis* Regulation, regardless of which jurisdiction was invoked by the parties—prompted a strong reaction from the Member States as well as from legal academics and practitioners.[92] Ultimately, the proposed instrument failed to attract the unanimity required for its adoption, with the result that enhanced co-operation measures were authorised in relation to the 14 Member States who voted to standardise their applicable law rules.[93]

Other proposals have focused largely on regulating the property rights of international families with a view to removing any anticipated obstacles to their

---

[90] Above n 57.

[91] Reg 1259/2010 [2010] OJ L343/10 (commonly referred to as Rome III). See also Dec 2010/405 authorising enhanced co-operation in the area of the law applicable to divorce and legal separation [2010] OJ L189/12.

[92] A Borras, 'From Brussels II to Brussels II*bis* and further' in K Boele-Woelki and C González Beilfuss (eds), *Brussels IIbis: Its Impact and Application in the Member States* (Antwerp, Intersentia, 2007); A Fiorini, 'Rome III—A Step too far for the Europeanisation of Private International Law?' (2008) 22 *IJLPL* 178 and M Harding, 'The Harmonisation of Private International Law in Europe: Taking the Character Out of Family Law?' (2011) 1 *Journal of Private International Law* 203.

[93] Spain, Italy, Luxembourg, Hungary, Austria, Romania, Slovenia, Bulgaria, France, Germany, Belgium, Latvia, Malta and Portugal. The remaining 13 states will continue to apply their own conflict of laws rules to determine which national laws will govern such matters. Reg 1259/2010 [2010] OJ L343/10 (commonly referred to as Rome III). See also Dec 2010/405 authorising enhanced co-operation in the area of the law applicable to divorce and legal separation [2010] OJ L189/12.

movement between the Member States. These include proposals in relation to the division of matrimonial property,[94] the property consequences of registered partnerships,[95] and succession.[96] All of these areas are of at least tangential reference to children as the ultimate beneficiaries of the legal predictability, autonomy and financial security generated by such instruments.

Further, child-related developments in the field of EU family justice have been triggered by the Lisbon Treaty, albeit in a subtle manner. The new legal basis on which EU family justice measures are enacted, Article 81 TFEU, is slightly broader in scope than the legal basis it replaced (ex Art 65 EC). Thus, while previously the EU was only authorised to enact family justice measures '*in so far as* is necessary for the proper functioning of the internal market', Article 81 TFEU allows the EU to enact measures '*particularly* when necessary for the proper functioning of the internal market'. This delicate change in wording suggests that the development of harmonised family justice measures need no longer be justified exclusively on the basis of removing obstacles to mobility between the Member States, but instead, can be proposed on any number of grounds not linked to the internal market at all. Such a prospect may well cause concern for those who have already objected strongly to EU intervention in the sacrosanct domain of domestic family justice, but the potential this creates for more effective regulation of child protection issues (such as child abuse or domestic violence) that straddle jurisdictional and geographical territories are indeed welcome.[97]

In relation to the legislative process, while the Lisbon Treaty has entrenched the more democratic 'ordinary legislative procedure' as the default legislative process in relation to most issues,[98] the rather more restrictive 'special legislative procedure'[99] is retained in relation to cross-border family law measures.[100] The restrictive nature of this process is partially offset by the option to introduce a

---

[94] Proposal for a Regulation on jurisdiction, applicable law and the recognition and enforcement of decisions in matters of matrimonial property regimes COM (2011) 126 final, 16 March 2011 (colloquially referred to as Rome IV). For a summary of some of the English practitioners' objections to proposed legislation in this area, see Karsten, 'The State' above n 25.

[95] Proposal for a Regulation on jurisdiction, applicable law and the recognition and enforcement of decisions regarding the property consequences of registered partnerships COM (2011) 127 final, 16 March 2011. This is a particularly welcome development given the divergence in Member States' approach to registered partnerships, only 14 of which legally recognise registered partnership.

[96] Proposal for a Regulation on jurisdiction, applicable law, recognition and enforcement of decisions and authentic instruments in matters of succession and the creation of a European Certificate of Succession COM (2009) 154 final, 14 October 2009.

[97] Spain, during its presidency of the EU in 2011, announced plans to develop an EU-wide protection order for victims of domestic violence to ensure that contact bans and injunctions issued in one Member State can be enforced in other Member States to which the victim (and her children) moves.

[98] It is more democratic because of the enhanced involvement of the European Parliament in the process as compared to other legislative processes.

[99] Art 289(1)–(3) TFEU. Otherwise referred to as 'consultation' or 'consent', these special procedures imply less input from the European Parliament and are typically accompanied by a requirement for unanimous voting in favour of a proposal by members of the Council.

[100] Art 81(3) TFEU.

so-called 'passerelle clause' which gives the Council the option to apply the ordinary legislative procedure to aspects of cross-border family law provision.[101]

While these procedural changes are unlikely to bring about any radical extension of EU competence in relation to family matters (indeed, it is questionable whether such an extension is desirable) the elevated status of fundamental rights following the Lisbon Treaty may prove particularly fruitful in enhancing children's rights in this context. Notably, it affords the same legal value to the Charter of Fundamental Rights as is attributed to the Treaties.[102] Chapter two has already explored the implications of this for children's rights, notably through the inclusion within Article 24 of the Charter of the normative children's rights principles of best interests and participation, as well as a right to maintain '... on a regular basis a personal relationship and direct contact with both his or her parents...'. However, it is not entirely clear whether the elevated constitutional status of the Charter will, of itself, impact in any tangible way on the protection and promotion of children's family rights at EU level. Certainly the Treaty emphasises that the more explicit reference to the Charter does not extend in any way the competences of the Union to enact measures which are not otherwise authorised by the Treaty.[103] Moreover, commentators have noted that the Charter merely embodies a series of 'exhortatory principles'[104]—of which Article 24 is a good example—rather than new, justiciable rights. Such principles, as Dougan notes:

> Cannot in themselves form the basis of directly effective individual rights, enforceable even in the absence of necessary implementing measures at Union or national level; but should instead act merely as useful yardsticks against which to measure the relevant success (or otherwise) of Union/national regulatory activity.[105]

The explicit reference to the Charter within the Treaty of Lisbon is probably more realistically to be viewed as a source of inspiration guiding the Union's interpretation of fundamental rights within the strict confines of EU regulatory competence[106] rather than as a source of additional rights. While accepting these limitations, the fact that children's rights are acknowledged as a discrete aspect of

---

[101] Art 81(2) TFEU. To do this, the national parliaments must be notified of the proposed deferral to the ordinary legislative process which they have a right to veto within six months (Art 81(3) TFEU). See further H Stalford and M Schuurman, 'Are We There Yet? The Impact of the Lisbon Treaty on the EU Children's Rights Agenda' (2011) 19 *International Journal of Children's Rights* 7, in which we note that: 'National parliaments' veto right could prove interesting in the context of children's rights, particularly given the political sensitivities surrounding EU measures in the field of family justice: on the one hand, we may well see national parliaments exploiting this opportunity to voice their objections to EU legislative provision relating to children if the legal basis for such action is questionable and if it is deemed to infringe too much on domestic sovereignty. On the other hand, however, national parliaments may well push for enhanced provision within EU instruments with a view to maximising the protection available for children implicated in cross-national family proceedings'.

[102] Art 6(1) TEU.

[103] Art 6(1) Treaty of Lisbon.

[104] M Dougan, 'The Treaty of Lisbon 2007: Winning Minds, Not Hearts' (2007) 45 *CML Rev* 617, 663.

[105] Dougan, ibid.

[106] As currently developed through the EU's general principles framework. See ch 2 for a full consideration of this process and its relevance to the development of children's rights.

fundamental rights within the Charter—which itself has been explicitly identified as a constitutional source by the Treaty of Lisbon—renders them significantly more visible and, consequently, much more difficult for the institutions to ignore in the development and interpretation of EU law. It is conceivable, therefore, that family law measures which do not sufficiently take into account the specific vulnerabilities and interests of children could be legitimately challenged in the future on the basis that they are incompatible with specific provisions of the Charter.[107]

Alongside more explicit reference to the Charter of Fundamental Rights is the conviction in Article 6(2) TEU that 'the Union shall accede to the European Convention for the Protection of Human Rights and Fundamental Freedoms'. Again, this issue has already been explored in chapter two. There it was noted that the children's rights implications of EU accession to the ECHR depends largely on the capacity of the ECHR itself to uphold and protect children's rights. Given the textual limitations of the ECHR, which contains only limited reference to children, the advancement of children's rights in this context has been achieved largely as a result of the interpretative ingenuity of the ECHR. Such ingenuity may pay dividends in the context of EU family justice, with Article 6 ECHR[108] and Article 8 ECHR,[109] offering a particularly abundant jurisprudence to support children's claims within the process.

CONCLUSION

The range and extent of legislative activity in the EU family arena highlight its potential as a platform for reform and co-operation between the Member States' authorities. The extent to which children's rights are integral to this process, however, remains in doubt. Certainly the mediation and maintenance instruments, while commendable for their attempts to facilitate the free movement of family-related decisions alongside the free movement of family members themselves, represent something of a step backwards as far as children's rights are concerned, particularly when compared to the achievements of the EU in governing international child custody and access.

The fact that any reference to children is largely absent from the mediation and maintenance instruments is not entirely attributable to EU ambivalence to children's rights, but rather, reflects a lack of conviction at the national level with regard to children's status in such processes. On the one hand, there is a profusion of research and commentary affirming that substantive developments in the field

---

[107] Provisions other than Art 24 may be equally significant, including Art 7 (the right to private and family life) and Art 47 (right to a fair and public hearing and to representation). It is noteworthy that the original proposal for the EU Mediation Directive recommended a more explicit reference to Art 47—which could have strengthened children's claims for more active involvement in such processes—although this was removed from the final approved instrument.

[108] Right to a fair trial.

[109] Right to private and family life.

of maintenance and, indeed, procedural developments in favour of more conciliatory alternatives to dispute resolution, are ultimately concerned with protecting and promoting children's rights. On the other, however, the bland articulation of these processes within formal measures obfuscates the overarching commitment to children's rights that drove reform in these areas in the first place. It is hardly surprising then that the EU remains equally silent on such issues. It would be constitutionally dubious and politically imprudent, not to mention futile, to seek to implement children's rights obligations if national authorities are ill-equipped or unwilling to give effect to them.

Having said that, the EU could have, at least, included a general reference to children's rights within these instruments without compromising itself constitutionally, if only to serve as a subtle reminder to Member States of their abiding obligation to address children's interests in the context of these national family laws and processes. Mere reference to children's rights can have a surprisingly motivating effect on Member States prompting a re-appraisal of national procedures by administrative and judicial authorities and others implicated in the family justice system whilst sending out a consistent message about how the EU values children's rights. It remains to be seen whether the enhanced status of the Charter and the ECHR following the Lisbon Treaty will help bring children's rights issues to the fore in future EU family law developments, but it should at least support a more persuasive alignment between the international jurisprudence in this area and that of the EU. Until then, however, efforts need to continue at the national level to ensure that children's interests are appropriately represented; a process that may, in turn, inspire their more explicit endorsement at the supra-national level in the future.

6

Education, Children's Rights and the EU

INTRODUCTION

THIS CHAPTER EXAMINES the extent to which children's right to education is upheld and promoted by the EU. It is trite to note that education is a central feature of children's lives, that it is a crucial forum for their personal, intellectual and social development and for nurturing a sense of civic and cultural awareness. Fundamentally, education is a context within which children's agency is most explicitly developed and expressed insofar as it equips children with the tools they need to engage their civil, political, economic, social and cultural rights.

The Commission identifies educational access and achievement as a central priority of broader children's rights strategy, the Agenda for the Rights of the Child.[1] Indeed, it is in the context of education that EU children's rights measures are most explicit and advanced, but it is also an area in which children's experiences and status vary dramatically too, not only according to the Member State or region in which they live, but in response to a range of socio-economic, cultural, personal and political factors. EU action in the field of education is, therefore, simultaneously universal (it targets all children in the EU in some way or another, unlike most other areas of EU law) as well as being highly specific (the scope of the EU's powers in the field of education provision, and the way in which those powers are exercised, depend on the specific context of children's lives). The main question underpinning this analysis is the extent to which the EU's intervention in all of these contexts reflects and accommodates children's right to education as endorsed by international law.

To contextualise the discussion of the extent to which EU education law and policy accommodates children's rights, the analysis begins by setting out the international human rights framework relating to education. It then considers the nature of the EU's competence to develop education measures before examining critically how this competence is exercised. In doing so, the discussion highlights how EU action in the field of education adheres to the following typology, each motivated by different considerations and governed by different regulatory

---

[1] COM (2011) 60 final.

tools: (1) as an aspect of the EU's wider Social Agenda; (2) through EU migration law and (3) through EU equality law.

A broader aim of the analysis is to consider how education, on the one hand, offers a context within which the EU can protect the rights of more marginalised and vulnerable children, and, on the other, enables children to fulfill their potential as social, political and economic contributors. In doing so, the chapter represents a conscious attempt to shift the debate from an exclusively paternalistic approach to children's rights—an approach that is so dominant in international and EU children's rights discourse—and, instead, to consider the extent to which EU provision endorses the positive and active role children can play in achieving the broader economic and social ideals to which the EU aspires.

THE SOURCE AND SCOPE OF CHILDREN'S 'RIGHT' TO EDUCATION

Children's fundamental right to education is firmly entrenched in international,[2] European[3] and domestic law. Most notably, Article 28 of the United Nations Convention on the Rights of the Child 1992 (UNCRC) requires that states parties recognise the right of the child to education by: making primary education compulsory and freely available to all; encouraging the development of and access to different forms of secondary education, including general and vocational education and taking measures to encourage regular attendance at schools and to reduce drop-out rates. Article 28(3) further requires that states parties promote and encourage international co-operation in education: 'with a view to contributing to the elimination of ignorance and illiteracy throughout the world and facilitating access to scientific and technical knowledge and modern teaching methods'.

Article 29 of the UNCRC spells out the fundamental objectives of children's education as being concerned with: the development of the child's personality, talents and mental and physical abilities to their fullest potential; inculcating a respect for human rights and fundamental freedoms; the development of respect for the child's parents, his or her own cultural identity, language and values, for the national values of the country in which the child is living, the country from which he or she may originate, and for civilisations different from his or her own; the preparation of the child for responsible life in a free society, in the spirit of understanding, peace, tolerance, equality of sexes, and friendship among all peoples, ethnic, national and religious groups and persons of indigenous origin and the development of respect for the natural environment. This catalogue of provision

---

[2] See notably: 1948 Universal Declaration of Human Rights, Art 26(1); International Covenant on Economic, Social and Cultural Rights 1966, Arts 13 and 14; International Convention on the Elimination of All Forms of Racial Discrimination 1965, Arts 5(e), 5(v) and 7; 2006 UN Convention on the Rights of Persons with Disabilities, Arts 7 and 24; International Convention on the Protection of the Rights of All Migrant Workers and Members of their Families, Arts(4), 30 and 45.

[3] Art 2, Protocol 1 of the 1950 European Convention on Human Rights; Arts 7, 15, 17 and 30 of the 1996 (revised) European Social Charter, ETS 163.

is underpinned by the philosophy that education provides an essential platform for realising other fundamental rights, for achieving personal, social and academic fulfilment, participating meaningfully in the life of the wider community, and for maximising young people's employment potential.[4]

The UN Committee on the Rights of the Child (UN Committee) has provided concrete guidance on how these aspirations might be achieved in practice, including through: systematic review of curricula, teaching materials and school policies to include the various aims of education; ongoing training for all those involved in the development and provision of children's education; adaptation of teaching methods to promote the values of inclusive education and the development of mechanisms to enable education to be routinely monitored and evaluated.[5] Children's right to education is further endorsed by a range of Council of Europe activities—underpinned largely by Article 2 Protocol 1 of the European Convention on Human Rights (ECHR)—although in a rather less explicit and direct way than other international provision.[6] Specifically, this states that:

> No person shall be denied the right to education. In the exercise of any functions which it assumes in relation to education and to teaching, the State shall respect the right of parents to ensure such education and teaching in conformity with their own religious and philosophical convictions.[7]

In an *EU* context, the fundamental right to education has been articulated most explicitly in Article 14 of the Charter of Fundamental Rights in the EU:

1. Everyone has the right to education and to have access to vocational and continuing training;
2. This right includes the possibility to receive free compulsory education;
3. The freedom to found educational establishments with due respect for democratic principles and the right of parents to ensure the education and teaching of their children in conformity with their religious, philosophical and pedagogical convictions shall be respected, in accordance with the national laws governing the exercise of such freedom and right.

While Article 14 reflects the main values and provisions established by the international human rights framework, the language it adopts is rather more clipped

---

[4] See UN Economic and Social Council, GC, *The Right to Education* (E/C 12/1999/10) 8 December 1999, 1.

[5] UN Committee on the Rights of the Child, GC 1, *The Aims of Education* (CRC/GC/2001/1) 17 April 2001.

[6] The scope and application of this provision will be considered later in this chapter.

[7] This provision underpins and is fleshed out by a framework of recommendations, charters and intergovernmental conventions. For example, linguistic diversity and both mother and host-tongue teaching is protected by the European Cultural Convention 1954, ETS 018; the European Charter for Regional or Minority Languages 1992, ETS 148, Art 8.1; the European Social Charter (revised 1996), Art 19; Recommendation 1740 (2006) of the Parliamentary Assembly, on the place of the mother tongue in school education; and the Framework Convention for the Protection of National Minorities 1995, ETS 157, Art 14.2.

and certainly less ambitious and exhaustive than some of the measures referred to above.[8] It is clearly inspired more by the ECHR's 'derivative' approach to education whereby rights are bestowed upon children at the behest of their parents rather than by the direct and more comprehensive formula of the UNCRC.[9]

This overview reveals that implicit in the right to education are a range of obligations, not only in terms of guaranteeing children's substantive rights to and within education, but also in terms of effecting the necessary institutional and pedagogical measures to accommodate their multifarious needs.

THE NATURE AND SCOPE OF CHILDREN'S EDUCATIONAL RIGHTS UNDER EU EDUCATION LAW AND POLICY

The extent to which substantive education law and policy at *EU* level endorse the rights to and within education can only be fully understood in the context of EU legal competence in the field. Until the early 1990s education was regarded as falling within EU competence only insofar as it impacted upon the labour market.[10] Thus, legislative intervention was limited to developing vocational training provision with a view to preparing young people for entry into employment. In 1992, the Treaty on European Union (TEU) broadened the scope of EU competence in the field of education by incorporating a new provision entitled Education, Vocational Training and Youth into the (then) EC Treaty.[11] This provision has been further extended following the Lisbon Treaty to reinforce the complementary, supportive role of the Union vis-à-vis the Member States:

> The Union shall contribute to the development of quality education by encouraging cooperation between Member States and, if necessary, by supporting and supplementing their action, while fully respecting the responsibility of the Member States for the content of teaching and the organisation of education systems and their cultural and linguistic diversity.[12]

Consistent with this more supportive, complementary role, the EU's approach to education has been, and continues to be, characterised less by top-down legal prescription and more by soft measures to encourage mutually agreed targets

---

[8] The reference in Art 14(2) to the 'possibility' to receive free compulsory education' is less compelling than an outright obligation on the part of states to provide access to free compulsory education for all children.

[9] For a critique of the ECHR's articulation of parents' right to educate rather than children's right to education, see J Roche, 'Children, Citizenship and Human Rights' (2008) 9 *Journal of Social Sciences* 43. The sparse case law of the ECHR also confirms that this article has been used primarily with a view to securing access to education rather than rights within education. See, eg *Belgian Linguistic Case* (1979–80) 1 EHRR 252. We will return to this issue later in the chapter.

[10] The original Treaty reference to education (Art 128 EEC) provided simply for the establishment of a 'common vocational policy capable of contributing to the harmonious development both of the national economies and of the common market'.

[11] Formerly Art 149 EC, now Art 165 TFEU.

[12] Art 165(1) TFEU.

between the Member States, to support exchange programmes and initiatives that seek to nurture a sense of civil and social responsibility as well as a more acute awareness of the role and scope of the EU in the lives of its citizens.[13] Any authority to adopt legally binding acts to regulate the content or organisation of the educational curriculum, on the other hand, remains exclusively a matter for the Member States in the light of their distinct historical, cultural and political context.

Despite these confines in legal competence, the EU has been surprisingly proactive in developing fairly robust protection as well as myriad opportunities for children in the context of education. This has been achieved in three discrete contexts: first, as an integral aspect of the EU's Social Agenda, aimed at developing the EU's labour and intellectual capital and engaging its citizens in the European project from an early age; second, as part of a 'package' of rights associated with migration and EU citizenship and third, as part of the broader EU equality/non-discrimination framework, particularly in relation to disability and race.

UPHOLDING CHILDREN'S EDUCATIONAL RIGHTS AS AN ASPECT OF THE EU'S SOCIAL AGENDA

The first main context in which children's educational rights are pursued is as an aspect of the EU's broader Social Agenda. Insofar as this is synonymous with the EU's overarching commitment to stimulating employment and economic growth, the Social Agenda epitomises the EU's strong historical association between education entitlement and the employment agenda. This is particularly evident since the introduction, in 2000, of the Lisbon Agenda. This heralded the launch of an ambitious new strategy aimed at making the EU into 'the most competitive and dynamic knowledge-based economy in the world'.[14] Although this agenda was not grounded in the EU legal basis pertaining to education,[15] improving education and training systems across the Member States was identified as a key means of achieving the ambitions of the Social Agenda, as was maximising opportunities for those on the margins of society.

The unveiling of the Lisbon Agenda affirmed the EU's view of education first and foremost as a rite of passage into active employment.[16] But equally significantly,

---

[13] Arts 2(5), 6 and 165 TFEU.

[14] Lisbon European Council, 23 and 24 March 2000, Presidency Conclusions.

[15] Measures to combat social exclusion are grounded in the social policy provisions of Arts 151–53 TFEU (ex Arts 136–37 EC), an area of shared competence between the EU and the Member States. Action in this regard is reinforced by Art 3(3) TEU which pledges the EU's general commitment to combating social exclusion alongside protecting the rights of the child. The value of pursuing children's rights within the broad context of social inclusion is considered in ch 2.

[16] Alongside the introduction of new legislation and programmes aimed at stimulating the mobility of students, researchers and other highly skilled professionals between the Member States other more localised policy and funding initiatives were also announced. These included the development of accessible, multi-purpose learning centres, learning partnerships, enhanced mobility and exchange

it signalled the integration of a new priority into the EU employment/education nexus: that of promoting social inclusion.[17] This process has not only served to enhance the legitimacy of EU interest in these areas, but has extended EU action to a range of broader social issues that affect participation in education and employment—notably poverty, health, well-being and culture—and sharpened the EU's focus on children in the process.[18] In that sense, the EU Social Agenda is a good example of the indirect route the EU typically takes before arriving at any meaningful consideration of children's rights. While the legal basis for EU initiatives in the field of education may be decidedly ambivalent to children's interests, the emergence of a causative chain—between education as a gateway to employment, and employment as an antidote to poverty and social exclusion—called for a more holistic, life-course approach to achieving social and economic cohesion. This, in turn, pulled children into the EU's line of vision: if compulsory education is the key stimulant of social advantage, so the focus of EU investment should be on that too with a view to forging the all-important social and economic contract between the individual and society at the earliest opportunity.

The successor to the Lisbon Agenda, the Europe 2020 Strategy, reflects further the intimate correspondence between education, social inclusion and employment by setting out a 10-year action plan aimed at, inter alia, expanding labour market access, and improving education and training throughout the life-course.[19] It comprises seven interlinked flagship initiatives to which both the EU and Member States commit, including:

> 'Youth on the Move' to enhance the performance of education systems and facilitate the entry of young people to the labour market ... and 'European Platform Against Poverty' to ensure social and territorial cohesion such that the benefits of growth and jobs are widely shared and people experiencing poverty and social exclusion are enabled to live in dignity and take an active part in society.[20]

By embedding the EU's education agenda within a wider employment, social inclusion and anti-poverty framework, the Europe 2020 Strategy could perhaps be celebrated for adopting a more holistic, long-term vision of education.

---

programmes, and an enriched skills and life-long learning agenda. HL Ackers and B Gill, *Moving People and Knowledge: Scientific Mobility in an Enlarging European Union* (London, Edward Elgar, 2008).

[17] European Commission, *Progress Towards the Lisbon Objectives in Education and Training: Indicators and Benchmarks*, Staff Working Document (Brussels, European Commission, 2007).

[18] See also: H Frazer and E Marlier, *Tackling Child Poverty and Promoting the Social Inclusion of Children in the EU: Key Lessons* (Luxembourg, European Commission, 2007); Social Protection Committee, *Child Poverty and Well-Being in the EU: Current Status and Way Forward* (Luxembourg, European Communities, 2008) and H Stalford, H Sax, and E Drywood, *Developing Indicators for the Protection, Respect and Promotion of the Rights of the Child in the European Union: Final Report* (Vienna, Fundamental Rights Agency, 2009).

[19] Commission, '2020: A Strategy for Smart, Sustainable and Inclusive Growth' (Communication) COM (2010) 2020 final, 5. The Commission proposes a target of 75% employment among those aged 20–64 by 2020, as well as 40% of young people achieving a degree at tertiary level.

[20] Ibid, 6.

However, provision relating to the education of children per se is by no means comprehensive; explicitly child-focused measures have evolved in a rather rambling and scattered fashion, and certainly in a way that has been peripheral to mainstream EU education provision to date. The random nature of this journey raises concerns as to whether the convergence of EU education measures with market-led objectives has limited the prospect of upholding and promoting *children's rights* in the here and now, thereby endorsing a decidedly instrumental and outdated perception of children as 'adults-in-the-making' or 'human becomings'—action that is concerned more with nurturing children's potential as future earners and producers.[21]

The following section suggests, perhaps optimistically, that this is not necessarily the case: whilst the strategic correlation between children's education and the pursuit of broader economic goals may be ideologically contentious, it carries with it significant methodological benefits that have enabled the EU to effect important changes in relation to issues that are hostile or ill-suited to top-down legal intervention.

EU EDUCATION POLICY AND THE OPEN METHOD OF CO-ORDINATION

It has already been noted that the EU exercises limited legal competence in the field of education: its role is confined to merely supporting the activities of Member States who remain solely responsible for curricula content and the organisation of their education systems.[22] While EU education provision is generally non-binding and supportive in nature, it has increased and diversified in more recent years in response to the EU's growing social inclusion agenda. More specifically, the Commission's interest in the field of compulsory education was galvanised following the introduction of the Lisbon Strategy at the turn of the millennium. This was not simply because education and training were explicitly prioritised as a means of achieving the employment and knowledge-based goals identified by the Strategy, but also because of the introduction of a new, more politically palatable working methodology to facilitate inter-state co-operation and exchange: the Open Method of Co-ordination (OMC).[23] Europe 2020, as the successor of the Lisbon Strategy, has taken up the baton in this regard, emphasising the importance of sustaining active cross-national links and best practice

---

[21] J Qvortrup, M Brady, G Sgritta and H Wintersberger (eds), *Childhood Matters: Social Theory, Practice and Politics* (Aldershot, Avebury, 1994); A James, C Jenks and A Prout, *Theorizing Childhood* (Oxford, Polity Press, 1998).

[22] Art 165(1) TFEU.

[23] See, more generally, F Beveridge and S Velluti (eds), *Gender and the Open Method of Coordination* (Dartmouth, Ashgate, 2008).

exchange between the Member States through regular national reporting, data collection and clearly defined benchmarks.[24]

Of course, the majority of EU educational measures continue to be driven by the ambition of producing a skilled and versatile workforce to enhance the EU's economic and knowledge-based competitiveness on a global scale. While it has already been noted that such features appear to respond rather grudgingly to the children's rights framework envisaged by international human rights law, they have proven to be surprisingly effective in addressing some of the more endemic, insidious inequalities facing children in the here and now.[25] For example, among the key benchmarks adopted by the Council under the Europe 2020 Strategy are: (1) that at least 95 per cent of children between four years old and the age for starting compulsory primary education should participate in early childhood education; (2) that the proportion of early leavers from education and training should be reduced to less than 10 per cent; and (3) that the proportion of low-achieving 15-year-olds in reading, mathematics and science should be less than 15 per cent.

This approach, based on mutually-agreed goals, a coherent action plan and regular national reporting is, in many respects, a much more efficient and effective way of mobilising Member States to respond to an EU-wide problem. Indeed, even if hard legal intervention was possible, it would take many more years to permeate national legal and policy systems and would be likely to produce much more divergent results depending on Member States' receptiveness and resourcefulness in meeting the obligations imposed. More broadly, the emergence of the education/employment/social inclusion nexus has encouraged the EU to foster a broader perspective of children and young people's education—one that views children's educational interests and attainment as inextricably linked with wider social, cultural and economic factors—and generated a new, more inclusive, positive and empowering rhetoric of intercultural understanding and exchange, youth citizenship and participation.[26]

---

[24] Prior to that, the European Commission launched a public consultation in 2007 to identify those aspects of school education on which joint action at EU level could be effective in supporting Member States in the modernisation of their systems. See Commission, 'Improving Competences for the 21st Century: An Agenda for European Cooperation on Schools' (Communication) COM (2008) 425 final.

[25] See later in this chapter, as well as: S Bouwsma, *Disability Policy in EU Member States and the Open Method of Co-ordination* (Twente, University of Twente, 2003) and W Bartlett, R Benini and C Gordon, *Measures to Promote the Situation of Roma EU Citizens in the European Union: Study* (Brussels, European Parliament, 2011) 189–90.

[26] It is worth noting that many of the child-related initiatives to have emerged from the social inclusion agenda make explicit reference to the right to education as enshrined in the UNCRC. See, eg Opinion of the European Economic and Social Committee, 'Education for Inclusion: A Tool for Fighting Poverty and Social Exclusion' (exploratory opinion) [2011] OJ C18/18, fn 2; Opinion of the European Economic and Social Committee, 'Early Childhood Care and Education' (own-initiative opinion) [2010] OJ C339/1, s 2.7 Poverty of Children in Europe.

PROMOTING CHILDREN'S AGENCY THROUGH EU EDUCATION
MEASURES: ACTIVE CITIZENSHIP AND CHILDREN'S
PERSONAL DEVELOPMENT

It is worth mentioning at this point that dovetailing with EU educational initiatives in the context of social inclusion is an ongoing campaign to engage with
children and young people on a more political and cultural level. Certainly, the
right to education has long been recognised as encompassing not only equal
access to educational provision and academic opportunities, but participation in a
forum that is crucial for the child's personal development, for promoting mutual
understanding, tolerance and friendship, and for nurturing a sense of social and
civic responsibility. In short, education is necessary for the fulfilment of all of the
civil, political, economic, social and cultural rights expressed in Article 29 of the
UNCRC.[27] EU law and policy has sought to achieve these broader objectives since
the 1990s through a variety of funding and policy initiatives focusing, on the one
hand, on stimulating cross-national exchange between the Member States and, on
the other, promoting young people's sense of civic duty and European identity.

The first set of initiatives, aimed to promote cross-national educational
exchange and the sharing of best practices, are integrated into a single Lifelong
Learning Programme (LLP). Allocated a budget of over €7 billion, the LLP spans
six years (2007–13) and covers both pupil and teacher exchange programmes,
as well as training for professionals involved in the delivery of education at all
levels.[28] Funding for children's education is delivered through the COMENIUS
scheme of the LLP which has the specific aim of developing 'knowledge and
understanding among young people and educational staff of the diversity of
European cultures, languages and values'.[29] This certainly responds to the broader
educational ideals of Article 29 of the UNCRC. However, the LLP's relatively low
prioritisation of child-related initiatives is revealed in the budgetary allocation:
COMENIUS receives less than 13 per cent of the LLP budget, the remaining
87 per cent allocated to adult-learning initiatives under the LLP.

The second set of initiatives that responds to the EU's broader vision of education is the anthology of measures aimed at promoting young people's sense of
civic duty and European identity. Certainly, the need to activate young people's
citizenship has been a leitmotif running through EU youth policies now for over
a decade. For instance, the Commission's 2001 White Paper, 'A New Impetus for
European Youth', noted:

> If young people have one clear message, it is that they want their voice to be heard and
> want to be regarded as fully-fledged participants in the process; they want to play their

---

[27] Stalford, Sax and Drywood, *Developing Indicators*, above n 18.

[28] Dec 1720/2006 establishing an integrated action programme in the field of lifelong learning
[2006] OJ L327/45.

[29] See European Commission Education and Training website: ec.europa.eu/education/lifelong-
learning-programme/doc84_en.htm.

part in building Europe; they want to influence the debate on the way it develops. It is time now to regard youth as a positive force in the construction of Europe rather than as a problem. In other words, we have to give young people the wherewithal to express their ideas, and to test them against similar ideas from other players in civil society.[30]

This commitment to 'giving young people the wherewithal to express their ideas' offers one of the most pronounced nods in the direction of Article 12 of the UNCRC. It has been articulated in a range of subsequent Commission schemes and recommendations, many of which have been administered through school-based initiatives. These include the European Youth Pact, aimed at promoting young people's social and professional integration and at mainstreaming youth issues into various EU policy areas,[31] and Youth in Action I, aimed at extending opportunities for exchange, volunteering and democratic participation to young people from less advantaged backgrounds.[32]

Such initiatives are laudable insofar as they provide a rare platform for directly engaging young people in shaping the political, cultural and economic priorities of the EU. In that sense, they bear some of the hallmarks of more empowering notions of children and young people's agency and contribution that are, on the whole, conspicuously absent from the EU's broader children's rights agenda. However, the reference to 'youth' belies the highly exclusive, adult-focused nature of these initiatives. 'Youth', in European parlance, refers largely to those in the 15 to 30 age-group and is, therefore, implicitly concerned with capturing the interests of those who are at the juncture between education and training or employment, that is, those who show some economic potential and therefore present themselves as worthy of EU investment.   Second, while the rhetoric of youth participation in decision-making is fairly persuasive, there is less concrete evidence of the EU actually embedding young people's views within legal and policy recommendations and less evidence still to attest to the longer term impact of all of these participatory measures on young people's personal and social development or sense of civic responsibility.[33] Having considered these broader, more policy-led aspects of EU education policy, the discussion now turns to some of the 'harder' legal expressions of children's right to education.

---

[30] COM (2001) 681 final, 5.

[31] Commission, 'Policies concerning Youth: Addressing the Concerns of Young People in Europe, implementing the European Youth Pact and Promoting Active Citizenship' (Communication from Mr Figel in association with Mr Špidla) SEC (2005) 693, COM (2005) 206 final; Resolution of the Council and of the Representatives of the Governments of the Member States, 'The Concerns of Young People in Europe: Implementing the European Pact for Youth and Promoting Active Citizenship' [2005] OJ C292/5.

[32] Dec 1719/2006 establishing the Youth in Action Programme for the period of 2007 to 2013 [2006] OJ L327/30. See further: eacea.ec.europa.eu/youth/index_en.php. See also, European Parliament Resolution, 'An EU Strategy for Youth: Investing and Empowering' (2009/2159(INI)) [2011] OJ C161E.

[33] The EU Agenda for the Rights of the Child refers to the importance of 'providing possibilities for greater participation of children in the development and implementation of actions and policies that affect them' (above n 1,13), but it offers very little concrete guidance on how this might be achieved in practice, and fails to link such an ambition with existing initiatives under the European youth agenda.

CHILDREN'S EDUCATIONAL RIGHTS UNDER EU MIGRATION LAW

Some of the most direct EU expressions of children's right to education largely coalesce around free movement and immigration provision, areas in which the EU exercises direct law-making powers.[34] The potential impact of EU intervention in relation to migrant children's education should not be underestimated: international comparative data reveals that between 10 and 15 per cent of pupils in the initial 15 EU Member States were either migrants themselves or the children of migrant parents. The population of migrant children in Member States such as Ireland, Italy and Spain has quadrupled since 2000, while in certain cities, such as Rotterdam, Brussels and Birmingham, migrant children account for approximately 50 per cent of the school population.[35]

While the limitations on the EU's competence still apply in this context—it is prohibited from determining the content and scope of national education systems and curricula—some important provisions have been introduced to uphold children's right to *access* schools in the Member State to which they move on an equal basis to nationals. In the context of legal migration, children have an unconditional right under EU law to access education in any Member State to which they move. This right applies equally to children of third country nationality[36] as it does to migrant children of EU nationality,[37] and extends also to refugees and asylum seekers.[38] These provisions have been interpreted to considerable effect, at least as far as *EU* migrant children are concerned, to secure children's right to receive education in the host Member State even when their family's normal residence entitlement has otherwise expired. For instance, in the

---

[34] The EU shares competence with the Member States to enact legal measures in these areas (Art 4 TFEU).

[35] P Stanat and G Christensen, *Where Immigrant Students Succeed: A Comparative Review of Performance and Engagement in PISA 2003* (Paris, OECD, 2006).

[36] Dir 2003/109 concerning the status of third country nationals who are long-term residents [2003] OJ L16/44, Art 11; Dir 2003/86 on the right to family reunification [2003] OJ L251/12, Art 14.

[37] Reg 492/2011 on freedom of movement for workers within the Union [2011] OJ L 141/1. Article 10 states: 'The children of a national of a Member State who is or has been employed in the territory of another Member State shall be admitted to that State's general educational, apprenticeship and vocational training courses under the same conditions as the nationals of that State, if such children are residing in its territory. Member States shall encourage all efforts to enable such children to attend these courses under the best possible conditions'. This right was previously enshrined in Art 12 of the former Reg 1612/68 [1968] OJ L257/2. See also Art 24(1) of Dir 2004/38 on the right of citizens of the Union and their family members to move and reside freely within the territory of the Member States [2004] OJ L158/77 which guarantees equality of access to education to all EU citizens and their family members who are lawfully resident in other Member States.

[38] Art 14 of Dir 2001/55 on minimum standards for giving temporary protection in the event of a mass influx of displaced persons and on measures promoting a balance of efforts between Member States in receiving such persons and bearing the consequences thereof [2001] OJ L212/12; Art 10 of Dir 2003/9 laying down minimum standards for the reception of asylum seekers [2003] OJ L31/18; Art 27 of Dir 2004/83 on minimum standards for the qualification and status of third country nationals or stateless persons as refugees or as persons who otherwise need international protection and the content of the protection granted [2004] OJ L304/12; Art 14(c) of Dir 2008/115 on common standards and procedures in Member States for returning illegally staying third country nationals [2008] OJ L348/98.

past, generous residence and educational rights could only be exercised under EU free movement law by children residing with at least one EU migrant parent in the host state.[39] Since the landmark decision in *Baumbast,* however, EU migrant children retain an independent right of residence in the host state for the specific purposes of pursuing their education even following the death or departure of their EU migrant parent.[40] Furthermore, if their primary carer is of third country nationality (and otherwise dependent on the EU spouse for accessing residence and other social rights in the host state), they too can retain a right of residence in the host state for the purposes of caring for their children while they remain in education.[41] The Court of Justice has thereby acknowledged that such is the importance of achieving continuity in children's education that it can effectively 'anchor' the family's residence in the host state for the duration of his or her studies:

> The right conferred by [ex] Article 12 of Regulation No 1612/68 on the child of a migrant worker to pursue, under the best possible conditions, his education in the host Member State necessarily implies that that child has the right to be accompanied by the person who is his primary carer and, accordingly, that that person is able to reside with him in that Member State during his studies. To refuse to grant permission to remain to a parent who is the primary carer of the child exercising his right to pursue his studies in the host Member State infringes that right.[42]

The guarantee of equal access to education for children regardless of nationality or of migration status is not only imperative to their intellectual and social development but also minimises the deleterious effects of moving on children. Encouragingly, current data confirms that such a policy has achieved generally equal participation rates in education among migrant and non-migrant children alike across Europe.[43] However, the formula endorsed by EU law is flawed in two

---

[39] Formerly Art 12 of Reg 1612/68.

[40] Case C-413/99 *Baumbast and R v Secretary of State for the Home Department* [2002] ECR I-7091.

[41] The *Baumbast* decision has now been codified in Dir 2004/38 Art 12(3) which provides that: 'The Union citizen's departure from the host Member State or his/her death shall not entail the loss of the right of residence of his/her children or of the parent who has actual custody of the children, irrespective of nationality, if the children reside in the host Member State and are enrolled at an educational establishment for the purpose of studying there, until the completion of their studies'. This is confirmed in a line of subsequent cases: Case C-34/09 *Zambrano v ONEm* [2011] CMLR 46; Case C-127/08 *Metock v Minister for Justice, Equality and Law Reform* [2008] ECR I-6241; Case C-310/08 *Harrow LBC v Ibrahim* [2010] ECR I-1065 and Case C-480/08 *Teixeira v Lambeth LBC* [2010] 2 CMLR 50. See also Case C-60/00 *Carpenter v Secretary of State for the Home Department* [2002] ECR I-6279 which, although not specifically concerned with the children's education, established an important precedent in anchoring an otherwise disqualified parent's right of residence in the host state. The 'anchoring' nature of children's rights under EU law are discussed further in chs 2 and 3.

[42] Para 37. Children's educational rights have also acted as a brake on deportations where the child's parents have died and the host state is acting in loco parentis, see Case C-7/94 *Landesamt für Ausbildungsförderung Nordrhein-Westfalen v Gaal* [1996] ECR I-1031.

[43] See European Commission, *Progress Towards the Common European Objectives in Education and Training: Indicators and Benchmarks 2010/2011,* Commission Staff Working Paper (Brussels, European Commission, 2011) 117–18.

main respects. First, while the strictures of EU legal competence prescribe that direct legal intervention is strictly limited to regulating children's educational rights following migration, a distinct hierarchy of entitlement has emerged according to the migration *category* into which the child falls. Furthermore, a formal equality approach—which does little more than ensure a basic right of access to education—fails to address some of the more functional inequalities facing migrant children thereafter.

THE LIMITATIONS OF A BASIC 'EQUALITY OF ACCESS' APPROACH TO EDUCATION

While all migrant children have a right to access some form of compulsory education in the host state, the scope of that right differs significantly according to the circumstances of the child's migration. Optimum entitlement is afforded to children who have migrated from another EU Member State with their EU migrant parents: formally, at least, they have unlimited access to all types and levels of education in the host state, including access to maintenance grants and other support that facilitates their access.[44] Migrant children from outside the EU enjoy more limited education-related rights: they can only generally access *state* education under the same conditions as nationals, and are excluded from peripheral benefits such as maintenance grants.[45] Entitlement is further diluted in relation to asylum-seeking children who, according to EU law, must be granted access to the host state's education system on *similar* but not necessarily the *same* terms as those that apply to nationals.[46] As such, education may be provided in accommodation centres rather than schools, and the authorities can postpone asylum-seeking children's full access to a school for up to three months and, in some cases, for up to a year, from the date of application for asylum.[47] An EU directive also rather vaguely enables Member States to offer 'other arrangements where the specific situation of the child makes access to the education system impossible'[48]

---

[44] Case 9/74 *Casagrande v Landehauptstadt München* [1974] ECR 773; Case C-3/90 *Bernini v Minister van Onderwijs en Wetenschappen* [1992] ECR I-1071. See further HL Ackers and H Stalford, *A Community for Children? Children, Citizenship and Migration in the European Union* (Aldershot, Ashgate, 2004).

[45] See the provisions referred to above at n 38, as well as Dir 2004/83 on minimum standards for the qualification and status of third country nationals or stateless persons as refugees or as persons who otherwise need international protection and the content of the protection granted [2004] OJ L304/12, Arts 23(2) and 27(1).

[46] Dir 2003/9 laying down minimum standards for the reception of asylum seekers [2003] OJ L31/18, Art 10(1). This is in spite of recommendations, in the original proposals for this legislation, to extend access to education to asylum-seeking children on the 'same' basis as nationals. See E Drywood, *The Child in EU Asylum and Immigration Law: A Socio-Legal Analysis of Regulatory and Governance Issues* (PhD, Liverpool, 2010) 118.

[47] Dir 2003/9, Art 10(2).

[48] Ibid Art 10(3).

without specifying what these 'other arrangements' might reasonably entail.[49] Notwithstanding that most migrant children enjoy at least a basic right to access education in the host state, a range of practical and administrative obstacles may hamper their exercise of this right and, indeed, their educational progress once installed in a school. For example, unless their move to the host state coincides with the start of the academic year, they are likely to experience difficulties or delays in obtaining a place in their school of choice. Moreover, economically disadvantaged migrants are unlikely to have the know-how or resources to secure residence within a catchment area of the most desirable state schools. Even if timely admission to a school is secured, this is unlikely on its own to provide children with the education they need unless it accommodates the child's specific linguistic, cultural, economic and emotional needs. For example, a young refugee from Somalia might have a right to access a school in Berlin but there is limited accompanying entitlement, under EU law at least, to receive additional language or academic tuition, or indeed, to receive specialist counselling to enable them to catch up and integrate with children in their age-group. In that sense, EU law falls far short of international human rights provision which clearly articulates the importance of supplementing access entitlement with measures that address such needs.[50] The availability of such provision, instead, depends very much on the resources and programmes in place at national or, indeed, at regional level. European data reveals a widespread inadequacy in this regard, however: young people of migrant background are significantly more at risk of being excluded from or exiting the education system without having obtained an upper second-ary qualification.[51] Furthermore, even after taking socio-economic and linguistic factors into account, there is still a considerable disparity between the achieve-ment rates of migrants when compared to non-migrant children: across the EU Member States, on average, migrant students are reported to be one-and-a-half years behind their native peers in their reading skills by the age of 15.[52]

[49] In a bid to address this ambiguity, proposals to amend the Asylum Reception Directive recom-mend imposing an explicit obligation on Member States to offer support such as 'preparatory classes, including language classes, aimed at facilitating the access of minors to the national education system, and/or specific education designed to assist their integration into that system'. See Commission, 'Proposal for a Directive of the European Parliament and of the Council Laying Down Minimum Standards for the Reception of Asylum-Seekers' COM (2008) 815 final, 23 and Drywood, *The Child in EU Asylum and Immigration Law*, above n 46, 120.

[50] Notably, Art 45 of the International Convention on the Protection of all Migrant Workers and Members of their Families 1990 guarantees all legally established migrants access to national educa-tional institutions in the host state. It also provides for but does not guarantee a right to reception teaching and mother-tongue teaching to facilitate integration and preserve cultural identity. Article 14 of the 1977 Council of Europe Convention on the Legal Status of Migrant Workers guarantees a right of access to education and Art 15 urges intergovernmental co-operation in the provision of mother-tongue teaching for migrants' children.

[51] Stanat and Christensen, above n 35.

[52] Ibid 119–20. See further European Commission, 'Migration and Mobility: Challenges and Opportunities for EU Education Systems' (Green Paper) COM (2008) 423 final, 1; European Commission, *Joint Council/Commission Report on the Implementation of the Education and Training 2010 Work Programme Delivering Lifelong Learning for Knowledge, Creativity and Innovation* (Brussels,

BEYOND A BASIC ACCESS: RIGHTS FOR MIGRANT CHILDREN

That is not to say that the EU has been completely impervious to the educational challenges facing migrant children. As far back as the 1970s, legislation was introduced requiring Member States to provide supplementary language tuition with a view to facilitating EU migrant children's integration both in the host state and in their country of origin should they subsequently return.[53] Given the ambitious scope of this instrument—it prescribes both host language and mother-tongue tuition—its implementation at the national level has been woefully inadequate.[54] It is this very observation that has prompted the Commission to re-open discussions as to how EU law and policy can best accommodate and reflect the educational needs of its increasingly multi-cultural, multi-lingual population. An important development in this regard has been the adoption by the Commission of a Green Paper addressing the situation of migrant children, particularly those of vulnerable socio-economic status, and the launch of a consultation to explore the merits of resurrecting and updating Directive 77/486 to respond to the educational needs of the EU's migrant population in the 21st century.[55] There is certainly some support for reinforcing the legal obligations set out in this instrument, not only as a means of achieving greater parity between children independent of their migration status, but also in view of the benefits migrant children bring to the social and learning environment of the host state.[56] However, the significant expansion of the EU, coupled with the diversification of the EU migrant population over the last 30 to 40 years, perpetuates concerns as to the feasibility of enforcing compliance with such legal obligations today. This brings us back to the question of whether legal prescription offers the most appropriate mechanism by which to achieve these goals. A range of integration programmes have already been instituted across the Member States to reflect the characteristics and needs of their individual

European Commission, 2008). See also K Pendakur and R Pendakur, 'Language Knowledge as Human Capital and Ethnicity' (2002) 36 *International Migration* Review 147.

[53] Dir 77/486 on the education of the children of migrant workers [1977] OJ L199/32. Note that this Directive only governs the linguistic needs of the children of *EU* migrant workers in the context of compulsory education, third country national migrant children are excluded from its scope.

[54] This was in spite of renewed pressure imposed on Member States by the European Parliament to implement the Directive properly. See European Parliament Resolution on the application of Dir 77/486 on the education of the children of migrant workers [1987] OJ C125/8, also Commission Reports on the implementation of Directive 77/486, COM (84) 54 final and COM (88) 787 final. For further analysis of the scope of the Directive, see: Ackers and Stalford, *A Community for Children*, above n 44; H Cullen, 'From Migrants to Citizens? European Community Policy on Intercultural Education' (1996) 45 *ICLQ* 109; Eurydice, *Integrating Immigrant Children into Schools in Europe* (Brussels, Eurydice Policy Unit, 2004) and Eurydice, *Integrating Immigrant Children into Schools in Europe: Measures to Foster Communication with Immigrant Families and Heritage Language Teaching for Immigrant Children* (Brussels, Eurydice Policy Unit, 2009).

[55] Above n 52.

[56] See further Stanat and Christensen, *Where Immigrant Students Succeed*, above n 35 and Eurydice, *Integrating Immigrant Children*, above n 54, 70–71.

migrant communities, most of which have evolved independently of any legal obligation but which, instead, are supported by broader, non-legal EU programmes and actions.[57] Indeed, many of the initiatives being pursued under the EU Social Inclusion Programme, Europe 2020 (referred to above), target the very same communities of children as the migration laws described here. Even in the absence of legal competence, however, Europe 2020 goes much further in seeking to address the root causes of educational under-achievement and exclusion, whilst also mobilising Member States to institute coherent remedial measures.

UPHOLDING EDUCATIONAL RIGHTS THROUGH
THE EU'S EQUALITY FRAMEWORK

The discussion up until now has emphasised that, as far as binding measures are concerned, the EU regulates education largely in the context of migration as an offshoot of its competence in the field of immigration, asylum and free movement and, even then, it is mainly with a view to achieving formal equality of access to education. The current limitations of the EU in addressing educational inequalities among such children are hardly surprising: insofar as it exercises a merely complementary role in the educational field, the EU simply does not have the competence to dictate, at the micro-level, the content of educational provision for children from minority and ethnic backgrounds or, indeed, to influence how educational resources should be distributed internally from region to region. That said, it is important to cast the net beyond distinctly educational measures and look to other EU legal mechanisms to challenge some of the most entrenched forms of educational segregation and marginalisation. With that in mind, a range of other binding and non-binding educational measures have emerged in the context of the EU's broader equality framework with a view to ensuring that children are not educationally isolated as a result of disability, race, ethnicity or gender. Two prominent illustrations of EU activity in this context relate to the education of disabled children and of children from the Roma community.

---

[57] The Commission has incorporated specific recommendations on education and migrant integration into its broader immigration strategy. See, eg Commission, 'A Common Agenda for Integration: a Framework for the Integration of Third Country Nationals in the European Union' (Communication) COM (2005) 389 final. Other lifelong learning initiatives such as COMENIUS and the Youth Programme support a range of projects related to intercultural education, school integration of migrant pupils and social inclusion for disadvantaged youth. These initiatives are summarised in the Commission's Green Paper, above n 52, s 4.

TACKLING DISCRIMINATION IN EDUCATION ON
GROUNDS OF DISABILITY

There are approximately 80 million people with disabilities in the EU,[58] including some 16 per cent of men and women aged 16 to 64.[59] Data also reveals
that disabled people, and particularly females, are significantly more likely to
be socially and economically disadvantaged as a result of long-term unemployment and poverty.[60] This, it is widely acknowledged, results largely from
the inaccessibility of appropriate educational support during childhood and
youth.[61] Unsurprisingly, therefore, discrimination against disabled children in
education has been the subject of EU initiatives for some time. This has been
driven, on the one hand, by a discrete EU disability publicity campaign and
strategy[62] together with support for specialist advocacy and research bodies,[63]
and, on the other hand, as an aspect of broader legal and policy pursuits.[64]
One of the most prominent examples of the latter is a proposal for a Directive
implementing the principle of equal treatment outside employment, based

[58] European Opinion Research Group, *Attitudes of Europeans to Disability. Eurobarometer 54.2*
(Brussels, European Commission, 2001).
[59] Applica, CESEP and Alphametrics, *Men and Women with Disabilities in the EU: Statistical
Analysis of the Labour Force Survey Ad Hoc Module and the EU-SILC* (Brussels, European Commission,
2007). Note that none of the European data is collected or disaggregated to reveal disability among
younger children: the focus is firmly on young people of working age.
[60] The employment rate of disabled people remains stable (50%) but is still well below that for
the rest of the population (68%), see Commission, 'Situation of Disabled People in the European
Union: the European Action Plan 2008–09 (Communication) COM (2007) 738 final, 2 and
European Parliament, 'Report on the Situation of Women with Disabilities in the European Union'
(2006/2277(INI)—A6-0075/2007) final.
[61] Ibid.
[62] 2003 marked a surge of measures in this regard: the Council of Ministers of Education adopted
a Resolution on equal opportunities for pupils and students with disabilities in education and training [2003] OJ C134/04, 6. 2003 was also designated The European Year of Persons with Disabilities
and coincided with the launch of the EU's Disability Action Plan 2003–10. This adopted a clear
'mainstreaming' ethic aimed at ensuring that the diverse needs of people with disabilities are understood and taken into account when developing all aspects of EU law and policy. This approach has
been carried forward into the follow-up EU Disability Strategy 2010–20. For a summary of activities pursued under these plans, see Commission, *European Disability Strategy 2010–20: A Renewed
Commitment to a Barrier-Free Europe*, Staff Working Document (Brussels, European Commission,
2010).
[63] See, notably, the European Agency for Development in Special Needs Education (european-
agency.org/) and the education-related campaigns of the European Disability Forum (edf-feph.org/).
[64] The EU's Lifelong Learning Programme (LLP) referred to above includes provision on the
education and training of disabled people. Some measures have been taken by the EU to support
educational opportunities for disabled children, building on previous projects carried out under the
Commission's SOCRATES, LEONARDO and YOUTH programmes. For example, in 2003 the Council
of Ministers of Education adopted the Resolution on equal opportunities (above n 62) and a hearing
was organised by the European Agency for Development in Special Needs Education in the European
Parliament for children and young people from 22 countries to come and share their experiences and
wishes with Commission officials and MEPs.

on Article 13 of the former EC Treaty (now Art 19 TFEU).[65] This instrument seeks to prohibit discrimination based on religion or belief, disability, age or sexual orientation in both the public and private sectors, including education. Specifically, Article 4 of the proposed directive obliges Member States to achieve effective access for disabled people to education and anticipates that 'reasonable accommodation may be necessary to ensure such effective access' provided that this would not impose a disproportionate burden on the education service provider.[66]

It is also important to note that these activities have coincided with and responded to the emergence of a more explicit *rights*-based approach to disability at EU level. Specifically, the introduction of the Charter of Fundamental Rights of the European Union in 2000,[67] followed by the EU's ratification in December 2010 of the UN Convention on the Rights of Persons with Disabilities,[68] both make explicit provision relating to children, disability discrimination and education.[69] Significantly, by ratifying the UN Convention on Disability, the EU institutions have committed unequivocally to upholding the values of the Convention—effectively catalysing the process of disability mainstreaming within all law and policy-making activities that fall within EU competence—and bringing EU activity in line with the disability rights agenda orchestrated by the Council of Europe.[70] But more could be done to draw on the expertise and resources of the UN Committee on the Rights of the Child too. For instance, the

[65] Commission, 'Proposal for a Council Directive on Implementing the Principle of Equal Treatment Between Persons Irrespective of Religion or Belief, Disability, Age or Sexual Orientation' COM (2008) 426 final.

[66] Taken from the European Disability Forum position on the proposal for a Council Directive on implementing the principle of equal treatment between persons irrespective of religion or belief, disability, age or sexual orientation, September 2008, on the EDF website: edf-feph.org. The EDF intends to use the new Citizens Initiative process, introduced by the Treaty of Lisbon (Art 11(4)) to lobby the Commission to improve the protection available to disabled people under the proposed legislation (1million4disability.eu). Details on the scope and conditions of this process are contained in Reg 211/2011 on the Citizen's Initiative [2011] OJ L 65/1. For a critique of the Citizens Initiative as a tool for promoting children's rights issues at EU level, see H Stalford and M Schuurman, 'Are We There Yet? The Impact of the Lisbon Treaty on the EU Children's Rights Agenda' (2011) 3 *International Journal of Children's Rights* 7.

[67] See the general non-discrimination provision in Art 21, as well as Art 26, whereby 'the Union recognises and respects the right of persons with disabilities to benefit from measures designed to ensure their independence, social and occupational integration and participation in the life of the community'.

[68] This marks the first instance in which an intergovernmental organisation has signed and ratified an international human rights treaty, see A Lawson, 'The UN Convention on the Rights of Persons with Disabilities and European Disability Law: A Catalyst For Cohesion?' in OM Arnardóttir and G Quinn (eds), *The UN Convention on the Rights of Persons with Disabilities: European and Scandinavian Perspectives* (Boston, Martinus Nijhoff, 2009) 81.

[69] Art 7(1) states that 'States Parties shall take all necessary measures to ensure the full enjoyment by children with disabilities of all human rights and fundamental freedoms on an equal basis with other children'. Article 24 sets out the right of disabled people to education and the associated obligations of states parties to realise that right.

[70] See, eg Council of Europe's Action Plan to promote the rights and full participation of people with disabilities in society: improving the quality of life of people with disabilities in Europe 2006–15,

Committee's General Comment no 9 on the rights of children with disabilities[71] pinpoints various procedural and substantive measures that could be put in place at national level, such as ring-fencing a proportion of the state budget to meet the educational needs of children with disabilities and to maximise opportunities for their integration into the social and cultural mainstream. These recommendations could usefully inform further OMC-driven intergovernmental initiatives, for example under the Europe 2020 Strategy, to complement the EU's ongoing legal and awareness-raising campaigns in this area.

TACKLING DISCRIMINATION IN EDUCATION ON GROUNDS OF ETHNICITY: ROMA

A further prominent example of educational marginalisation, and an area in which the EU has shown increasing interest, relates to children from the Roma community.[72] Roma represent the biggest ethnic minority in Europe with an estimated population of 10 to 12 million present across all 27 EU Member States. Within this population, there are approximately three million Roma children of school-age in the EU.[73] Their social—including educational—marginalisation is particularly evident in some of the more recent EU accession states of Central and Eastern Europe which have a higher Roma population with many children there failing to complete even their primary education.[74] A minority reach secondary or tertiary education, while in Bulgaria and Romania, up to 15 per cent of Roma children are estimated as having received no education at all.[75]

Research has attributed chronic educational under-performance by the Roma to a history of institutionalised discrimination by school systems and continuing large-scale truancy, as Pogány notes:

> The educational needs of Roma children ... are acute and wide-ranging, and inextricably bound up with the abject poverty experienced by a significant proportion of Roma in

---

Rec (2006) 5. See further Lawson, above n 68, for a full overview of EU and Council of Europe activities in relation to disability.

[71] General Comment no 9, 'The Rights of Children with Disabilities' CRC/C/GC, 27 February 2007.

[72] The term 'Roma' is most commonly used in EU policy documents and discussions to refer to a variety of groups of people who describe themselves as Roma, Gypsies, Travellers, Manouches, Ashkali, Sinti, as well as other titles.

[73] L Farkas, *Segregation of Roma Children in Education: Addressing Structural Discrimination Through the Race Equality Directive* (Brussels, European Commission, 2007).

[74] See D Ringold, MA Orenstein and E Wilkens, *Roma in an Expanding Europe: Breaking the Poverty Cycle* (Washington, World Bank, 2003) 12; A Tremlett, "Gypsy Children Can't Learn': Roma in the Hungarian Education System' in J Goddard, S McNamee and A James (eds), *The Politics of Childhood* (Palgrave Basingstoke, MacMillan, 2005) 145. See also ch 8 for more detailed discussion of the impact of EU accession on children's status and experiences.

[75] See European Commission, *The Situation of Roma in an Enlarged European Union* (Brussels, European Commission, 2004).

the transition from communism, as well as the absence amongst many Roma subgroups of an established culture of commitment to formal education.[76]

Such observations are supported by European Commission funded research which has revealed that Roma children suffer both 'intra-school' segregation through the organisation of separate Roma classes, or 'intra-class' segregation, manifested in differing levels of curricular standards within the same class. [77]

As in the context of disability, a range of legal and non-legal initiatives have been developed at EU level to address this issue. Targeted institutional and budgetary measures include the establishment of the EURoma network in 2007 to promote the use of the EU's Structural Funds to enable Member States to share strategies and best practice with a view to standardising approaches.[78] For the most part, and consistent with the EU's mainstreaming approach to tackling inequalities, Roma-related measures are instituted as part of the broader social inclusion agenda.[79] For example, the educational inclusion of Roma children and young people is a discrete priority within the European Social Fund,[80] the EU's Lifelong Learning Programme, the Youth in Action Programme, the pre-accession programme (Phare)[81] and the public health programme.[82]

Alongside these co-operation initiatives some rather sharper legal techniques are at the EU's disposal to challenge educational discrimination against Roma children. Again, these can be categorised into human rights-based measures on the one hand, and equality measures on the other. In terms of the former, the general non-discrimination provision in the Charter of Fundamental Rights (Art 21, which prohibits discrimination on the basis of, inter alia, race, ethnic origin or membership of a national minority), coupled with Articles 22 (respect for cultural diversity), 24 (rights of the child), and 14 (right to education) provide a normative basis for challenges to EU and national measures that disadvantage Roma

---

[76] I Pogány, 'Minority Rights and the Roma of Central and Eastern Europe' (2006) 6 *Human Rights Law Review* 1, 19–20.

[77] For a detailed review of the educational rights of Roma in a Romanian context, see M Roth and F Moisa, 'The Right to Education of Roma Children in Romania: European Policies and Romanian Practices' (2011) 19 *International Journal of Children's Rights* 127.

[78] See euromanet.eu/.

[79] European Commission, 'An EU Framework for National Roma Integration Strategies up to 2020' (Communication) COM (2011) 173 final.

[80] The European Social Fund, in particular, has provided substantial support for human resources development in Roma education, depending on the particular needs of each Member State. For example, it has been used to support the training of Romani school assistants in Finland and minority education projects in Greece. See further, European Commission, *Improving the Tools for the Social Inclusion and Non-Discrimination of Roma in the EU* (Brussels, European Commission, 2010).

[81] See, eg EMS Consortium, *Review of the European Union Phare Assistance to Roma Minorities: Interim Evaluation of Phare Support Allocated in 1999–2002 and Implemented until November 2003* (Brussels, European Commission, 2004).

[82] For a review of Member States' achievements in responding to these measures, see: European Commission, 'Roma in Europe: The Implementation of European Union Instruments and Policies for Roma Inclusion—Progress Report 2008–10', Commission Staff Working Document, SEC (2010) 400 final and European Commission, 'Roma Integration: First Findings of Roma Task Force and Report on Social Inclusion' MEMO/10/701, Brussels, 21 December 2010.

children in the context of education. These EU fundamental rights measures are bolstered by the activities of the Council of Europe in relation to Roma: dovetailing with its wider, ongoing campaign to promote inclusive education for Roma,[83] the European Court of Human Rights has issued some important decisions, based on Article 2 Protocol 1 of the ECHR, to support the educational rights of this community.[84] Two landmark cases, in particular, shifted the legal landscape in this regard. In the first case — *DH v Czech Republic*[85]—the Court found that there was a violation of Article 2 Protocol 1 in conjunction with Article 14 of the ECHR[86] when it was established that an unusually high proportion of Roma children were placed in schools for children with learning disabilities. The subsequent case of *Sampanis v Greece*[87] was brought by a group of Roma school children against the Greek authorities. The children had, due to enrolment difficulties, missed a full year of primary school education and, subsequently, were placed in preparatory classes in a separate building away from the rest of the school population. The Court concluded that the school should have paid particular attention to the vulnerable position of the Roma and should have facilitated the Roma children's initial enrolment.[88]

While these decisions tackle deeply entrenched institutional prejudice against Roma children, their potential to effect change within the EU legal order is limited in two respects. First, insofar as the decisions relate to the organisation of national education systems, they fall outside the EU's law-making powers: EU intervention is somewhat confined to informing the way in which the EU develops its co-operation programmes or allocates funding for national Roma inclusion projects. Second, the ECHR provision on education is explicitly framed as a *parental* right to educate their children in conformity with their own religious and philosophical convictions rather than a right ascribed directly to the children. In reality, however, the 'philosophical convictions' of many Roma parents actually implies an aversion to mainstream education or a preference for 'home schooling' such that many Roma children experience educational exclusion directly as a result of parental prescription rather than in spite of it.

---

[83] See, eg Council of Europe Recommendation (2000) 4 on the education of Roma/Gypsy children in Europe, adopted by the Committee of Ministers on 3 February 2000.

[84] This states that 'no person shall be denied the right to education. In the exercise of any functions which it assumes in relation to education and to teaching, the State shall respect the right of parents to ensure such education and teaching in conformity with their own religions and philosophical convictions'. The discussion in ch 2 reveals the impact of international human rights instruments and jurisprudence on EU measures insofar as they relate to matters that fall within EU competence.

[85] *DH and others v Czech Republic* App no 57325/00 (2008) (unreported) Judgment of the Grand Chamber, 7 February 2006.

[86] This provision sets out a general prohibition of discrimination: 'The enjoyment of the rights and freedoms set forth in this Convention shall be secured without discrimination on any ground such as sex, race, colour, language, religion, political or other opinion, national or social origin, association with a national minority, property, birth or other status'.

[87] *Sampanis and others v Greece* App no 32526/05, Judgment 5 June 2008.

[88] The more recent ECtHR decision in *Oršuš v Croatia* App no 15766/03 (unreported) Judgment of 16 March 2010, found a similar violation of Art 2 of Protocol 1 ECHR when Roma children were placed in Roma-only classes owing to their allegedly poor command of the Croatian language.

It is for these reasons that the European Commission has expressed a preference for deploying the EU equality framework, rather than the human rights framework, to protect Roma children from educational disadvantage. Specifically, the Race Equality Directive[89] offers a comprehensive framework within which to challenge the range of discriminatory processes and institutional mechanisms that hinder Roma children's educational progress. It is necessarily broad, covering educational provision at all levels in both the public and private sectors, and in an informal or formal setting.[90] An immediate strength of the Race Equality Directive in comparison to the ECHR is that direct discrimination against Roma children generally cannot be justified on the basis of parental consent under the Directive, unlike in the context of the latter.[91] Moreover, it requires that equal treatment is ensured in relation not only to the conditions in which education is provided, but also in relation to the *content* of education. One might therefore envisage this provision being used to challenge Member States who fail to integrate sufficient minority language provision or culturally-sensitive material into their curriculum, or whose curriculum contains elements that are insensitive to the specific needs and culture of the Roma community. In that sense, the EU's broader non-discrimination framework has the potential to activate substantive changes to Member States' education systems in a manner that would otherwise be impossible in the context of more explicit EU education provision or, indeed, in the context of human rights provision.

The status and experiences of Roma children, like disabled children, are shaped by an array of social, ethnic, economic, legal and cultural variables: on one level, their educational marginalisation may be characteristic of unchallenged exclusionary laws and policies (segregation policies, inappropriate access and streaming procedures) at the national or even regional level; yet on another level, it is likely to be borne out of more deeply-embedded structural obstacles and social or cultural prejudices (absenteeism, drop-out, residential segregation or the itinerant lifestyle).[92] The multifarious nature of discrimination and social exclusion, even within particular communities, reinforces the need for a mixed strategy at European level: one that deploys a blend of legal and non-legal initiatives, including top-down legal prescription, coupled with the OMC and complemented by bottom-up awareness-raising and grass-roots advocacy. The EU seems to have achieved a good combination in this regard, but the extent to which it is successful in enabling children to actually receive a sufficient standard of education remains to be seen. Certainly, existing research at the national level reveals pervasive inequalities in education, inequalities that are intrinsically linked with poverty and social exclusion and which, so far, have been largely impervious to national

---

[89] Dir 2000/43 implementing the principle of equal treatment between persons irrespective of racial or ethnic origin [2000] OJ L180/22.

[90] Art 3(1).

[91] Farkas, *Segregation of Roma Children*, above n 73.

[92] Roth and Moisa, above n 77.

social inclusion initiatives. It is for this reason that the goals and monitoring processes established by the EU, embedded within its broader social inclusion agenda, are to be welcomed as enhancing Member States' accountability for the persistent underachievement of certain socially, economically and ethnically marginalised groups.

CONCLUSION

In exploring the contexts in which children's educational rights are upheld at EU level, this chapter has sought to make some broader observations about the various regulatory and political factors that drive or, indeed, hinder the EU's approach to children's rights. The educational rights and needs of children are as vast as they are diverse and are, therefore, necessarily pursued in various contexts, using a variety of governance tools. This is no less so at EU level which adopts a multi-methods approach that is sensitive to but not particularly constrained by the boundaries between Member State and EU competence. On the one hand, we see some modest binding measures—enacted primarily through equality and migration legislation—establishing a 'floor' of rights upon which Member States can implement additional measures to reflect their individual social, cultural, religious, economic and political contexts. This operates in tandem with soft law, funding initiatives and the OMC, whereby the EU works with and supports Member States in developing their policies within an integrated framework.

In some cases, education is pursued as a discrete and targeted policy area but, more often than not, it is mainstreamed into the EU's rather broader social and economic agendas. This typical approach, whereby education is mainstreamed throughout virtually all aspects of EU social and rights-related law, carries with it specific benefits both in terms of the increased resources available and the heightened political impetus to achieve those goals. In the process, education acts as a vehicle by which children's rights are drawn into the very heart of the EU polity.

Certainly, the measures referred to in this chapter offer useful illustrations of how different EU regulatory tools and contexts can be used together to address the range of educational needs that children have. Collectively, they respond quite well to the complex mix of welfare-related needs on the one hand (particularly in relation to the economically and socially marginalised), and to a vision of children and young people as active protagonists in the present and future of Europe, on the other. However, there is always the risk that in embedding education within broader political, economic and social frameworks, the EU risks obscuring or compromising children's *rights* to and within education. Inevitably, therefore, the EU is forced to grapple with various tensions depending on the regulatory context in which education is pursued. In the context of the EU's Social Agenda, we see a tension between enhancing children's experiences in the here and now whilst maximising their potential to contribute to the future economic, cultural and political capital of the EU. The trade off here is that the rights and experiences of younger children are often sidelined in favour of those with a more realistic, imminent capacity to contribute directly to the economic and political life of the EU. By the same token, education-related measures aimed at promoting opportunities for 'active citizenship', while they provide a political discourse with which the EU can engage more positively with young people, have yet to reach significantly beyond the relatively privileged, already educated and politically savvy European mainstream. Similarly, education rights pursued in the context of migration, while they support children's fundamental right to access compulsory education whatever their circumstances, remain vulnerable to the political sensibilities of the Member States who may be keen to constrain the rights of children from migrant communities that threaten to destabilise national welfare regimes.

The educational measures achieved under the EU's equality framework perhaps chime more persuasively with the children's rights ideology in that concerns to protect and promote the interests of the most marginalised groups are at the forefront of the legislative measures, with little scope for compromise.

Importantly, however, a more prominent rights rhetoric is now creeping into all contexts in which EU educational measures have been developed. EU equality measures are now increasingly informed by international and European human rights instruments, such that the two discourses have almost converged. Equally, the social inclusion process and the nurturing of active citizenship is now explicitly associated with the fulfilment of the objectives identified in the Charter of Fundamental Rights, and developments within the immigration and free movement framework are now commonly scrutinised for their compatibility with human rights standards.[93] Procedurally, too, we see greater potential for the EU to pool resources with and learn from parallel international human rights initiatives in the field of education, notably the Council of Europe and the United Nations. The extent to which such developments will impact materially on children's experiences on the ground remains to be seen: detailed and comparable data revealing the true extent of *children's* educational status across all the Member States has yet to be achieved, and the true impact of EU measures on the lived experiences of children has yet to be comprehensively evaluated. Notwithstanding these limitations, education is one area in which the EU seems to be moving in the right direction, applying a flexible and responsive regulatory methodology which is genuinely informed by human rights, which embodies distinct participatory elements, and from which other aspects of EU children's rights could usefully learn.

---

[93] Notably by virtue of the European Commission, 'Strategy for the Effective Implementation of the Charter of Fundamental Rights by the European Union' (Communication) COM (2010) 573, 4 discussed further in ch 2.

7

Child Protection and EU Law

INTRODUCTION

CHILD PROTECTION COVERS a multitude of issues. It can denote the protection of children's rights in general terms, but more commonly it refers specifically to the protection of children against the worst forms of exploitation, abuse, violence and neglect. It is this second interpretation that will inform the discussion in this chapter, the aim of which is to analyse the nature and scope of EU intervention in different aspects of child protection.

The international legal framework offers a useful benchmark against which to evaluate EU child protection measures. Indeed, it is the international framework that has informed the development of child protection initiatives at national and regional level. A key provision in this regard is Article 19 of the United Nations' Convention on the Rights of the Child (UNCRC) which provides that states parties shall take all appropriate legal, administrative, social and educational measures to protect children from all forms of abuse. The provision identifies a range of responses that should be initiated to enable states parties to fulfil these obligations, including programmes aimed at spotting, protecting and treating victims, and at identifying, investigating and prosecuting perpetrators.[1]

Child protection is, therefore, an inherently multi-faceted endeavour, associated very much with the development of national and local systems, standards and procedures aimed at preventing, identifying, investigating and treating instances of child abuse or neglect. Furthermore, their successful implementation implies a coherent, multi-agency co-operation between the educational, social welfare, investigative and judicial authorities.[2] The question for this chapter is the extent to which such approaches have permeated the EU regulatory framework. Certainly, child protection issues have grabbed and sustained the EU's attention to a much greater extent than other aspects of children's rights. There has been significant EU investment in research, legal and policy measures aimed at exposing and addressing some of the most serious violations of children's rights. In fact, the proliferation of EU measures in the field of

---

[1] C Forder, 'Family Rights and Immigration Law: A European Perspective' in H Schneider (ed), *Migration, Integration and Citizenship: A Challenge for Europe's Future*, vol II (Maastricht, Forum Maastricht, 2005).

[2] J Fortin, *Children's Rights and the Developing Law* (Cambridge, Cambridge University Press, 2005).

child protection stands in stark contrast to the EU's reluctance to engage with children's rights more generally. The standard rationale for non-intervention—based on limited competence and the political opposition to EU engagement in issues that are regarded as more appropriately addressed at the national and local level—seems to present less of a barrier in the context of child protection. It seems, somehow, more politically palatable for the EU to intervene to safeguard the most vulnerable of children.

Given the broad scope of this area, the aim of this chapter is not simply to summarise EU child protection measures. Rather it will address broader questions relating, first, to the basis and remit of the EU's role in this regard. Secondly, it will critically assess the coherence and utility of the EU child protection agenda and whether it is truly compatible with children's rights. This will involve some consideration of the extent to which EU intervention complements, overlaps with or, indeed, undermines other international child protection efforts. The third section suggests some methodological and institutional changes that need to be put in place to enhance the effectiveness of the EU's response in this area.

AN OVERVIEW OF THE LEGAL AND POLICY FRAMEWORK UNDERPINNING EU CHILD PROTECTION MEASURES

Any analysis of the nature and scope of the EU child protection agenda demands some scrutiny of the source of EU competence to implement measures in this regard. Such competence is derived both from the EU's broader commitment to adhere to fundamental rights as part of the general principles of EU law framework,[3] and more recently, from specific measures enshrined within the treaties. As to the former, in general terms, international conventions relating to the protection of children inform the development and interpretation of EU law in the same way as other aspects of fundamental rights. The extent of this commitment should not be underestimated: a range of international instruments contain detailed provisions on child protection.[4] Virtually every article of the UNCRC, for example, contains some provision of relevance to child protection to supplement the general framework established in Article 19. It includes measures that endorse state intervention in family affairs, for example by removing a child from a violent or neglectful home if it is in his/her own best interests (Art 9), as well as the provision of alternative care arrangements (Arts 20–21). Other measures are aimed at attaining and maintaining high standards in child care/child protection institutions (Art 3(3)), and at regularly scrutinising the treatment of children who have been taken into

---

[3] Discussed in ch 2.

[4] Eg the European Court of Human Rights (ECtHR), the Convention on the Elimination of All Forms of Discrimination against Women (CEDAW—now regulated by the Office of the High Commissioner for Human Rights in Geneva), the International Declaration of Children's Rights, the UN Disability Convention, to name but a few. See Forder, *'Family Rights'*, above n 1 for further details about this international framework.

care (Art 25). Articles 32 to 39 further elaborate on the standards that should be applied to combat economic and sexual exploitation, including trafficking. The provisions and principles set out in the UNCRC are complemented by a range of Practice Guides, General Comments,[5] Protocols[6] and Recommendations targeting specific aspects of child protection[7] and responding to particular national child protection regimes.[8]

The extent to which the EU institutions—and, indeed the Member States— have to adhere to such international standards in the formulation, application and interpretation of EU law has already been discussed at length in chapter two. This obligation is reinforced by the EU constitution itself: Article 3(3) TEU, as amended by the Lisbon Treaty, establishes 'protection of the rights of the child' as one of the Union's core values, while Article 3(5) TEU identifies protection of the rights of the child as an important aspect of the EU's external relations policy. These developments, in turn, reaffirm the child protection obligations inherent in the Charter of Fundamental Rights of the European Union (the Charter), which is now afforded the same legal status as the treaties.[9] While many of the substantive rights contained within the Charter are applicable to child protection,[10] Article 24 acknowledges more generally children's inherent vulnerability and need for protection. (1) children shall have the right to such protection and care as is

---

[5] The UN Committee on the Rights of the Child has so far published 12 General Comments which are essentially detailed guidelines on its interpretation of discrete provisions of the UNCRC. While all of these touch upon some aspect of child protection, those with a more explicit child protection agenda include: General Comment no 10, 'Children's Rights in Juvenile Justice' CRC/C/GC/10, 25 April 2007; General Comment no 8, 'The Right of the Child to Protection from Corporal Punishment and Other Cruel or Degrading Forms of Punishment' CRC/C/GC/8, 2 March 2007; General Comment no 6, 'Treatment of Unaccompanied and Separated Children Outside Their Country of Origin' CRC/GC/2005/6, 1 September 2005 and General Comment no 3, 'HIV/AIDS and the Rights of the Child' CRC/GC/2003/3, 17 March 2003.

[6] The United Nations General Assembly adopted two Optional Protocols to the Convention in 2000 to enhance levels of protection against and awareness of specific, extreme abuses against children: the Optional Protocol on the Sale of Children, Child Prostitution and Child Pornography and the Optional Protocol on the Involvement of Children in Armed Conflict.

[7] See, eg the Report of the Independent Expert for the United Nations study on violence against children, UN Doc A/61/299, 29 August 2006, and the more elaborate World Report on Violence Against Children (PS Pinheiro, *Report on Violence Against Children* (Geneva, UN, 2006)). Furthermore, Art 32 UNCRC provides for the integration into the child rights' context of standards against economic exploitation of children developed by the International Labour Organisation (ILO), such as the ILO Conventions 138 (1973) concerning a Minimum Age for Admission to Employment, and ILO Convention 182 (1999) on the Worst Forms of Child Labour.

[8] See further T Buck, A Gillespie, L Ross and S Sargent, *International Child Law*, 2nd edn (Abingdon, Routledge, 2010), and for further guidance on how the child protection-related provisions of the UNCRC are implemented and monitored see R Hodgkin and P Newell, *Implementation Handbook for the Convention on the Rights of the Child*, 3rd edn (Geneva, UNICEF, 2007).

[9] Art 6(1) TEU.

[10] Substantive protective rights include Art 3 (right to the integrity of the person); Art 4 (prohibition of torture and inhuman or degrading treatment or punishment); Art 5 (prohibition of slavery and forced labour); Art 18 (right to asylum); Art 19 (prohibition of slavery and forced labour); Art 32 (prohibition of child labour and protection of young people at work). See further H Cullen, 'Children's Rights' in S Peers and A Ward (eds), *The EU Charter of Fundamental Rights: Politics, Law and Policy* (Oxford, Hart, 2004) 323.

necessary for their well-being and (2) in all actions relating to children, whether taken by public authorities or private institutions, the child's best interests must be a primary consideration.

While the EU's constitutional commitment to protecting children's welfare is bold and unequivocal, substantive EU measures in this area have emerged in a characteristically gradual and piecemeal fashion and have necessarily been confined to key areas that intersect with the operation of EU law. In that sense, legislative attention has largely concentrated on the child protection implications of EU internal market measures such as the free movement of goods, services and persons and latterly, with the growing asylum and immigration acquis.[11] Accompanying this, however, is a raft of non-legislative measures which have proved equally, if not more effective, in tackling various forms of child abuse and exploitation.

Before embarking on a more detailed presentation of these provisions, it is important to note that the legal force and scope of EU child protection law and policy has been affected quite significantly by the structural and institutional changes brought about by the Lisbon Treaty. Most notably, the Lisbon Treaty dissolved the 'three pillar structure' established by the 1992 Maastricht Treaty, with the effect that all measures that had previously been formulated on an intergovernmental basis under pillars two[12] and three[13] are now integrated into a single system and governed primarily by the Treaty on the Functioning of the European Union (TFEU).[14] This includes all matters relating to child protection (notably measures to combat child trafficking and sexual exploitation), all of which were previously regulated under pillar three, but which are now regulated under Title V (Arts 67–80) TFEU entitled 'Area of Freedom Security and Justice'. This constitutional restructuring simplifies and streamlines the legislative process, reducing the former menu of legal instruments available to a choice of just three—directives, regulations or decisions[15]—the implementation of which are subject to scrutiny of the Court of Justice. Consequently, any child protection instruments that were adopted (typically as framework decisions) under the former pillar three will now have to be recast in one of these three forms, with the potential to produce much more uniform, legally forceful effects across the Member States.[16]

---

[11] A range of other, more sporadic initiatives have emerged in the context of consumer protection and health and safety, the details of which fall outside the scope of this book.

[12] Formerly the pillar governing common foreign and security policy.

[13] Governing police and judicial co-operation in criminal matters.

[14] Formerly the first 'EC' pillar.

[15] Arts 288–92 TFEU.

[16] All framework decisions have to be updated and transformed into directives before they can have effect under the regime of the Lisbon Treaty (Art 10 of Protocol 36). See further H Stalford and M Schuurman, 'Are We There Yet?: The Impact of the Lisbon Treaty on the EU Children's Rights Agenda' (2011) 3 *International Journal of Children's Rights* 7; S Peers, 'Mission Accomplished? EU Justice and Home Affairs Law After the Treaty of Lisbon' (2011) 48 *CML Rev* 661.

EU CHILD PROTECTION LEGISLATION

EU intervention to protect children in a cross-border context is rationalised on very much the same grounds as EU family justice measures (as explored in chapters four and five): the free circulation of goods, services and people, facilitated through the liberalisation of internal border checks, particularly from the early 1990s onwards,[17] has served the more nefarious objectives of those engaged in illegal cross-border activity. Human trafficking, child abduction and sex tourism are obvious examples of such crimes. These phenomena have been compounded by the further expansion of the EU to include the Central and Eastern European states from 2004 onwards: what were formerly hotbeds of such activities in the 'external' world are now firmly located within the EU, while common 'source' countries such as the Russian Federation, Ukraine, Belarus, Turkey, Moldova and the Western Balkans now enjoy easier access to the EU territory as border countries. In particular, individuals from these countries are now routinely identified in the course of EU law enforcement investigations as either trafficking victims or perpetrators.[18] EU action to combat such issues is, therefore, seen as offering the most appropriate means of addressing the unintended consequences of the economic, legal and geographical expansion of the EU. However, the development of child protection law in this area represents more than just the EU's acknowledgement of its accountability for facilitating cross-border child exploitation. It also reflects nation states' impotence to tackle some of the most odious forms of child abuse and exploitation by themselves, and is concerned with harnessing the EU's unique political and economic resources to formulate a supra-national response to what are typically trans-national phenomena.

EU EFFORTS TO COMBAT CHILD TRAFFICKING

Up until very recently, the sole constitutional basis for EU action in relation to child protection was limited to an isolated reference to human trafficking and 'offences against children' under the former 1992 Treaty on European Union (TEU). The former Article 29 TEU specifically identified 'trafficking in persons

---

[17] Member States' commitment to the gradual abolition of checks at their common borders can be traced back to the Schengen Agreement of 14 June 1985. This subsequently led to the 1990 Schengen Convention which came into effect in March 1995 [2000] OJ L239/19. Measures aimed at abolishing controls on internal borders between the signatory countries were also accompanied by so-called 'compensatory measures' intended to ensure a high level of security within this zone. These measures involved the development of a common visa regime, improving co-ordination between the police, customs and the judiciary and co-ordinating efforts to combat problems such as terrorism and organised crime. For further analysis of the scope and impact of Schengen, see S Peers and N Rogers (eds), *EU Immigration and Asylum Law: Text and Commentary* (Leiden, Martinus Nijhoff, 2006) ch 1.

[18] Europol, *Trafficking in Human Beings in the European Union: A Europol Perspective*, December 2009: europol.europa.eu/publications/Serious_Crime_Overviews/Trafficking%20in%20Human%20Beings%20June%202009.pdf.

and offences against children' as particular priority areas for closer co-operation between Member States in the former third pillar context of police and judicial co-operation in criminal matters.[19] This was reinforced subsequently by the Charter, which introduced an explicit prohibition of trafficking in human beings.[20] As far as secondary legislation is concerned, the former Article 29 TEU gave rise to the Framework Decision 2002/629 of 19 July 2002 on combating trafficking in human beings,[21] the aim of which was to harmonise Member States' criminal responses to perpetrators of child trafficking and to achieve a level of consonance between EU law and the international trafficking regulatory framework. Significantly, this framework decision is the first of the EU child protection instruments enacted under the former pillar three to have undergone the transposition into an EU directive[22] (hereafter the Trafficking Victims Directive) in response to the constitutional changes brought about by the Lisbon Treaty.[23]

The EU has also addressed trafficking through its competence in the field of visas, asylum and immigration, although in a much more instrumental way.[24] This is an implicit acknowledgement that the factors driving 'forced' migration— political or civil unrest, or financial hardship—may be the very factors that expose people to trafficking.[25] The most notable achievement in this regard was the introduction of Directive 2004/81[26] (hereafter 'the Trafficking Co-operation Directive'). This Directive enables third country nationals who are victims of trafficking or of an illegal immigration to be issued with a residence permit by the host state on the condition that they co-operate with the competent authorities in identifying the perpetrators of the crime. Significantly, children are excluded from the scope of this instrument unless individual Member States decide otherwise.[27] In the event that a Member State choses to incorporate some protection for minors, they are obliged to implement further protective measures to ensure that child victims' needs are met; for example, due account must be taken of the child's best interests in seeking their co-operation with any investigation. The Directive also provides scope for enhanced national provision on education,

---

[19]   This provision was included within the TEU by the Treaty of Amsterdam 1997. Note that following the Treaty of Lisbon, all measures relating to police and judicial co-operation in criminal matters are integrated into a new Title V of the Treaty of the Functioning of the EU (TFEU) (Area of Freedom, Security and Justice). As such, the former Art 29 TEU is now replaced by Art 67 TFEU. This is rather more general than the former Art 29 TEU in that it does not make any explicit reference to trafficking in persons or offences against children. Explicit references to trafficking are included, however, within Ch 2, Title V on Border Checks, Asylum and Immigration (Art 79), and within Ch 4, Title V TFEU relating to Judicial Co-operation in Criminal Matters (Art 83).

[20]   Art 5(3).

[21]   [2002] OJ L203/1.

[22]   Dir 2011/36 on preventing and combating trafficking in human beings and protecting its victims [2011] OJ L101/1 and replacing Council Framework Decision 2002/629.

[23]   The implications of these changes are discussed below.

[24]   Formerly under Arts 61–69, Title IV Pt III EC; now regulated under Arts 77–80 TFEU.

[25]   IOM, *Trafficking in Unaccompanied Minors in the European Union* (Paris, IOM, 2002).

[26]   [2004] OJ L261/19.

[27]   Art 3.

family reunification and legal representation, as well as an obligation to make efforts to establish the minor's identity.[28]

CHILD PROTECTION LAW AND THE EU INTERNAL MARKET

Child protection has also featured, albeit in a much more subtle way, in EU free movement law governing the mobility of both EU nationals and goods between the Member States. Specifically, legislation governing the free movement of persons protects migrant children against expulsion from the host state, even if this would otherwise be justified on grounds of public policy or public security. This is based on a desire to protect children's welfare by preventing any unnecessary separation from their family in the host state.[29] Similarly, the regulatory framework governing the free movement of goods between the EU Member States,[30] while it does not contain an explicit reference to protecting children, does allow national restrictions to be imposed on imports or exports on grounds of, inter alia, 'public morality, public policy or public security; the protection of health and life of humans'.[31] The Court of Justice has demonstrated a willingness to interpret this proviso with a view to safeguarding children's welfare, even if doing so might serve to undermine the EU's single market ethos. The case of *Dynamic Medien*, for example, concerned an action by one German company (Dynamic Medien) to prohibit another German company (Avides) from importing DVDs and videos of Japanese 'Anime' cartoons from the UK. Dynamic Medien argued that even though the cartoons had been classified as suitable for children of 15 years and older by the UK film classification authorities, they had not been subject to the same approval in accordance with German law. The respondents, Avides, contended that this additional requirement constituted a disproportionate infringement on the free movement of goods—effectively imposing a prohibited double regulatory burden on goods moving between the Member States. The Court of Justice found in favour of Dynamic Medien, however, affirming that the restrictions could be justified on the grounds of public policy or public morality. In reaching its conclusion, the Court of Justice relied on key children's rights principles enshrined in both the Charter (Art 24) and in the UNCRC. In particular, whilst acknowledging children's Article 13 UNCRC right to freedom of information, the Court attached persuasive force to Article 17 UNCRC which encourages signatory states to

---

[28] Art 10.
[29] Para 24, Preamble and Art 28(3) Directive 2004/38 on the right of citizens of the Union and their family members to move and reside freely within the territory of the Member States [2004] OJ L158/77.
[30] Title II, Pt III (Arts 28–37) TFEU (ex Title I, Pt III (Arts 23–31) EC).
[31] Art 36 TFEU (ex Art 30 EC).

develop 'appropriate guidelines for the protection of the child from information and material injurious to his or her well-being'.[32]

Significantly, the decision in *Dynamic Medien* represents the only example to date of the UNCRC being used by the Court of Justice to trump the fundamental freedoms associated with the free circulation of goods between the Member States.[33] In addition, however, it emphasises the EU's sensitivity to different Member States' regulatory responses to child protection issues; responses that are informed by potent cultural, social, political and religious factors that may vary significantly from one context to another.

EU CHILD SEXUAL EXPLOITATION AND ABUSE LEGISLATION

The third main context in which legally binding EU child protection measures have been developed is in the area of sexual exploitation and abuse, again under the former third pillar framework of police and judicial co-operation in criminal matters. Most notable in this regard was the Framework Decision on combating the sexual exploitation of children and child pornography, introduced in 2004 aimed to achieve a level of co-ordination between Member States' criminal justice responses to the sexual exploitation of children.[34] To achieve this, the instrument sought to approximate Member States' investigative and judicial approaches to criminal activities by introducing common provisions to regulate the creation of sexual exploitation offences, penalties, aggravating circumstances, jurisdiction and extradition. The Framework Decision also called for the sensitive treatment and protection of child victims in the investigation and prosecution of such offences.[35] In response to the changes brought about by the Lisbon Treaty, the Commission transposed this instrument into a directive and, in the process, seised the opportunity to review and update its content to address the impact of technological developments on child sexual exploitation.[36]

THE DEVELOPMENT OF AN EU CHILD PROTECTION INFRASTRUCTURE

These legislative and judicial developments present only part of the EU child protection framework and reflect those issues that intersect very clearly with the EU's

---

[32] Case C-244/06 *Dynamic Medien Vertriebs GmbH v Avides Media AG* [2008] ECR I-505.

[33] On the tensions created between the need to safeguard fundamental internal market freedoms on the one hand and fundamental rights on the other, see ch 2.

[34] Council Framework Decision 2004/68 [2004] OJ L 13/44.

[35] Para 11 Preamble and Art 9(2). This is consistent with Art 13 of Framework Decision 2001/220 on the standing of victims in criminal proceedings with respect to sexually exploited children.

[36] Directive 2011/93/EU of the European Parliament and of the Council of 13 December 2011 on combating the sexual abuse and exploitation of children and child pornography, and replacing Council Framework Decision 2004/68/JHA, OJ L 18, 21.1.2012, p 7–7.

competence in relation to immigration control or to achieve cross-national police co-operation in criminal matters. The EU has always acknowledged, however, that this body of law can only operate if supported by a robust child protection infrastructure to facilitate the cross-national gathering and exchange of information relating to both victims and perpetrators. Throughout the 1990s, for instance, the Commission supported a series of joint action programmes aimed at promoting international co-operation between law-enforcement authorities.[37] This initial investment eventually led to the establishment of a number of cross-national bodies. Notably, EUROJUST was set up in February 2002 as a judicial co-operation body responsible for co-ordinating investigations and prosecutions across the Member States. Its activities primarily focus on organised criminal activity that crosses borders, particularly human trafficking. Similarly, the European Law Enforcement Agency (EUROPOL) facilitates co-operation between the investigative authorities in the Member States with a view to preventing and combating serious organised crime, including criminal activities involving children. Both of these bodies are assisted by the data-gathering activities of the Schengen Information System (SIS) which allows the competent authorities in the Member States to obtain information regarding certain categories of persons and property that have moved across borders.[38]

2002 also saw the introduction of the European Arrest Warrant (EAW),[39] a fast-track extradition procedure enabling the national judicial authorities of one Member State to secure the arrest and return of a person to their territory to answer charges of an offence. While the EAW was initially driven largely by a desire to track down suspected terrorists, it has also assisted in bringing to justice perpetrators of crimes against children following their move to another Member State.[40] However, its success in this regard remains limited, mainly because it operates only in relation to those who have already been identified to the police and are being prosecuted for an offence.[41] In that sense, it is less a tool for *child*

---

[37] For a summary, see B Hebenton and T Thomas, *Policing Europe: Co-operation, Conflict and Control* (New York, St Martin's Press, 1995) and B Hebenton and T Thomas, 'Capacity Building Against Transnational Organised Crime: Measures to Combat Sexual Offenders' (1999) 7 *European Journal of Crime, Criminal Law and Criminal Justice* 150.

[38] For details of the history and scope of the SIS, see B Hayes, *From the Schengen Information System to SIS II and the Visa Information (VIS): the Proposals Explained* (London, Statewatch, 2004).

[39] Council Framework Decision 2002/584 on the European Arrest Warrant and the surrender procedures between Member States—statements made by certain Member States on the adoption of the Framework Decision. This has subsequently been amended by Council Framework Decision 2009/299 amending Framework Decisions 2002/584, 2005/214, 2006/783, 2008/909 and 2008/947, thereby enhancing the procedural rights of persons and fostering the application of the principle of mutual recognition to decisions rendered in the absence of the person concerned at the trial [2009] *OJ L 81/24*.

[40] Most notoriously, in March 2010, Liam Adams, a prominent member of the Irish Republican Party, Sinn Fein, (and brother of its leader, Gerry Adams), was issued with a EAW in the Irish Republic to answer claims of sexual abuse committed against his daughter for over a decade whilst living in Northern Ireland.

[41] The EAW is limited to cases in which a final sentence of imprisonment has been imposed for a period of at least four months or for offences for which the maximum period of the penalty is at least a year in prison.

protection—insofar as the offence has already been committed—but rather one of accountability and retribution.

Arguably, a more effective cross-national child protection procedure is provided by an interconnected, transparent criminal records system that ensures that those with convictions for offences against children in one Member State can be prevented from working with children in any other state to which they move. Campaigners have been calling for such measures for many years now, arguing that existing international provision[42] is out-of-date and difficult to enforce in an area as vast and diverse the EU. Certainly fluid free movement policy and practice make it increasingly difficult to track the activities of EU migrant workers who pose a threat to children. The NSPCC, for instance, have observed that:

> There is evidence to suggest that people who have been convicted of sexual offences against children are increasingly travelling to other countries. What we know about the behaviour of sex offenders indicates that convicted offenders may seek to exploit differences between countries' systems to evade detection, or obtain employment with children and abuse again. In some EU member states it is easier to get jobs that provide access to children than it is in others.[43]

This was illustrated to devastating effect by the case of Michel Fourniret, a French forest warden who murdered and raped seven young women and children during his time as a caretaker on both sides of the Franco–Belgian border between 1987 and 2001. Fourniret moved to Belgium in the late 1980s after being jailed in France for child sex offences, but was offered a job in a school by the Belgian authorities who were unaware of his criminal record. He subsequently murdered one woman and attempted to abduct another young girl in Belgium until his wife (an accessory in many of his previous crimes) reported him to the police. Fourniret is still being investigated for similar crimes against young girls in other parts of Europe.[44]

The EU has only recently responded to the child protection threats posed by the free movement of workers provisions, initially in the form of Framework Decision 2009/315 on the organisation and content of the exchange of information extracted from criminal records between Member States.[45] While this instrument, like the EAW, was primarily designed to identify and track convicted or suspected terrorists, its potential as a child protection tool is clear:

> The mechanism established by this Framework Decision aims at ... ensuring that a person convicted of a sexual offence against children should no longer ... be able to conceal

---

[42] Notably, the European Convention on Mutual Assistance in Criminal Matters 1959.

[43] K Fitch, K Spencer-Chapman and Z Hilton, *Protecting Children from Sexual Abuse in Europe: Safer Recruitment of Workers in a Border-Free Europe* (London, NSPCC, 2007) 3.

[44] H Samuel, 'Michel Fourniret Jailed for Life Over Ardennes Sex Murders' *The Telegraph*, London, 28 May 2008.

[45] [2009] OJ L93/23. Prior to this, the EU funded some small-scale initiatives, concentrated within the individual Member States. See, eg the CUPISCO (Collection and Use of Personal Information on Child Sex Offenders) Programme reported in Hebenton and Thomas, *Capacity Building*, above n 37, 155.

this conviction … with a view to performing professional activity related to supervision of children in another Member State.[46]

EU attempts to approximate rules on the format and transmission of criminal records across all of the Member States are further supported by the Directive on combating the sexual abuse, sexual exploitation of children and child pornography.[47] This provides that, to avoid the risk of repeat offences, Member States shall take the necessary measures to ensure that any person who has been convicted of child sex offences may be temporarily or permanently prevented from exercising activities involving regular contact with children. It further states that Member States shall take the necessary measures to ensure that such disqualifications are entered into the criminal records of any other Member State to which the offender moves. [48]

ADDED VALUE OR EMPTY RHETORIC? ASSESSING THE EFFECTIVENESS OF EU ACTION IN THE FIELD OF CHILD PROTECTION

The activities detailed so far present an impressive portfolio of EU child protection measures, one that makes an unequivocal commitment to preventative and protective action in the field of child exploitation and abuse. The success of these measures in actually achieving those goals, however, depends on the following key factors: (1) whether the EU initiatives outlined above truly endorse a *children's rights* approach that captures and accommodates children's lived experiences; (2) whether EU child protection measures add *value* to the patchwork of parallel international and, indeed, national initiatives and (3), whether they can be persuasively enforced to produce tangible effects on the ground.

IS EU CHILD PROTECTION LEGISLATION COMPATIBLE WITH CHILDREN'S RIGHTS?

Despite the proliferation of EU child protection measures, a number of factors are identified as undermining their capacity to impact meaningfully on children's rights and welfare. First, it can be argued that the internal market logic underpinning the EU will almost always prevail over child protection objectives such that any provision designed to uphold and protect children's rights struggles to compete with the other more dominant agendas it endorses. For example, EU immigration and asylum legislation has effected a fairly pronounced shift away from the early focus on upholding international human

---

[46] Ibid para 12 Preamble.
[47] Above n 36.
[48] Ibid Art 10.

rights standards that seek to protect the rights of immigrants—as enshrined in the Geneva Convention, for example—towards a more resolute preoccupation with safeguarding external borders in the name of national security and economic rationalisation.[49] Children's rights are an inevitable casualty of this trend, as evidenced most poignantly in the 'selective' right of children to join their families in the host state offered by the EU Family Reunification Directive,[50] and the 'conditional' protection offered by the Directive granting residence to the victims of trafficking.[51] The objection here is not to the pursuit of public security and economic stability—undeniably important prerogatives—but rather to the sidelining or displacement of children's interests that commonly ensues. As the Fundamental Rights Agency have noted in the context of child trafficking: 'States have an important interest in prosecuting child traffickers and in regulating immigration. However these policy goals should not be allowed to overshadow the best interests of child victims of trafficking'.[52]

This is always a danger in the context of securitisation in particular, whereby the interests of a largely 'invisible' group of children can be so readily subjugated to the broader interests of safeguarding external borders. Indeed, this process can be legitimately rationalised as a policy that prioritises the greater (national) interests over the interests of a (non-national) minority: an approach that is aimed at enhancing national security in times of unprecedented vulnerability to terrorist attacks, and at minimising the burden on national social and welfare systems in times of acute economic fragility.

The more explicit child protection objective of EU trafficking and sexual exploitation legislation has, in the past, risked being circumscribed by its overarching 'criminalisation' agenda. For instance, the previous incarnation of the Framework Decision on child sexual exploitation[53] and of the Trafficking Victims Directive[54] were criticised for focusing primarily on approximating national approaches to defining offences and prosecuting perpetrators, with relatively little

---

[49] Although the latter priorities remain prominent. For an analysis of how the EU and Member States respectively have responded to the security challenges associated with the freedom, security and justice, particularly in the wake of the Lisbon Treaty, see Peers, above n 16; T Obokata, 'Key EU Principles to Combat Transational Organised Crime' (2011) 48 *CML Rev* 801; A Hinarejos, 'Law and Order and Internal Security Provisions in the Area of Freedom, Security and Justice: Before and After Lisbon' in C Eckes and T Konstadinides (eds), Crime Within the Area of Freedom, Security and Justice: A European Public Order (Cambridge, Cambridge University Press, 2011).

[50] Dir 2003/86 on the right to family reunification [2003] OJ L251/12, notably Arts 4(1) and 4(6), discussed further in ch 4. See further E Drywood, 'Giving with One Hand, Taking with the Other: Fundamental Rights, Children and the Family Reunification Decision' (2007) 32 *EL Rev* 396.

[51] The Trafficking Co-operation Directive, above n 26.

[52] FRA, *Child Trafficking in the European Union: Challenges, Perspectives and Good Practices* (Luxembourg, Office for Official Publications of the European Communities, 2009) 12. See also E Drywood, '"Child-Proofing" EU Law and Policy: Interrogating the Law-Making Processes Behind Asylum and Immigration Provision' (2011) 3 *International Journal of Children's Rights* 31.

[53] Above n 34.

[54] Above n 22.

attention devoted to protecting or rehabilitating the victims of such crimes.[55] The protective potential of this law was further diluted by its tendency to generalise or, worse still, homogenise the status and experiences of child 'victims'. The initial Framework Decision on trafficking victims, for example, was premised on a single, dominant discourse of child trafficking: that of the involuntary removal of children from their country of origin for purposes of sexual or labour exploitation. While this may characterise a significant proportion of child trafficking, it obscured the complexity of trafficked children's lives, the variety of childhood cultures from which they emerge, and the reality of the 'choices' they and their families make.[56] The original instrument was also confined to child trafficking for the purposes of labour or sexual exploitation, whilst ignoring other, equally prominent 'pull' factors associated with trafficking such as adoption, domestic work, forced marriage or organ extraction.

Thankfully, there are positive signs that the EU has reflected on and is addressing these weaknesses: the revised Trafficking Victims Directive, as well as the revised sexual exploitation legislation, for instance, both include much more extensive and explicit measures aimed at protecting victims, including facilitating access to legal remedies and adapting criminal proceedings to address child victims' inherent vulnerabilities.[57] Further resources have also been invested in developing an extensive, empirically-verified evidence base for the development of more responsive child protection measures,[58] which involve more active consultation with national and international child protection experts. While all of these developments suggest a greater level of coherence with the international child protection framework referred to at the beginning of this chapter, they also signal an attempt to link the different areas

---

[55] Measures were limited to requiring, rather vaguely, that all Member States ensure 'appropriate measures' are in place to assist child victims and their families in the course of criminal proceedings against perpetrators (Art 7 Trafficking Framework Decision and Art 9 of the Sexual Exploitation Decision). See further, Save the Children, *Initial Comments on the Revision of 2002 EU Trafficking Framework Decision* (14 October 2008) savethechildren.net/alliance/europegroup/archives.html.

[56] For a detailed discussion of the various contexts in which child trafficking takes place, as well as a profile of traffickers, victims and those that exploit victims following trafficking, see I Staiger, 'Trafficking in Children for the Purpose of Sexual Exploitation in the EU' (2005) 13/14 *European Journal of Crime, Criminal Law and Criminal Justice* 603.

[57] Sexual Exploitation Directive, above n 36, notably Arts 17–20; Trafficking Victims Directive, above n 22, notably Arts 11–17.

[58] Eg through the Commission's Action Plan on Unaccompanied Minors COM (2010) 313, 3 which includes series of protective measures in relation to child trafficking; the EU Fundamental Rights Indicators on the rights of the child, which includes child trafficking as a specific indicator domain: H Stalford, H Sax et al, *Indicators for the Protection, Respect and Promotion of the Rights of the Child in the European Union* (Vienna, EU Fundamental Rights Agency, 2010); the Fundamental Rights Agency's attempts to achieve more co-ordinated and comprehensive data-collection in the field of trafficking—Eurasylum Ltd, *The Protection of the Rights and Special Needs of Trafficked Children: A Thematic Discussion Paper Prepared for the European Union Agency for Fundamental Rights* (Vienna, Fundamental Rights Agency, 2008) and the research, data-collection and legal and policy initiatives implemented under the anti-trafficking aspect of the EU's Stockholm Programme, 'Action Plan Implementing the Stockholm Programme' COM (2010) 171 final.

of EU law together with a more consistent and prominent human rights 'thread'. For example, the Trafficking Victims Directive cross-references to a number of other instruments, including the EU Framework Decision regulating victims' rights in criminal proceedings,[59] the Trafficking Co-operation Directive[60] and the Framework Decision on the European Arrest Warrant,[61] thereby suggesting a much more sensitive balance between the securitisation and criminalisation priorities associated with this law, and upholding the safety and dignity of the individual.[62]

However, these instruments, and the Trafficking Victims Directive in particular, is still stubbornly limited in certain respects. First, despite its attempts to encapsulate a broader definition of 'trafficking',[63] the instrument is still largely premised on the erroneous presumption that trafficking is overwhelmingly motivated by organised criminal networks across countries.[64] In doing so, it fails to account for the arguably more common situation in which family or acquaintances engineer the trafficking informally or, indeed, where the child him or herself actively 'colludes' in the arrangement, usually for financial or educational reasons.[65] EU provision also fails to capture cases where the child is trafficked internally within a Member State, perhaps plucked out of the child protection or asylum system (although it is acknowledged that this raises sensitive competence issues). Such limitations perpetuate fears, therefore, that a significant proportion of trafficked children continue to fall between the gaps in EU trafficking law, a consequence that is only reinforced by variations and gaps in legal definitions of trafficking at the domestic level.[66]

---

[59] Council Framework Decision 2001/220 on the standing of victims in criminal proceedings [2001] OJ L82/1. For an illustration of how this instrument has been used to protect children's rights, see Case C-105/03 *Pupino* [2005] ECR I-5285.

[60] Above n 26.

[61] Above n 39.

[62] For a broader discussion of how this balancing act is performed, see S Krieg, 'Trafficking in Human Beings: The EU Approach between Border Control, Law Enforcement and Human Rights' (2009) 6 *European Law Journal* 775.

[63] Above n 22, para 11 Preamble.

[64] Although this is primarily due to the fact that the legislation is inspired by the UN Trafficking Protocol to Prevent, Suppress and Punish Trafficking in Persons, Especially Women and Children, supplementing the United Nations Convention Against Transnational Organised Crime, which offers an equally narrow perspective of the perpetrators of child trafficking.

[65] See D Scullion, 'Gender Perspectives on Child Trafficking: A Case Study of Child Domestic Workers' in H Stalford, S Currie and S Velluti (eds), *Gender and Migration in 21st Century Europe* (Surrey, Ashgate, 2009), 45. See also H Askola, 'Foreign National Prisoners, Deportations and Gender' in Stalford, *Gender*, 163. Askola's typology of trafficking in the context of adults can also be applied to children.

[66] FRA, *Child Trafficking*, above n 52, 13; R Huijsmans and S Baker, 'Child Trafficking: Worst Form of Child Labour, or Worst Approach to Child Migrants?' (unpublished paper presented to conference, Easier Said than Done: 20 Years of Children's Rights Between Law and Practice, Institute of Child Health, London, 11–12 June 2009); M-H Chou, 'The European Union and the Fight against Human Trafficking: Comprehensive or Contradicting?' (2008) 1 *St Antony's International Review* 76.

ADDED VALUE OF EU INTERVENTION IN INTERNATIONAL CHILD PROTECTION

The campaign to protect children against abuse and exploitation is extensive and ubiquitous, operating on multiple jurisdictional levels through a range of legal, political, educational and economic initiatives. There are now so many international child protection programmes that it would be impossible to summarise them exhaustively in this chapter. Suffice to say that the most prominent of these have been developed by the United Nations and the Council of Europe.

At UN level, the International Labour Organisation (ILO) has played a central role for the past 90 years in raising awareness of and campaigning for the elimination of child labour. It has established widely endorsed international standards on child labour,[67] and, in 1992, established the International Programme on the Elimination of Child Labour (IPEC).[68] Other UN bodies play an equally prominent role in the global child protection arena. Indeed, the UN Children's Fund (UNICEF) is defined by its mandate to protect and promote the rights of all children which it achieves through political lobbying, delivering practitioner training, administering basic health and sanitation services, educating and supporting community groups and families, and through research and data-gathering on the situation and experiences of children.[69] All such activities are underpinned by the provisions and principles enshrined in the UNCRC and its two Optional Protocols.[70]

The Council of Europe (CoE), for its part, has actively pursued enhanced child protection provisions for over half a century, most notably through the development of child-sensitive legal instruments and jurisprudence.[71] Such activities culminated in the 2008 launch of the ambitious, multi-annual strategic programme: Building a Europe For and With Children. The first phase of this programme (2009–11) adopted violence against children as a key

---

[67] ILO Minimum Age Convention 1973 (no 138); the ILO Worst Forms of Child Labour Convention 1999 (no 182).

[68] This now operates at the grass-roots level in nearly 90 countries across five continents, supporting field projects with technical advice, data collection, research and evaluation, all of which is aimed at developing a comprehensive body of knowledge on child labour and identifying the means of tackling it. See further ILO, *The International Programme on the Elimination of Child Labour: What It Is and What It Does* (Geneva, ILO, 2010).

[69] Deatiled in UNICEF's annual State of the World's Children Reports: unicef.org/sowc.

[70] See above n 6.

[71] In addition to the 1950 Convention for the Protection of Human Rights and Fundamental Freedoms (ECHR), notable CoE instruments include the Convention on Action against Trafficking in Human Beings (2005), the Convention for the Protection of Children against Sexual Exploitation and Sexual Abuse (CETS no 201, 2007), the Convention on Contact Concerning Children (2003), the Convention on Cybercrime (2001), the Convention on the Exercise of Children's Rights (1996). These are supplemented by a plethora of themed Guidelines and training manuals, as well as Recommendations, Resolutions and Declarations from the Committee of Ministers.

theme, including the instigation of a three-year action plan to address the sexual exploitation of children.[72]

This very brief snapshot of just some of the co-ordinated activities being undertaken at the international level—themselves the product of years of extensive investment, significant expert capacity not to mention an unequivocal commitment to promoting and protecting children's rights and welfare—raises questions as to the purpose, capacity and added value of the EU child protection agenda. There is no doubt that the EU framework remains underdeveloped and deficient, and that there is still a woeful dearth of experienced children's rights specialists employed within the EU institutions.[73] Even more fundamentally, the vague and relatively tenuous legal basis for child protection legislation significantly limits opportunities for direct EU intervention in this area. But notwithstanding these limitations, the potential for the EU to make a distinctive, global contribution to child protection should not be underestimated. For a start, it exercises significant political and legal leverage to garner the support of Member States to ensure effective, uniform implementation of international recommendations and obligations. Furthermore, EU child protection measures should not be viewed as operating on a distinct, parallel path to other international endeavours: rather, there is strong evidence of a concerted effort on the part of the EU to draw upon the achievements and expertise of the UN and the CoE, as well as various children's rights non-governmental organisations (NGOs) working in the field of child protection.

The synergy between EU child protection measures and international provision is also reflected in the ongoing process of legislative reform, particularly in the wake of the Lisbon Treaty. For example, the directive to replace the 2004 Framework Decision on combating the sexual abuse, sexual exploitation of children and child pornography explicitly incorporates and develops aspects of the CoE Convention for the Protection of Children against Sexual Exploitation and Sexual Abuse.[74] In doing so, the Commission confidently asserted that the revised EU instrument will add value to the level of protection offered by the CoE Convention.[75] Similarly, the revised Trafficking Victims Directive claims to be modelled on, whilst also 'adding value' to, the 2000 United Nations Trafficking Protocol[76] and the 2005 CoE Convention on Action Against Trafficking in Human Beings.

---

[72] See further: coe.int/children.

[73] Hebenton and Thomas, *Capacity Building*, above n 37.

[74] Above n 36. In fact, the Commission even considered the option of foregoing the opportunity to revise the Framework Decision in favour of simply encouraging Member States to adopt the CoE Convention instead.

[75] Explanatory Memorandum acompanying proposal for a Directive on combating the sexual abuse, sexual exploitation of children and child pornography, repealing Framework Decision 2004/68 COM (2010) 94 final.

[76] Above n 64.

Arguably, however, the true test as to the 'added value' of EU intervention in child protection lies in the extent to which such measures can be enforced and produce positive effects on the ground. Of course, this is contingent on a range of factors: how receptive Member States are to implementing such measures at the domestic level,[77] on the specific resources at the EU's disposal to support effective implementation, and on how responsive the phenomenon itself is to legal intervention.

THE ENFORCEABILITY OF EU CHILD PROTECTION MEASURES

The EU's endorsement and enforcement of international child protection norms and practice is essential, not least to ensure that the obligations imposed on the Member States by EU law do not conflict with the measures by which they are simultaneously signatories under international law. Of course, the difference between EU measures and international instruments is that the former are generally much more easily enforced, insofar as they are subject to judicial scrutiny and sanction. Many international instruments, on the other hand, whilst legally binding, rely largely on political pressure from the international community and on the willingness of individual Member States to actually implement them appropriately. Paradoxically, therefore, by incorporating all of the fundamental elements of international instruments into its own laws, the EU implicitly assumes the role of human rights sentinel, enforcing Member States' compliance with their international obligations simply by casting the same obligations within an EU instrument. In the process, the EU can, in theory, impose international obligations on Member States regardless of whether or not they have signed or ratified the international instrument by which the EU measure is informed.[78] This produces a striking irony: notwithstanding the EU's historical ambivalence to child protection, by entrenching EU instruments within international children's rights norms, the EU offers one of the most direct and efficient means of enforcing such obligations.

Whether this is actually achieved in practice, however, depends on a number of factors. On a more technical level, the extent to which Member States are bound by EU child protection measures depends very much on the legislative form that they take. For instance, some of the instruments described above are framed within a

---

[77] Evidence suggests that despite extensive ratification of the international instruments summarised above, they have yet to be fully and effectively incorporated into national child protection systems. This raises inevitable concerns that the EU will face similar resistance when it comes to Member States' implementation of parallel EU measures.

[78] Of course, the scope of these integrated, internationally-inspired measures will be limited to areas in which the EU can competently legislate, such that the EU instrument will necessarily be more limited than the international instrument by which it is inspired. In that sense, achieving a comprehensive and consistent commitment to international child protection measures still demands that Member States sign the various international conventions in their own right.

directive, whilst others are formulated within a framework decision. Both types of instrument are binding upon Member States as to the result to be achieved, but leave to the national authorities the choice of form and method for implementation.[79] Framework decisions do not have direct effect, however, and the Commission cannot take legal action before the Court of Justice to *enforce* their transposition. Rather, the Court of Justice's role in the enforcement of framework decisions has been limited to determining their interpretation or validity at the request of a national court whose Member State has voluntarily accepted the Court's jurisdiction. This distinction would have been significant in the past insofar as national courts were not obliged to apply directly an EU framework decision relating to child protection; they could only have been compelled to interpret national law as far as possible in compliance with a framework decision.[80] Since the entry into force of the Lisbon Treaty, however, this distinction is rather more academic. Under the new TFEU, framework decisions have been abolished along with the 'three pillar' structure of the EU and replaced with a more streamlined categorisation of legal instruments comprised of regulations, directives and decisions.[81] The legal effect of framework decisions that are already in existence—including their lack of direct effect—will be preserved until they are repealed, annulled or amended in accordance with the revised legislative structure. Moreover, for a period of up to five years from 1 December 2009, pre-existing framework decisions will remain immune from any action for enforcement by the Commission and will be shielded from full judicial scrutiny by the ECJ (in accordance with the former Art 35 TEU).[82]

As a result of the Lisbon Treaty, therefore, future legislative measures in the field of child protection will most likely take the form of directives, as already evidenced in the directive replacing the Framework Decision on Trafficking in Human Beings and the sexual exploitation Directive.[83] But even if EU child protection provision assumes the more authoritative legal form of the directive, the extent to which it produces binding effects on the Member States that will benefit children will depend on the nature and content of the specific provisions.[84] For instance, the Trafficking Co-operation Directive contains provisions on emergency health care and access to the education system for victims. However, only those Member States that have exercised their discretion to apply this Directive to children are obliged, by EU law at least, to extend such rights to them.[85] Moreover, other directives in this area

---

[79]   Ex Art 34(2) TEU and ex Art 249 EC.

[80]   See Pupino, above n 59.

[81]   There is still a distinction drawn between 'legislative acts' (regulations, directives and decisions) and 'non-legislative acts' (such as recommendations and opinions), the latter being adopted outside the 'ordinary' or 'special' legislative procedure (Arts 288–89 TFEU). See further M Dougan, 'The Treaty of Lisbon 2007: Winning Minds, Not Hearts' (2008) 45 *CML Rev* 617.

[82]   See Arts 9–10, Protocol on Transitional Provisions, attached to the Treaty of Lisbon.

[83]   Above n 22 and n 36 respectively.

[84]   Directives adopted in the context of EU criminal law will still not have direct effect such that, in practice, the transposition of framework decisions into directives will probably have little impact on their practical implementation.

[85]   Above n 27.

grant extensive leeway to Member States to *limit* as much as to extend provision for child immigrants. For example, the Reception Conditions Directive reinforces the Member States' prerogative to place children in accommodation centres that are adapted to meet their needs,[86] in spite of the fact that international NGOs and the European Court of Human Rights have forcefully condemned the placing of children in any form of detention.[87]

These observations reinforce a more general point about the precincts of EU competence in addressing the inadequacies of domestic child protection systems. EU law operates on the presumption that adequate child protection systems are in place at the national level to give effect to the provisions contained within its secondary legislation. Its role is not to scrutinise those systems or hold Member States to account for their violation of international human rights laws to which they are signatories. Such functions fall firmly within the mandate of human rights bodies such as the European Court of Human Rights and the UN Committee on the Rights of the Child. Furthermore, the examples referred to above are indicative of the EU's defensive approach to child protection. The EU does not have a positive obligation to implement measures that actively uphold children's rights, nor is it competent to dictate to Member States how they should manage domestic child protection systems. Rather, it has an obligation to avoid acting in a way that undermines or conflicts with existing international children's rights norms, if only to ensure that its measures do not contravene international standards by which Member States are bound.

The unpredictable effect of EU child protection legislation, both in terms of its domestic implementation and enforceability, offers a persuasive case in favour of a more multi-faceted approach to this complex area: one that captures not only the negative outcomes of child exploitation and abuse, but that addresses its root causes too.

ADOPTING A MULTI-LEVELED, 'ROOTS AND BRANCHES' APPROACH TO CHILD PROTECTION

The analysis so far has evaluated the legal, policy and institutional scaffolding supporting EU intervention in child protection issues. This area is more multifarious than almost any other area of children's rights and, therefore, calls for a

---

[86] Dir 2003/9 laying down minimum standards for the reception of asylum seekers [2003] OJ L 31/18, Arts 10(1) and 19. Note, however, that Art 19 endorses the placement of over 16s in adult accommodation centres.

[87] See Separated Children in Europe Programme, Statement of Good Practice, 3rd edn (Brussels, Save the Children, 2004). Moreover, in January 2010, the ECtHR concluded that the detention of a Chechen family of four children and their mother in a closed reception centre constituted a violation of Art 3 of the ECHR (*Muskhadzhiyeva v Belgium* App no 41442/07 (unreported) Judgment of 19 January 2010). The case follows the previous ECtHR ruling in 2006 which condemned Belgian authorities for their detention of a five–year-old unaccompanied minor in a closed reception centre (*Mubilanzila Mayeka and Kaniki Mitunga v Belgium* App no 13178/03 (unreported) Judgment of 12 October 2006).

multi-leveled response. The top-down EU legislative measures described above can achieve some consistency in how the Member States organise aspects of their child protection systems, but it is limited in two fundamental respects. First, it is necessarily confined to areas for which there is a clear legal basis for EU action (primarily those child protection issues that straddle geographical boundaries and intersect with EU immigration and asylum law). Secondly, EU law in these areas is commonly motivated by a range of other political and economic priorities— such as curbing illicit migration and safeguarding national welfare systems—the very achievement of which may serve to obscure or, worse still, undermine children's welfare. However, it does not necessarily follow that such issues could be adequately addressed simply by introducing more legislation. Indeed, the root causes of children's vulnerability—notably factors such as poverty, gender, ill-health and even social or cultural norms—extend far beyond the formal parameters of legal prescription. Equally essential in tackling such issues, therefore, are the non-legislative measures which have *prevention* and rehabilitation as their ultimate aim: those that support capacity-building, awareness-raising, education, data-gathering and developing a sound knowledge base. The emphasis here then is less exclusively on top-down instruction and more on grass-roots intervention, harnessing the expertise of a range of actors working on the front line, so that children's needs are identified through the lived experiences and perspectives of children themselves, and indeed, the social, cultural and economic norms of the families and communities in which they live.

Thankfully, the EU has started to endorse this more nuanced approach in the context of child protection to a greater extent than almost any other area of EU children's rights provision. There has been significant EU investment since the early 1990s in research, campaigning and knowledge exchange initiatives spanning issues such as online child abuse,[88] missing children[89] and violence.[90] The Daphne Programme is one of the most prominent illustrations of such activities.

---

[88] Council Decision 2000/375 to combat child pornography on the internet [2000] OJ L 138/1. This provides for enhanced co-operation between the Member States to facilitate the investigation and prosecution of internet-based offences against children. It includes provision for co-operation with Europol, constructive dialogue between the Member States and industry, and adapting criminal law to account for technological developments. For a review of EU developments in the field of online safety, see J Savirimuthu, 'The EU, Online Child Safety and Media Literacy' (2011) 19 *International Journal of Children's Rights* 173.

[89] Commission Decision of 15 February 2007 on reserving national six-digit telephone numbers beginning with '116' for harmonised services of social value included the EU-wide common number (116 000), OJ [2007] L 49, 17.2.2007; see also Council Resolution on the contribution of civil society in finding missing or sexually exploited children (9 October 2001), by addressing, for example, information exchange of tracing missing children, OJ [2001] C 283/01

[90] Past programmes include STOP which, until 2003, supported exchanges, training and co-operation between organisations and practitioners working to combat trade in human beings and the sexual exploitation of children. See Council Decision of 28 June 2001 establishing a second phase of the programme of incentives, exchanges, training and cooperation for persons responsible for combating trade in human beings and the sexual exploitation of children, OJ [2001] L186/07. AGIS ran until 2006 and was aimed at facilitating cross-national co-operation between the police, the judiciary and other professionals in relation to criminal matters. See Council Decision of 22 July 2002 establishing

Launched in 1997 and conducted over successive phases, with an annual budget now in excess of €17 million,[91] this programme funds a range of actions to combat all types of violence against children, young people and women and to protect victims and groups 'at risk'. Such actions include research, data-collection, training, networking, programme development and implementation and dissemination of good practice. These might be conducted by small organisations and groups working at the grass-roots level, research institutions, or larger, cross-national campaign NGOs working to effect change at policy level. It advocates wide dissemination of good practice examples with a view to encouraging 'policy-borrowing' between the Member States, thus raising standards of prevention and protection from violence across the EU.[92]

Another good example of non-legislative support for child protection is the Safer Internet Programme, a multi-annual initiative established in 1999 on the basis of the former Article 153 EC.[93] This is aimed at facilitating collaboration between various stakeholders, from the NGO, governmental, law-enforcement, academic and technological industry sectors, to enhance online child safety. The current programme runs from 2009 to 2013 and, with a budget of €55 million, is focusing on combating illegal online content, online grooming and bullying.[94]

One of the most striking features of these non-legislative initiatives is that, insofar as they do not impose any binding obligations on the Member States, they enable the EU to support issues that are outside the scope of the EU's legislative competence, arguably with much greater effect than many binding legal measures referred to earlier. The Daphne Programme, for instance, covers myriad issues that have traditionally fallen firmly within the *domestic* legal and policy sphere, including domestic violence, corporal punishment, harmful traditional practices, self-defence and bullying in schools.[95] In many instances, it has provided essential pump-priming funding for small-scale regional projects enabling them to gather a sufficient knowledge-base and profile to qualify for longer-term financial support thereafter.

a framework programme on police and judicial co-operation in criminal matters (AGIS), OJ [2002] L 203/5.

[91] Decision No 779/2007/EC of 20 June 2007 of the European Parliament and the Council establishing for the period 2007–2010 a specific programme to prevent and combat violence against children, young people and women and to protect victims and groups at risk (Daphne III programme) as part of the General Programme Fundamental Rights and Justice, OJ [2007] L 173/19.

[92] For a history of the Daphne Programme, at least until 2003, see Daphne, *The Daphne Experience 1997–2003: Europe Against Violence Towards Children and Women* (Luxembourg, European Commission, 2005).

[93] 'In order to promote the interests of consumers and to ensure a high level of consumer protection the Union shall contribute to protecting the health, safety and economic interests of consumers, as well as to promoting their right to information, education and to organise themselves in order to safeguard their interests'. This provision is now enshrined in Art 169 TFEU.

[94] Decision 1351/2008 [2008] OJ L 348/118.

[95] 'Europe Against Violence: Campaign Messages and Materials from Daphne Programme Projects' ec.europa.eu/justice_home/funding/2004_2007/daphne/project_daphne_en.htm.

Consistent with this approach, in its proposals to amend the Framework Decision on Child Sexual Exploitation, the Commission suggested that the focus should lie not in amending existing laws but in implementing non-legislative measures aimed at facilitating the exchange of information and experience in the field of child protection, awareness-raising, or in establishing tighter mechanisms for data collection.[96]

The sustainability and impact of these activities ultimately depends on the EU's willingness to address some persistent institutional and procedural weaknesses. These weaknesses relate, in particular, to inadequate cross-departmental collaboration within the Commission, the dearth of child protection experts in key EU positions, and insufficient data.

IMPORTANCE OF CROSS-DEPARTMENTAL AND CROSS-INSTITUTIONAL COLLABORATION IN CHILD PROTECTION

The discussion up to now has highlighted the achievements of the EU in ensuring that EU child protection measures are informed by the existing international child protection framework, a process that demands ongoing consultation and relationship building with relevant child protection stakeholders at international, EU institutional and domestic level. Evidence of systematic and meaningful engagement with international and domestic stakeholders in this regard is somewhat patchy; and evidence of effective *internal* collaboration and communication, particularly between the various Directorate Generals (DGs) of the European Commission, is even patchier still.[97] This is reinforced by the Commission's tendency to apportion substantive themes to discrete departments. Specifically, DG Justice's mandate in relation to immigration, asylum and cross-national co-operation in criminal matters has placed it at the vanguard of cross-national child protection issues, and indeed, of the development of the Agenda on the Rights of the Child more broadly.[98] In practice, however, child protection issues can rarely be addressed under a single thematic banner by a single department. Rather it is intrinsically linked with and underpinned by wider issues, particularly poverty,[99] that fall within the remit of other

---

[96] Above n 36. See also R V Lindo, '*The Trafficking of Persons into the European Union for Sexual Exploitation: Why it Persists and Suggestions to Compel Implementation and Enforcement of Legal Remedies in Non-Complying Member States*' (2006) 29 Boston College International and Comparative Law Review 135.

[97] J Grugel and I Iusmen, 'The European Commission as Guardian Angel: Agenda-Setting for Children's Rights' (forthcoming 2012) *Journal of European Public Policy*.

[98] Commission, 'An EU Agenda for the Rights of the Child' (Communication) COM (2011) 60 final.

[99] Poverty is defined here in the broader sense to cover not only material deprivation but also factors that prevent children from accessing basic social, recreational, educational and health resources on an equal basis to adults or, indeed, to other children. For further details on the EU's extensive work in this area, see: *The Social Protection Committee Child Poverty and Well-Being in the EU: Current Status and Way Forward* (Luxembourg, Office for Official Publications of the European Communities, 2008);

Commission departments (such as DG Employment, Social Affairs and inclusion DG External Relations[100] and even DG Education and Culture). Yet despite the synergy between these agendas there is little evidence of an ongoing, co-ordinated exchange of knowledge or methodologies between them. For example, those responsible for developing child protection initiatives within DG Justice rarely call upon the monitoring expertise of DG Employment, Social Affairs and Inclusion—which co-ordinates the EU's anti-poverty/social inclusion agenda or, indeed the former DG External Relations (RELEX) which co-ordinates EU action in the context of development—to assist them in identifying the factors that make children most vulnerable to abuse and exploitation.

The absence of more effective cross-departmental communication within the Commission is not the only weakness in the EU's child protection framework. Equally central to a comprehensive child protection strategy is an identifiable coherence and dialogue between the various types of activity undertaken. For example, the EU's extensive investment in the various phases of the Daphne Programme has been highly successful in creating partnerships, building capacity and sharing best practice between the Member States.[101] By disseminating the findings and key messages of such activities, the EU serves as a kind of children's rights oracle, imparting its wisdom to policy-makers, social workers, teachers, NGOs, health workers and legal advisors across the Member States. However, there is no clear rationale for the choice of priorities for each phase of the Daphne Programme, nor is there any indication of the EU adopting a more reflective approach and applying the findings of this rich knowledge resource to its own internal legal and policy planning.

ENHANCING THE KNOWLEDGE BASE

This last point reinforces the need to develop EU child protection measures in a way that responds directly and meaningfully to children's needs. To achieve this,

H Stalford, H Sax et al. *Developing Indicators for the Protection, Respect and Promotion of the Rights of the Child in the European Union: Summary Report* (Vienna, Fundamental Rights Agency, 2009) 38–43; Eurochild, *Fact Sheet on Child Poverty in the EU* (Belgium, Eurochild, 2007); Eurochild, *Ending Child Poverty within the EU: A Review of the 2006–08 National Reports on Strategies for Social Protection and Social Inclusion* (Belgium, Eurochild, 2007); H Frazer and E Marlier, *Tackling Child Poverty and Promoting the Social Inclusion of Children in the EU: Key Lessons* (Luxembourg, European Commission, 2007) and J Bradshaw, P Hoelscher and D Richardson, 'An Index of Child Well-Being in the European Union' (2007) 80 *Social Indicators Research* 133.

[100] DG External Relations has been merged with the European External Action Service following the Treaty of Lisbon. This comes under the authority of a new High Representative for Foreign Affairs and Security Policy.

[101] Commission, 'Daphne Programme (2000–03)'(Final Report) COM (2004) 824 final; see also Decision 779/2007 on the Daphne III Programme [2007] OJ L173/19 'to prevent and combat violence against children, young people and women and to protect victims and groups at risk'.

there has to be some mechanism both for measuring the nature and extent of a particular child protection issue and for testing how effectively existing laws, policies and processes respond to that issue. This poses a number of challenges. At a fundamental level, the complexity of child protection makes it difficult to evaluate any aspect of it in a linear, comprehensive way. Children are vulnerable to harm not because of one isolated factor, but through the interaction of a range of economic, social, political, legal and procedural variables. By the same token, children are protected from harm, not necessarily by virtue of a single legal intervention, but rather through the application of different measures by different actors in different contexts. This complexity is further compounded in relation to the *cross-national* child protection issues typically regulated by the EU insofar as further layers of legal, political and cultural variables are brought to bear on such matters.

To even begin the process of assessing need and identifying solutions demands clear, detailed and comparable information, information that has long since been identified as considerably lacking. For example, the European Commission, in assessing Member States' implementation of EU law on child sexual exploitation and pornography, conceded that 'it is difficult to provide an exhaustive evaluation in respect of legislation concerning particularly vulnerable victims due to the limited information received by Member States'.[102] Similar observations have been made in relation to data on trafficking in human beings too.[103]

The perennial problem of insufficient and unreliable data is attributable first and foremost to the difficulties inherent in identifying and quantifying child abuse and exploitation: children in extreme situations of vulnerability are notoriously 'invisible'. We are, as a consequence, forced to work with wildly inconsistent 'guesstimates' of the nature and extent of such problems: guesstimates that are then presented as statistically sound. Representations of the incidence of trafficking provide a good illustration of this point. Data from international offices such as the UN Development Programme (UNDP),[104] the ILO,[105] the International Organisation for Migration (IOM) and UNICEF commonly present a global estimation of trafficking which draws on a range of disparate sources, many of which are mere estimates of other national or local organisations. For instance, in 2002, the ILO estimated that in the year 2000, 1.2 million of the children in the worst forms of child labour had been trafficked. This figure represented the total number of children in the worst forms of child labour who were believed to have been trafficked at that point in time. The estimate of 1.2 million was subsequently

---

[102] Commission, 'Art 12 of the Council Framework Decision of 22 December 2003 on combating the sexual exploitation of children and child pornography' (Report) COM (2007) 716 final, 9.

[103] Commission, 'Fighting trafficking in human beings—an integrated approach and proposals for an action plan' (Communication) COM (2005) 514 final, 9.

[104] Eg UNDP, Europe and the CIS, Bratislava Regional Centre, *Trafficking in Human Beings: A Guidance Note* (New York, UNDP, 2004) 7.

[105] Eg ILO, *Action Against Trafficking in Human Beings* (Geneva, ILO, 2008).

repeated by others but incorrectly interpreted to mean that 1.2 million children were being trafficked *each year*.[106]

We know very little of the evidence underpinning such conclusions. In fact, they stand in stark contrast to data generated by EU bodies: Eurojust registered 74 cases of human trafficking in 2009, only three more than those registered in 2007, and compared to 29 in 2006.[107] Similarly, the Fundamental Rights Agency found relatively little concrete evidence of child trafficking through their research conducted in 2008 to 2009. In some Member States, such as Poland and Lithuania, there was no record of a single victim of child trafficking. The study also revealed that prosecution rates for child trafficking offences are derisory in comparison to the projected scale of the phenomenon:

> Final convictions based on child trafficking could only be detected in four Member States in the period 2000–2007. These available figures indicate that there are generally very few final convictions in child trafficking cases. In five Member States it emerges that no final convictions were issued in the period 2000–2007. In one Member State no case of child trafficking was even identified and/or prosecuted in the named period. In some Member States statistics concerning the convictions for child trafficking are conflated with statistics for convictions for trafficking in human beings in general or other offences like smuggling and prostitution. Thus it is not possible to state how many child trafficking cases ended in conviction in these countries.[108]

Whilst acknowledging that the paucity of data is symptomatic of the hidden nature of the phenomenon, such findings prompt suggestions that reporting on child trafficking at best sensationalises or, at worst, grossly inflates the problem. But, more crucially, we have very little evidence on which to base concrete recommendations for legal, policy and research developments. As Europol has noted, 'in the absence of solid data it is obviously difficult to formulate effective counter-trafficking policies'.[109]

Data gaps such as these are not just specific to the more 'invisible' and extreme forms of child exploitation, however. Commentators have, for some years now, identified a palpable failure on the part of the EU to collect data on children in almost every aspect of EU activity, attributing it largely to the EU's traditional indifference to most things child-related.[110] It is for that reason that the progress made in very recent years to further disaggregate demographic, migration and

---

[106] Reported in M Dottridge, *Child Trafficking for Sexual Purposes: A Contribution of ECPAT to the World Congress III Against Sexual Exploitation of Children and Adolescents* (Brazil, ECPAT International, 2008).

[107] Eurojust, 'Trafficking in Human Beings' (2010) 2 *Eurojust News* 2.

[108] FRA, *Child Trafficking*, above n 52, 14. Similar observations are made by Huijsmans and Baker, above n 49.

[109] FRA, *Child Trafficking*, above n 52, 9.

[110] S Ruxton, *Children in Europe* (London, NCH Action for Children, 1996); H Stalford, H Sax et al, above n 100, 22.

labour force data by age is to be welcomed.[111] There is also a growing body of EU statistical evidence relating to families, child poverty, education and generational inequalities.[112] That said, these statistics rarely adopt children as the unit of analysis, and when they do, they often focus on young people aged 11 or above, to the exclusion of younger children.[113] The position of children is routinely subsumed within more general statistical groupings, and any child-related data is rarely disaggregated further to reveal the distinct experiences of different childhood age groups.[114] Even where there are attempts to extrapolate the specific situation of children from general data, such efforts have yet to be achieved with any consistency across all of the Member States, making it virtually impossible to draw cross-national comparisons or, indeed, to inform a coherent cross-national response.[115]

Further concerns—and these are no less prevalent at the international level—relate to the tendency to 'sanitise' data by presenting it in isolation from the political, economic and cultural context from which it is derived. This is a common feature of cross-national comparison which can often overlook or, at least, undermine the importance of national or regional context in favour of statistical comparability.[116] This is particularly critical in assessing the vulnerability of children to a particular form of abuse or exploitation—something that can only be fully understood within the broader cultural, economic, legal and policy context in which they are situated.[117] For example, statistics revealing the proportion of child asylum seekers reported across the Member States will vary significantly according to how domestic systems process such cases. In Greece, Italy and Cyprus, for example, child asylum seekers are automatically processed through the child protection system as opposed to the immigration system and, therefore, are often not even registered as asylum seekers. As far as the rest of Europe are concerned,

[111] Eg by virtue of Reg 862/2007 on Community statistics on migration and international protection and repealing Reg 311/76 on the compilation of statistics on foreign workers [2007] OJ L199/23, Art 3(1) imposes an obligation on Member States to disaggregate immigration statistics in accordance with age.

[112] Eg see European Commission, *The Social Situation in the European Union 2009* (Luxembourg, Publications Office of the European Union, 2010).

[113] See, eg the EU Statistics on Income and Living Conditions (SILC) and the WHO Health Behaviour in School-Age Children (HBSC) data sets. Similar observations have been made by the Commission, 'Fighting trafficking in human beings: an integrated approach and proposals for an action plan' (Communication) COM (2005) 514 final, 9.

[114] Stalford, Sax and Drywood, *Developing Indicators*, above n 100, 22.

[115] Some of these issues are discussed in J Ennew, 'Has Research Improved the Human Rights of Children? Or have the Information Needs of the CRC Improved Data About Children?' in A Invernezzi and J Williams, *The Human Rights of Children: From Visions to Implementation* (Fanham, Ashgate, 2011) 133.

[116] L Hantrais and S Mangen (eds), *Cross-National Research Methodology and Practice* (London, Routledge, 2007).

[117] J Boyden, 'Childhood and the Policy Makers: A Comparative Perspective on the Globalization of Childhood' in A James and A Prout (eds), *Constructing and Deconstructing Childhood: Contemporary Issues in the Sociological Study of Childhood* (Basingstoke, Falmer, 1990).

there are no, or at least very few, child asylum seekers in these countries![118] Some Member States record a higher incidence of trafficked children, simply because they have much more efficient mechanisms for identifying such children.

Such observations reinforce the need not only to situate data within the legal, political and institutional infrastructure of the Member State in question, but to view it alongside other forms of non-statistical research and information.[119] This takes us back to the point raised earlier regarding the importance of marrying up such data with the extensive internal research archive already at the EU's disposal (through funded programmes such as Daphne), and with the rich empirical resources available at academic, NGO and governmental level.

THE FUTURE OF EU CHILD PROTECTION

To conclude this chapter, it is worth speculating a little further on the impact of some key constitutional and policy developments—specifically the Lisbon Treaty and the Stockholm Programme—on the EU's child protection 'agenda'.

The Lisbon Treaty, which came into force on 1 December 2009, marks a minor victory in the campaign for a more forceful EU commitment to children's rights. Indeed, chapter two has already referred to the increased prominence of human rights provision within the revised EU treaties as a result of this development and the potential for this to reinforce the EU's allegiance to international children's rights instruments. But the Treaty of Lisbon also represents a particular triumph as far as child *protection* is concerned. Significantly, the 'protection of the rights of the child' is ordained as one of the core objectives of the EU,[120] and as a specific priority shaping its external relations policy.[121] Also incorporated into the new TFEU is an explicit legal basis for the adoption of protection and preventative measures in the area of child-related crime. This is achieved both in the context of the EU's immigration and asylum acquis,[122] as well as through measures aimed at stimulating cross-national judicial co-operation in criminal matters,[123] and now appears to be focused as much on the protection and rehabilitation of victims as on the identification and prosecution of perpetrators, as the analysis in this chapter

---

[118] UNHCR, *2007 Global Trends: Refugees, Asylum Seekers, Returnees, Internally Displaced and Stateless Persons* (Geneva, UNCHR, 2008).

[119] U Kilkelly, 'Operationalising Children's Rights: Lessons from Research' (2006) 1 *Journal of Children's Services* 36.

[120] Art 3(3) TEU [2010] OJ C 83/13.

[121] Art 3(5) TEU.

[122] Specifically, anti-trafficking measures previously enshrined in Art 29 of the TEU have now been incorporated and expanded upon in Art 79 TFEU (Ch2, Title V—Policies on Border Checks, Asylum and Immigration).

[123] Arts 82(2) and 83(1)TFEU (Ch 4 of Title V TFEU—Judicial Cooperation In Criminal Matters).

has illustrated.[124] Public health also remains a high priority for the EU, with an expression of ongoing support for national and cross-national activities (such as Daphne) aimed at 'obviating sources of danger to physical and mental health'.[125] Such measures are further complemented by enhanced support for external development co-operation and humanitarian aid allowing implementation of measures to tackle the root causes of some of the worst abuses of children.[126]

These substantive changes, coupled with the enhanced prominence of human rights in the EU constitution more generally, have established a firm mandate for ongoing EU action to protect children, particularly in the context of abuses with a cross-border element. This mandate resonates with the EU's latest multi-annual programme: the Stockholm Programme.[127] As the successor of the Tampere and Hague Programmes, Stockholm is aimed at pursuing, whilst also meeting the challenges of, an area of freedom, security and justice. It acknowledges from the outset the delicate balance that must be struck between 'respecting fundamental freedoms and integrity while guaranteeing security in Europe'.[128] In doing so, it also emphasises the importance of making allowance for the 'special needs of vulnerable people' both within and outside the EU.[129] A number of 'tools' are identified as essential for this process including: full and effective implementation, enforcement and evaluation of existing legal instruments; a review of the quality, clarity and accessibility of existing legislation; greater coherence between the activities both internal and external to JLS departments, including improved co-ordination with EU agencies such as Europol, Eurojust and the FRA; more pertinent evaluation of the implementation of policies in this area; the development of better training for all professionals and other stakeholders involved in the implementation of the area of freedom, security and justice; more fluid and responsive dialogue with representative associations and civil society; and more strategic funding and programming of initiatives.[130] These priorities echo many of the points made throughout this chapter and are bolstered by more specific, child-focused recommendations in the Stockholm Programme, particularly 'victims of sexual exploitation and abuse as well as children that are victims of trafficking and unaccompanied minors in the context of immigration policy'.[131]

---

[124] Indeed, it is these very measures that have formed the basis for the Directives replacing the framework decisions on trafficking and on sexual exploitation and child pornography, discussed above n 22 and 36 respectively.

[125] Art 168 TFEU.

[126] Art 208 TFEU.

[127] Council of the European Union, 'The Stockholm Programme: an open and secure Europe serving and protecting the citizen' (Notice) [2010] OJ C115/1.

[128] Ibid, Annex, 3.

[129] Ibid, Annex, 4.

[130] Ibid, Annex, 5–10.

[131] Ibid, Annex, 15.

CONCLUSION

Child protection is intrinsic to children's rights insofar as every decision relating to children is underpinned by a fundamental concern to uphold and protect their welfare. For the purposes of this chapter, a narrower definition of child protection has been adopted to define measures and systems—falling within the scope of EU competence—that seek to address the needs of children in the most vulnerable of situations. However, even this covers an array of issues. While the discussion above by no means claims to provide an exhaustive account of the extent and diversity of EU child protection measures, it has drawn out some of the EU's key achievements and challenges in this area. In fact, EU intervention has been more inventive and extensive in relation to 'children in crisis' than almost any other area of EU children's rights, reinforcing the hegemony of the child *protection* narrative at EU level, over and above children's *rights* or *empowerment* more broadly. This is perhaps attributable to Member States' receptiveness to the EU's input in this area. The politics of harm, poverty and deprivation are not exclusively owned or, indeed, claimed by the nation state: no one wants to shoulder the burden, responsibility and expense of assisting vulnerable and marginalised children. As such, we see Member States readily relinquishing sole responsibility for such issues and deferring to the EU and international community for support.

An obvious starting point in evaluating the effectiveness of EU action was to analyse the content and scope of child protection provision within 'hard' EU legislative instruments and jurisprudence. This analysis has revealed three main tensions in this body of law which are largely the product of the EU's limited legal competence in this area and of the need to accommodate various other political and public needs, often through the same instrument. First, the development of specific child protection measures within more generic free movement, immigration and asylum instruments, as well as through more tailored instruments in the field of trafficking and labour and sexual exploitation, indicate a growing acknowledgement by the EU of its responsibility to ensure that its internal market objectives should not be pursued at the expense of children's welfare. In that sense, EU child protection measures are typically defensive in nature, implying a negative obligation to develop and apply EU law in a manner that does not impact injuriously on children's welfare, rather than a positive obligation to implement measures that actively promote children's welfare. But this is a powerful commitment nonetheless, ensuring that even the most generic of provisions do not produce effects that harm children's welfare. Indeed, isolated cases such as *Dynamic Medien* relating to restrictions on the free movement of goods provisions, highlight the potential for this 'negative' obligation to be interpreted in a manner that upholds children's rights very effectively indeed.

Linked to this point is an identifiable tension between the EU's duty to respond to the political, economic and securitisation issues posed by increasing cross-border mobility, on the one hand, and to accommodate the specific needs of children implicated in such processes on the other. The common result is a distinct prioritisation of the former, even if it means undermining or disregarding children's rights. Indeed, the discussion has highlighted the ease with which children's rights can be trumped by a desire to protect political sensitivities, particularly in the more contentious areas of immigration and asylum.

These factors could be regarded as significantly limiting the possibility of EU legislation alone having a meaningful impact on children's experiences on the ground. Certainly the Lisbon Treaty represents a reinforced commitment to child protection, but whether this will be able to stand firm in the face of pressing political and economic pursuits remains to be seen. The changes made in relation to human trafficking and sexual exploitation suggest, albeit tentatively, that it will. In any case, it is important to remember that legislative intervention is only one of several tools at the EU's disposal to tackle the many complex issues that threaten children's welfare. The proliferation of knowledge exchange and information sharing, data collection and capacity building initiatives all reveal a more nuanced, multi-levelled and multi-disciplinary child protection strategy.

But the analysis in this chapter has also drawn attention to some persistent institutional and methodological issues that threaten the coherence of the EU's child protection strategy. First, and perhaps paradoxically, the inexorable 'chaos' of child protection has to be acknowledged before any strategic approach can be formulated. This demands acceptance of the fact that it cannot be confined to the mandate of a single DG within the Commission, or packaged into neat, isolated action plans. Rather, child protection has to be addressed within the broader social, political, economic and cultural context within which children are situated. It has to adopt a more pre-emptive approach: one which takes action to minimise those factors that most commonly expose children to exploitation and abuse in the first place, notably poverty and social exclusion. To achieve this, the EU has to pursue a more integrated approach which genuinely engages with a range of external stakeholders from the NGO, welfare services, legislative, political, judicial and investigative sectors. But this has to be complemented also with a greater openness to cross-departmental collaboration and exchange *internal* to the EU, as well as a more effective 'joining up' of the resources and data generated by the EU's various activities that impact upon child protection. This level of collaboration is critical, not simply to achieve a level of consensus on how to formulate appropriate legal and policy responses, but to maximise the potential for pooling financial and expert resources, and to avoid unnecessary duplication or, worse still, damaging contradiction vis-à-vis international and domestic efforts in this critical aspect of children's rights.

8

Children's Rights and EU Enlargement

INTRODUCTION

THIS CHAPTER EXPLORES the implications of EU enlargement for children. In particular, it considers the extent to which children's rights are articulated in the accession negotiations and whether EU membership affects children's status and experiences. More broadly, the enlargement process is a valuable context for assessing the currency of children's rights at EU level since it lays bare the legal, economic and political standards to be achieved by a candidate country to gain EU membership. In that sense, we can interrogate whether children's rights are sufficiently valued by the EU to warrant inclusion within the pre-accession criteria. Carrying this analysis through to post-accession experience, we can explore how the process of social and political adjustment implied by accession—for the acceding state, the other Member States and for the EU institutions—manifests itself in relation to children. In short, EU enlargement offers a lens through which to explore how domestic children's rights regimes respond to the dynamics of EU integration, and how children are really affected on the ground. Equally, the process of accession provides us with some insight into the EU's relations and standing with the outside world, of the values it endorses and seeks to propagate on the international scene, and of candidate states' receptiveness to such standard setting. [1]

The chapter begins by setting out the current accession framework, including the conditions for EU membership, critically assessing the extent to which it provides a mechanism for promoting children's rights issues. It then moves on to assess the impact of the accession process on children's rights before and after membership is achieved. It also discusses some of the more constitutional and ideological tensions created by a process that seeks to promote children's rights in ways that seem otherwise unattainable on a purely internal scale. Finally it questions, in particular, whether the EU is sufficiently equipped to live up to and sustain the children's rights standards it imposes on accession states and on the extent to which the accession of new states act as a catalyst for internal developments in children's rights protection at EU level.

[1] M Cremona, 'EU Enlargement: Solidarity and Conditionality' (2005) 30 *EL Rev* 3, 4.

The reflections in the chapter draw principally on the post-millennium waves of enlargement. 2004 saw the accession of 10 new Member States to the European Union: Cyprus, the Czech Republic, Estonia, Hungary, Latvia, Lithuania, Malta, Poland, Slovakia and Slovenia. EU membership was then extended to Bulgaria and Romania in 2007. These enlargements are unprecedented, in terms of the number of countries involved, the political, economic and cultural diversity they brought to the EU, and the sheer length and complexity of the accession negotiations.[2] As well as highlighting some particular children's rights concerns arising out of these particular periods of enlargement, the analysis aims to draw out some broader lessons for the next wave of EU expansion. Reference will therefore be made to the extent to which children's rights feature in the negotiations currently underway with candidate[3] and potential candidate states.[4]

MEMBERSHIP 'CONDITIONALITY' AS A MECHANISM FOR PROMOTING CHILDREN'S RIGHTS

Accession to the EU has evolved into an increasingly complex and lengthy process, involving a series of pre-accession stages aimed at preparing candidate countries and, indeed, the EU itself, for full EU membership. Negotiations have, since 1993, been conducted—formally at least—on the basis of a set of political, economic and legal conditions collectively known as the 'Copenhagen Criteria'[5] coupled with an assessment of whether the EU has the capacity to absorb new members. The political conditions are formulated broadly requiring the state concerned to have achieved the stability of institutions guaranteeing democracy, the rule of law, human rights and respect for and protection of minorities. The economic criteria require states to demonstrate the existence of a functioning market economy as well as the capacity to cope with competitive pressure and market forces within the Union. Finally, states must be able to 'take on the obligations of membership and to adhere to the aims of political, economic and monetary union' (the EU acquis).[6] These criteria—or 'Membership Conditionality'[7]—are regarded as the key to safeguarding EU integration and have been further developed and formalised by the

---

[2] Ibid 8. See also C Hillion (ed), *EU Enlargement: A Legal Approach* (Oxford, Hart, 2004).

[3] Turkey, Croatia, the Former Yugoslav Republic of Macedonia, Iceland, Montenegro and Serbia.

[4] Other potential candidate countries of the Western Balkans include Albania, Bosnia and Herzegovina, and Kosovo under UN Security Council Resolution 1244.

[5] Presidency Conclusions of the Copenhagen European Council (21–22 June 1993). Note that legal, economic and political conditions for accession also applied to previous accessions but were less formalised, and certainly not as strictly applied as the current conditions. See further C Hillion, 'The Copenhagen Criteria and their Progeny' in Hillion, *EU Enlargement*, above n 2, 1.

[6] For a more detailed exposition of how the pre-accession process has developed, see M Maresceau, 'Pre-accession' in M Cremona (ed), *The Enlargement of the European Union* (Oxford, Oxford University Press, 2003) 9.

[7] Cremona, above n 1, 15.

European Council to respond to ongoing and far-reaching eastward expansion. Thus, the 1995 Madrid European Council meeting underlined the importance not only of transposing EU law and policy into national measures, but of adapting administrative and judicial structures to ensure their effective application.[8] Moreover, in 1997, the Luxembourg European Council[9] stressed the need to clearly define, in the form of accession partnerships, which aspects of the Copenhagen Criteria should be prioritised by the candidate state and to identify areas in which pre-accession assistance should be targeted.[10] This Council also instituted an annual reporting process to chart states' progress towards meeting the Copenhagen Criteria.[11] For its part the Commission issued a Communication in 1997, 'Agenda 2000', in which it provided the first detailed explanation of what each aspect of the accession conditions entail.[12] Collectively, these documents reveal the extent to which children's rights operate as a pre-condition for accession, and catalogue the advancements made by states to develop and promote children's rights regimes. The following sections explore precisely how this membership conditionality has been used for this purpose.

CHILDREN'S RIGHTS AND THE POLITICAL CRITERIA: USING HUMAN RIGHTS 'CONDITIONALITY' TO ENHANCE CHILDREN'S RIGHTS

The ideals reflected in the political aspect of the Copenhagen Criteria have always been an important precondition for membership since the very inception of the European Economic Community (EEC).[13] While these conditions as they

---

[8] Presidency Conclusions of the Madrid European Council (15–16 December 1995).

[9] Presidency Conclusions of the Luxembourg European Council (12–13 December 1997).

[10] Financial assistance for EU accession states has largely been administered through PHARE, originally created in 1989 as the Poland and Hungary: Assistance for Restructuring their Economies Programme and subsequently extended to other Central and Eastern European candidate states. Assistance for the countries of the Western Balkans (Albania, Bosnia-Herzegovina and the former Yugoslav Republic of Macedonia) was initially provided through the Community Assistance for Reconstruction, Development and Stability in the Balkans (CARDS) Programme. This was replaced in 2007 by a single framework for financial assistance, the Instrument for Pre-accession Assistance (IPA). See further E Gateva, 'Post Accession Conditionality: Support Instrument for Continuous Pressure?' Working Paper no 18 (Berlin, KFG, 2010).

[11] The latest progress reports for current candidate and potential candidate states are available to view at: ec.europa.eu/enlargement/how-does-it-work/progress_reports/index_en.htm.

[12] Agenda 2000 for a Stronger and Wider Union COM (97) 2000 final, vol I, 15 July 1997; and Agenda 2000: The Challenge of Enlargement COM (97) 2000 final, vol II, 15 July 1997.

[13] For a brief summary of the application of the political criteria to previous enlargements see K Smith, 'EU Membership Conditionality' in Cremona (ed), *The Enlargement*, above n 6, 109 and C Hillion, 'The Copenhagen Criteria and their Progeny' in Hillion (ed), *EU Enlargement*, above n 2, 3–7. These requirements are expressed in Art 2 TEU: 'The Union is founded on the values of respect for human dignity, freedom, democracy, equality, the rule of law and respect for human rights, including the rights of persons belonging to minorities. These values are common to the Member States in a society in which pluralism, non-discrimination, tolerance, justice, solidarity and equality between women and men prevail'. This provision is further alluded to in Art 49 TEU which sets out the basic procedure for applying for EU membership.

exist today—the stability of institutions, guaranteeing democracy, the rule of law, human rights and respect for and protection of minorities—are ill-defined and extremely broad, they have licensed the EU to scrutinise the human rights infrastructure of candidate states, including, inter alia, their ratification of international human rights law, adherence to associated reporting obligations, and the accessibility and fairness of justice and political, including electoral, processes.[14]

This call to accountability has provided applicant states with 'a unique opportunity to introduce democracy and to benefit from greater freedom',[15] a particular priority as far as the most recent post-Communist accession states are concerned. The degree of optimism as to the liberalising potential of the political criteria have been somewhat tempered, however, by the perceived enormity of the task of transforming systems of former dictatorship and oppression into more moderate democracies. Dupré, for instance, presents the ambitions of the criteria as something of a 'quantum leap', ideologically, politically and culturally, for these states and questions whether such a shift can be achieved over the course of the negotiations period.[16]

Notwithstanding the ambitious scope of the political criteria, and perhaps even because of it, they have offered arguably the most fertile grounds for holding states to account on children's rights issues. Indeed, children's rights feature much more prominently in the 'political' sections of the progress reports of the most recent accession states, contrasting markedly with the often perfunctory reference to children in the economic and legal (EU acquis) updates. The progress reports relating to Romania and Bulgaria made particularly extensive reference to children's rights, emphasising the need to reduce the number of children in residential care, to implement measures to combat child trafficking and street begging, and to promote the social inclusion of Roma children.[17] This in turn prompted an extensive review of these states' child protection regimes, with a particular emphasis on reform in Romania. As a result, in 2001, the Romanian Government established the National Authority for Child Protection and Adoption to address the most prominent children's rights concerns raised by the EU. Following accession, this Authority was subsequently divided into two distinct institutions: the National Agency for Protection of Children's Rights (NAPCR), charged with enforcing and monitoring a number of child protection reforms, including the de-institutionalisation of children in residential care

---

[14] Agenda 2000, above n 12.

[15] C Dupré, 'After Reforms: Human Rights Protection in Post-Communist States' (2008) 5 *European Human Rights Law Review* 621, 622.

[16] Ibid 623.

[17] Regular Report on Romania's Progress Towards Accession 2003, 12, 23–24 and 32; Regular Report on Bulgaria's Progress Towards Accession 2003, 13, 21, 23–24, 25. See also: 'Continuing Enlargement: Strategy Paper and Report for the European Commission on the Progress Towards Accession by Bulgaria, Romania and Turkey' COM (2003) 676 final. I Iusmen, 'Human Rights Developments beyond the EU Acquis: the Child Protection Case in Romania' in 'The EU and Child Protection in Romania: Accession Conditionality and Feedback Effects' (PhD thesis, University of Sheffield, 2009) see ch 5.

and the Romanian Office for Adoptions, charged with regulating internal and international adoption.

Similarly, the adoption of the Child Protection Act by Bulgaria in 2000 gave rise to the establishment of the State Agency for Child Protection (SCAP) in 2001. SCAP's mandate was to develop a more coherent approach to reforming the child protection system across Bulgaria with an immediate focus on addressing the notoriously high number of children in institutionalised care and, later, the needs of unaccompanied minors seeking asylum and child victims of trafficking.[18] However, a coherent campaign of de-institutionalisation was not implemented in Bulgaria until 2007.[19]

Children's rights occupy an increasingly prominent place in the progress reports for the current candidate states also, covering an equally diverse range of issues. These reports indicate that EU evaluations of these states' progress towards accession are not necessarily commensurate with the progress they have made in relation to children's rights. For instance, Croatia is distinguished as having met the political criteria for membership, such that accession is anticipated in 2013. This is in spite of Croatia's explicit admission that 'limited progress' has been made in relation to children's rights. Identified failings include the persistent educational exclusion of children with developmental difficulties and of children from the Roma community.[20] A similar observation is made in relation to the Former Yugoslav Republic of Macedonia which reveals an over-representation of Roma children in schools for children with learning disabilities, as well as high drop-out rates, particularly among Roma girls.

Even though progress in relation to children's rights may not be a decisive factor in determining a candidate state's readiness for EU membership, however, it is clear that pre-accession political conditions have prompted nation states to reflect on how they respond to the most endemic children's rights abuses and to instigate reform accordingly. Macedonia, for example, has reported some prog ress in relation to child labour and sexual exploitation, most notably through the adoption of a three-year action plan (2009–12) to combat child trafficking.[21] Similarly, while the Commission recommends that 'significant further efforts are

---

[18] See Plan for Decreasing the Number of Children Placed in Specialised Institutions in the Republic of Bulgaria (Ordinance no 602 of the Council of Ministers, 2 September 2003). Bulgarian State Agency for Child Protection, *Report on the Status of Specialised Institutions for Children with Physical and Mental Disabilities* (Bulgaria, SCAP, 2006).

[19] This was through the use of the EU Structural Funds, financial instruments that the European Commission uses as part of its regional policy to reduce disparities in development and promote economic and social cohesion in the European Union. For a critical analysis of Bulgaria's reform of institutionalised care in the process of accession, see V Sotiropoulou and D Sotiropoulos, 'Childcare in Post-Communist Welfare States: The Case of Bulgaria' (2007) 36 *Journal of Social Policy* 141 and for a children's rights perspective, V Todorova, 'Children's Rights in Bulgaria after the End of Communism' (2009) 17 *International Journal of Children's Rights* 623.

[20] Commission, 'Enlargement Strategy and Main Challenges 2011–12' (Croatia Progress Report accompanying the Communication) COM (2011) 666 final, 12, 9 November 2010.

[21] Ibid 18 and 21.

required to guarantee fundamental rights' in Turkey,[22] the country has reported some far-reaching changes in the field of children's rights, covering themes such as participation rates in primary education and the proportion of children below the poverty threshold. It has also implemented a number of institutional and procedural amendments to protect child victims of abuse and violence and to rehabilitate children involved in criminal activities whilst making a concerted effort to align the Turkish juvenile justice system with international standards.[23] Children's rights feature in all of the progress reports and Commission conclusions for the potential candidate countries too, with particular scrutiny of the quality and inclusivity of compulsory education, levels of poverty and social exclusion (particularly of Roma children and other minority ethnic groups), provision for disabled children, and the protection of child victims of labour and sexual exploitation.[24] In fact, Iceland is the only candidate country to have remained relatively silent on children's rights issues; there are just two cursory references to children in its 46 page progress report for 2010.[25]

Notwithstanding the persuasiveness of human rights conditionality in prompting important children's rights reforms, it has been criticised on a number of grounds, two of which are highlighted for the purposes of this discussion. First, the human rights framework underpinning the political criteria lacks coherence and persuasiveness, primarily because of the relatively fragile nature of the EU's reputation in this regard; and secondly, the human rights conditionality is highly selective, prioritising certain (largely political and economic) rights over others.

THE IMPORTANCE OF CONTEXT IN APPLYING THE EU'S HUMAN RIGHTS CONDITIONALITY

Commentators have derided the insensitivity of the political criteria to the cultural, political and, indeed, the children's rights contexts of the accession states and their tendency to draw unrealistic and unfair comparisons between the Member States.[26] Linked to this is the assertion that the human rights standards applied in the accession process are not modelled on a distinct set of EU human rights standards. Rather, it is argued that they are entrenched in Western states' interpretations of human rights norms and practices which Central and Eastern European countries are expected to appropriate regardless of their distinct

---

[22] Ibid 18, 20.

[23] Turkey 2010 Progress Report, above n 20, 2–3.

[24] See the individual 2010 Progress Reports on Albania, Bosnia and Herzegovina, Montenegro, Serbia and Kosovo, all accompanying the Commission, 'Enlargement Strategy and Main Challenges 2011–12' (Communication) COM (2011) 666 final.

[25] Iceland 2010 Progress Report, above n 20.

[26] M Koinova, 'Challenging Assumptions of the EU Enlargement Literature: The Impact of the EU on Human and Minority Rights in Macedonia' (2011) 63 *Europe-Asia Studies* 807.

contexts. Lataianu illustrates this point by reference to children in institutionalised care in Romania:

> It is obvious that comparison between the Romanian childcare residential institutions and those in the EU countries shows a wide gap. In these conditions, the real progress made by Romania in this field becomes almost invisible. The situation of children in Romanian residential institutions should be compared to the general state of Romanian society. It is very hard to conceive a prosperous situation of institutionalized children when almost half the population lives in poverty (on less than US$40 a month).[27]

Lataianu points to the need to interpret children's situation in the light of the widespread nature of poverty in Romania and the reality of children's family lives which, in many cases, offers significantly worse conditions and prospects for children than institutionalised care:

> There will be numerous cases of children living with their families in extreme poverty but, on the other hand, there will also be cases of residential institutions offering conditions of the best western standards where children enjoy better conditions than those living with their families.[28]

Her critique therefore calls for a more context-sensitive approach that evaluates progress over time by reference to the social and economic 'dynamics' of each new candidate state as opposed to the more diverse standards of the established Member States.[29] This supports the contention that the true challenge of the accession process lies not simply in engaging governments' commitment to the principles expressed in the Copenhagen Criteria, but in penetrating attitudinal differences and challenging deeply embedded prejudices and inequalities from the bottom up—stimulating internal dialogue and adjustments to render states sufficiently receptive to top down intervention. In that sense local and grassroots-level campaigns are as important as those targeting political procedures and institutional mechanisms if the process is to amount to more than a mere 'hollow rhetoric of rights'.[30]

Such observations are illustrated by a range of children's rights issues. For instance, pre-accession conditions and recommendations aimed at achieving the integration of disabled children within mainstream education nobly respond to the requirements of the UN Convention on the Rights of Persons with Disabilities (to which the EU is a signatory). Their effective implementation, however, depends on a far-reaching social shift in the way that disability is perceived within that particular country, coupled with dramatic adjustments to the welfare services, transport and architectural infrastructure of the environments in which disabled

---

[27] CM Lataianu, 'Social Protection of Children in Public Care in Romania from the Perspective of EU Integration' (2003) 17 *International Journal of Law, Policy and the Family* 99, 118.

[28] Ibid 119.

[29] See further Iusmen, above n 17, who argues that Romania has effected particularly dramatic improvements in relation to child protection.

[30] Dupré, 'After Reforms', above n 15, 631.

people live. Similarly, the removal of children from institutionalised care can only be effectively achieved through a deeper understanding of the economic and cultural factors that precipitated their abandonment in the first place and through the development of effective long-term re-socialisation and care strategies.

Of course, imposing Western benchmarks of rights protection can be particularly problematic in relation to post-Communist states where the culture and language of 'human rights', and certainly children's rights, has largely been absent or where there are limited mechanisms, institutional and otherwise, to ensure they are enforced systematically. For instance, Thomas, acknowledging the role of human rights in precipitating the end of the Cold War and the collapse of Communism, comments on the 'instrumentalist' approach adopted by many reformists who, despite the rhetoric of human rights, have demonstrated a reluctance to embrace democratic values of equality, inclusivity and accountability in practice.[31] This reluctance is, in many cases, heightened in relation to children.

Even these observations, however, are based on the presumption that the EU itself represents a paragon of human rights and, indeed, child protection—that it is eminently qualified to diagnose problems in the children's rights systems of applicant states and prescribe improvements accordingly. Iusmen makes a similar observation in the broader context of the EU's human rights mandate in which she highlights the disjunction between the 'EU's real involvement with human rights' and its 'external projection', a disjunction that has been referred to as a 'human rights EUtopia'.[32] This disjunction, Iusmen argues, undermines the plausibility of the EU's human rights conditionality in the context of pre-accession:

> Credibility rests on the consistency between what is being projected externally and what is being practiced at the internal level when it comes to human rights, which is consistent with the theological urge that the EU should 'do unto others as it does unto itself'.[33]

The resulting 'bifurcation'[34] between the internal and external elements of the EU's human rights agenda is arguably less marked given the elevated status of human rights, particularly the ECHR and the Charter, following the Treaty of Lisbon.[35] It is still apparent, however, in the context of children's rights: the EU

---

[31] D Thomas, 'Human Rights Ideas, the Demise of Communism, and the End of the Cold War' (2005) 7 *Journal of Cold War Studies* 110.

[32] I Iusmen, '"Do as I say not as I do": EUtopia, the CEECs and the Credibility of the EU Human Rights Regime' (2009) 9 *Romanian Journal of European Affairs* 54; K Nicolaidis and R Howse, 'This is My EUtopia ... : Narrative as Power' (2002) 40 *Journal of Common Market Studies* 767.

[33] Ibid.

[34] A Williams, 'Enlargement of the Union and Human Rights Conditionality: A Policy of Distinction?' (2000) 25 *EL Rev* 601; A Albi, 'Ironies in Human Rights Protection in the EU: Pre-Accession Conditionality and Post-Accession Conundrums' (2009) 15 *European Law Journal* 46; B de Witte, 'The Impact of Enlargement on the Constitution of the European Union' in M Cremona (ed), *The Enlargement of the European Union* (Oxford, Oxford University Press, 2003) 240; W Hale, 'Human Rights and Turkey's EU Accession Process: Internal and External Dynamics, 2005–10' (2011) 2 *South European Society And Politics* 323.

[35] Art 6 TEU. The status of fundamental rights in the EU legal order is explored fully in ch 2.

remains decidedly hesitant as regards concrete internal action in matters relating to children, a hesitance that is largely attributable to the fragility of the legal basis on which to enact directly justiciable measures. Consequently, as previous chapters have illustrated, EU children's rights provision is typically characterised by ad hoc, non-committal aspirations rather than by specific obligations, even in relation to issues that fall squarely within the legislative competence of the EU. This raises questions as to the precise frame of reference and methodology used by the EU when prioritising particular children's rights issues in the pre-accession negotiations. Specifically, what is the rationale for prioritising certain children's rights issues over others? And how can the EU legitimately encroach upon such issues in respect of external countries in the absence of any legal competence to regulate them internally? While it might seem counterintuitive to raise such questions in the context of an analysis that advocates a more pro-active and sensitive EU response to children's rights issues, they do draw attention to the highly selective, almost arbitrary nature of the political aspect of the Copenhagen Criteria.

THE SELECTIVE NATURE OF EU HUMAN RIGHTS CONDITIONALITY

The highly selective nature of the political criteria is largely attributable to the twists and turns of the enlargement process and to the distinct historical, political and social trajectory of each new state. While earlier accessions were rather more concerned with securing economic alignment, the subsequent expansion to incorporate the CEEC states presented more acute challenges of economic, cultural, social and political integration. The political criteria were adapted to meet these challenges, focusing primarily on securing some of the more basic (exclusively adult) political and civil rights that had been subverted during the communist regime. Consequently, some of the more entrenched inequalities, including those affecting children, were sidelined, at least initially. Dupré comments:

> Due to the nature of the previous regimes and the post-communist countries' aspirations to become liberal democracies, the fundamental civil and political right was the most visible item on the overall law reform agenda. It arguably became the priority, with a concentration of efforts and resources on the judiciary, on the promotion of free and fair elections and freedom of expression (i.e. dissent) and assembly. It is suggested, however, that this was only the tip of the iceberg and that the breadth of human rights reforms was sometimes underestimated … The collapse of communist regimes did not automatically put an end to human rights violations, and it is argued that it triggered other types of rights problems that equally deserve attention, but that were not always included in any kind of comprehensive reform agenda.[36]

The emergence of a more prominent children's rights dimension in the accession negotiations can be traced back to the preparations for Romania's accession to the

---

[36] Dupré, 'After Reforms', above n 15, 624.

EU. Extensive media and international NGO coverage of the plight of children in Romanian institutions and the concerns relating to the proliferation of the international adoption industry in particular, prompted scrutiny of children's rights in the accession process in a way that had previously seemed unnecessary, unjustified even. This, in turn, prompted a radical overhaul of Romania's child protection system between 1999 and 2005, including the replacement of old-style child care institutions with alternative care arrangements, enhanced social and economic support for families to prevent child abandonment, as well a moratorium on international adoptions.[37]

These developments were not only significant for children in Romania, but had important knock-on effects for how children's rights featured within the EU's accession negotiations with Bulgaria. Indeed, Romania's accession experience is now widely regarded as providing the ultimate template for child protection reform in relation to *all* successive accessions to the EU.[38] But while the Romanian experience sets a firm precedent for future accession negotiations as regards candidates' children's rights accountability, this appears to be confined to children 'in crisis'. It follows then that similar negotiations with other candidate states are likely to be limited to (a relative minority of) children on the margins of society. The implications of this are two-fold: first, the overarching emphasis on protecting children rather than protecting their rights in an external context both reflects and consolidates the hegemony of child protection that has now come to epitomise EU children's rights internally;[39] and secondly, it implies that the accession process will remain largely indifferent to some of the more subtle yet endemic inequalities affecting the majority of children in the candidate states.[40]

CHILDREN'S RIGHTS AND THE ECONOMIC CRITERIA

The second group of conditions under the Copenhagen Criteria focuses on the candidates' economic 'fitness', assessed on the basis of whether there is a liberalised and competitive market, a healthy reliance on private enterprise, a sufficiently robust regulatory framework, and the existence of ample human and material capital fed by a sturdy energy, telecommunications and transport infrastructure.[41]

---

[37] Iusmen, *Human Rights Developments*, above n 17, reports that the closure of old-style institutions was accompanied by the development and implementation of modern child protection services, such as family-type modules, day care centres, maternal centres, recuperation centres or foster care networks.

[38] Ibid 49.

[39] The EU child *protection* hegemony is discussed further in ch 7.

[40] The difficulties common to children more generally are reflected in UNICEF, *Child Poverty in Perspective: An Overview of Child Well-Being in Rich Countries—Innocenti Report Card 7, 2007* (Florence, UNICEF, 2007).

[41] Hillion, above n 5, 12.

At first glance, the extent to which these conditions might be used to address children's rights is perhaps unclear. There are a number of ways, however, in which children are implicated in the economic criteria. The fact that any market economy demands sufficient human capital reinforces the need to invest in compulsory education and appropriate training to ensure that individuals are equipped with the necessary skills and knowledge to sustain it in the long term.[42] Additionally, the emphasis on private enterprise and competing in the global market demands some scrutiny of whether children's rights are sufficiently protected in the pursuit of such practices and of whether they are appropriately regulated to guard against exploitative child labour both in the applicant state's own region and in the countries with which it conducts business. Children are implicated also in any measures that seek to maximise (adult) participation in the labour market insofar as such participation, for women in particular, is largely dependent on the accessibility and affordability of suitable childcare. Indeed, this has been explicitly acknowledged in the context of the EU's current growth strategy, Europe 2020.[43]

Despite the evident links between children's interests and the economic element of membership conditionality, however, it has yet to be exploited as a means of monitoring and promoting children's rights in the accession process. The absence of any reference to children in the context of the economic criteria—as evidenced most clearly in the candidate states' progress reports—may be attributable to the simple fact that they are afforded less attention than the other Copenhagen Criteria generally in the reporting process. Indeed, states have always been granted a certain level of 'slippage' as regards their fulfilment.[44] Additionally, many of the requirements implied by the economic criteria are also addressed and to a degree, absorbed by the legal criteria, an issue to which the discussion now turns.

CHILDREN'S RIGHTS AND THE LEGAL CRITERIA

The adoption and implementation of the legal aspects of the Copenhagen Criteria—the EU acquis—is central to the accession process. The EU acquis comprises the entire body of common rights and obligations that is binding on all EU Member States, notably: the content, principles and political objectives of the treaties; legislation adopted pursuant to the treaties and the case law of the Court of Justice; declarations and resolutions adopted by the Union as well as other soft

---

[42] For an analysis of children as 'investments' see C Piper, 'Investing in a Child's Future: Too Risky?' (2010) 22 *Child and Family Law Quarterly* 1.

[43] Commission, 'Europe 2020—A strategy for smart, sustainable and inclusive growth' (Communication) COM (2010) 2020 final, 18. See also Commission, 'Early childhood education and care: providing all our children with the best start for the world of tomorrow' (Communication) COM (2011) 66 final.

[44] Smith, above n 13, 114. It is telling that the Commission was relatively vague and brief on what the economic conditions entailed in its Agenda 2000 Communication, above n 12.

law measures.[45] Also included within the acquis are international agreements concluded by the European Union and those entered into by the Member States among themselves within the sphere of the Union's activities.[46]

For the next wave of EU enlargement, the acquis is divided into 35 sub-themes or 'chapters' which correspond to the main themes of EU activity.[47] The negotiations set priorities for, and monitor the adoption of, measures relating to each chapter within the candidate country. While virtually all of these areas contain aspects of relevance to children, those areas in which children's rights might be promoted in the most explicit and direct way include: free movement for workers (Ch 2); information society and media (Ch 10); statistics (Ch 18); social policy and employment (Ch 19); judiciary and fundamental rights (Ch 23); justice, freedom and security (Ch 24); education and culture (Ch 26); consumer and health protection (Ch 28); external relations (Ch 30); and foreign, security and defence policy (Ch 31). As the discussion in previous chapters has highlighted, explicit children's rights measures have been enacted across all of these areas, in the form of binding legislation, soft law and policy initiatives. In theory, therefore, the EU acquis offers a coherent and exhaustive mechanism for monitoring candidate countries' receptiveness to EU children's rights provision. In practice, however, the accession negotiations touch on only a small number of these measures: the progress reports contain surprisingly scant reference to children in the sections relating to the acquis, at least when compared to the reports on their progress towards meeting the political criteria. In fact most references are confined to the occasional brief statement which bears little correspondence to specific EU legal and policy instruments.[48] For example, the level of children's rights scrutiny of the acquis in Croatia's 2010 progress report is confined to two brief sentences under Chapter 23 (judiciary and fundamental rights) and Chapter 24 (justice, freedom and security). The former notes, rather blandly, that 'The Ombudsman for Children became more active in promoting and protecting children's rights, but it lacks appropriate office space and staff resources to carry out its mandate'; while the latter is marginally more revealing, reporting that:

> In October 2009, the ministries of the Interior and Health have signed a protocol defining the standard operation procedure for reception and return of unaccompanied

---

[45] Some scholars have distinguished between the 'hard (legislative) acquis' and the 'soft acquis' but collectively it can be termed the 'EU acquis'. See further E O'Hagan, 'Too Soft to Handle? A Reflection on Soft Law in Europe and Accession States' (2004) 26 *Journal of European Integration* 379.

[46] Above n 12. eg the 2006 UN Convention on the Rights of Persons with Disabilities.

[47] For a full list of chapters, see: ec.europa.eu/enlargement/the-policy/process-of-enlargement/mandate-and-framework_en.htm. For the previous fifth round of enlargement—in 2004 and 2007—the acquis was comprised of 31 chapters although the themes were largely the same as the current acquis.

[48] Curiously, one of the only and most frequently cited pieces of legislation is Dir 77/486 on the education of the children of migrant workers [1977] *OJ L199/32*. This is in spite of the fact that implementation of this Directive across the Member States has been notoriously weak, a situation to which the EU, itself, has been largely indifferent. See further HL Ackers and H Stalford, *A Community for Children? Children, Citizenship and Migration in the European Union* (Aldershot, Ashgate, 2004) ch 9.

minors. However, nomination of guardians for this vulnerable group, in line with the internationally recognised principle of the best interests of the child, is uneven.[49]

The Turkish progress report is rather more detailed, providing specific information on improvements to pre and compulsory schooling provision,[50] and on legislative amendments to enable children accused of committing terrorist crimes to be tried in juvenile courts.[51] Other references, however, are typically trite such as 'the provision of affordable child care is insufficient'[52] and 'as regards the rights of the child, there has been progress with the legal framework on children's rights, juvenile justice and the gender pay gap in primary education. Nevertheless, efforts need to be further strengthened in all areas, including education, child labour, health, juvenile justice, administrative capacity and co-ordination'.[53]

As far as the potential candidate countries are concerned, Bosnia and Herzegovina's progress on the children's rights aspects of the EU acquis is confined to two general recommendations for enhanced child health provision and educational integration.[54] This contrasts with Montenegro's significantly more comprehensive approach: their report catalogues specific institutional, procedural and substantive legal and policy developments that have been implemented to give effect to children's rights.[55] Kosovo and Serbia's progress reports, while less detailed, are also peppered with references to a range of children's rights developments and recommendations—references that were conspicuously absent from previous reports.[56]

Overall, children's rights issues are gradually finding their way into the reporting process for both candidate and potential candidate states, no doubt reflecting the increasing priority attached to children's rights since the accession of Romania and Bulgaria, and indeed, within internal EU law and policy. This is still far from being achieved in any systematic or coherent way, however; there is no clear interrogation of specific children's rights issues within the context of the various chapters such that the information provided by different states varies significantly. This largely reflects the Commission's failure to identify precisely the nature and scope of children's rights-related provision within the various chapters of the EU acquis. As it tends to be embedded in more generalised instruments, more rigorous auditing of children's rights during the accession negotiations implies a rather

---

[49] Commission, 'Enlargement Strategy and Main Challenges 2011–12' (Communication) COM (2011) 666 final, 52 and 54.

[50] Ibid 79, under Ch 23 on Judiciary and Fundamental Rights.

[51] Ibid.

[52] Ibid 71 under Ch 19 on Social Policy and Employment.

[53] Ibid 79 under Ch 23 on Judiciary and Fundamental Rights.

[54] Boznia and Herzegovina 2010 Progress Report accompanying the Commission, 'Enlargement Strategy and Main Challenges 2011–12' (Communication) COM (2011) 666 final, 43.

[55] Montenegro 2010 Analytical Report accompanying the Commission, 'Opinion on Montenegro's application for membership of the European Union' (Communication) COM (2010) 670.

[56] Kosovo and Serbia 2010 Progress Reports, above n 24. The 2008 Reports contained virtually no reference to children: Kosovo and Serbia's 2008 Progress Reports accompanying Commission, 'Enlargement Strategy and Main Challenges 2008–09' (Communication) COM (2008) 674, 40–41.

labour-intensive process of dissecting such instruments to unearth the relevant children's rights measures. In that sense, children's rights proofing pre-accession is much messier than it would be in relation to gender, for example. There is no identifiable EU 'children's rights acquis' comparable to the EU gender acquis; there is no neat corpus of EU children's rights legislation and policy on which to hang explicit accession criteria. Instead we have a sprawling, sometimes insipid range of provisions contained within broader, adult-focused laws which are rarely intended to produce the same harmonising effects as comparable provisions such as those in the field of gender equality.[57]

COMPLEMENTING EU CONDITIONALITY WITH ACTION 'ON THE GROUND'

Of course, the accession process is not simply a matter of the EU imposing and candidate states adopting a series of conditions: there has to be evidence of their actual implementation.[58] Closer scrutiny of whether EU law and policy is being implemented at the domestic level is potentially much more constructive and far-reaching since it focuses efforts on the structural and systemic deficiencies that hamper operationalisation of the acquis at the national level. Once such deficiencies are identified, EU investment is likely to follow. In order to improve implementation of the gender aspects of the EU acquis, for instance, the EU has invested considerable funding in the accession states to support judicial and administrative capacity-building projects, to establish and sustain women's networks, and to develop more vigorous gender monitoring processes.[59] In the same token, effective implementation of the acquis relating to children demands ongoing self-reflection on the part of the Member States as to how existing shortfalls in their child-related laws, policies and processes might be addressed. It requires collaboration with other international children's rights institutions and NGOs, as well as investment in training and other capacity-building tools for professionals who work directly with children and young people in a judicial, social and investigative capacity.

The EU has and continues to invest substantial financial support in such processes under its pre-accession assistance programmes. For instance, the 2009 annual work programme for CARDS[60] provided €1,400,000 to support a second

---

[57] Of course it could be argued that since children's rights are effectively more integrated in a variety of EU instruments, albeit with varying degrees of persuasiveness, this may lend itself to a more effective, mainstreamed approach to protecting and promoting children's rights in the context of enlargement. Indeed, proponents of gender equality at EU level have been critical of the fact that gender has yet to be addressed in this kind of integrated manner. See further S Steinhilber, *Women's Rights and Gender Equality in the EU Enlargement. An Opportunity for Progress*, WIDE Briefing (Brighton, Siyanda, 2002) 4 and F Beveridge, 'Gender, the Acquis and Beyond' in M Dougan and S Currie (eds), *50 Years of the European Treaties: Looking Back and Thinking Forward* (Oxford, Hart, 2008) 401.

[58] See para 30, Presidency Conclusions of the Luxembourg Council, above n 9.

[59] For specific examples, see Beveridge, 'Gender, the Acquis and Beyond', above n 57, 398–400.

[60] Above n 10.

national programme, co-ordinated by UNICEF, aimed at enhancing the social protection and inclusion system for children in Bosnia and Herzegovina. The EU also provided €600,000 to fund the European Instrument for Democracy and Human Rights (EIDHR) programme in the Former Yugoslav Republic of Macedonia. This programme aims to strengthen the role of civil society and raise awareness of human rights issues within the country, identifying children's rights as a particular priority. €1,700,000 has been allocated to a similar programme in Kosovo, with an emphasis on the provision of social services to abused children and children with special needs. Furthermore, UNICEF has been provided with €2 million funding to address the situation of disabled children in institutionalised care within Serbia through a number of capacity building initiatives.[61]

All of these examples highlight the unique transformative and, to some extent, untapped potential of membership conditionality to stimulate political, economic and structural re-alignment in the interests of children. The longer term durability and impact of such processes on children, however, is predicated on two fundamental presumptions: first, that the EU child-relevant measures with which compatibility is being sought are, themselves, compatible with normative children's rights standards; and secondly, that the EU has the constitutional, political and institutional resources to uphold the children's rights standards set by the Copenhagen Criteria following accession.

UPHOLDING CHILDREN'S RIGHTS POST-ACCESSION

There is no disputing the impact of the accession process on children's rights at the national level, at least in relation to some of the former Communist states. In many respects change has been swift and dramatic to meet the accession deadlines and to avoid shameful exposure in the annual reporting process. These advancements have been effected primarily through the political as opposed to the legal or economic criteria and centre on some core priorities, notably the integration of Roma children, the plight of children in institutionalised care and juvenile justice. Romania provides a noteworthy illustration in this respect, as Lataianu explains:[62]

> Considering the living conditions of children in public care as a human rights issue, the European Commission paid special attention to this topic in all the reports provided about Romania's application for membership of the EU. Appreciating that the conditions of children living in residential institutions is a matter for concern in Romania, in 1997 the EU spent almost 70 million ecu (much of it by means of the PHARE programmes) to improve this situation. [Accordingly] the reports of 1997 and 1998 showed

---

[61] See further: ec.europa.eu/enlargement/pdf/how_does_it_work/grants_tenders/grants/list_of_grants_after_isc_adopted_until_05_09_en.pdf.

[62] Much of this change was driven by the new Department for Child Protection (DCP) established in January 1997.

positive appreciation of the decentralization of the institutional management and the increased interest in placing children in alternative forms of care.[63]

As a result of this investment and the pressure exerted by the Commission, not to mention by national and international children's rights advocates, by the turn of the millennium Romania had managed to reduce by almost 50 per cent the number of children in institutionalised care and to increase the corresponding proportion of children within family-type care.[64] By the end of 2005, over 170 children's institutions had been closed down and by June 2006 statistics indicated a 75 per cent reduction in the number of children left in institutionalised care compared to a decade previously.[65]

Similarly, in Bulgaria, the number of children in specialised institutions has fallen by 42.3 per cent since 2001, a trend that was undoubtedly precipitated by the pre-accession negotiations.[66] At the end of 2008, 7,276 children were residing in a total of 140 institutions, with many of the old residential programmes having been replaced by new types of alternative community-based schemes for children and young adults.[67] The same report, however, revealed a persistent lack of coherence between the various agencies within the child protection system, in terms of an unclear division of roles, poor levels of communication and ineffective referral procedures between them.[68] Moreover, despite the apparent reduction in the number of children in old-style orphanages, there remains a widespread policy of segregation across the public sector: schools for children with learning and physical disabilities are run by the Ministry of Labour and Social Policy (MLSP); medico-social institutions for abandoned and orphaned children are run by the Ministry of Health; and rehabilitative boarding schools for children with behavioural problems or a history of criminal activity are run by the Ministry of Education.[69] Such evidence highlights the persistence of Bulgaria's infrastructure of institutionalisation and casts doubt over the extent of the accession process' achievements in transforming deeply-embedded cultural attitudes towards children's rights and needs and, indeed, in addressing the root causes of child abandonment in the first instance.

These stubborn shortcomings in national children's rights systems reinforce the potential of EU enlargement to trigger (rather than provide an instantaneous

---

[63]   Lataianu, 'Social Protection', above n 27, 109.

[64]   Ibid 117.

[65]   Whether these changes go far enough is another matter: it is still estimated that there are over 25,000 children living in institutions across Romania. Furthermore, there is as yet little empirical evidence to support the presumption that children who have been moved into alternative forms of care (including family and foster care) are better looked after, emotionally, physically or materially, or that their prospects for the future are significantly improved. See National Authority for the Protection of Children's Rights, *Child Welfare in Romania* (Romania, Children's Rights Romania, 2006).

[66]   United Nations Children's Fund, *Draft Country Programme Document—Bulgaria* (New York, UNICEF, 2009).

[67]   Above n 17, paras 5–6.

[68]   Ibid, para 7.

[69]   ARK Bulgaria, *Briefing Note: Institutions in Bulgaria* (Bulgaria, ARK, 2008).

panacea for) a long and difficult process of reform in ways that are otherwise impossible in a purely internal situation. But to do this persuasively demands not only adaptations to domestic systems and processes, but also ongoing scrutiny and refinement of the EU children's rights measures with which candidate states are expected to comply. Moreover, it demands some consideration of and receptiveness to the influence that the accession states themselves can have on the culture of children's rights within the EU.

ACCEDING TO WHAT? SCRUTINISING THE QUALITY OF EU
CHILDREN'S RIGHTS MEASURES TO WHICH ACCESSION
STATES ARE EXPECTED TO CONFORM

Focusing more attention on the specific requirements of EU child-relevant measures within the accession negotiations may go some way towards promoting children's rights at EU level more broadly. The likely effects of this are limited, however, primarily because adoption of such measures by accession states are only ever going to be as effective as the EU provisions from which they extrapolate. Previous chapters have already highlighted that children's rights provision can be decidedly vague, imposes few binding obligations on the Member States and, in some cases, may even diminish or undermine the level of children's rights protection already available at the national level. Indeed, some EU measures of direct relevance to children have been heavily criticised for falling short of international human rights standards. For example, chapter three has already highlighted how, in the field of immigration, EU legislation imposes more restrictive conditions on family reunification for children over the age of 12 years old than it does for younger children,[70] thereby conflicting with international human rights principles such as Article 10 of the UNCRC[71] and Article 8 of the European Convention on Human Rights, not to mention Articles 7 and 24 of the Charter of Fundamental Rights of the European Union. Conflicts such as this present something of a paradox within the accession process: by unreservedly adopting certain children's rights measures under the legal criteria, accession states may actually fall foul of the human rights standards contained within the political criteria by virtue of the fact that the EU measures themselves are inherently deficient. This reinforces the need to precede any campaign to promote the adoption of EU children's rights measures at the national level with more detailed scrutiny

---

[70] Dir 2003/86 on the right to family reunification [2003] OJ L251/12 (known as the Family Reunification Directive), Art 4(1). See also E Drywood, 'Giving with One Hand, Taking with the Other: Fundamental Rights, Children and the Family Reunification Decision' (2007) 32 *EL Rev* 396.

[71] Art 10(1) UNCRC reads 'applications by a child or his or her parents to enter or leave a State Party for the purpose of family reunification shall be dealt with by States Parties in a positive, humane and expeditious manner. States Parties shall further ensure that the submission of such a request shall entail no adverse consequences for the applicants and for the members of their family'.

of their content and scope at the source, a process that necessarily entails assessing their compatibility with key international children's rights norms.[72]

Aside from the isolated examples referred to above as to the impact of EU accession on child protection issues, it is difficult to gauge the wider impact of EU accession on children, particularly in the absence of any coherent, longitudinal evaluation. In reality, EU accession is likely to affect all children to varying degrees, although not always in a positive way. On a very general level, the stabilising effect of EU membership on accession states' economies will pay dividends for children directly as well as indirectly, as manifested in more opportunities and incentives for foreign investment, a rise in parental employment and living standards, enhanced access to goods and services and, ultimately, better resourced welfare, health and education systems. By the same token, children benefit from new states' legal alignment with the EU following accession in the sense that they will be brought within the scope of the Treaty, EU secondary legislation and other soft-law measures and policy initiatives.[73] As the discussion has already highlighted, however, the extent to which this process impacts positively on children's rights depends largely on whether EU measures offer substantially better provision for children than that which already exists at the national level, and whether it is appropriately transposed. Where EU law offers less than what is available at the national level, EU accession may technically imply a downgrading of children's rights. Take EU measures aimed at reconciling work and family life, for instance: the automatic application of EU gender equality laws entitle mothers to a continuous period of maternity leave of at least 14 weeks following the birth or adoption of a child.[74] They also allow parents to work flexibly to enable them to manage their domestic and caring responsibilities more effectively and to take up to four months unpaid leave to care for children up until they reach the age of eight.[75] While these initiatives may have significantly enhanced employment

---

[72] While the EU's expression of children's rights may be inherently flawed, wider concerns around the 'lack of rigour' when scrutinising compliance with the acquis has also been expressed. For more discussion of this see F Beveridge, 'Gender, the Acquis and Beyond' referring to gender issues above n 57; and M Maresceau, 'Pre-accession' in Cremona (ed), above n 6, 21–23 discussing the relevance of accession negotiations to environmental issues.

[73] EU equality legislation that prohibits discrimination in relation to access to services such as education is a case in point and is discussed further in ch 6.

[74] Dir 92/85 on the introduction of measures to encourage improvements in the safety and health at work of pregnant workers and workers who have recently given birth or are breastfeeding [1992] OJ L348/1, Art 8. See also recent proposals to extend this period of leave to 18 weeks: Proposal for a Directive of the European Parliament and of the Council amending Council Directive 92/85 COM (2008) 600/4. These provisions are further supported by the Dir 2006/54 on the implementation of the principle of equal opportunities and equal treatment of men and women in matters of employment and occupation (recast) [2006] OJ L204/23. This Directive prohibits 'any less favourable treatment of a woman related to pregnancy or maternity leave' (Art 2(c)).

[75] Dir 96/34 on the framework agreement on parental leave concluded by UNICE, CEEP and the ETUC [1996] OJ L145/4. This was revised in June 2009 to increase parental leave from three to four months. See more recently Commission, 'A Roadmap for Equality between Women and Men, 2006–10' (Communication) COM (2006) 92 final. Also, the Commission's proposal to amend the Pregnant Workers Directive includes a right to *request* flexible working patterns after a period of maternity leave

protection for working parents in the more established Member States, with inevitable benefits for their children, a number of the more recent accession states already offered markedly more generous provision. In the Czech Republic, Latvia and Poland, for example, parents can take long periods of statutory leave until the child is three or four years old (albeit with limited financial support). The Hungarian system provides a moderately high earnings-replacement rate for the first two years followed by a flat-rate payment for the third year; while in Slovenia fathers benefit from a long paternity leave entitlement of 90 days, of which 75 days can be taken after maternity leave supported by a low flat-rate allowance.[76] In theory, therefore, these states could legitimately reduce entitlement and still comply with the minimum requirements of EU law following accession.[77]

THE MIXED BLESSING OF ENHANCED MOBILITY RIGHTS FOLLOWING EU ACCESSION

A further subtle illustration of the double-edged and, perhaps unanticipated, impact of EU membership for children can be seen in another area of adult-targeted law: the free movement of persons provisions. One of the most attractive and controversial effects of EU accession is the opportunity to access other Member States' systems for the purposes of work, study, travel, retirement, receipt of services, or simply for personal reasons.[78] Although primarily targeted at encouraging adult mobility, the free movement provisions can carry significant benefits for children, including greater educational opportunities in the host state, as well as opening up new cultural and linguistic horizons. But what of the more negative consequences of gaining access to freedom of movement? Evidence

(above n 60, Art 11(5)). See further E Caracciolo di Torella and A Masselot, *Reconciliation of Work and Family Life in EU Law and Policy* (Basingstoke, Palgrave Macmillan, 2010) 50.

[76] D Anxo, C Fagan, M Smith, MT Letablier and C Perraudin, *Parental Leave in European Companies: Establishment Survey on Working Time 2004–05* (Dublin, European Foundation for the Improvement of Living and Working Conditions, 2007) 5. See further A Hatland and E Mayhew, 'Parental Rights and Obligations' in J Bradshaw and A Hatland (eds), *Social Policy, Employment and Family Change in Comparative Perspective* (Cheltenham, Edward Elgar, 2006) 79; N Finch, 'Childcare and Parental Leave' in Bradshaw and Hatland, *Social Policy*, above, 119; E Drew, *Parental Leave in Council of Europe Member States* (Strasbourg, Directorate General of Human Rights, 2005); OECD, *Babies and Bosses: Reconciling Work and Family Life—A Synthesis of Findings for OECD Countries* (Paris, OECD, 2007).

[77] Albi, 'Ironies in Human Rights Protection', above n 34, reveals instances in which the post-Communist constitutional courts have been faced with the prospect of having to downgrade the level of protection they offer after accession in order to conform with EU law. See, however, the decision of Case C-144/04 *Mangold* [2005] ECR I-9981which significantly reduces Member States' capacity to level down provision in the ways anticipated above.

[78] Dir 2004/38 on the right of citizens of the Union and their family members to move and reside freely within the territory of the Member States amending Reg 1612/68 and repealing Dirs 64/221, 68/360, 72/194, 73/148, 75/34, 75/35, 90/364, 90/365 and 93/96 [2004] OJ L158/77. For a detailed, social-legal analysis of the impact of enlargement on mobility entitlement and practices in the EU, see S Currie, *Migration, Work and Citizenship in the Enlarged European Union* (Ashgate, Aldershot, 2008).

suggests that in the post-accession environment, parents are choosing to leave children behind while they work for a temporary period abroad.[79]

The increasing trend in family dispersal for the sake of migration is motivated by a range of social, legal and economic factors, including: the inaccessibility of appropriate and affordable childcare arrangements in the host state (particularly for 'dual career' couples); the insecurity associated with fixed, short-term employment contracts (a characteristic of an increasing number of migrants' posts now); the financial benefits to be gained from sending remittances 'back home' to family;[80] and concerns as to the potential impact of moving on the child's education or the other parent's career. Such considerations frequently result in long periods of parental separation from children and, in some cases, separation of children from their siblings.[81] While parents may have the child's best interests at heart by adapting migration decisions to account for their educational, care and social needs, familial separation of this nature sits uncomfortably with wider normative principles and research that underline the importance of 'active parenting' and every day, direct familial interaction for children's well-being and development.[82]

SUSTAINING CHILDREN'S RIGHTS PROTECTION IN THE POST ACCESSION ENVIRONMENT

The final observation relating to the effects of the accession process on children is more constitutional in nature and questions the longer-term capacity of the EU to enforce Member State compliance with the standards set down by the Copenhagen Criteria. In particular, the political conditionality enables the EU to scrutinise and enforce human rights standards in relation to prospective accession states even though it does not possess similar powers in relation to its existing states. In other words, the accession process licenses the EU to exercise something

[79] HL Ackers and H Stalford, 'Managing Multiple Life-Courses: The Influence of Children on Migration Processes in the European Union' in K Clarke, T Maltby and P Kennett (eds), *Social Policy Review 19* (Bristol, Policy Press, 2007) 317.

[80] M Sana and D Massey, 'Household Composition, Family Migration and Community Context: Migrant Remittances in Four Countries' (2005) 86 *Social Science Quarterly* 509; N Glystos, 'The Role of Migrant Remittances in Development: Evidence from Mediterranean Countries' (2002) 40 *International Migration* 5.

[81] For further discussion of empirical research analysing the impact of highly-skilled migration on family life in the context of enlargement, see H Stalford, 'Parenting, Care and Mobility in the European Union: Issues Facing EU Migrant Scientists' (2005) 18 *Innovation: The European Journal of Social Science Research* 361 and Ackers and Stalford, 'Managing Multiple Life-Courses', above n 79.

[82] C Smart, 'From Children's Shoes to Children's Voices?' (2002) 40 *Family Court Review* 305; C Smart, 'Towards an Understanding of Family Change: Gender Conflict and Children's Citizenship' (2003) 17 *Australian Journal of Family Law* 1. See also J Brannen, E Heptinstall and K Bhopal, *Connecting Children: Care and Family Life in Later Childhood* (London, Routledge, 2000) and A Bainham, B Lindley and M Richards (eds), *Children and Their Families: Contact, Rights, and Welfare* (London, Hart, 2003). Some of these issues are explored further in ch 3.

of a human rights monitoring function in a way that would be legally ill-founded and politically untenable at the internal level. By way of illustration, Brandtner and Rosas highlight that the explicit demands imposed by the political criteria concerning the protection of minority rights, while welcome, have no grounding in the treaties and were never a particular focus of EU internal activities.[83] Similarly, Williams points to the emphasis in the accession partnerships for Romania, Bulgaria and the Czech Republic, on implementing social and educational programmes to integrate Roma children in spite of the limited scope of EU internal actions in favour of this group.[84] This dilemma—diagnosed by Alston and Weiler as 'the schizophrenia that afflicts the Union between its internal and external policies'[85]—is especially relevant to children's rights: it seems the EU can legitimise scrutinising countries' children's rights systems in the lead up to accession as a sine qua non of membership but, once entry is achieved, it suffers acute amnesia in relation to children's rights regulation and monitoring. If children's rights are not routinely monitored in an internal context, however, surely compliance with children's rights as a precondition for membership seems unnecessary and even artificial, tokenistic even?

Two principal arguments justify the EU's requirement that new Member States implement and uphold the pre-accession recommendations relating to children's rights in the absence of any specific legal competence to do so internally. First, the purpose of the accession process is to do what is necessary to bring accession states in line with existing Member States, including in matters relating to children's rights, given how critical social, civil, economic and political coherence is to EU integration. Since full accession is based on the presumption that the minimum standards have been achieved, there is no legitimate reason to monitor states' performance indefinitely. Indeed, it is precisely the fact that children's rights violations remain relatively impervious to sanction through EU internal enforcement mechanisms that enhances the need to bring states up to speed before they join.[86]

---

[83] See B Brandtner and A Rosas, 'Human Rights and the External Relations of the European Community: An Analysis of Doctrine and Practice' (1998) *European Journal of International Law* 468.

[84] A Williams, 'Enlargement of the Union and Human Rights Conditionality: A Policy of Distinction?' (2000) 25 *EL Rev* 601, 612.

[85] P Alston and J Weiler, 'A European Union Human Rights Policy' in P Alston, M Bustelo and J Heenan (eds), *The European Union and Human Rights* (Oxford, Oxford University Press, 1999) 9.

[86] The EU can rely on a number of mechanisms to monitor states' ongoing compliance with the obligations undertaken during the accession process. These include the imposition of a range of sanctions under Art 7 TEU on Member States found to be in breach of their fundamental rights obligations (from financial penalties to suspension of certain privileges and in extreme cases, even expulsion from the EU). The Co-operation Verification Mechanism (CVM) was also established to monitor the post-accession progress of Romania and Bulgaria towards meeting the benchmarks agreed prior to their accession (specifically in relation to addressing crime and corruption and in reforming the judicial system). Finally, the EU can institute infringement proceedings pursuant to Art 258 TFEU in relation to Member States that fail to comply with their obligations under the treaties. It is hardly surprising, given the relatively low priority attached to children's rights in EU law more generally, that none of these mechanisms have, to date, been used to challenge accession

A second argument justifying the enhanced level of EU scrutiny of human rights in applicant states points to the fact that the criteria for membership is a product of the climate in which they were developed: that of post-Communist Europe. In that sense, the pre-accession human rights standards could be seen as a compensatory mechanism aimed at addressing the withdrawal of human rights standards from many states following the collapse of Communism.[87] As Pogány notes:

> One of the defining features of the Communist system was that it accorded rights with respect to employment, education, healthcare, pensions, housing, etc. as a matter of constitutional entitlement. The abrupt removal of these rights, on which many ... had come to depend, was an inevitable consequence of the transition from command to market economies. However, the substitution of minority rights (along with civil and political rights) has scarcely compensated for the disappearance of a wide range of socio-economic guarantees that had assured ... a relatively secure way of life and a modest standard of living that many, accustomed to severe hardship in the inter-war era and before, considered acceptable.[88]

These arguments may go some way towards explaining the apparent 'double-standard' in the EU's approach to children's rights as far as accession states are concerned: the children's rights conditionality introduced in relation to Romania and Bulgaria's accession sought to address the abject violations of children's rights epitomised by the child care institutions. While such images remain so vivid, surely any effort by the EU to prompt national action in favour of children should be welcomed regardless of the legal, ideological and political anomalies it may create. Certainly, as the discussion has already highlighted, the EU's achievements in prompting national reform of structures and procedures through the process of accession should not be underestimated. The prospect of EU membership offers an incentive for change, and once this process gathers momentum, individual, national as well as global expectations are raised. These expectations can exert a much more potent pressure on individual states to uphold standards than any enforcement mechanism at the EU internal level. After all, it is rather more difficult for states to justify an active reduction in existing children's rights provision than it is to justify a simple failure to develop children's rights provision further. This observation prompts further

---

states' compliance with their children's rights obligations. See further, E Gateva, *Post Accession Conditionality*, above n 10.

[87] I Pogány, 'Minority Rights and the Roma of Central and Eastern Europe' (2006) 6 *Human Rights Law Review* 1, 12.

[88] Ibid 12. See also I Pogány, 'Refashioning Rights in Central and Eastern Europe: Some Implications for the Region's Roma' (2004) 10 *European Public Law* 89. Pogány concedes that although formally included in the constitutions of Communist states, social and economic 'rights' (like other types of rights) were ultimately subject to curtailment or withdrawal on political grounds at the absolute discretion of the authorities.

consideration of the positive 'feedback'[89] effects that accession states can have on the development of children's rights in the EU.

ASK NOT WHAT THE EU CAN DO FOR CHILDREN'S RIGHTS IN THE ACCESSION STATES, BUT WHAT THE ACCESSION STATES CAN DO FOR CHILDREN'S RIGHTS IN THE EU

While much of the academic commentary has focused on the achievements of accession conditionality for the new Member States, there has been relatively little scrutiny of the repercussions of the accession process at EU legal and policy level. De Búrca, in particular, attributes many of the dramatic changes to the EU's fundamental rights framework since the turn of the millennium to the institutions' desire to 'lead by example' in setting the human rights standards of candidate states.[90] More specifically, the growing prominence of minority rights in internal EU law and policy-making has coincided with, and undoubtedly responded to, the enhanced scrutiny of minority rights in the accession negotiations, particularly in the context of Roma integration.[91]

A similar trend can be identified in relation to children's rights. It is probably no coincidence that Romania and Bulgaria's accession to the EU, which is accredited with rendering the accession process more permeable to child protection issues, was sandwiched between the Commissions two flagship Communications on internal children's rights issues.[92] Iusmen notes more generally:

> The experience of the EU child protection conditionality implemented in Romania created a precedent in terms of the extent and depth of EU action in this policy area. The accumulation of EU know-how on and experience in children's rights ... contributed to the shaping of the EU's current enlargement policy and, crucially, had feedback effects on the EU's internal approach to children's rights ... [In] the light of the expertise and practical knowledge garnered at the Commission level ... the normative perspective on

[89] Iusmen, above n 17.

[90] G De Búrca, 'Beyond the Charter: How Enlargement has Enlarged the Human Rights Policy of the EU' (2004) 27 *Fordham International Law Journal* 679.

[91] Noteworthy internal developments include the extension of the non-discrimination principle on grounds of race and ethnicity (Art 19 TFEU) which has, in turn, provided the basis for a new race equality legislation, Dir 2000/43 implementing the principle of equal treatment between persons irrespective of racial or ethnic origin [2000] OJ L180/22. There has been a proliferation of measures aimed at promoting understanding and improving the integration of Roma throughout the EU, including the launch by the European Commission of an EU Strategy on Roma Inclusion: 'An EU Framework for national Roma Integration Strategies up to 2020' (Communication) COM (2011) 173 final. For the Macedonian perspective, see M Koinova, 'Challenging Assumptions', above n 26.

[92] Commission, 'Towards an EU Strategy on the Rights of the Child' (Communication) COM (2006) 367 final and Commission, 'An EU Agenda for the Rights of the Child' (Communication) COM (2011) 60 final.

EU involvement with children's rights has shifted from a 'terra nova' stance to one of 'déjà vu'.[93]

The creeping effects of the accession conditionality vis-à-vis children's rights are also evidenced in the priorities pursued by the Member States during their presidency of the EU. Hungary, for instance, adopted early childhood education as a key issue during its presidency in the first half of 2011,[94] in addition to bringing experts together to consider how to address the problem of children running away from care. Similarly, Belgium, during its presidency in 2010, supported a range of networking events and campaign activities under the theme 'Matching international agendas on children, youth and children's rights', with a particular focus on combating child poverty.[95]

CONCLUSION

The accession process has undergone gradual change and extension, particularly since the early 1990s in response to the increasing diversity of the new applicant states. The formalisation of the process following the Treaty of Amsterdam has enhanced the weight of the Copenhagen Criteria enabling them to be applied by the EU as a stick-shaped carrot. The EU can legitimately set standards for states which they must meet prior to entry, but provides concrete support to enable them to achieve those standards, the ultimate incentive being EU membership. The broad scope and detailed nature of the negotiations has transformed it into one of the most effective sites for promoting children's rights in particular. This has been achieved much more effectively through some aspects of the criteria than others, however. The EU legal (acquis) and economic criteria demand comparatively little accountability as far as children's rights are concerned, primarily because of the extensive range of other issues that they cover, and the difficulty of mining children's rights obligations from the broader instruments in which they are routinely enshrined. The political criteria, on the other hand, have provided a clearer, more constructive articulation of children's rights, succeeding in transposing the vague obligation to respect human rights and uphold democracy, into concrete structural and policy recommendations, obligations, priorities and benchmarks. Insofar as these are expressed in unequivocal terms, they offer little room for manoeuvre with the effect that they impose a high degree of accountability on candidate states. The reforms generated by this process provides fresh insight into the true capacity of the EU to advance children's rights that is otherwise impossible in a purely internal context. The process is not just about piecemeal compliance with isolated EU provisions but instead demands that states

---

[93] Iusmen, 'Human Rights Developments', above n 17, 55.
[94] See: eu2011.hu/news/kulcsszerepet-szan-tanacs-az-oktatasnak.
[95] See: eutrio.be/search/apachesolr_search/children?filters=language%3Aen.

reflect upon and implement significant institutional reform to children's rights systems. This can, as the examples above demonstrate, have a dramatic and trans-formative impact on how children's rights are prioritised at the state level mak-ing any subsequent retreat from the standards set very difficult indeed. But the relationship is by no means unilateral: the accession states themselves can offer new insights and stimulate new policy reflections within the European Union. Romania's candidacy, in particular, marked a pivotal point in the integration of a more prominent children's rights element within the enlargement process and no doubt contributed to the development of the EU's broader children's rights strategy internally.

There is still considerable scope, however, to make the accession process more child-sensitive, not least by exploiting further the economic and legal elements of the Copenhagen Criteria. This demands a much more rigorous assessment of the nature and scope of children's rights obligations across the different chapters that constitute the EU acquis so that states can report on progress in a more coherent, detailed way. This has to be accompanied by closer scrutiny of the structural and systemic deficiencies that hamper effective application of EU children's rights measures at the national level, including the wide-spread lack of child-sensitive data, poor formal representation for children at NGO and governmental level, and insufficient training for those dealing with children in formal judicial and investigative processes. This demands a rather more positive endorsement of the EU's role in prescribing children's rights standards in the external world; one that sees this apparent double-standard as a unique opportunity to harness the EU's resources to effect significant, sustainable changes to children's rights systems at the domestic level. The hope is, ultimately that such reforms will then exert a posi-tive influence on existing Member States and, indeed, catalyse more meaningful reform in the way that children's rights are developed and administered at the EU level.

Conclusion:
The Future of Children's Rights
in the European Union

THIS BOOK HAS coincided with and indeed, responded to, a pivotal point in the development of EU measures relating to children. While traditionally children's rights and EU law and policy have been viewed as mutually exclusive enterprises, more recent constitutional, legal and policy developments have firmly etched issues relating to child welfare and rights on the EU legal and policy agenda.

The adoption, in February 2011, of the EU Agenda for the Rights of the Child marks the crystallisation of EU efforts in relation to children into an actual strategy on the rights of the child, driven largely by the lobbying activities of international children's rights NGOs and campaign networks. This, in turn, has benefited from the constitutional reinforcement of fundamental rights brought about by the Treaty of Lisbon. Such developments are clearly welcome, not least for exposing the EU to international censure should it fail to deliver on its goals. Indeed, there is every suggestion that the EU has entered into a more constructive, collaborative and holistic phase of child law and policy-making. Its approach is certainly more ambitious: implicit in the EU Agenda for the Rights of the Child and related activities is a desire to embed international children's rights norms more firmly within EU regulatory processes. This both complements, but also contrasts with, the more subtle, timid approach that has characterised previous EU activities relating to children. Historically, cognisant of the structural and constitutional limitations of the EU, modest changes have been effected largely within a legislative context by nudging gently at the parameters of competence and highlighting the instrumental value of children within and to the EU internal market project. Both approaches have their merits and pitfalls: the former may ultimately lead to less in the way of binding measures and present an uncomfortable challenge to national sovereignty, but make a significantly greater global impact; the latter, on the other hand, perhaps offers more realistic, sustainable outcomes in terms of binding law, thereby impacting upon nation states to a greater degree, but with a more limited topical 'reach'.

Ultimately, the future of EU children's rights lies in a combination of these two approaches: one that adopts international children's rights standards as a benchmark by which to measure, and thereby challenge current EU provision affecting children, whilst grounding suggestions for development in a realistic appraisal of EU competence and the political will of both the institutions and the Member States. Such has been the aim of this book—to present a detailed overview of the content and scope of children's rights at EU level across various areas of law and policy whilst exploring whether existing structural and procedural mechanisms adequately accommodate them. This analysis has revealed some progress, at least in the development of more explicit and far-reaching child-related measures, and a more acute consciousness of the importance and validity of EU intervention in relation to children's rights. It has also drawn attention to the vast and valuable resources at the EU's disposal to assist this process. But the analysis has also unearthed a number of fundamental limitations that risk undermining the EU's prospects of making a meaningful impact on children's lives. These can be summarised as follows: first, the EU's conceptualisation of children's rights is flawed; second the EU lacks conviction as to its own role in relation to children's rights; and third, the institutional, political and procedural mechanics of the EU are still insufficiently amenable to children's rights.

THE EU'S FLAWED CONCEPTUALISATION OF CHILDREN'S RIGHTS: FROM SUBVERSION TO INSERTION TO PERVERSION

The EU's journey towards the children's rights Agenda that exists today has been characterised by political detours, legal dead ends and campaign blind alleys. For at least the first 10 years following its inception, the EU was decidedly ambivalent, antipathetic even, to the impact it might have on children's lives. In that sense, one could argue that children's rights were positively subverted—subjugated to the primary, economic, adult-focused aims of the EU. On recognising that children are, in fact, instrumental to the achievement of the EU's broader goals, reference to their needs and rights were cautiously inserted into a handful of key internal market instruments. While the number of concrete legislative references to children has expanded considerably, some are rather less effective than others in giving rise to tangible, enforceable entitlement. The changes effected to the fundamental rights framework following the implementation of the Charter and the Lisbon Treaty offered new opportunities for the EU to further children's rights. The constitutional and ideological implications of this are explained fully in chapter two, but subsequent chapters cast doubt on the capacity or, indeed, the willingness of the EU to achieve the aspirations set out in these instruments in practice. This raises concerns as to whether instruments such as the Lisbon Treaty, the Charter and, indeed, the EU Agenda in which campaigners are investing such hope, are simply further evidence of the EU's 'add children and stir' approach to children's rights: reference to 'children's rights' adds an appealing flavour to the EU framework, but is it sufficiently forceful to affect the substance and outcomes for children? Indeed, in embracing the language of children's rights so dramatically as a result of these developments without the necessary insight into how they can operate, there is a concern that the EU risks perverting children's rights. This is illustrated by an identifiable preoccupation with child protection that dominates much of the EU's activity relating to children.

THE HEGEMONY OF THE CHILD PROTECTION AGENDA AT EU LEVEL

An important aim of this book has also been to challenge the prevailing tendency, particularly in international and EU children's rights research and campaigning, to focus almost exclusively on children 'in crisis'—to prioritise those in the most vulnerable of economic, social and legal situations. This is accompanied by an inherent perception that any focus, in research or political terms, on children who enjoy a relatively privileged socio-economic and legal status, are well cared-for by their parents and are educated, is a futile indulgence. This 'deficit-oriented' approach pervades EU children's rights law and policy, and is most evident in the priorities for action, identified by DG Justice, since its initial 2006 Communication, 'Towards a Strategy on the Rights of the Child'. It is equally evident in the priorities set by the European Forum on the Rights of the Child, established shortly after the 2006 Communication.[1] Virtually all of the meetings convened by the Forum since 2006 have focused largely on children in the most extreme of vulnerable situations.[2] The subsequent EU Agenda for the Rights of the Child reaffirms the EU's preoccupation with child protection. Thus, despite its standard mantra of 'promoting, protecting and fulfilling the rights of the child in all relevant EU policies', the Agenda singles out children on the very margins of society by prioritising issues such as juvenile justice, abduction, poverty, sexual and labour exploitation, forced migration and children in armed conflict. Significantly, the Treaty of Lisbon has served to set in constitutional stone the hegemony of child protection; the references to 'protection of the rights of the child', now peppered sparingly across the revised TEU[3] and TFEU,[4] are in danger of being construed merely as an obligation to reinforce measures to protect 'vulnerable' children rather than to protect children's *rights* more broadly in areas that fall within EU competence.

Whilst the EU's preoccupation with addressing the needs of the most socially and economically marginalised children is, in some respects, to be welcomed (after all, who can criticise the EU for wanting to help children in need?), it carries with it some less positive consequences. First, it risks sentimentalising and homogenising the EU's children's rights agenda by focusing on a limited number of children

---

[1] Discussed in ch 2.

[2] Themes of the meetings have included: protecting children against sexual exploitation (meeting one, June 2007); missing children, child poverty and social exclusion (meeting two, March 2008); violence against children (meeting three, December 2008) and child labour (meeting four, June 2009).

[3] Art 3(3) and (5) TEU.

[4] Art 79(2)(d) TFEU; Art 83(1) TFEU.

in a limited range of circumstances. In the process, it excludes from the research and political mainstream the experiences of (the majority of) children in the EU who enjoy a relatively privileged socio-economic and legal status, are well cared-for by their parents and are educated. Secondly, it fails to account for the complexity of children's lives; those who are economically and politically secure may still be vulnerable and in need, albeit in different ways to those who are not.[5] And thirdly, it attaches prominence to children's inherent vulnerability and helplessness whilst overlooking their achievements, capacity and, indeed, desire to make active, positive contributions to society on a par with adults.

Aspects of this book, therefore, have deliberately explored children's capacity and contribution as economic, political and social actors, in a private context, in local settings as well as in a national and, indeed, supra-national context. In doing so, the intention has been to illustrate the ways in which EU law and policy can celebrate and facilitate children and young people's agency.

MORE THAN JUST A WEBSITE: CHILDREN'S PARTICIPATION IN THE EU

Similar concerns as to the 'perversion' of children's rights are raised in relation to the EU's attempts to enhance children's participation and engagement. It is telling that child participation features as the last priority in the EU Agenda for the Rights of the Child. There is some attempt to define what child participation implies in practice—providing children with the opportunity to voice their opinions and participate in decisions that affect them[6]—but the action to which the Commission commits reveals a rather narrower interpretation. The sole commitment to enhancing the level of information available to children about their rights and relevant EU policies is based on the misguided presumption that children want access to this information, or that access to information will trigger an immediate sense of engagement and identification with the EU project. In reality, while the connection can be made in abstract legal and political terms, the regulatory activities of the EU that touch upon any aspect of children's lives are far removed from the issues facing children on a day-to-day basis. Children are no more interested in what the EU is working on or how it functions than adults are unless it touches their lives in a meaningful and personal way. Thus, as a number of chapters in this book have highlighted, the participatory ethic has to be firmly embedded in EU measures that will be transposed at the domestic level. This, in turn should bolster participatory opportunities in the national and regional

[5] This point has been addressed, in more recent years, by the development of child 'well-being' indicators that have sought to ascertain the experiences of children more generally across developed ('rich') countries. While the methodologies surrounding these endeavours remain contentious they have highlighted the complexity of children's lives and needs and endorsed more inclusive, representative data gathering and analysis. These issues are discussed further in ch 1.

[6] Commission, 'An EU Agenda for the Rights of the Child' (Communication) COM (2011) 60 final, 13–14.

systems with which children interact, whether that be the family justice process, the immigration process, educational opportunities, or civic activism.

SQUARE PEGS AND ROUND HOLES?: EXPECTATIONS OF THE EU'S ROLE IN RELATION TO CHILDREN'S RIGHTS

A second fundamental limitation hampering the furtherance of children's rights at EU level relates to the confused perception of the EU's role in this regard, a confusion that is perpetuated by the EU as much as by external stakeholders. Such has been the level of input from children's rights NGOs and lobbyists, and such is the EU's desire, at least recently, to respond to children's rights and to legitimise its role in the field, that it has developed an unsettling tendency to calibrate its children's rights agenda in accordance with the demands and priorities of the international community—often as something of a knee-jerk reaction to the children's rights scandal of the day. It is important to remember, however, that the EU is operating within an entirely different, rather more restricted constitutional framework than other international institutions. Its primary objective is to achieve a sustainable level of political and economic convergence and stability across the Member States. It was never intended to be a children's rights body, any more than it was intended to be a human rights body. Ultimately, therefore, the strictures of EU competence and the principle of subsidiarity will never allow the EU to interact with domestic children's rights issues in quite the same way as international law.

But that does not mean to say that the EU does not have a critical role to play in upholding and promoting children's rights standards. There is a clear need for a more coherent approach to children's rights at this level, but it has to be strategic rather than reactive. It has to bow to the reality of EU competence and to the very real political and ideological objections that Member States may raise to potentially reckless and wide-spread intervention in matters that have no identifiable link with the EU's core functions and objectives.

THE EU AS REGULATOR, CO-ORDINATOR AND SUPPORTER

This demands a more confident assertion on the part of the EU of what it cannot do as much as what it can do. Only then is it likely to position itself as a legitimate international legal and political force in the field of children's rights. With this in mind, the EU should be regarded as playing a multi-faceted role in promoting children's rights, as regulator, co-ordinator and supporter. The regulatory role involves top-down legislative and policy intervention that can be transposed at the Member State level in accordance with specific domestic interests. The co-ordinating role involves acting as a catalyst and correspondent between the Member States, mobilising rather than dictating domestic responses to universal children's rights issues.

Finally, the supportive role involves bolstering the activities of parallel international legal and campaign networks such as the Council of Europe, the United Nations, the World Health Organisation, UNICEF and, indeed, NGOs and practitioners at the domestic level.

Implicit in this conceptualisation of the EU's role is that abstract children's rights principles or declarations have merely a rhetorical force unless they are integrated into normative or procedural frameworks with which the EU is familiar and which have a firm grounding in the EU's constitutional order. Chapter two has demonstrated, for instance, that the language of the UNCRC is important in framing the EU's commitment to children's rights, but it needs a constitutional vehicle too to enable the instrument to be persuasively embedded in and pursued by EU law and policy. The analysis suggested the familiar and successful frameworks of citizenship, non-discrimination and social inclusion as effective (albeit not exhaustive) vehicles in this regard. Indeed, the EU has a vast range of similar governance tools and resources which can support and entrench children's rights in a range of other contexts.

INSTITUTIONAL, PROCEDURAL AND POLITICAL BLOCKAGES

A final, fundamental obstacle hampering the development of an effective system of EU children's rights are what have been referred to as the institutional, procedural and political 'blockages' within the EU.[7] These blockages are particularly apparent in the context of the EU's children's rights activities. The coherence of the EU Agenda for the Rights of the Child belies the highly fragmented and disparate way in which children's rights are actually developed within the EU. This is partly symptomatic of the way in which the Commission, as the primary instigator of EU children's rights measures, is organised. While the thematic allocation of mandates to the various Directorate Generals makes administrative sense, it is insensitive to the interaction between different aspects of children's rights. In the absence of clear correspondence between the assorted activities of the DGs, children's rights are dealt with in isolation from some of the bigger contexts and variables that may impact on them. This, in turn, skews the EU's perspective of the issues such that any responses are likely to be inadequate. Illustrations of this are provided in chapter seven: child trafficking is addressed as part of DG Justice's mandate. As a result of this, it is divorced from the wider context and variables which contribute to this phenomenon, notably poverty. To achieve a more informed, comprehensive and effective response in this area demands routine co-operation between DG Justice and those with the expertise and empirical insight into child poverty issues, for example, within DG Employment, Social Affairs and Inclusion. In reality, and in spite of the institutional amendments discussed in

[7] G Grugel and I Iusmen, 'The European Commission as Guardian Angel: Agenda-Setting for Children's Rights' (forthcoming 2012) *Journal of European Public Policy*.

chapter one aimed at easing communication between these internal actors, there is still a clear tendency, particularly within DG Justice, to pursue children's rights rather too much in isolation from other DGs.

With better internal co-ordination, these departments could usefully learn from one another: DG Education and Culture has amassed an impressive portfolio of expertise in relation to child participation and empowerment; a coherent model for mainstreaming children's rights has been formulated in the context of the EU's external relations agenda;[8] and DG Employment, Social Affairs and Inclusion is at the vanguard of new co-operative methods of governance and monitoring by virtue of its social inclusion agenda.

Aside from these institutional sticking points, are the blockages that exist between the EU's policy-making actors and those engaged in commissioning, managing and archiving research, and in monitoring the implementation and impact of EU law and policy at Member State level. Chapters one and seven have referred to an identifiable evidence base on which to develop informed and responsive children's rights measures. This could be partly addressed if there was simply better 'feedback' between these different enterprises which together constitute a rich empirical resource providing useful insights into the impact of existing EU measures on children's experiences, whilst also revealing gaps in provision. In the same token, further efforts could be made to exploit the links already forged with external stakeholders, particularly those in international institutions such as the UN or the Council of Europe. There is significant potential to extend these collaborations with a view to identifying and developing more compatible, synergistic monitoring mechanisms, and with a view to pooling skills and resources more effectively to facilitate the collection of information and avoid unnecessary duplication of effort.[9]

ACHIEVING BETTER ACCOUNTABILITY—FOR WHAT AND TO WHOM?

So what broader conclusions can be drawn from the analysis presented in this book as to the EU's accountability for children's rights?

Accountability in an EU context implies a process by which the EU institutions or, indeed, a Member State, is held to account for any activities that undermine or threaten the rights and welfare of children within the scope of EU competence. That might, in turn, require the implementation of pre-emptive or remedial

---

[8] See, eg Commission, 'A special place for children in EU external action' (Communication) COM (2008) 55 final (not published in the *Official Journal*) and General Affairs Council, 'Update of the EU guidelines on children and armed conflict' 16 June 2008 (not published in the *Official Journal*).

[9] Save the Children, for example, has illustrated how the UNCRCs General Measures of Implementation can be adapted to an EU context to achieve a coherent and comprehensive approach to child mainstreaming. See further S Ruxton, *Governance Fit for Children. To What Extent have the General Measures of Implementation of the UNCRC Been Realised in Five European Countries?* (Brussels, Save the Children, 2010).

measures, often in the form of legislation, but also by virtue of judicial prescription or sanctions. But this also presumes that there are mechanisms by which potential or actual abuses of children's rights can be identified, reported and addressed. A number of formal and informal mechanisms exist in this regard. Some are institutional, such as the European Ombudsman or the Court of Justice but these are notoriously difficult for children to access because of the time, finances and information required to fully exploit them. Some involve longer-term collective lobbying, such as the EU Citizens' Initiative,[10] but this requires substantial resources and planning, and is certainly not designed to address individual children's issues.[11] Others involve infringement actions[12] or financial sanctions[13] in relation to Member States that fail to meet the obligations undertaken under EU law although, as was noted in chapter eight, the institutions have been reluctant to use any of these sanctions in child-related matters.

The challenge of rendering these mechanisms more accessible is not exclusive to the EU nor, indeed, is it exclusive to children but rather is a challenge pervading all legal orders at all levels. Furthermore, the process of developing, implementing and monitoring children's rights is not just a question of the EU acting alone, but implies a joint responsibility of a range of actors: at the most basic level the EU can initiate and enact laws but it is for the Member States to actually implement them. Indeed, there have been many examples presented in this book of EU legislative measures pertaining to an aspect of children's rights but in a manner that relies entirely on the amenability of Member States' existing children's rights procedures to implement them effectively.

These issues reinforce the importance of more evidence-based mechanisms for holding the EU to account on children's rights issues. Such mechanisms respond equally well to areas in which the EU exercises a more complementary role (such as social policy or education) and where accountability has rather more constructive connotations in terms of implying a responsibility to support action at the domestic level. They include monitoring programmes, impact assessments, national reporting, or children's rights indicators. The EU has made some progress in adapting these processes to the specific needs and interests of children and has asserted a strong commitment to sustaining them in the future.[14] The extent to which they will give rise to a period of reflection and responsive reform at EU level, however, remains to be seen.

---

[10] Arts 11(4) TEU and 24 TFEU.

[11] For an analysis of the Citizens' Initiative from a children's rights perspective see H Stalford and M Schuurman, 'Are We There Yet? The Impact of the Lisbon Treaty on the EU Children's Rights Agenda' (2011) 3 *International Journal of Children's Rights* 381. For a more general overview of how the Citizens Initiative operates, see B Davies, 'Giving EU Citizens a Voice: Regulation 211/2011 on the EU Citizen's Initiative' (2011) 3 *Journal of Social Welfare and Family Law* 289.

[12] Art 258 TFEU.

[13] Art 7 TEU.

[14] EU Agenda for the Rights of the Child, above n 6, 5.

By way of conclusion, notwithstanding the obstacles to the future progress of EU children's rights, it is important to acknowledge the significant advancements that have already been made in this regard, and in a relatively short period of time. Children's rights take time to evolve, relationships between the key protagonists both internal and external to the EU take time to become established and effective, and some time needs to pass before the true impact of EU measures on the ground can be monitored and evaluated. This book, therefore, ends on a note of high optimism as to the future role of the EU in developing and upholding children's rights. The raw materials are in place and there is an unprecedented political momentum at international and national level for joining forces with the EU to formulate a more effective response to children's rights issues that simply cannot be addressed by nation states acting alone. The EU is still adjusting to the ideological and methodological shifts demanded by this role. By harnessing the extensive legal, economic and political resources already at its disposal, however, it has the potential, not only to avert any injurious effects that EU action might have on children, but to position itself at the forefront of the global campaign to protect and promote children's rights.

Bibliography

Ackers, HL and Gill, B, *Moving People and Knowledge: Scientific Mobility in an Enlarging European Union* (London, Edward Elgar, 2008)

Ackers, HL, and Stalford, H, 'Children, Migration and Family Policy in the European Union: Intra-Community Mobility and the Status of Children in EC Law' (1999) 21 *Children and Youth Services Review* 699

——, *A Community for Children? Children, Citizenship and Migration in the European Union* (Aldershot, Ashgate, 2004)

——, 'Managing Multiple Life-Courses: The Influence of Children on Migration Processes in the European Union' in Clarke, K, Maltby, T and Kennett, P (eds), *Social Policy Review 19* (Bristol, Policy Press, 2007)

Ahmed, T and Butler, I de Jesús, 'The European Union and Human Rights: An International Perspective' (2006) 17 *European Journal of International Law* 771.

Aiyagari, A, Greenwood, J and Seshandri, A, 'Efficient Investment in Children' (2002) 102 *Journal of Economic Theory* 290

Albi, A, 'Ironies in Human Rights Protection in the EU: Pre-Accession Conditionality and Post-Accession Conundrums' (2009) 15 *European Law Journal* 46

Alderson, P and Goodwin, M, 'Contradictions within Concepts of Children's Competence' (1993) 1 *International Journal of Children's Rights* 303

Alles, S, 'Franco-German Family Mediation: From the Experiences of a Parliamentary Pilot Project to New Prospects' (Seventh European Conference on Family Law, Strasbourg, Council of Europe, 16 March 2009)

Alston, P, 'The Best Interests Principle: Towards a Reconciliation of Culture and Human Rights' (1994) 8 *International Journal of Law Policy and the Family* 1

—— 'Ships Passing in the Night: The Current State of the Human Rights and Development Debate seen Through the Lens of the Millennium Development Goals' (2005) 27 *Human Rights Quarterly* 755

—— and Weiler, J, 'A European Union Human Rights Policy' in Alston, P, Bustelo, M and Heenan, J (eds), *The European Union and Human Rights* (Oxford, Oxford University Press, 1999)

Anderson, B and O'Connell Davidson, J, 'Border Troubles and Invisibility: Child Rights and Migration in Europe' (Save the Children Sweden Seminar on Rightless Migration, 1 June 2005)

Andreß, HJ, Borgloh, B, Brockel, M, Giesselmann, M and Hummelsheim, D, 'The Economic Consequences of Partnership Dissolution: A Comparative Analysis of Panel Studies from Belgium, Germany, Great Britain, Italy and Sweden' (2006) 22 *European Sociological Review* 533

Andrews, S, Armstrong, D, McLernon, L, Megow, S and Skinner, C, *Maintenance: Research on Instigating Behaviour Change*, vol 1–Main Report (London, Child Maintenance and Enforcement Commission, 2011)

Anxo, D, Fagan, C, Smith, M, Letablier, MT and Perraudin, C, *Parental Leave in European Companies: Establishment Survey on Working Time 2004–05* (Dublin, European Foundation for the Improvement of Living and Working Conditions, 2007)

Applica, CESEP and Alphametrics, 'Men and Women with Disabilities in the EU: Statistical Analysis of the Labour Force Survey Ad Hoc Module and the EU-SILC' (Brussels, European Commission, 2007)

Archaud, D, *Children: Rights and Childhood*, 2nd edn (London, Routledge, 2004)

—— and Skivenes, M, 'Balancing a Child's Best Interests and a Child's Views' (2009) 17 *International Journal of Children's Rights* 1

Aries, P, *Centuries of Childhood: A Social History of Family Life* (New York, Vintage Books, 1962)

ARK Bulgaria, 'Briefing Note: Institutions in Bulgaria' (Bulgaria, ARK, 2008)

Arnull, A, 'From Charter to Constitution and Beyond: Fundamental Rights in the New European Union' (2003) Public Law 774

—— 'Family Reunification and Fundamental Rights' (2006) 31 EL Rev 611

—— Dashwood, A, Ross, M, Wyatt, D, Spaventa, E and Dougan, M, *European Union Law*, 5th edn (London, Sweet & Maxwell, 2006)

Askola, H, 'Foreign National Prisoners, Deportations and Gender' in Stalford, H, Currie, S and Velluti, S (eds), *Gender and Migration in 21st Century Europe* (Surrey, Ashgate, 2009) 163

Bailey, A and Boyle, P, 'Untying and Retying Family Migration in the New Europe' (2004) 30 *Journal of Ethnic and Migration Studies* 229

Bailey, AJ and Cooke, TJ, 'Family Migration, Migration History and Employment' (1998) 21 *International Regional Science Review* 99

Bainham, A, Lindley, B and Richards, R (eds), *Children and their Families: Contact, Rights and Welfare* (London, Hart, 2003)

Balton, D, 'The Convention on the Rights of the Child: Prospects for International Enforcement' (1990) 12 *Human Rights Quarterly* 120

Bandman, B, *Children's Right to Freedom, Care, and Enlightenment* (London, Routledge, 2007)

Barlow, A, Duncan, S, James, G and Parks, A, *Cohabitation, Marriage and the Law: Social Change and Legal Reform in the 21st Century* (Oxford, Hart, 2005)

Barnard, C, *The Substantive Law of the EU: The Four Freedoms* (Oxford, Oxford University Press, 2007)

Barret, G, 'Family Matters: European Community Law and Third Country Family Members' (2003) 40 *CML Rev* 369

Bartlett, W, Benini, R and Gordon, C, *Measures to Promote the Situation of Roma EU Citizens in the European Union: Study* (Brussels, European Parliament, 2011)

Beaumont, P, 'International Family Law in Europe: The Maintenance Project, the Hague Conference and the EC—A Triumph of Reverse Subsidiarity' (2009) 73 *RabelsZ Bd* 509

Beveridge, F, 'Gender, the Acquis and Beyond' in Dougan, M and Currie, S (eds), *50 Years of the European Treaties: Looking Back and Thinking Forward* (Oxford, Hart, 2008)

—— and Velluti, S (eds), *Gender and the Open Method of Coordination* (Dartmouth, Ashgate, 2008)

Boele-Woelki, K, (ed) *Common Core and Better Law in European Family Law* (Netherlands, Intersentia, 2005)

—— Braat, B and Curry-Sumner, I (eds), *European Family Law in Action*, vol II (Antwerp, Intersentia, 2003)

—— Braat, B and Curry-Sumner, I (eds), *European Family Law in Action*, vol III (Antwerp, Intersentia, 2005)

Borras, A, 'From Brussels II to Brussels II*bis* and Further' in Boele-Woelki, K and González Beilfuss, C (eds), *Brussels IIbis: Its Impact and Application in the Member States* (Antwerp, Intersentia, 2007)

Bouwsma, S, *Disability Policy in EU Member States and the Open Method of Co-ordination* (Twente, University of Twente, 2003)

Boyd, M, 'Family and Personal Networks in International Migration: Recent Developments and New Agendas' (1989) 23 *International Migration Review* 638

Boyden, J, 'Childhood and the Policy Makers: A Comparative Perspective on the Globalization of Childhood' in James, A and Prout, A (eds), *Constructing and Deconstructing Childhood: Contemporary Issues in the Sociological Study of Childhood* (Basingstoke, Falmer, 1990)

Boyle, P, Cooke, TJ, Halfacree, K and Smith, D, 'A Cross-National Comparison of the Impact of Family Migration on Women's Employment Status' (2001) 38 *Demography* 201

Boyle, PJ, Cooke, TJ, Gayle, V and Mulder, CH, 'The Effect of Family Migration on Union Dissolution in Britain' in Stalford, H, Currie, S and Velluti, S (eds), *Gender and Migration in 21st Century Europe* (Aldershot, Ashgate, 2009) 11

Bradley, C, 'Briefings' (2006) 3 *International Family Law Journal* 162

—— 'Resolution: Resolution's International Committee' (2009) 3 *International Family Law Journal* 201

Bradshaw, J, Hoelscher, P and Richardson, D, 'An Index of Child Well-Being in the European Union' (2007) 80 *Social Indicators Research* 133

Brandtner, B and Rosas, A, 'Human Rights and the External Relations of the European Community: An Analysis of Doctrine and Practice' (1998) 9 *European Journal of International Law* 468

Brannen, J, Heptinstall, E and Bhopal, K, *Connecting Children: Care and Family Life in Later Childhood* (London, Routledge, 2000)

Bray, R, Lenaerts, K and Van Nuffel, P (eds), *Constitutional Law of the European Union*, 2nd edn (London, Sweet and Maxwell, 2005)

Breen, C, 'The Emerging Tradition of the Best Interests of the Child in the European Convention on Human Rights' in Breen, C, *The Standard of the Best Interest of the Child* (Dordrecht, Martinus Nijhoff, 2002) page number

—— *Age Discrimination and Children's Rights: Ensuring Equality and Acknowledging Difference* (Oxford, Hart, 2005)

Bryceson, D and Vuorela, U (eds), *The Transnational Family: New European Frontiers and Global Networks* (New York, Berg, 2002)

Buck, T, Gillespie, A, Ross, L and Sargent S, *International Child Law*, 2nd edn (Abingdon, Routledge, 2010)

Bulgarian State Agency for Child Protection, *Report on the Status of Specialised Institutions for Children with Physical and Mental Disabilities* (Bulgaria, SCAP, 2006)

Burgess, A, *The Costs and Benefits of Active Fatherhood. Evidence and Insights to Inform the Development of Policy and Practice* (Wiltshire, The Fatherhood Institute, 2006)

Butler, I, Scanlan, L, Robinson, M, Douglas, GF and Murch, MA, *Divorcing Children: Children's Experience of Their Parents' Divorce* (London, Jessica Kingsley, 2003)

Campbell, J and Oliver, M, *Disability Politics: Understanding our Past, Changing our Future* (London, Routledge, 1996)

Caracciolo di Torella, E and Masselot, A, *Reconciliation of Work and Family Life in EU Law and Policy* (Basingstoke, Palgrave Macmillan, 2010)

Case Comment, 'Children's Rights, Parental Autonomy and Article 5' (1989) 14 *EL Rev* 254

Cashmore, J, 'Children's Participation in Family Law Matters' in Hallett, C and Prout, A (eds), *Hearing the Voices of Children: Social Policy for a New Century* (Bodmin, Routledge Falmer Press, 2003) 158

Cholewinski, R, 'Family Reunification and Conditions Placed on Family Members: Dismantling a Fundamental Human Right' (2002) 4 *European Journal of Migration and Law* 271

Commission of the European Communities, *Progress Towards the Common European Objectives in Education and Training: Indicators and Benchmarks 2010/2011*, Commission Staff Working Paper (Brussels, European Commission, 2011)

Connor, T, 'Case C-303/06 *Coleman v Attridge Law and Steve Law* Judgment of the ECJ' (2010) 32 *Journal of Social Welfare and Family Law* 57

Corsaro, W, *The Sociology of Childhood*, 2nd edn (London, Sage, 2005)

Costa, JP, *International Justice for Children* (Strasbourg, Council of Europe, 2009)

Costello, C, '*Metock*: Free Movement and "Normal Family Life" in the Union' (2009) 46 *CML Rev* 587

Cremona, M, 'EU Enlargement: Solidarity and Conditionality' (2005) 30 *EL Rev* 3

Cullen, H, 'From Migrants to Citizens? European Community Policy on Intercultural Education' (1996) 45 *ICLQ* 109

—— 'Children's Rights' in Peers, S and Ward, A (eds), *The EU Charter of Fundamental Rights: Politics, Law and Policy* (Oxford, Hart, 2004) 323

—— '*Siliadin v France*: Positive Obligations under Article 4 of the European Convention on Human Rights' (2006) 6 *Human Rights Law Review* 585

Currie, S, *Migration, Work and Citizenship in the Enlarged European Union* (Surrey, Ashgate, 2008)

—— 'Accelerated Justice or a Step Too Far? Residence Rights of Non-EU Family Members and the Court's Ruling in *Metock*' (2009) 34 *EL Rev* 310

—— 'The Transformation of Union Citizenship' in Currie, S and Dougan, M (eds), *50 Years of the European Treaties: Looking Back and Thinking Forward* (Oxford, Hart, 2009) 365

Curry-Sumner, I, 'Transnational Recovery of Child Maintenance in Europe: The Future is Bright, The Future is Central Authorities' in Masaryk University, *Days of Public Law: Collection of Articles* (Brno, Masaryk University, 2007)

Daphne, *The Daphne Experience 1997–2003: Europe Against Violence Towards Children and Women* (Luxembourg, European Commission, 2005)

Dashwood, A, Dougan, M, Rodger, B, Spaveta, E and Wyatt, D, *Wyatt and Dashwood's European Union Law*, 6th edn (Oxford, Hart, 2011)

Davies, B, 'Giving EU Citizens a voice: Regulation 211/2011 on the EU Citizen's Initiative' (2011) 33 *Journal of Social Welfare and Family Law* 289

De Búrca, G, 'The Language of Rights and European Integration' in Shaw, J and More, G (eds), *New Legal Dynamics of European Union* (Oxford, Clarendon Press, 1995)

—— 'Beyond the Charter: How Enlargement has Enlarged the Human Rights Policy of the EU' (2004) 27 *Fordham International Law Journal* 679

De Maris, A and MacDonald, W, 'Premarital Cohabitation and Marital Instability: A Test of the Unconventionality Hypothesis' (1993) 55 *Journal of Marriage and Family* 399

de Witte, B, 'The Impact of Enlargement on the Constitution of the European Union' in Cremona, M (ed), *The Enlargement of the European Union* (Oxford, Oxford University Press, 2003) 240

Dennison, G, 'Is Mediation Compatible with Children's Rights?' (2010) 32 *Journal of Social Welfare and Family Law* 169

Dey, I and Wasoff, F, 'Mixed Messages: Parental Responsibilities, Public Opinion and the Reforms of Family' (2006) 20 *International Journal of Law, Policy and the Family* 225

DG Education and Culture, *Looking Behind the Figures of the Main Results of the Eurobarometer 2007 Survey on Youth* (Brussels, European Commission, 2007)

Dingwall, R, 'Divorce Mediation: Should We Change our Mind?' (2010) 32 *Journal of Social Welfare and Family Law* 107

—— and Eeklaar, J, *Rethinking Child Protection* (Oxford, Centre for Socio-Legal Studies, 1984)

Dottridge, M, *Child Trafficking for Sexual Purposes: A Contribution of ECPAT to the World Congress III Against Sexual Exploitation of Children and Adolescents* (Brazil, ECPAT International, 2008)

Dougan, M, 'The Treaty of Lisbon 2007: Winning Minds, Not Hearts' (2007) 45 *CML Rev* 617

—— and Spaventa E, '"Wish You Weren't Here"…New Models of Social Solidarity in the European Union' in Spaventa, E and Dougan, M (eds), *Social Welfare and EU Law* (Oxford, Hart, 2005)

Douglas, GF and Murch, MA, 'Taking Account of Children's Needs in Divorce: A Study of Family Solicitors' Responses to New Policy and Practice Initiatives' (2002) 14 *Child and Family Law Quarterly* 57

Drew, F, *Parental Leave in Council of Europe Member States* (Strasbourg, Directorate General of Human Rights, 2005)

Dronkers, J, Kalmijn, M and Wagner, M, 'Causes and Consequences of Divorce: Cross-national and Cohort Differences' (2006) 22 *European Sociological Review* 479

Drywood, E, 'Giving with One Hand, Taking with the Other: Fundamental Rights, Children and the Family Reunification Decision' (2007) 32 *EL Rev* 396

—— 'Challenging Concepts of the "Child" in Asylum and Immigration Law: The Example of the EU' (2010) 32 *Journal of Social Welfare and Family Law* 309

—— *The Child in EU Asylum and Immigration Law: A Socio-Legal Analysis of Regulatory and Governance Issues* (PhD thesis, Liverpool, 2010)

—— '"Child-Proofing" EU Law and Policy: Interrogating the Law-Making Processes Behind Asylum and Immigration Provision' (2011) 19 *International Journal of Children's Rights* 31

Dubout, E, 'Interprétation Téléologique et Politique Jurisprudentielle de la Cour Européenne des Droits de L'homme' (2008) 19 *Revue Trimetrielle des Droits de L'Homme* 383

Duncan, W, 'The Development of the New Hague Convention on the International Recovery of Child Support and Other Forms of Family Maintenance' (2004) 38 *Family Law Quarterly* 663

—— 'The Hague Convention of 23 November 2007 on the International Recovery of Child Support and Other Forms of Family Maintenance: Comments on its Objectives and Some of its Special Features' in Buono, G and Volken, P (eds), *Yearbook of Private International Law*, vol X 2008 (Germany, Sellier, 2009)

Dupré, C, 'After Reforms: Human Rights Protection in Post-Communist States' (2008) 5 *European Human Rights Law Review* 621

Dworkin, R, 'Rights as Trumps' in Waldron, J (ed), *Theories of Rights* (Oxford, Oxford University Press, 1984) 153

Eames, D, 'Maintenance Enforcement: The 2007 Hague Convention and the EC Regulation' (2008) 1 *International Family Law Journal* 47

Eekelaar, J, *The Emergence of Children's Rights* (Oxford, OUP, 1986)

—— 'The Interests of the Child and the Child's Wishes: The Role of Dynamic Self-determinism' (1994) 8 *International Journal of Law Policy Family* 42

Ellis, E, *EU Anti-Discrimination Law* (Oxford, Oxford University Press, 2005)

EMS Consortium, *Review of the European Union Phare Assistance to Roma Minorities: Interim Evaluation of Phare Support Allocated in 1999–2002 and Implemented until November 2003* (Brussels, European Commission, 2004)

Ennew, J, 'Has Research Improved the Human Rights of Children? Or have the Information Needs of the CRC improved data about children?' in Invernezzi, A and Williams, J (eds), *The Human Rights of Children: From Visions to Implementation* (Fanham, Ashgate, 2011) 133

Eurochild, *Ending Child Poverty within the EU: A Review of the 2006–08 National Reports on Strategies for Social Protection and Social Inclusion* (Belgium, Eurochild, 2007)

—— *Fact Sheet on Child Poverty in the EU* (Belgium, Eurochild, 2007)

—— *Policy Position: EuroChild's proposals for the development of the EU's Strategy on the Rights of the Child* (Belgium, Eurochild, 2010)

Eurojust, 'Trafficking in Human Beings' (2010) 2 *Eurojust News* 2

European Commission, *The Situation of Roma in an Enlarged European Union* (Brussels, European Commission, 2004)

—— *Progress towards the Lisbon Objectives in Education and Training: Indicators and Benchmarks*, Commission Staff Working Document (Brussels, European Commission, 2007)

—— *Joint Council/Commission Report on the Implementation of the Education and Training 2010 Work Programme 'Delivering Lifelong Learning for Knowledge, Creativity and Innovation'* (Brussels, European Commission, 2008)

—— *Improving the Tools for the Social Inclusion and Non-Discrimination of Roma in the EU* (Brussels, European Commission, 2010)

—— *The Social Situation in the European Union 2009* (Luxembourg, Publications Office of the European Union, 2010)

—— *Impact Assessment Accompanying Document to the Communication from the Commission to the European Parliament, the Council, the European Economic and Social Committee and the Committee of the Regions Bringing Legal Clarity to Property Rights for International Couples*, Commission Staff Working Paper (Brussels, European Commission, 2011)

—— *The Social Dimension of the Europe 2020 Strategy: A Report of the Social Protection Committee 2011* (Brussels, European Commission, 2011)

European Court of Human Rights and the European Union Agency for Fundamental Rights, *Handbook on European Non-Discrimination Law* (Luxembourg, Publications Office of the European Union, 2011)

European Evaluation Consortium, *Evaluation of the Functioning of the European Judicial Network in Civil and Commercial Matters: Final Report* (Brussels, European Commission, 2005)

European Opinion Research Group, *Attitudes of Europeans to Disability: Eurobarometer 54.2* (Brussels, European Commission, 2001)

Eurydice, *Integrating Immigrant Children into Schools in Europe* (Brussels, Eurydice Policy Unit, 2004)

—— *Integrating Immigrant Children into Schools in Europe: Measures to Foster Communication with Immigrant Families and Heritage Language Teaching for Immigrant Children* (Brussels, Eurydice Policy Unit, 2009)

Fahey, E, 'Going Back to Basics: Re-embracing the Fundamentals of the Free Movement of Persons in Metock' (2009) 36 *Legal Issues of Economic Integration* 83

Farkas, L, *Segregation of Roma Children in Education: Addressing Structural Discrimination through the Race Equality Directive* (Brussels, European Commission, 2007)

Feller, E, Türk, V and Nicholson, F, *Refugee Protection in International Law: UNHCR's Global Consultations on International Consultation* (Cambridge, Cambridge University Press, 2003)

Ferreira, N, 'The Harmonisation of Private Law in Europe and Children's Tort Liability: A Case of Fundamental and Children's Rights Mainstreaming' (2011) 19 *International Journal of Children's Rights* 571

Finch, F, 'Childcare and Parental Leave' in Bradshaw and Hatland (eds), *Social Policy, Employment and Family Change in Comparative Perspective* (Cheltenham, Edward Elgar, 2006)

Fiorini, A, 'Rome III: A Step Too Far For the Europeanisation of Private International Law?' (2008) 22 *International Journal of Law Policy and the Family* 178

Fitch, K, Spencer-Chapman, K and Hilton, Z, *Protecting Children from Sexual Abuse in Europe: Safer Recruitment of Workers in a Border-Free Europe* (London, NSPCC, 2007)

Fottrell, D, (ed), *Revisiting Children's Rights: 10 Years of the UN Convention on the Rights of the Child* (Dordrecht, Kluwer, 2000)

FRA, *Child Trafficking in the European Union: Challenges, Perspectives and Good Practices* (Luxembourg, Office for Official Publications of the European Communities, 2009)

Frazer, H and Marlier, E, *Tackling Child Poverty and Promoting the Social Inclusion of Children in the EU: Key Lessons* (Brussels, European Commission, 2007)

Fredman, S, 'The Age of Equality' in Fredman, S and Spencer, S (eds), *Age as an Equality Issue: Legal and Policy Perspectives* (Oxford, Hart, 2003) 21

Freeman, M, 'The Best Interests of the Child? Is The Best Interests of the Child in The Best Interests of Children?' (1997) 11 *International Journal of Law, Policy and the Family* 360

—— *International Child Abduction: The Effects* (Leicester, Reunite, 2006)

—— 'Why It Remains Important to Take Children's Rights Seriously' (2007) 15 *International Journal of Children's Rights* 5

Forder, C, 'Seven Steps to Achieving Full Participation of Children in the Divorce Process' in Willems, JCM (ed), *Developmental and Autonomy Rights of Children: Empowering Children, Care-Givers and Communities* (Antwerp, Intersentia, 2002)

—— 'Family Rights and Immigration Law: A European Perspective' in Schneider, H (ed), *Migration, Integration and Citizenship: A Challenge for Europe's Future*, vol II (Maastricht, Forum Maastricht, 2005)

Fortin, J, 'Rights Brought Home for Children' (1999) 62 *MLR* 350

—— *Children's Rights and the Developing Law* (Cambridge, Cambridge University Press, 2005)

Foster, N, 'Family and Welfare Rights in Europe: The Impact of Recent European Court of Justice Decisions in the Area of Free Movement of Persons' (2003) 25 *Journal of Social Welfare and Family Law* 291

Franklin, R (ed), *The Handbook of Children's Rights: Comparative Policy and Practice* (London, Routledge, 1995)

Frazer, H and Marlier, E, *Tackling Child Poverty and Promoting the Social Inclusion of Children in the EU: Key Lessons* (Luxembourg, European Commission, 2007)

Freeman, M, *The Rights and Wrongs of Children* (London, Frances Pinter, 1983)

—— *The Moral Status of Children: Essays on the Rights of the Child* (The Hague, Kluwer Law International, 1997)

Garde, A, *EU Law and Obesity Prevention* (The Netherlands, Kluwer Law International, 2010)

—— 'Advertising Regulation and the Protection of Children–Consumers in the European Union: In the Best Interest of…Commercial Operators?' (2011) 19 *International Journal of Children's Rights* 523

—— 'The Best Interests of the Child and EU Consumer Law and Policy: A Major Gap between Theory and Practice?' in Kenny, M and Devenney, J (eds), *European Consumer Protection: Theory and Practice* (Cambridge, Cambridge University Press, 2012)

Gateva, E, 'Post Accession Conditionality: Support Instrument for Continuous Pressure?' *Working Paper No 18* (Berlin, KFG, 2010)

Glystos, N, 'The Role of Migrant Remittances in Development: Evidence from Mediterranean Countries' (2002) 40 *International Migration* 5

Goldson, B and Muncie, J, 'Rethinking Youth Justice: Comparative Analysis, International Human Rights and Research Evidence' (2006) 6 *Youth Justice* 91

—— (eds) *Youth Crime and Juvenile Justice—Volume 1: The 'Youth Problem'* (London, Sage, 2009)

Granath, K, *Study to Inform a Subsequent Impact Assessment on the Commission Proposal on Jurisdiction and Applicable Law in Divorce Matters—Draft Final Report to the European Commission DG Justice, Freedom and Security* (Brussels, European Policy Evaluation Consortium, 2006)

Grugel, G and Iusmen, I, 'The European Commission as Guardian Angel: Agenda-Setting for Children's Rights' (forthcoming 2012) *Journal of European Public Policy*

Guggenheim, M, *What's Wrong with Children's Rights* (Cambridge, Harvard University Press, 2005)

Hailbronner, K and Thym, D, 'Case C-34/09, *Gerardo Ruiz Zambrano v Office National de l'emploi (ONEm)*, Judgment of the Court of Justice (Grand Chamber) of 8 March 2011' (2011) 48 *CML Rev* 1253

Hale, W, 'Human Rights and Turkey's EU Accession Process: Internal and External Dynamics, 2005–10' (2011) 16 *South European Society and Politics* 323

Hantrais, L and Mangen, S (eds), *Cross-National Research Methodology and Practice* (London, Routledge, 2007)

Harding, M, 'The Harmonisation of Private International Law in Europe: Taking the Character out of Family Law?' (2011) 1 *Journal of Private International Law* 203

Harper, M, 'An English (Law) View of Brussels I and Brussels II' (2006) 9 *International Family Law Journal* 9

Harris-Short, S, 'Family Law and the Human Rights Act 1998: Judicial Restraint or Revolution' (2005) 17 *Child and Family Law Quarterly* 329

Hatland, A and Mayhew, E, 'Parental Rights and Obligations' in Bradshaw, J and Hatland, A (eds), *Social Policy, Employment and Family Change in Comparative Perspective* (Cheltenham, Edward Elgar, 2006)

Hayes, B, *From the Schengen Information System to SIS II and the Visa Information (VIS): The Proposals Explained* (London, Statewatch, 2004)

Hebenton, B and Thomas, T, *Policing Europe: Cooperation, Conflict and Control* (New York, St Martin's Press, 1995)

—— 'Capacity Building Against Transnational Organised Crime: Measures to Combat Sexual Offenders' (1999) 7 *European Journal of Crime, Criminal Law and Criminal Justice* 150

Herman, E, 'Migration as Family Business: The Role of Personal Networks in the Mobility Phase of Migration' (2006) 44 *International Migration* 191

Hervey, T (ed), 'Thirty Years of EU Sex Equality Law' (2005) 12 *Maastricht Journal of European and Comparative Law* 307

Hickman, T, 'Beano No More: The EU Charter of Rights After Lisbon' (2011) 16 *Judicial Review* 113

Hillion, C (ed), *EU Enlargement: A Legal Approach* (Oxford, Hart, 2004)

—— 'The Copenhagen Criteria and their Progeny' in Hillion, C (ed), *EU Enlargement: A Legal Approach* (Oxford, Hart, 2004)

Hinarejos, A, 'Law and Order and Internal Security Provisions in the Area of Freedom, Security and Justice: Before and After Lisbon' in Eckes, C and Konstadinides, T (eds), *Crime within the Area of Freedom, Security and Justice: A European Public Order* (Cambridge, Cambridge University Press, 2011)

Hodgkin, R and Newell, P, *Implementation Handbook for the Convention on the Rights of the Child*, 3rd edn (Geneva, UNICEF, 2007)

Hodson, D, 'Fairness in Family Law Across Europe: A Pan European Ideal or a Pandemonium of Cultural Clashes?' (European Regional Conference of the International Society of Family Law, University of Chester, 17–21 July 2007)

Holt, J, *Escape from Childhood: The Needs and Rights of Children* (Harmondsworth, Penguin, 1975)

House of Commons, Work and Pensions Committee, and Child Support Reform, *Report of Session 2006–07 Together with Formal Minutes* (London, The Stationery Office, 2007)

House of Lords European Union Committee, *Schengen Information System II (SIS II): Report with Evidence* (London, The Stationary Office, 2007)

Hujisman, R, 'Free Movement of Workers and an Expanding EU: Time to Think about Child Migration' in Swärd, S and Bruun, L (eds), *Conference Report—Focus on Children in Migration: From a European Research and Method Perspective* (Stockholm, Save the Children Sweden, 2007)

Hunt, M, 'The Horizontal Effect of the Human Rights Act' (1998) *PL* 423

Hunter, R, 'Close Encounters of a Judicial Kind: "Hearing Children's Voices" in Family Law Proceedings' (2007) 3 *Child and Family Law Quarterly* 283

ILO, *Action against Trafficking in Human Beings* (Geneva, ILO, 2008)

—— *The International Programme on the Elimination of Child Labour: What It Is and What It Does* (Geneva, ILO, 2010)

IOM, *Trafficking in Unaccompanied Minors in the European Union* (Paris, IOM, 2002)

Iusmen, I, 'Do as I Say Not as I Do': EUtopia, the CEECs and the Credibility of the EU Human Rights Regime' (2009) 9 *Romanian Journal of European Affairs* 54

—— 'Human Rights Developments beyond the EU *Acquis*: the Child Protection Case in Romania' in, *The EU and Child Protection in Romania: Accession Conditionality and Feedback Effects* (PhD thesis, University of Sheffield, 2009)

Jacobs, FG, 'Human Rights in the European Union: The Role of the Court of Justice' (2001) 26 *EL Rev* 331

James, A, Jenks, C and Prout, A, *Theorizing Childhood* (Oxford, Polity Press, 1998)

Kaczorowska, A, *Public International Law*, 4th edn (Oxford, Routledge, 2010)

Kanics, J and Sutton, D, *Save the Children and the Separated Children in Europe Programme Position Paper on Returns and Separated Children* (Norway, Save the Children, 2004)

Karsten, I, 'The State of International Family Law Issues: A View from London' (2009) 1 *International Family Law Journal* 35

Kiernan, K, 'Cohabitation in Western Europe: Trends, Issues and Implications' in Booth, A and Crouter, A (eds), *Just Living Together: Implications of Cohabitation on Families, Children and Social Policy* (New Jersey, Lawrence Erlbaum Associates, 2002)

Kilkelly, U, *The Child and the European Convention on Human Rights* (Aldershot, Ashgate, 1998)

—— 'The Impact of the Convention on the Case Law of the European Court of Human Rights' in Fottrell, D (ed), *Revisiting Children's Rights: 10 Years of the UN Convention on the Rights of the Child* (Dordrecht, Kluwer, 2000) 87

—— 'The Best of Both Worlds for Children's Rights: Interpreting the European Convention on Human Rights in the Light of the UN Convention on the Rights of the Child' (2001) 23 *Human Rights Quarterly* 308

—— 'Effective Protection of Children's Rights in Family Cases: An International Approach' (2002) 12 *Transnational Law and Contemporary Problems* 336

—— 'Operationalising Children's Rights: Lessons from Research' (2006) 1 *Journal of Children's Services* 36

King, R, 'Towards a New Map of European Migration' (2002) 8 *International Journal of Population Geography* 89

Koball, H and Principe, D, 'Do Non-Resident Fathers Who Pay Child Support Visit Their Children More?' Series B, no B-44 (Washington DC, The Urban Institute, 2002) 1

Kofman, E, 'Family-Related Migration: A Critical Review of European Studies' (2004) 30 *Journal of Ethnic and Migration Studies* 243

—— Phizacklea, A, Raghuram, P and Sales, R, *Gender and International Migration in Europe: Employment, Welfare, and Politics* (London, Routledge, 2000)

Koinova, M, 'Challenging Assumptions of the EU Enlargement Literature: The Impact of the EU on Human and Minority Rights in Macedonia' (2011) 63 *Europe-Asia Studies* 807

Kränzl-Nagl, R and Zartler, U, 'Children's Participation in School and the Local Community' in Percy-Smith, B and Thomas, N (eds), *A Handbook of Children and Young People's Participation: Perspectives from Theory and Practice* (London, Routledge, 2010)

Krieg, S, 'Trafficking in Human Beings: The EU Approach between Border Control, Law Enforcement and Human Rights' (2009) 15 *European Law Journal* 775

Krisch, N, 'The Open Architecture of European Human Rights Law' (2008) 71 *MLR* 183

Kumar, C, 'A Fast-Track to Europe: The Urgent Procedure for Preliminary Rulings' (2008) 3 *International Family Law* 180

Lamont, R, 'Habitual Residence and Brussels II *bis*: Developing Concepts for European Private International Family Law' (2007) 3 *Journal of Private International Law* 261

—— '*Re M* and Beyond: Managing Return When a Child has Settled Following Abduction' (2009) 31 *Journal of Social Welfare and Family Law* 73

Lansbergen, A and Miller, N, 'European Citizenship Rights in Internal Situations: An Ambiguous Revolution? Decision of 8 March 2011, Case C-34/09 *Gerardo Ruis Zambrano v ONEM*' (2011) 7 *European Constitutional Law Review* 287

Lansdown, G, *The Evolving Capacities of the Child* (Florence, UNICEF Innocenti Research Centre, 2005)

—— *What's the Difference? Implications of a Child Focus in Rights Based Programming—A Discussion Paper* (London, Save the Children, 2005)

Lansky, DT, Swift, LH, Manley, E, Elmore, A and Gerety, C, 'The Role of Children in Mediation' (1996) 14 *Conflict Resolution Quarterly* 147

Lataianu, CM, 'Social Protection of Children in Public Care in Romania from the Perspective of EU Integration' (2003) 17 *International Journal of Law, Policy and the Family* 99

Lavalette, M, *Child Employment in the Capitalist Labour Market* (Aldershot, Avebury, 1994)

Lawson, A, 'The UN Convention on the Rights of Persons with Disabilities and European Disability Law: A Catalyst For Cohesion?' in Arnardóttir, OM and Quinn, G (eds), *The UN Convention on the Rights of Persons with Disabilities: European and Scandinavian Perspectives* (Boston, Martinus Nijhoff, 2009) 81

Lindo, RV, 'The Trafficking of Persons into the European Union for Sexual Exploitation: Why It Persists and Suggestions to Compel Implementation and Enforcement of Legal Remedies in Non-Complying Member States' (2006) 29 *Boston College International and Comparative Law Review* 135

Lister, R, 'Unpacking Children's Citizenship' in Invernizzi, A and Williams, J (eds), *Children and Citizenship* (London, Sage, 2008) 9

Litcher, DT, 'Household Migration and the Labour Market Position of Married Women' (1980) 9 *Social Science Research* 83

Locke, J, 'Some Thoughts Concerning Education' in Adamson, J (ed), *The Educational Writings of John Locke* (London, Edward Arnold, 1912)

Lowe, N, 'New International Conventions Affecting the Law Relating to Children: A Cause for Concern?' (2001) *International Family Law* 171

—— 'The 1996 Hague Convention on the Protection of Children: A Fresh Appraisal' (2002) 14 *Child and Family Law Quarterly* 191

—— 'The Growing Influence of the EU in International Family Law: A View from the Boundary' (2003) 56 *Current Legal Problems* 439

—— 'A Review of the Application of Article 11 of the Revised Brussels II Regulation' (2009) *International Family Law* 27

—— Everall, M and Nicholls, M, *International Movement of Children: Law, Practice and Procedure* (Bristol, Jordan Publishing, 2004)

—— and Horosova, K, 'The Operation of the 1980 Hague Abduction Convention: A Global View' (2007) 41 *Family Law Quarterly* 59

Lundy, L, '"Voice is Not Enough": Conceptualising Article 12 of the United Nations Convention on the Rights of the Child' (2007) 33 *British Education Research Journal* 927

Maclean, M, (ed), *Parenting after Partnering: Containing Conflict after Separation* (Oxford, Hart Publishing, 2007)

—— 'Family Mediation: Alternative or Additional Dispute Resolution? An Editorial' (2010) 32 *Journal of Social Welfare and Family Law* 1

Marcu, M, 'Population and Social Conditions' in, *Statistics in Focus*, 38/2011 (Brussels, Eurostat, 2011)

Maresceau, M, 'Pre-accession' in Cremona, M (ed), *The Enlargement of the European Union* (Oxford, Oxford University Press, 2003) 9

Mastekaasa, A, 'Marital Status, Distress and Well-being: An International Comparison' (1994) 25 *Journal of Comparative Family Studies* 183

McEleavey, P, 'The Brussels II Regulation: How the European Community has Moved into Family Law' (2002) *International and Comparative Law Quarterly* 883

—— 'The Communitarisation of Family Law: Too Much Haste Too Little Reflection?' in Boele-Woelki, K (ed), *Perspectives for the Unification and Harmonisation of Family Law in Europe* (Antwerp, Intersentia, 2003) 509

—— 'The Communitarisation of Divorce Rules: What Impact for English and Scottish Law' (2004) *ICLQ* 605

—— 'Evaluating the Views of Abducted Children: Trends in Appellate Case Law' (2008) *Child and Family Law Quarterly* 230

McGlynn, C, 'Ideologies of Motherhood in European Sex Equality Law' (2000) 6 *European Law Journal* 29

—— *Families and the European Union: Law, Politics and Pluralism* (New York, Cambridge University Press, 2006)

McGoldrick, D, 'The Charter and United Nations Human Rights Treaties' in Peers, S and Ward, A (eds), *The EU Charter of Fundamental Rights: Politics, Law and Policy* (Oxford, Hart, 2004) 83

—— 'The Boundaries of Justiciability' (2010) 59 *ICLQ* 981

Meulders, D and Gustafsson, S, *The Rationale of Motherhood Choices: Influence of Employment Conditions and of Public Policies* (Brussels, European Commission, 2004)

Mincer, J, 'Family Migration Decisions' (1978) 86 *Journal of Political Economy* 749

Mnookin, RH, 'Child Custody Adjudication: Judicial Functions in the Face of Indeterminacy' (1975) 39 *Law and Contemporary Problems* 226

Mowbray, A, *The Development of Positive Obligations under the European Convention on Human Rights by the European Court of Human Rights* (Oxford, Hart Publishing, 2004)

National Authority for the Protection of Children's Rights, *Child Welfare in Romania* (Romania, Children's Rights Romania, 2006)

Neale, B, 'Dialogues with Children: Children, Divorce and Citizenship' (2002) 9 *Childhood* 455

—— *Young Children's Citizenship: Ideas into Practice* (York, Joseph Rowntree Foundation, 2004)

Nicolaidis, K and Howse, R, 'This is my EUtopia ... Narrative as Power' (2002) 40 *Journal of Common Market Studies* 767

Norrie, K, 'Human Rights and the Children's Hearing System: An Assessment of Which Aspects of the Children's Hearing System Might be Subject to Challenge under the European Convention' (2000) *The Journal Online* 19

O'Brien, C, 'Case C-310/08 *Ibrahim*, Case C-480/08 *Teixiera*' (2011) 48 *CML Rev* 203

O'Connell Davidson, J and Farrow, C, *Child Migration and the Construction of Vulnerability* (Stockholm, Save the Children Sweden, 2007)

O'Hagan, E, 'Too Soft to Handle? A Reflection on Soft Law in Europe and Accession States' (2004) 26 *Journal of European Integration* 379

Obokata, T, 'Key EU Principles to Combat Transational Organised Crime' (2011) 48 *CML Rev* 801

OECD, *Babies and Bosses: Reconciling Work and Family Life—A Synthesis of Findings for OECD Countries* (Paris, OECD, 2007)

—— *PISA 2006: Science Competencies for Tomorrow's World—Volume 1 Analysis* (Paris, OECD, 2007)

Olivier, B and Herman Reestman, J, 'European Citizens' Third Country Family Members and Community Law' (2007) 3 *European Constitutional Law Review* 463

Opromolla, A, 'Children's Rights under Articles 3 and 8 of the European Convention: Recent Case Law' (2001) 26 *EL Rev, Human Rights Supplement* 46

Parker, S, 'The Best Interests of the Child: Principles and Problems' (1994) 8 *International Journal of Law, Policy and the Family* 26

Parkinson, L, *Family Mediation: Appropriate Dispute Resolution in a New Family Justice System*, 2nd edn (London, Jordan Publishing, 2011)

Peers, S, 'Legislative Update EU Immigration and Asylum Law 2010: Extension of Long-term Residence Rights and Amending the Law on Trafficking in Human Beings' (2011) 13 *European Journal of Migration and Law* 201

—— 'Mission Accomplished? EU Justice and Home Affairs Law after the Treaty of Lisbon' (2011) 48 *CML Rev* 661

—— and Rogers, N (eds), *EU Immigration and Asylum Law: Text and Commentary* (Leiden, Martinus Nijhoff, 2006)

Pendakur, K and Pendakur, R, 'Language Knowledge as Human Capital and Ethnicity' (2002) 36 *International Migration Review* 147

Percy-Smith, B and Thomas, N, *A Handbook of Children and Young People's Participation: Perspectives from Theory and Practice* (London, Routledge, 2009)

Pinheiro, PS, *Report on Violence against Children* (Geneva, UN, 2006)

Piper, C, 'Assumptions about Children's Best Interests' (2000) 22 *Journal of Social Welfare and Family Law* 261

—— 'Investing in a Child's Future: Too Risky?' (2010) 22 *Child and Family Law Quarterly* 1

Pogány, I, 'Refashioning Rights in Central and Eastern Europe: Some Implications for the Region's Roma' (2004) 10 *European Public Law* 89

—— 'Minority Rights and the Roma of Central and Eastern Europe' (2006) 6 *Human Rights Law Review* 1

Potter, M, 'The Voice of the Child: Children's "Rights" in Family Proceedings' (2008) 3 *International Family Law Journal* 140

Purdy, LM, 'Why Children Shouldn't Have Equal Rights' (1994) 2 *International Journal of Children's Rights* 223

Qvortrup, J, Brady, M, Sgritta, G and Wintersberger, H (eds), *Childhood Matters: Social Theory, Practice and Politics* (Aldershot, Avebury, 1994)

Raghuram, P, 'The Difference that Skills Make: Gender, Family Migration Strategies and Regulated Labour Markets' (2004) 30 *Journal of Ethnic and Migration Studies* 303

Raitt, FE, 'Hearing Children in Family Law Proceedings: Can Judges Make a Difference?' (2007) 2 *Child and Family Law Quarterly* 204

Redmond, G, 'Child Poverty and Child Rights: Edging Towards a Definition' (2008) 14 *Journal of Children and Poverty* 63

Reunite, *Mediation in International Parental Child Abduction: The Reunite Mediation Pilot Scheme* (Leicester, Reunite, 2006)

Ridge, T, 'Supporting Children? The Impact of Child Support Policies on Children's Well-being in the UK and Australia' (2005) 34 *Journal of Social Policy* 121

Ringold, D, Orenstein, MA and Wilkens, E, *Roma in an Expanding Europe: Breaking the Poverty Cycle* (Washington, World Bank, 2003)

Roberts, M, *Mediation in Family Disputes: Principles of Practice* (Farnham, Ashgate, 2008)

Roche, J, 'Children, Citizenship and Human Rights' (2008) 9 *Journal of Social Sciences* 43

Rodríguez, R, *Study on Child Labour and Protection of Young Workers in the European Union: Final Report* (Brussels, DG Employment, Social Affairs and Equal Opportunities, 2006)

Roker, D, Player, K and Coleman, J, 'Young People's Voluntary and Campaigning Activities as Sources of Political Education' (1999) 25 *Oxford Review of Education* 185

Roth, M and Moisa, F, 'The Right to Education of Roma Children in Romania: European Policies and Romanian Practices' (2011) 19 *International Journal of Children's Rights* 127

Rubellin-Devichi, J, 'The Best Interests Principle in French Law and Practice' (1994) 8 *International Journal of Law, Policy and the Family* 259

Ruxton, S, *Children in Europe* (London, NCH Action for Children, 1996)

—— *What About Us? Children's Rights in the European Union: Next Steps* (Brussels, The European Children's Network, 2005)

—— *Governance Fit for Children. To What Extent Have the General Measures of Implementation of the UNCRC Been Realised in Five European Countries?* (Brussels, Save the Children, 2010)

Sana, M and Massey, D, 'Household Composition, Family Migration and Community Context: Migrant Remittances in Four Countries' (2005) 86 *Social Science Quarterly* 509

Saposnek, D, 'The Value of Children in Mediation: A Cross-Cultural Perspective' (1991) 8 *Conflict Resolution Quarterly* 325

Save the Children, *Child Rights Programming: How to Apply Rights-Based Approaches in Programming* (Stockholm, Save the Children, 2002)

Savirimuthu, J, 'The EU, Online Child Safety and Media Literacy' (2011) 19 *International Journal of Children's Rights* 173

Sawyer, C, 'Citizenship is Not Enough: The Rights of Children of Foreign Parents' (2005) 35 *Family Law* 224

Schulz, A, 'Guidance from Luxembourg: First ECJ Judgment Clarifying the Relationship between the 1980 Hague Convention and Brussels II Revised' (2008) 4 *International Family Law Journal* 221

Schuz, R, 'Habitual Residence of Children under the Hague Abduction Convention: Theory and Practice' (2001) 13 *Child and Family Law Quarterly* 1

Scullion, D, 'Gender Perspectives on Child Trafficking: A Case Study of Child Domestic Workers' in Stalford, H, Currie, S and Velluti, S (eds), *Gender and Migration in 21st Century Europe* (Surrey, Ashgate, 2009) 45

Separated Children in Europe Programme, *Statement of Good Practice*, 3rd edn (Brussels, Save the Children, 2004)

Shah-Kazemi, S, 'Cross-Cultural Mediation: A Critical View of the Dynamics of Culture in Family Disputes' (2000) 14 *International Journal of Law, Policy and the Family* 302

Shuibhne, N, 'Free Movement of Persons and the Wholly Internal Rule: Time to Move On?' (2002) 39 *CML Rev* 731

—— 'Margins of Appreciation: National Values, Fundamental Rights and EC Free Movement Law' (2009) 34 *EL Rev* 230

Siehr, K, 'The 1980 Hague Convention On The Civil Aspects Of International Child Abduction: Failures And Successes in German Practice' (2000) 33 *New York University Journal of International Law and Politics* 207

Skinner, C, Bradshaw, J and Davidson, J, *Child Support Policy: An International Perspective—Research Report No 405* (Leeds, Department for Work and Pensions, 2007)

—— and Davidson, J, 'Recent Trends in Child Maintenance Schemes in 14 Countries' (2009) 1 *International Journal of Law, Policy and the Family* 23

Smart, C, 'From Children's Shoes to Children's Voices?' (2002) 40 *Family Court Review* 305

—— 'Towards an Understanding of Family Change: Gender Conflict and Children's Citizenship' (2003) 17 *Australian Journal of Family Law* 1

—— Neale, B and Wade, A, *The Changing Experience of Childhood: Families and Divorce* (Cambridge, Polity Press, 2001)

Smith, K, 'EU Membership Conditionality' in Cremona (ed), *The Enlargement of the European Union* (Oxford, Oxford University Press, 2003)

Social Protection Committee, *Child Poverty and Well-Being in the EU: Current Status and Way Forward* (Luxembourg, European Communities, 2008)

Solberg, A, 'Negotiating Childhood: Changing Constructions of Age for Norwegian Children' in James, A and Prout, A (eds), *Constructing and Reconstructing Childhood* (Basingstoke, Falmer Press, 1990)

Sotiropoulou, V and Sotiropoulos, D, 'Childcare in Post-Communist Welfare States: The Case of Bulgaria' (2007) 36 *Journal of Social Policy* 141

Spaventa, E, 'Federalisation versus Centralisation: Tensions in Fundamental Rights Discourse in the EU' in Dougan, M and Currie, S (eds), *50 Years of the European Treaties* (Oxford, Hart Publishing, 2009) 343

Spielmann, D, 'Human Rights Case Law in the Strasbourg and Luxembour Courts: Conflicts, Inconsistencies and Complementarities' in Alston, P (ed), *The EU and Human Rights* (Oxford, Oxford University Press, 1990) 757

Staiger, I, 'Trafficking in Children for the Purpose of Sexual Exploitation in the EU' (2005) 13/14 *European Journal of Crime, Criminal Law and Criminal Justice* 603

Stalford, H, 'The Citizenship Status of Children in the European Union' (2000) 8 *International Journal of Children's Rights* 101

—— 'Concepts of Family under EU Law: Lessons from the ECHR' (2002) 1 *International Journal of Law, Policy and the Family* 410

—— 'Brussels II and Beyond: A Better Deal for Children in the European Union?' in Boele-Woelki, K (ed), *Perspectives for the Unification and Harmonisation of Family Law in Europe* (Antwerp, Intersentia, 2003)

—— 'Old Problems, New Solutions? EU Regulation of Cross-National Child Maintenance' (2003) 15 *Child and Family Law Quarterly* 269

—— 'Parenting, Care and Mobility in the European Union: Issues Facing EU Migrant Scientists' (2005) 18 *Innovation: The European Journal of Social Science Research* 361

—— 'European Union Family Law: A Human Rights Perspective' in Meeusen, J, Straetmans, G and Pertegas-Sender, M (eds), *International Family Law for the European Union* (Antwerp, Intersentia, 2006) 119

—— 'The Relevance of European Union Citizenship to Children' in Invernizzi, A and Williams, J (eds), *Children and Citizenship* (London, Sage, 2008) 159

—— 'Crossing Boundaries: Reconciling Law, Culture and Values in International Family Mediation' (2010) 32 *Journal of Social Welfare and Family Law* 155

—— 'For Better, For Worse: The Relationship between EU Citizenship and the Development of Cross-border Family Law' in Shuibhne, N, Dougan, M and Spaventa, E (eds), *Empowerment and Disempowerment of the EU Citizen* (Oxford, Hart Publishing, forthcoming 2012)

—— and Drywood, E, 'The Use of the UNCRC in EU Law and Policy-Making' in Invernizzi, A and Williams, J (eds), *The Human Rights of Children: From Visions to Implementation* (Aldershot, Ashgate, 2011) ch 9

—— Sax, H and Drywood, E, *Developing Indicators for the Protection, Respect and Promotion of the Rights of the Child in the European Union: Summary Report* (Vienna, Fundamental Rights Agency, 2009)

—— Sax, H et al, *Developing Indicators for the Protection, Respect and Promotion of the Rights of the Child in the European Union: Final Report* (Vienna, Fundamental Rights Agency, 2009)

—— Sax, H et al, *Developing Indicators for the Protection, Respect and Promotion of the Rights of the Child in the European Union: Updated Post-Lisbon Treaty Conference* (Vienna, Fundamental Rights Agency, 2010)

—— and Schuurman, M, 'Are We There Yet? The Impact of the Lisbon Treaty on the EU Children's Rights Agenda' (2011) 3 *International Journal of Children's Rights* 381

Stanat, P and Christensen, G, *Where Immigrant Students Succeed: A Comparative Review of Performance and Engagement in PISA 2003* (Paris, OECD, 2006)

Steiner, HJ and Alston, P, *International Human Rights in Context,* 2nd edn (Oxford, Oxford University Press, 2000)

Steinhilber, S, *Women's Rights and Gender Equality in the EU Enlargement. An Opportunity for Progress,* WIDE Briefing (Brighton, Siyanda, 2002)

Stevens, D, 'Asylum-Seeking Families in Current Legal Discourse: A UK Perspective' (2010) 32 *Journal of Social Welfare and Family Law* 5

Szcszyzak, E, 'Experimental Governance: The Open Method of Coordination' (2006) 12 *European Law Journal* 486

TÁRKI, *Child Poverty and Child Well-Being in the European Union: Report for the European Commission* (Budapest, TÁRKI, 2010)

Thomas, D, 'Human Rights Ideas, the Demise of Communism, and the End of the Cold War' (2005) 7 *Journal of Cold War Studies* 110

Thomas, N, Gran, BB and Harnson, KC, 'An Independent Voice for Children's Rights in Europe? The Role of Independent Children's Rights Institutions in the EU' 19 *International Journal of Children's Rights* 429

—— and O'Kane, C, 'When Children's Wishes and Feelings Clash with their Best Interests' (1998) 6 *International Journal of Children's Rights* 137

Thorpe, M, 'London: The Divorce Capital of the World' (2009) 39 *Family Law* 21

Thym, D, 'Respect for Private and Family Life under Article 8 ECHR in Immigration Cases: A Human Right to Regularize Illegal Stay?' (2008) 57 *ICLQ* 87

Tidimas, T, *The General Principles of EU Law,* 2nd edn (Oxford, Oxford University Press, 2007)

Tobin, J, 'Beyond the Supermarket Shelf: Using A Rights Based Approach to Address Children's Health Needs' (2006) 14 *International Journal of Children's Rights* 275

—— 'Understanding A Human Rights Based Approach to Matters Involving Children: Conceptual Foundations and Strategic Considerations' in Invernezzi, A and Williams, J (eds), *The Human Rights of Children: From Visions to Implementation* (Farnham, Ashgate, 2011) 61

Todorova, V, 'Children's Rights in Bulgaria after the End of Communism' (2009) 17 *International Journal of Children's Rights* 623

Tomasi, L, Ricci, C and Bariatti, S, 'Characterisation in Family Matters for the Purposes of European Private International Law' in Meeusen, J, (ed), *International Family Law for the European Union* (Antwerp, Intersentia, 2007) 341

Townsend, P, *The Concept of Poverty: Working Papers on Methods of Investigation and Life-Styles of the Poor in Different Countries* (Michigan, Heinemann Educational, 1970)

—— *The International Analysis of Poverty* (New York, Harvester Wheatsheaf, 1993)

Tremlett, A, '"Gypsy Children Can't Learn": Roma in the Hungarian Education System' in Goddard, J, McNamee, S and James, A (eds), *The Politics of Childhood* (Basingstoke, MacMillan, 2005) 145

Trinder, L, 'Conciliation, the Private Law Programme and Children's Wellbeing: Two Steps Forward, One Step Back?' (2008) 38 *Family Law* 338

—— 'Maternal Gatekeeping and Gate-Opening in Post Divorce Families: Strategies, Contexts and Consequences' (2008) 29 *Journal of Family Issues* 1298

Tryfonidou, A, '*Kunqian Catherine Zhu and Man Lavette Chen v Secretary of State for the Home Department*: Further Cracks in the "Great Wall" of the European Union?' (2005) 11 *European Public Law* 527

—— 'Jia or "Carpenter II": The Edge of Reason' (2007) 33 *EL Rev* 908

—— 'Family Reunification Rights of (Migrant) Union Citizens: Towards a More Liberal Approach' (2009) 15 *European Law Journal* 634

Tun, AA, Cave, G, Trotter, D and Bell, B, 'The Domestic Fulfilment of Children's Rights: Save the Children's Experience in the Use of Rights-Based Approaches' in Alen, A, Bosely, H and De Bie, M (eds), *The UN Children's Rights Convention: Theory Meets Practice* (Netherlands, Intersentia, 2007) 33

UNDP, Europe and the CIS, Bratislava Regional Centre, *Trafficking in Human Beings: A Guidance Note* (New York, UNDP, 2004)

UNICEF, *Early Marriage: A Harmful Traditional Practice—A Statistical Exploration* (New York, UNICEF, 2005)

—— *The State of the World's Children 2006* (New York, UNICEF, 2005)

—— *Child Poverty in Perspective: An Overview of Child Well-Being in Rich Countries— Innocenti Report Card 7, 2007* (Florence, UNICEF, 2007)

—— *Draft Country Programme Document—Bulgaria* (New York, UNICEF, 2009)

UN High Commissioner for Refugees, *Refugee Children: Guidelines on Protection and Care* (Geneva, UNICEF, 1994)

UNHCR, *Trends in Unaccompanied and Separated Children Seeking Asylum in Europe 2000* (Geneva, UNHCR, 2001)

—— *2007 Global Trends: Refugees, Asylum Seekers, Returnees, Internally Displaced and Stateless Persons* (Geneva, UNCHR, 2008)

Wagner, W and Weiß, B, 'On the Variation of Divorce Risks in Europe: Findings from a Meta-Analysis of European Longitudinal Studies' (2006) 22 *European Sociological Review* 483

Walker, L, 'The Impact of the Hague Abduction Convention on the Rights of the Family in the Case Law of the European Court of Human Rights and the UN Human Rights Committee: The Danger of *Neulinger*' (2010) 6 *Journal of Private International Law* 629

—— and Beaumont, P, 'Shifting the Balance Achieved by the Abduction Convention: The Contrasting Approaches of the European Court of Human Rights and the European Court of Justice (2011) 7 *Journal of Private International Law* 231

Wall, K and São José, J, 'Managing Work and Care: A Difficult Challenge for Immigrant Families' (2004) 38 *Social Policy and Administration* 591

Weitzman, LJ and Maclean, M, *Economic Consequences of Divorce: The International Perspective* (London, Clarendon Press, 1992)

White, R, 'Conflicting Competences: Free Movement Rules and Immigration Laws' (2004) 29 *EL Rev* 385

Williams, A, 'Enlargement of the Union and Human Rights Conditionality: A Policy of Distinction?' (2000) 25 *EL Rev* 601

Williams, J, 'Incorporating Children's Rights: The Divergence in Law and Policy' (2007) 27 *Legal Studies* 261

Wikeley, N, 'Case Commentary: *R (Kehoe) v Secretary of State for Work and Pensions*: No Redress When the Child Support Agency Fails to Deliver' (2005) 17 *Child and Family Law Quarterly* 113

—— 'A Duty But Not a Right: Child Support after *R (Kehoe) v Secretary of State for Work and Pensions*' (2006) 2 *Child and Family Law Quarterly* 287

—— *Child Support: Law and Policy* (Oxford, Hart, 2006)

—— Ireland, E, Bryson, C and Smith, R, *Relationship Separation and Child Support Study: DWP Research Report No 503* (Norwich, HMSO, 2008)

Wintersberger, H, 'Work, Welfare and Generational Order: Towards a Political Economy of Childhood' in Qvortrup, J (ed), *Studies in Modern Childhood* (Basingstoke, Palgrave Macmillan, 2005) 201

Xanthaki, H, 'The Judiciary-Based System of Child Support in Germany, France and Greece: An Effective Suggestion?' (2000) 22 *Journal of Social Welfare and Family Law* 295

Zelizer, VA, 'The Priceless Child Revisited' in Qvortrup, J (ed), *Studies in Modern Childhood* (Palgrave, Macmillan, 2005) 184

Index